Banking Industry in 21st Century: Challenges and Opportunities

Banking Industry in 21st Century: Challenges and Opportunities

Edited by Elian Harvey

LANRYE
INTERNATIONAL
www.clanryeinternational.com

Clanrye International,
750 Third Avenue, 9th Floor,
New York, NY 10017, USA

ISBN: 978-1-64726-667-7

Cataloging-in-Publication Data

Banking industry in 21st century : challenges and opportunities / edited by Elian Harvey.
    p. cm.
Includes bibliographical references and index.
ISBN 978-1-64726-667-7
1. Banks and banking--History--21st century. 2. Financial institutions--History--21st century. I. Harvey, Elian.
HG1573 .B36 2023
332.1--dc23

For information on all Clanrye International publications
visit our website at www.clanryeinternational.com

Contents

Chapter 11   **Peer-to-Peer Lending and Bank Risks: A Closer Look**...**186**
Eunjung Yeo and Jooyong Jun

Chapter 12   **How to Achieve Sustainable Development of Mobile Payment through
Customer Satisfaction — The SOR Model**...**203**
Su-Chang Chen, Kuo Cheng Chung and Ming Yueh Tsai

Chapter 13   **Digital Financial Inclusion and Farmers' Vulnerability to Poverty**..**218**
Xue Wang and Guangwen He

               Permissions

               List of Contributors

               Index

Preface

A bank is a financial institution which has the authority to accept deposits and lend money. The other main activities involved in banking include clearing of cheques, remittance of funds, lockers and safe deposits, overseas banking services, wealth management, investment banking, etc. The banking industry is going through a transformation due to various reasons such as compliance pressures and increased regulation, increased competition from new fintech companies, disruptive technology, and evolving business models. The international banking industry faces various challenges such as consolidating in the face of shifting global growth balances, increased global financial volatility, and weak growth in developed nations. Some of the upcoming technologies which find application in the banking industry are blockchain technology and artificial intelligence. This book unfolds the innovative aspects of banking, its challenges and opportunities. It will also provide interesting topics for research, which interested readers can take up. The book will serve as a valuable source of reference for graduate and postgraduate students.

All of the data presented henceforth, was collaborated in the wake of recent advancements in the field. The aim of this book is to present the diversified developments from across the globe in a comprehensible manner. The opinions expressed in each chapter belong solely to the contributing authors. Their interpretations of the topics are the integral part of this book, which I have carefully compiled for a better understanding of the readers.

At the end, I would like to thank all those who dedicated their time and efforts for the successful completion of this book. I also wish to convey my gratitude towards my friends and family who supported me at every step.

Editor

CSR, Co-Creation and Green Consumer Loyalty: Are Green Banking Initiatives Important? A Moderated Mediation Approach from an Emerging Economy

Huidong Sun [1], Mustafa Raza Rabbani [2], Naveed Ahmad [3], Muhammad Safdar Sial [4], Guping Cheng [1,*], Malik Zia-Ud-Din [5] and Qinghua Fu [1]

[1] Economics and Management School, Wuhan University, Wuhan 430072, China; 2015101050086@whu.edu.cn (H.S.); 2016101050084@whu.edu.cn (Q.F.)

[2] Department of Finance and Accounting, College of Business Administration, Kingdom University, Riffa 40434, Bahrain; m.rabbani@ku.edu.bh

[3] UCP Business School, University of Central Punjab, Lahore 54000, Pakistan; naveeddgk2010@gmail.com

[4] Department of Management Sciences, COMSATS University Islamabad (CUI), Islamabad 44000, Pakistan; safdarsial@comsats.edu.pk

[5] Faculty of Law, Islamia University, Bahawalpur 63100, Pakistan; malikziaudin@yahoo.com

* Correspondence: 2016101050114@whu.edu.cn

Abstract: The homogenization of the banking segment has made it difficult for banking institutions to practice the quality of services that are needed in order to retain consumers. Thus, these days, finding ways to increase consumer loyalty—especially green loyalty—has become a challenge for the banking industry around the planet. Research has long acknowledged that corporate social responsibility (CSR) is a strategic concern that could help organizations to increase consumer loyalty. However, the impact of CSR practices on green consumer loyalty is rarely addressed in the extant literature. Hence, the present research investigated the impact of CSR on green consumer loyalty with the mediating effect of co-creation in the banking industry of Pakistan. The study also introduced green banking initiatives as a moderator between the mediated relation of CSR and green consumer loyalty, with the intention that such a moderator would strengthen this indirect relationship. The structural equation modeling technique was used for the data analysis. The results confirm that CSR enhances consumer loyalty, and that co-creation partially mediates this relationship. Furthermore, green banking initiatives further strengthen this relation. The results of the current survey could help banking institutions learn how they can develop core strategic considerations based on the integration of CSR co-creation and green banking initiatives.

Keywords: corporate social responsibility; green consumer loyalty; co-creation; bank; Pakistan; sustainability; green banking initiatives

1. Introduction

Broadly speaking, the concept of corporate social responsibility is deeply rooted in the idea of the long-term 'footprint' that an organization leaves on society, and can be seen in areas such as environmental responsibility/ sustainability [1], employee relations [2], and targeted marketing [3]. Sustainability is a concept that can be interpreted in different ways, with no clear and rigorous meaning for the general public [4]. Sustainability is often attributed as an end in itself, an ideal condition framed in absolute terms. However, sustainability is stronger than it seems, because it can be determined in different ways [5].

Consumers value the behavior of companies for the products they buy. More and more companies are taking on their corporate social responsibilities (CSR) voluntarily, or in response to external forces [6]. Participation in CSR is rewarded not only for the business operations, but also for loyalty [7], identification [8], and an increased procurement process [9]. In recent years, consumers have become more concerned about environmental friendliness practices and the ethical standards of businesses, but interestingly, this has not significantly increased the commercial success of sustainable products [10]. As a result, there is no balance between what consumers expect from businesses and the level at which consumers are willing to pay more, as per the wish of businesses; we refer this as a co-creation gap [11]. The customer's intentions and actions can be explained in many ways, one of which is the probable personal responsibility, and another is the lack of customer information. The gap between speech and action is an obstacle to sustainable development [12]. To close this gap, a push and pull partnership is required between the consumers and the company. In other words, this gap will exist forever if the customer and the company will not collaborate with each other (co-creation) in order to produce a product that is eco-friendly and acknowledged by consumers [13]. As a result of this collaborative approach, consumers can make more stable and realistic choices that are clearly visible and easily accessible.

Every organization wants to build a type of relationship with consumers that would encourage them to buy its products for a long period of time. Identification [8], especially customer identification with a company via co-creation [14], creates this type of choice, and raises issues such as strong attitude, honesty, and consistency. Co-creation creates a sense among consumers that they share the same values as those of the company. Co-creation (CC) can be regarded as an efficient, flexible and social process that aims to create relevant new products or services through communication and interaction with consumers [15]. The perception of co-creation is that it is attractive in nature, as it can lead to many resources for the organization, including economic efficiency [16], risk reduction [17], relationship marketing [18], and better understanding and competitiveness [19]. In addition, co-creation is an inspiring experience for many consumers in different ways [8]. First, consumers can establish warm, deep, and exclusive relationships with other members of the collaborative community. Second, when firms participate in a co-creation project, consumers always feel that they are growing as individuals, learning and being creative with the community [20]. Most importantly, engaging in co-creation activities offers consumers opportunities for self-development, and social and hedonic [21] resources that lead them to feel close to the brand. Remarkably, the same can be said about CSR, which seeks to ensure the value of the environment in which most participants interact.

Customers respond to CSR in different ways, and what works for one user may not work for another. Consumers also appear to be more sensitive to 'negligent' behavior than to 'responsible' company behavior [7]. However, consumers need to have a clear understanding of the company's efforts. They can develop (or provide an opportunity to know) a positive attitude only after learning about the company's CSR policy [22]. CSR creates a situation in which the consumer evaluates the company and the products, and attaches themselves to the company directly or indirectly [23,24]. The evaluation of the company, in turn, impacts consumer preferences. This is where social responsibility comes into play. It is clear that the relationship established between a socially responsible business and its customers ensures consistency [25].

Green banking initiatives refer to any banking practice that creates environmental benefits [26]. In other words, it means the promotion of environmentally friendly processes and the reduction of the carbon footprint of banking operations [27]. The leading financial institutions of a country can improve the quality of their services and social responsibility through green initiatives and financing [28]. Many modern banks in the world, at the local and international levels, are now making intensive and genuine effort to promote different technologies in line with green banking initiatives. Thus, green banking initiatives have become a prevalent trend in the modern banking world.

In brand policy, green positioning is achieved by combining functional characteristics and emotional resources. The same is true for the level of products as there are several product levels, in which, several groups can add values [29]. This combination of 'users' and 'non-users' forces businesses to move from a traditional, one-sided concept of sustainability to a broad conception. This, in turn, reduces the risk to the company's future. Due to the growing concern of environmentalism, consumers are more interested in purchasing products and services that have little impact on the environment [11]. In addition, different studies have concluded that the environmental image of an organization can improve sales and competitiveness, while satisfying consumers [30,31]. Accordingly, the search for new information on various aspects of green banks has increased among consumers in the recent era, which indicates that consumers are concerned enough to monitor environmental practices of an organization [32].

Going green has become an essential norm in the global banking industry. The idea of green banking has prompted banking institutions to introduce paperless, technology-based services, and to maintain their role as a responsible entity in sustainable development while minimizing the impact on the environment [33]. It is important for banks to understand the need for green practices, because the main success or failure of this investment will affect the satisfaction and loyalty of their end consumers [34]. We conceive of green consumer loyalty in line with the definition of Oliver [35]: "the green loyalty is the preference of buyers to repurchase a product or service prompted by strong commitment of organization towards environment".

With the growing inclination towards green banking, most researchers have studied issues in various areas, such as green banking initiatives [33], the impact of green banks on sustainable development [36], consumer information of green banks [37], customer satisfaction in green banks [38], green consumer loyalty [33], green bank acceptance [39], consumers' green attitude [40], and environment up-gradation through green banking initiatives [41]. Accordingly, the search for new information on various aspects of green banks has increased among consumers in the recent era, which indicates that consumers are concerned with the monitoring of the environmental practices of an organization [32]. Likewise, the transition to sustainability will change the character of banks, especially their products, services, and stakeholder relationships. Banks are one of the key players in supporting the transformation into a sustainable economy. The Goal for Sustainable Development has turned into a substantial goal for governments and businesses. This is due to a change in the understanding of the sustainable practices of organizations and the expansion of business objectives from profitability to sustainability [42]. New economic developments are already taking place, as we have sustainable banks, environmental taxes, green investment, green purchases, industrial production, a low carbon economy, friendly-energy sources, and more. Banks are no longer impartial mediators between businesses and customers. They are seen as active participants in economic and social processes. The Responsible Banks of recent times demonstrate their social and environmental responsibility through their annual social responsibility report [43].

The banking sector was especially chosen for the present study because of its large investment in CSR after the worldwide financial crunch in 2008, in order to restore consumer confidence and to enhance their image [44]. Due to increased pressures from different stakeholders, including consumers, banking institutions have started to report their efforts to preserve the natural environment. In this regard, green banking initiatives can lead a bank toward consumer satisfaction, which ultimately enhances green consumer loyalty [45–47]. Likewise, well-reputed banks in the banking industry began to engage in co-creation activities which aimed to improve the consumer experience. Consumer loyalty has a strong impact on corporate efficiency, as it is directly related to lower marketing expenses and greater revenues [48]. Likewise, in today's highly competitive era, organizations are trying to fight their counterparts through a variety of marketing tools, emphasizing that the inclusion of corporate social responsibility (CSR) as a core business strategy can move business forward [49].

The homogenization of the banking segment has made it difficult for banking institutions to practice the quality of services needed in order to retain consumers. Thus, finding ways to gain the loyalty of consumers has become a challenge for the banking industry around the planet. Research has long-established that CSR is an impressive marketing approach to increase the loyalty of consumers [8].

It has also been noted that consumers can reciprocate CSR based on their beliefs, brand identity, quality, and eventually loyalty [50,51]. Hence, companies involved in CSR activities can improve their institutional performance by improving consumer loyalty [52].

The contributions of the present study are many; first, the previous research has focused on emotional integration, such as affective engagement, with limited empirical studies of consumer behavior, particularly loyal consumer behavior [53,54]. Second, there are different studies confirming that consumer loyalty is a complex phenomenon, and the assumption that CSR alone will predict loyalty significantly is not wise thinking, as different studies have shown that the relationship of CSR and loyalty is made more significant by the introduction of moderators or mediators [24,55–58]. In line with these arguments, we propose that the inclusion of co-creation variable as a mediator between CSR and consumer loyalty better explains this relationship, as supported by the extant literature [8,14]. Third, we argue that the green banking initiatives of a bank moderate this indirect relationship, such that green initiatives strengthen this indirect relationship and enhance green consumer loyalty. Hence, this study employs a moderated mediation approach. Fourth, there are limited evidences that CSR and co-creation can enhance the loyalty consumers in an Asian context, particularly in a developing country such as Pakistan [8]. Fifth, much of the CSR research has been conducted on consumer behavior in advanced nations [14,15,59], and the findings from such studies suggest that additional research is obligatory in the context of developing countries. The developing nations are comprised of developing economies which are expected to be more inclined to produce a social and environmental effect compared to developed nations.

The results of the current survey will help banking institutions to understand how they can develop core strategic considerations based on the integration of CSR, co-creation, and green initiatives to boost green consumer loyalty. The rest of the article is comprised of the theory building and hypothesis, research methodology, analysis of data, discussion, conclusion, and finally implications for policy makers.

2. Theory and Hypotheses

2.1. CSR and Co-Creation

The theory of social identity [59] can be used to shed light on the effect of CSR on consumer behavior. The main elements of the theory of social identification are the conception of self- categorization and the theory of social identity [60]. The theory of self-categorization suggests that people should facilitate the social world by dividing it into groups (for example, profession, nationality, clubs, social groups). People consider themselves to belong to a certain class. According to the definition of social identity, everyone strives for self-reliance by improving their personality. The role of CSR in the attractive, meaningful renewal of consumer identity has been studied in terms of the theory of social identity [61]. When consumers see that the prices reflected by the organization's activities correspond to their value, the organization's identification increases. In terms of social identity, each person should be different from others in terms of social status, so they tend to look for participation groups that differ in their values. Therefore, when consumers assume that an entity has characteristics—such as CSR—that they value, they determine to identify them with that entity [62]. The relationship between CSR and co-creation can be considered as an effective level of activity and a community identification process. CSR, which takes into consideration the interests of all stakeholders, can reinforce the association amongst consumers and the organization, and facilitates sales with consumers and the organization based on key service information [15].

CSR is not workable for managers and experts if it is inconsistent with value creation [15,63]. In different business sectors, including the banking sector, CSR is known to help companies achieve specific long term goals, rather than short-term goals [64,65]. This means that CSR not only aims to address the changing social problems of stakeholders, but also provides key business-related benefits for organizations [66], in particular through the creation of a common value [67]. The solution of these two goals, in fact, requires managers not only to know that their organizations pursue both economic and social goals, but also to strengthen their relationships with stakeholders, especially consumers. These types of relationships with stakeholders are considered 'value co-creation areas' [68]. The content is integrated and co-designed with stakeholders and organizations, and creates a favorable environment for CSR research, as the actual value is based on both the participants and their relationships [69]. Adamik and Nowicki [70] argue that the creation of sustainable value by an organization for its members involves the examination of the ways in which co-responsibility can be incorporated into a coherent value chain. Shared responsibility and co-creation assumes that companies should not only take responsibility as a priority in the overall strategy of the organization, but that other stakeholders involved in the value chain should contribute to the ethical development and economic dimensions of the joint venture [71]. This approach recognizes that CSR plays a role as a link between stakeholders and social goals, and in the realization of social expectations [72]. A number of studies in the banking sector [67,71–74] have found that participants (especially consumers and shareholders) changed their behavior and inspected their banks more after the global financial crisis [44]. CSR communication plays an important role in convincing consumers of the bank's economic, social, and environmental performance [73]. Therefore, it is reasonable to assume that consumers will be able to contribute to co-creation events with companies that they consider are socially responsible. Hence, we propose the following hypothesis:

Hypothesis 1 (H1). *CSR positively affects co-creation.*

2.2. Co-Creation and Consumer Loyalty

Consumer satisfaction is a lifeline for businesses, especially those involved in services, but at the same time it can be challenging. Satisfaction promotes consumer loyalty as a source of long-term profitability for organizations [14]. In addition, loyal consumers are less attentive to other products offered by rival firms in the market. This has been found to increase consumer satisfaction and reduce the need to challenge the company and its products or services [74]. In addition, companies need to understand the importance of consumer satisfaction, as retaining existing consumers is cheaper than finding new consumers. In order to provide consumer satisfaction, co-creation in the banking sector is regarded as a crucial factor for the efficient handling of competition [8]. Consumer support has increased as the internet and other technologies have become available, and these resources encourage consumers to learn, enjoy, and use new products. In the recent era, consumers have been provided with more options for the purchase of goods and services than ever before, but still, they seem dissatisfied. Organizations focus on the production of a variety of products and services, but they are currently unable to meet the needs of consumers in an exact way. This gap can be overcome by sitting together and listening to each other [21]. At the same time, it is difficult to determine the essence of a cost-effective business design. Beirão, et al. [75] suggest that the key to the basic knowledge of the service depends on the consumer. They focus on the growth of the client–supplier relationship through communication and dialogue.

More recently, Buhalis and Sinarta [76] mentioned that co-creation is the mechanism that companies can use in order to develop products which consumers accept happily. It helps companies innovate, change products or designs, and explore changes in line with the consumer experience. Co-creation can be used as a way to promote transparency in production, and as a means of increasing organization and consumer confidence and reaping the full benefits. At the same time, Mainardes, et al. [77] mentioned an important co-creation feature which ensures that the deployment and transparency service is part of a network of shared features. Mainardes, Teixeira and da Silveira Romano [77] also state co-creation helps in making the information available which is difficult otherwise. By understanding the opportunities and risks, consumers can help reduce uncertainty and make informed decisions in the current stiff environment [78]. The details of this process increase consumer confidence for investment in the products offered by banks. Other researchers have highlighted the benefits of consumer involvement in an organization in terms of increasing consumers' satisfaction [79] and loyalty [80]. In services, the consumer–service provider relationship and the potential benefits of consumer communication help users to engage in co-creation [81].

In order to successfully co-create, consumers must provide resources to banks, such as information in line with the use of the value co-creation process [77]. Without important information from consumers, banks may not be able to perform their functions in an efficient manner. By sharing information with banks, consumers can assure that the bank will provide services in accordance with their needs [82]. Careful behavior occurs when consumers perceive themselves as part of the banking staff who are responsible for sharing valuable information and feedback in order to contribute to the co-creation process [83]. In terms of the value of building partnerships between consumers and banks, consumers need to collaborate, follow rules and policies, and receive guidance from banks about how to collaborate in the co-creation process with a bank [84]. To conclude, we argue that this partnership provides an opportunity to build a relationship that helps to build trust and reduces the chance for consumers to end the relationship with the bank. From this viewpoint, co-creation activities may help to achieve fair competition with loyal consumers. Hence, the following hypothesis is proposed:

Hypothesis 2 (H2). *Co-creation positively affects consumer loyalty.*

2.3. CSR and Consumer Loyalty

In today's highly competitive environment, corporations face many challenges. Consumers want to buy new products for as little money as possible, and opponents are attempting to snatch the market share [80]. Conversely, maintaining a strong consumer base is a matter of life for businesses, and increasing the quantity of loyal consumers is the most cost-effective strategy [82]. The correlation between CSR and consumer loyalty is defined in the theory of social exchange [85]. It states that the organization has a socially ethical response, which creates social mutuality [86]. It has been proposed that the general belief of repetition can be used to define organization's CSR actions with regard to consumer behavior. The general body of knowledge recognizes that following social policies can help businesses to form and maintain long-term relationships with consumers. Consistently, research on the perception of resilience in loyal consumer is broadly defined in CSR literature [87,88]. In this way, in the banking industry, Ramlugun and Raboute [89] showed the positive impact of CSR on loyal consumers. In the same vein, in the banking industry, Shabbir, et al. [90] found CSR to be positively correlated with consumer loyalty.

CSR has been recognized as a major source of interest for businesses, as it has many corporate advantages. Some of these benefits include the improvement of consumer satisfaction [91], producing a competitive advantage over competitors [92], encouraging sales growth [93], and building a strong brand image [94]. Based on above facts, businesses and academics began to consider CSR as a marketing tool [3,95–98]. For example, Alkitbi, et al. [95] showed that a company's product experience is not the only factor that makes up a positive customer rating. Conversely, CSR functions can be used for this purpose [24]. Similarly, Arli and Lasmono [96] further stated that consumers are interested in the activities of their CSR firms, and the positive outlook of the firm allows them to test the performance of their services. Today, companies are not only trying to feel socially responsible, but also to expand their CSR knowledge to their customers by letting them know about the company's CSR activities through different media [97].

For example, in today's digital age, socially responsible firms are interested in reporting their CSR actions on their websites and in online media communications. In addition, new successful plans continue to emerge as these firms invest in CSR services as part of their marketing strategy [98]. Therefore, the role of CSR adoption today is related to the quality of service indicators in long-term relationships and the restoration of positive customer attitudes after service failure and recovery. Most importantly, this seems to be an important factor in the expansion of the customer base.

According to previous research, consumers have good intentions when they learn about the activities of their CSR firms [99]. In their research work, Shabbir, Shariff, Yusof, Salman and Hafeez [90] describe the positive relationship between the bank's CSR activities and consumer loyalty. It is reported in the existing literature that the CSR practices of banks are directly related to loyalty [55], commitment [100], and company identification [101]. CSR has also been identified as having the potential to increase consumer confidence in many businesses, including hypermarkets [102] and the financial sector [103] of Pakistan. Likewise, CSR has a positive link with marketing communication prospects. In the current situation, it is necessary to understand why and how the credibility of the people is affected by CSR. Hence, we propose the following hypothesis:

Hypothesis 3 (H3). *CSR positively affects consumer loyalty.*

2.4. Co-Creation as Mediator

The concept of co-creation is emerging as a new frontier in marketing. Based on new service-oriented logic, value co-creation design is understood as a method of value formation through the process of cooperation between an organization and its customers (or other players related to the organization). This partnership involves the exchange of resources, such as knowledge and skills, for mutual gains [81]. As banking consumers become more knowledgeable, educated, and engaged in a wide range of marketing offerings by different banks, banking institutions strive to satisfy customers, build trust, and maintain long-term relationships with them in order to increase revenue [77]. In general, loyalty in a banking context is characterized as the extent to which consumers are committed to a particular bank and do not consider rivals [81]. The bank and customer may co-create in order to form a mutual bond, which ultimately leads consumers toward loyalty. Increasing and maintaining consumer loyalty is the sacred foundation of business philosophy [104]. From the perspective of marketing activities, consumer loyalty can be described as the inclination of a consumer to establish a long-term affiliation with a particular brand and endorse it to others [8]. Researchers recommend consumer loyalty as a strategy to make profits, as well as increasing the frequency of transactions and deliveries, agreeing to higher payments, and reducing costs [14]. In addition, the existing literature identifies the most common elements of consumer loyalty, such as consumer trust [51] and consumer commitment [105].

However, although previous research has linked it more broadly to emotions (e.g., consumer affective commitment), the existing literature still lacks due consideration as to how co-creation can enhance consumer loyalty [80]. Similarly, one study by Cossío-Silva, et al. [106], on personal care, found that co-creation increases behavioral outcomes such as consumer loyalty. As such, Chen et al. [107] mentioned that co-creation improves consumer loyalty through participation in the online marketing community, where consumer trust in the brand development process is enhanced through co-creation. Accordingly, Cambra-Fierro, Pérez and Grott [81] confirmed that co-creation activities have a positive impact on consumer loyalty in the banking sector.

In general, it can be said that the collective or integrated basis of CSR is related to the co-creation function, due to its interactional nature [8]. Thus, Iglesias, Markovic, Bagherzadeh and Singh [14] assumed, in the banking context, that the co-creation is the extent to which consumers contribute with businesses to the refining of current solutions, or to finding new solutions to make them valuable to consumers and the company. Many studies support the role of CSR as an important stimulant for co-creation [14,15,108–112]. CSR can strengthen consumer relationships, and organizations—taking into account the interests of different stakeholders—can motivate consumers to create value together with the organization based on key business information [8]. According to the basic principle of service, if companies believe that the consumer relationship is stable, rather than a transaction according to the CSR plan, they are better able to attract consumers to be creative. Once consumers engage in the co-creation process with companies, mutual relationships emerge that lead to consumer loyalty [106]. Shabbir, Shariff, Yusof, Salman and Hafeez [90] concluded that, when banking consumers learn about a company's CSR activities, they become an effective tool for the company through their actions, and this behavior of the participants leads to consumer loyalty. Based on the above arguments, we propose the following hypothesis:

Hypothesis 4 (H4). *Co-creation mediates the relationship between CSR and consumer loyalty.*

2.5. Green Banking Initiatives as a Moderator

Understanding the various factors that affect consumer satisfaction remains a concern for banks and the financial service business, as satisfaction plays a key role in building and developing stable, profitable, long-term customer relationships [108]. In addition, Green Banking initiatives are responsible for energy efficiency [109], environmental management [110], green construction [111], compliance with environmental rules [33], green financing [112], and so on. However, most of these studies have focused on consumers' perceptions of environmental issues in green banks, rather than involving consumers in product/service decisions in line with CSR activities. Most green banking activities are green deposits, green loans, green credit cards, green accounts, green money market operations, online banking, mobile banking, or environmental issues such as energy management, energy use, and recycled paper and waste [27,33,39,41,113–115]. Sustainability investment and green banking awareness programs are tools that are driven or supported by new technologies. These environmental initiatives measure customer satisfaction and green consumer loyalty [45,108].

When it comes to the importance and performance of a green banking system, consumers are now turning their attention to those banks that are responsible and interested in protecting the environment [113]. Accordingly, current consumers' or investors' considerations of banks depend not only on the security of their deposits or investments, but also on the accounting and expectations of the deposit or investment being used to improve the environment and social well-being [114]. Likewise, consumers are more likely to prefer those banking institutions which involve them in decision making through co-creation, as involving customers in decision making related to the environment builds a sense in consumers that this bank is concerned about the environment in real terms, which ultimately boosts their green loyalty [46]. A similar study found a positive effect of green value on consumer confidence [115]. The incorporation of environmental concerns into marketing strategies is seen as a tool to increase green loyalty [14,33].

Thus, the adoption of a green banking initiative, as a means of improving sustainability, is seen as an appropriate step in shaping a positive image of banks [116]. Green banking ensures the environmental efficiency of banks, and thus reduces the internal and external carbon footprint [109]. The banking industry is not regarded as a polluting industry, but it affects the environment through increased energy usage—such as the use of light and air-conditioning—and the huge usage of paper. It is therefore important to integrate CSR with the green initiatives of business operations in order to ensure sustainable economic development [41,117]. It can be said that banks are business citizens who, like any other business, are responsible for the preservation of the natural environment. Consumers' perceptions of the green value of a company have a significant effect on their green loyalty. A similar study has shown that consumers' perceptions of a company's green initiatives have a significant impact on post-purchase behavior [118]. In addition, Chen [47] has shown that there is a positive relationship between green practices and green loyalty. Based on the above requirements, we propose the following hypothesis:

Hypothesis 5 (H5). *Green banking initiatives moderate the indirect relationship of CSR and green consumer loyalty through co-creation, such that the relationship is stronger in the presence of green banking initiatives.*

Based on above discussion with the support of related literature, we propose the following research model (see Figure 1).

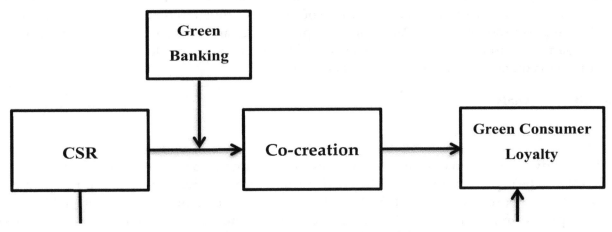

Figure 1. Proposed Research Model.

3. Methods

3.1. Sampling Procedure and Strategy

The proposed research model was applied in the banking industry of Pakistan. The information was gathered for the field research in three major cities, in particular Islamabad, Faisalabad, and Lahore. Islamabad is the capital city of Pakistan. Lahore is the second biggest city in Pakistan, and the capital of the largest province (in terms of population) of Punjab whereas, Faisalabad is also one of the largest city of Pakistan. A total of 800 surveys were disseminated and 529 were returned, among which 489 were useable for the data analysis. In our examination, all individuals beyond 18 years old with a bank account were considered as respondents. We used a multi-stage sampling method for the sake of the data collection; in this regard, at the primary stage, banks in all of the regions of Pakistan with an excess of 600 branches were searched, based on their investment in CSR. Six banks, including the National Bank of Pakistan (1450 branches), Habib Bank Limited (1500 plus branches), United Bank Limited (1380 branches), Muslim Commercial Bank Limited (1100 plus branches), Allied Bank Limited (1100 plus branches), and Meezan Bank (600 plus branches) met these measures and were chosen to proceed with the data collection. In the subsequent stage, different areas in every city were randomly chosen. The authors visited the selected areas all week long and at various times in order to gather information from the clients. The bank account holders were reached when they left a bank office or automated teller machine (ATM) administration territory. Conducting consumer correspondence in such a way is also in line with research of Khan, et al. [119], Shah and Khan [120], and Raza, Saeed, Iqbal, Saeed, Sadiq and Faraz [8]. Preceding the field study, a survey was conducted in order to discover these banks. Dedicated visits were made to obtain answers concerning the CSR exercises of the chosen banks and how they educate their consumers about their CSR experience. The Qualification Criteria for the banks were that they must have a CSR activity page on their website, and they must distribute a CSR update on paper and through electronic media, in which they must plainly mirror their CSR administrations in their yearly annual reports. These chosen banks are the biggest banks in the nation, and are spread over 80% of Pakistan's area.

3.2. Measures

The present research study adapted already existing scales which were reliable and validated by different researchers. For instance, the scale of CSR was adapted form Eisingerich, Andreas B, Rubera, Gaia Seifert, Matthias Bhardwaj and Gunjan [86]: the scale consists of three items; a sample item is: "This bank is a socially responsible bank". Similarly, the items for co-creation were adapted from Nysveen and Pedersen [121]. There were four items for the measurement of the co-creation construct. A sample item is: "I often find solutions to my problems together with my bank". The scale of consumer loyalty was adapted from Oliver [35], and includes four items. A sample item is: "I am willing to repurchase this product (bank) because of its (environmental) functions". Lastly, the items of green banking were adapted from Patterson and Spreng [122], and Khan, et al. [123], and include four items. A sample item is: "This bank's (environmental) functions provide very good value for me". All of the items were rated on a five point Likert scale.

4. Results and Analysis

4.1. Handling of Social Desirability

This study is based directly on consumer responses for data collection, so the social desirability bias (SDB) may be high in the questionnaire [124]. Various measures were taken to control and mitigate the SDB effect proposed by Grimm [125]. First, the researchers remained directly engaged in the data collection procedure, verifying the CSR awareness of respondents and obtaining their permission, then moving on to the research instrument. In addition, scales that were previously known and validated were used for all four variables of CSR, co-creation, green consumer loyalty, and green banking initiatives. The data were collected from different branches of the banks in different areas of the selected cities. In addition, all of the items were tested by experts, and the items of all three constructs were randomly scattered in the questionnaire in order to break any anticipated sequence developed by the respondents. Table 1 presents the demographic profile of the study respondents in which we report gender, age and education related information of the respondents of present study (see Table 1).

Table 1. Demographic profile of respondents.

	Frequency	%
Gender		
Male	357	73.0
Female	132	27.0
Age		
18–20	46	9.4
21–30	138	28.2
31–40	210	42.9
Above 40	95	19.4
Education		
Matric	39	7.9
Intermediate	78	15.9
Graduate	136	27.8
Master	189	38.6
Higher	47	9.6

4.2. Common Method Variance

This examination is liable to common method variance (CMV), since the information for all of the variables were collected from same individual. In order to limit the potential CMV impact, the items of all four variables were scattered randomly in the questionnaire. This approach reduces the probability of respondents liking a specific variable, and consequently restricts the probability that their answers to one variable would influence the others. In order to affirm that CMV didn't mirror our outcomes, we executed CFA based on a Harmon single-factor test [126] utilizing the maximum likelihood strategy. We set all of the items of the examination to load on a single factor. This one-factor estimation model didn't give consistent lists in their standard range of acceptability. Our four-factor estimation model altogether improved the chi-square, and furthermore gave preferable consistence of model fit indices over the one-factor estimation model.

Second, following Lindell and Whitney [127], we utilized the marker variable technique and utilized employee incivility as our marker variable (i.e., a variable that is hypothetically inconsequential to others in this examination). The lowest level of correlation between employee incivility and our four factor model was viewed as the CMV esteem (rs). Employee incivility is related to CSR (r = 0.011), Co-creation (r = −0.113), Green banking initiatives (r = 0.015), and Green consumer loyalty (r = −0.192). Likewise, the CMV estimate was observed as r = 0.011, which demonstrates an overall low common variance shared amongst the structures. In order to control likely CMV, the correlation coefficients between the three variables were adjusted depending on rs = 0.011. All of the adjusted coefficients after rectification for CMV were significant. These outcomes propose that CMV is not a potential issue in our study (see Table 2).

Table 2. Results of the CMV-adjusted correlations.

	Unadjusted Correlation	CMV-Adjusted Correlation
CSR–CC	0.514	0.511 *
CC–GCL	0.623	0.620 *
CSR–GCL	0.492	0.491 *
CSR–GBI	0.392	0.390 *
CC–GBI	0.421	0.419 *
GBI–GCL	0.543	0.540 *

* CMV-adjusted estimates using rs = 0.011.

The researchers performed factor analysis in order to assess whether the items are well-loaded on their respective variables. The results are shown in Table 3. According to these results, all of the items were loaded significantly on their respective construct, as the cut-off values for all of the items were beyond 0.05, as recommended by Fornell and Larcker [128]. Similarly, we also tested the Cronbach alpha values and composite reliability values for our four major constructs. All of the values produced good enough results to establish that there is no issue of reliability in instrument. Furthermore, the values of average variance extracted (AVE) were also calculated, which showed that all of the values are beyond the threshold level of 0.05 (see Table 4). Finally, we examined the discriminant validity, for which we compared the square root values of the AVE for each construct with the values of the correlations, and we found that all of the values of the square root of the AVE were greater than the correlation values (see Table 5).

In order to test the hypotheses of the present research study, we applied a covariance-based structural equation modeling (SEM) technique using the maximum likelihood method. Table 6 shows the results of the model fit indices for three models, among which model 1 tests the direct effects, model 2 shows the results for the mediation, and model 3 is concerned with the model fit result for the moderated mediation. As can be seen, all of the fit indices for model 3 are above the threshold values. If the below table is analyzed carefully, then it becomes obvious that the model fit indices are most appropriate in model 3. Model 1 is a model in which we only calculated for the direct effect of the CSR activities on CC and CL, and GBI on GCL, whereas in model 2, the hypothesized model is reproduced for the mediation results. The table further elaborates that model 3 produces the most suitable values of the fit indices and χ^2/df, which is indicative of the fact that our hypothesized model is well fitted to the data. Furthermore, we also conducted a χ^2 difference test in comparison to the alternate model 1, in order to establish the argument that our hypothesized model is better fitted to the data in comparison to models 1 and 2. The results show that the value of χ^2 is significantly improved from model 1 to 2 ($\Delta\chi2 = 1423.94$, Δdf = 5, p-value < 0.05), and from model 2 to 3 ($\Delta\chi2 = 15.66$, Δdf = 2, p-value < 0.05).

Table 3. Items with factor loadings.

Construct	Items	Factor Loading
CSR	This bank is a socially responsible bank	0.76
	This bank is more beneficial to society's welfare than other brands	0.88
	This bank contributes to society in positive ways	0.83
Co-creation	I often express my personal needs to this brand (bank)	0.73
	I often find solutions to my problems together with my brand (bank)	0.86
	I am actively involved when the brand (bank) develops new solutions for me	0.90
	The brand (bank) encourages customers to create new solutions together	0.77
Loyalty	I am happy about my decision to choose this product (bank) because of its (environmental) functions	0.87
	I believe that I do the right thing to purchase this product (bank) because of its (environmental) performance	0.89
	Overall, I am glad to buy this product (bank) because it is (environmentally) friendly	0.83
	Overall, I am satisfied with this product (bank) because of its (environmental) concern	0.81
Green Banking Initiatives	This bank's (environmental) functions provide very good value for me	0.82
	This bank is very concerned about environmental sustainability	0.79
	This bank management is serious about green banking projects and willing to finance green projects	0.86
	The daily operations of our bank are safe for the environment	0.82

Table 4. Factor loadings, reliability and AVE.

Variable	Items	[b] FL (Min-Max)	*t*-Value (Min-Max)	α [b]	CR [b]	AVE [b]
CSR	3	0.76–0.88	10.08–17.25	0.77	0.81	0.58
CC	4	0.73–0.90	11.72–20.19	0.75	0.79	0.61
GCL	4	0.81–0.89	13.81–21.71	0.78	0.82	0.59
GBI	4	0.79–0.86	19.76–27.88	0.86	0.86	0.64

[b] FL: factor loading; α [b]: Cronbach's α coefficient; CR [b]: composite reliability; AVE [b]: average variance extracted.

Table 5. Discriminant validity.

	Mean	SD	CSR	CC	GCL	GBI
CSR	3.22	1.20	0.76 [a]			
CC	3.18	1.29	0.51 **	0.78 [a]		
GCL	3.76	1.06	0.49 **	0.62 **	0.77 [a]	
GBI	3.49	1.11	0.39 **	0.42 **	0.54 **	0.80 [a]

[a] Squared root of the AVE.; ** significant value.

Table 6. Model fit indices comparison between the hypothesized model and the alternate models.

	Model—1 Direct effect Model	Model—2 Mediation model	Model—3 Moderated mediation model
χ^2 (df)	1622.37 (56)	214.09 (53)	198.43 (51)
χ^2/df	28.97	4.04	3.89
GFI	0.822	0.926	0.942
CFI	0.798	0.903	0.976
RMSEA	0.126	0.063	0.053

The results of the hypothesis testing significantly supported all five of the hypotheses of the study. Additionally, the bootstrap method—using 5000 bootstrapping samples—provided support to accept all of the hypotheses of the present research. CSR has a positive and significant impact on CC (β = 0.66) and GCL (β = 0.62), leading the authors to accept hypotheses H1 and H3. Similarly, CC has a positive and significant impact on GCL (β = 0.47), supporting H2 (see Table 7).

Table 7. Direct effects.

	Coefficients	SE	*p*-Value	95% Bias Corrected CI	Decision
H1: CSR⟶CC	0.66	0.062	<0.05	0.73; 0.79	Supported
H2: CC⟶CL	0.62	0.241	0.05	0.032; 0.21	Supported
H3: CSR⟶CL	0.47	0.218	<0.05	0.132; 0.38	Supported

The results of the significant direct effects for H1, H2, and H3 give support to the partial mediation effect of CC between CSR and CL. In order to test the mediation effect, we executed bootstrapping by using 5000 samples to generate a bias-corrected confidence interval for the mediation effect. The indirect effect (b = 0.41) was positive and significant, as indicated by its $p < 0.05$, but its value is reduced, which is indicative of the fact that there is a partial mediation of CC between CSR and CL. Furthermore, almost 46% of the total effect of CSR on CL happens through our mediator, CC. Lastly, in Table 8, we report the indirect effect of CSR on GCL through CC by applying bootstrap method recommended by Preacher and Hayes [129]. According to the results, the indirect effect is 0.41, which is reduced but remains significant, as indicated by the values of the bias-corrected confidence interval (0.128–0.802). As such, all of these results suggest that CC partially mediates the relationship between CSR and GCL. Lastly, we checked the results of the moderated mediation analysis in Table 8.

Table 8. Indirect effect.

	Standardized Indirect Effects	95% Bias Corrected CI *	Result
H4: CSR⟶CC⟶GCL	**0.41 (0.142)** *	0.128–0.802	Supported
H4: CSR⟶CC↓GCL	**0.54 (0.144)** *	0.137–0.887	Supported

* bootstrap standard error in bold.

For this purpose, we introduced GBI as a moderator between the indirect relation of CSR and GCL through CC; we used a multi-group analysis and $\chi2$ difference test along with the bootstrapping. The $\chi2$ values for both the constrained and unconstrained model were assessed for any meaningful differences. The results showed a difference of 26.33 in the $\chi2$ value, and a difference of 19 in the degree of freedom between the two models (constrained vs. unconstrained), which means that GBI acts as a moderator between the indirect relation of CSR and GCL. Additionally, the bootstrapping results confirmed that GBI moderates our indirect relation, such that the indirect relation of CSR and GCL is stronger after the inclusion of GBI as a moderator (the Beta value increased from 0.41 to 0.54). Hence, in line with the statement of Hypothesis 5, it is statistically proven that GBI moderates the indirect relationship of CSR and GCL through CC.

5. Discussion and Conclusions

The objective of the present study was to investigate the impact of CSR activities on green consumer loyalty in the context of the banking industry of Pakistan, with the mediating effect of co-creation and the moderating effect of green banking initiatives. The results confirm that CSR activities positively predict banking consumer loyalty (beta = 0.66, $p < 0.05$), which means that banks can use the CSR strategy to enhance consumer loyalty in the Pakistani banking sector. These findings are in line with previous research [24,52,58,92] studies which also support our argument that CSR can boost loyalty. Likewise, our findings also confirm that the development of co-creation is an enabler between the indirect relationship of CSR and green consumer loyalty, as co-creation partially mediates this relationship (standardized beta = 0.41 (0.142). This finding also received support from the existing literature [8,14]. Finally, we tested the moderation effect of green banking initiatives on the mediated relationship of CSR and consumer loyalty via co-creation. The results provide sufficient grounds to accept that green banking initiatives moderate this mediated relation. Hence, there is confirmation of the moderated mediation effect (standardized beta = 0.54 (0.144). In the coming section, we discuss and conclude our findings in detail.

The banking sector of Pakistan participates in CSR activities including charity, cause-and-effect marketing, and environmental safety. This industry is facing fierce competition, leading to an ever-increasing stiff environment. In order to increase the efficiency of their services, banks are looking for additional marketing strategies—such as CSR, green banking initiatives, and co-creation—in order to foster a favorable attitude in consumers. Technology is changing the traditional banking with a fast pace. As a result, banks pay more attention to both consumers and financial technologies in order to create products that meet the needs of consumers. Nowadays, consumers themselves are in great demand, as vanilla solutions from the banks have already been rejected by consumers. The consumers want to see the initiatives of their banking partners, especially green initiatives.

It's not just the digital power of financial technologies that banks need to adopt in their product development programs; consumers themselves have more access to information than ever before, and this increases their ability to understand their own needs. Banks need to understand that diversified partnerships will be the standard for future of financial services. The emergence of collaborative design (co-creation) caused a paradigm transition to a typical product development model in which marketing / sales departments conduct market research and then submit it to engineers in order for them to develop a product or service. However, the danger associated with the traditional approach is that these products may not meet the needs of the market in actual terms, and hence money is wasted and time runs out, which may lead to the failure of the whole organization. The new approach (co-creation) proactively involves consumers in the product development process and receiving feedback from consumers. This iteration cycle continues several times, as organizations have to produce a product that has a much higher level of reliability than the traditional model beyond the consumer's perception. Alignment with this approach requires the constant participation of consumers in order to build their belief that their organization is a caring organization, on the one hand, and that it takes into account social responsibility on the other hand. The above discussion is also supported by the extant literature [78,107,111,128,129]. Likewise, sustainability is a big trend in recent times, as eco-friendliness has become the new norm for modern consumers, who are increasingly choosing well-made ethical products and services over cheap and mass-produced ones.

Green banking initiatives are one of the most imperative aspects driving green consumer loyalty. This is because modern consumers feel a kind of stewardship regarding the environment. All of these efforts eventually contribute towards building a higher level of consumer loyalty. These findings are also in line with previous researchers [14,82,110]. The importance of consumer loyalty from a green perspective is reflected in the many marketing benefits that result from increased engagement. Once a banking institution understands consumers, it is important to understand the various benefits of consumer loyalty in order to better understand how to deal with them. In today's business, consumer trust is everything, and CSR is an important strategy for financial institutions to win the trust of consumers.

Social responsibility allows businesses to use their strengths to benefit the local community. The diffusion of CSR efforts to all stakeholders is essential, in that it allows individuals to contribute to the public account in their own way, and reduces the investment needed to benefit the organization and the community. This, in turn, has a measurable impact on all departments, as banks invest indirectly in public effort, financial literacy, diversity of access and supply, and the environment. The advantage of social responsibility beyond branding is that it establishes the perception among consumers that the brand is socially responsible and contributing to preserve nature through green initiatives. Good CSR work carefully improves the ability of individuals and consumers to engage in meaningful (co-creation) organizational approaches.

CSR is one of the ways to increase confidence through targeted, community-oriented approaches, rather than large and distant investments in resources. These results are also supported by previous research [14,51,92,108,112]. This means offering financial literacy programs to local schools, providing access and financial assistance to older and caring adults, and offering community days for free financial counseling. It also means participation in private communities, and the allocation of CSR funds for public festivals, clean-ups, and environmental activities. This is because going local means that the efforts of a bank, that has the opportunity to do business, are visible to the public. If the bank can build trust through CSR and co-creation efforts that are not marketing-centric, but instead aimed at improving the community, then the bank has taken one of the biggest steps to protect long-term consumers and increase social benefits.

The benefits of consumer loyalty can enhance repeat business, sales opportunities, high purchase prices, and positive word of mouth. Loyal consumers continue to purchase banking services on a regular basis. As the power to build relationships with this type of consumer increases, their purchase price increases in value or volume (or, more often, in both). This is sometimes natural, but the organization may choose to implement other incentive programs in order to encourage consumer loyalty, or to increase their spending levels, which in turn increases profits. Loyal consumers not only bring in new consumers, but also come back, depending on the quality of services and their relationship with a particular bank. However, as sales grow and consumers become more diverse, there are alternatives to the creation of consumer preferences.

Co-creation is different from assembling the same; rather, the banks and their consumers work together to create good ideas, improve services, and create new products based on consumer feedback. The idea is to let participants, especially consumers, know that they are working directly and independently to improve the services of a particular bank, especially in the context of environmentalism. This not only increases their presence, but also their green loyalty, as consumers who see themselves as part of the company are determined to continue using its services. The paybacks of co-creation are many, and can affect sustainability, marketing results, and overall profitability. We conclude that the most interested consumers in the company are an unexploited tool to increase the level of success, which means that cooperation and consumer resilience will help build the brand.

5.1. Implications and Suggestions

The present study has some important implications for theory, and for people in practice. For theory, this study accentuates the role of CSR in building loyal consumers in the Pakistani banking sector. That is, while companies are committed to CSR, they do everything they can to build meaningful relationships with their consumers, employees, and the environment. Consumers support organizations with their positive attitudes. Investing in CSR ensures that banks do more humanitarian work, and the interest of all stakeholders is vital for them. Therefore, they communicate reliably with the consumer through the branding process, which ultimately leads to greater loyalty, especially green loyalty. In a similar vein, CSR strengthens co-creation activities along with the general consumer base, which motivates consumers to participate in the bank's code of conduct in communication, and provides consumers with a lot of useful information on improving the quality of products and services. A bank's CSR gives consumers a platform to report directly to banks, which increases their self-esteem and pushes them to cross boundaries of behavior. In addition, social identity theory reinforces the power of the ethical value-based marketing model in defining the relationship between CSR co-creation and green initiatives.

Additionally, there are some practical implications for financial policy makers in this study. If bank policy makers need to be honest with people through CSR, they need to communicate with consumers through consumer engagement activities (co-creation). Banks should encourage discussions with consumers on new products, development services, and innovations. Banks can use co-creation activities as a tool to improve consumer's participation in the development of credit, pensions, car loans, and future investment plans. In this way, banks can easily obtain new ideas through experienced consumers. Our research also confirms that when companies understand the needs of their consumers, and involve them in the process of integration (co-creation), their loyalty increases. In addition, CSR activities not only allow consumers to identify with the organization, but to formally lead to consumer behavior. Therefore, banks need to secure this recognition through CSR-related programs, as this type of recognition is more robust than others. Banks' CSR guidelines should translate into actions that are appropriate for different partners, such as personnel growth, consumer handling policies, ethics and regulatory policies, and working in a better environment for the community. In the end, banks should try to build a culture that accepts the experience and understanding of valued consumers. In addition, banks need to maintain close relationships with consumers based on trust and brand strength. Banks need to see them as a source of innovation. This collaborative development approach has the best potential to turn CSR models into loyal consumers.

Our research further suggests that banking institutions need to realize the importance of green initiatives from a broader perspective; rather than assuming them to be an ethical responsibility, the banks are encouraged to include green initiatives in their core business practices, as the results of present study confirm that going green induces consumer loyalty from a green perspective. Hence, the policy makers are recommended to promote green initiatives in order to reap long term benefits in the form of induced consumer loyalty. In this regard, the following suggestions may be helpful for banking institutions:

(1) Banks need environmental impact assessment as part of the bank's overall consumer assessment (especially corporate consumers) before granting a loan if the consumer re-examines the environmental risk model and assesses the environmental impact of the consumer's business.

(2) Green offices should be established in order to implement the green banking guidelines and to introduce environmental culture as part of the organizational culture.

(3) The recycling of office waste using a recycling environment should be encouraged.

(4) An environmental campaign needs to be launched in order to commemorate environmental days such as World Water Day, Earth Day and Environmental Day.

(5) Banks should choose ways to eliminate / reduce the use of paper in their day-to-day operations. These steps include a gradual transition to paperless banking.

(6) Banks should install solar energy systems, which will prevent the release of greenhouse gases to reduce environmental degradation.

5.2. Limitations and the Way Forward

Like any other study, this study has its limitations. First, this research was limited to the banking institutions of Pakistan, so it is logical for future researchers to conduct the same in other areas of services, such as hospitality and tourism. In addition, some researchers may also be able to take into account the manufacturing industry and compare their results with those of the service sector. Second, this study is only representative of Pakistan's population, and its results cannot be generalized to all developing countries. In addition, since CSR activities are perceived differently by consumers in different cultures, repeating this type of research in other developing countries may generate different results. Therefore, in order to increase the integration of the research, it is recommended that researchers reproduce the present study in other developing countries.

Third, since all of the information in this study was collected through surveys, there are concerns of mono-method bias. Future research should reduce this issue by better understanding the impact of CSR on consumer loyalty, through grouping or in-depth interviews using qualitative insights. Fourth, this study only takes into account the attitudinal facet of CSR standards, co-creation, green banking, and green consumer loyalty; other studies could further strengthen our research by developing behavioral facets together with attitudinal ones. In addition to removing these limitations, there are other possibilities for future research. For example, it would be interesting to explore the ways in which employees affect the CSR opinion of consumers. This is true for service industries, as these types of services often have more communication between consumers and employees in order to build the consumer experience. Fifth, this study involves the development of co-creation with consumer loyalty; future research may involve brand-related variables, including brand equity, which is one of the most discussed variables in the world of marketing and brand management. It will be interesting to see what kind of brand equity, consumer-based brand equity, or financially-based brand equity is most affected by co-creation and green initiatives. Finally, cross-sectional data with random samples were used in this study; other studies could be performed using time series data and other sampling methods.

Author Contributions: All of the authors contributed to conceptualization, formal analysis, investigation, methodology and writing and editing the original draft. All authors have read and agreed to the published version of the manuscript.

References

1.   Shahzad, M.; Qu, Y.; Javed, S.A.; Zafar, A.U.; Rehman, S.U. Relation of environment sustainability to CSR and green innovation: A case of Pakistani manufacturing industry. *J. Clean. Prod.* **2020**, *253*, 119938. [CrossRef]

2.   Ahmad, R.; Ahmad, S.; Islam, T.; Kaleem, A. The nexus of corporate social responsibility (CSR), affective commitment and organisational citizenship behaviour in academia. *Empl. Relat.* **2020**, *42*, 232–247. [CrossRef]

3.   Zatwarnicka-Madura, B.; Siemieniako, D.; Glińska, E.; Sazonenka, Y. Strategic and Operational Levels of CSR Marketing Communication for Sustainable Orientation of a Company: A Case Study from Bangladesh. *Sustainability* **2019**, *11*, 555. [CrossRef]

4.   Abubakr, M.; Abbas, A.T.; Tomaz, Í.V.; Soliman, M.S.; Luqman, M.; Hegab, H. Sustainable and Smart Manufacturing: An Integrated Approach. *Sustainability* **2020**, *12*, 2280. [CrossRef]

5.   Samul, J. Spiritual Leadership: Meaning in the Sustainable Workplace. *Sustainability* **2019**, *12*, 267. [CrossRef]

6.   Han, H.; Al-Ansi, A.; Chi, X.; Baek, H.; Lee, K.-S. Impact of Environmental CSR, Service Quality, Emotional Attachment, and Price Perception on Word-of-Mouth for Full-Service Airlines. *Sustainability* **2020**, *12*, 3974. [CrossRef]

7.   Kim, Y.; Lee, S.S.; Roh, T. Taking Another Look at Airline CSR: How Required CSR and Desired CSR Affect Customer Loyalty in the Airline Industry. *Sustainability* **2020**, *12*, 4281. [CrossRef]

8.   Raza, A.; Saeed, A.; Iqbal, M.K.; Saeed, U.; Sadiq, I.; Faraz, N.A. Linking Corporate Social Responsibility to Customer Loyalty through Co-Creation and Customer Company Identification: Exploring Sequential Mediation Mechanism. *Sustainability* **2020**, *12*, 2525. [CrossRef]

9.   Knebel, S.; Seele, P. Introducing public procurement tenders as part of corporate communications: A typological analysis based on CSR reporting indicators. *Corp. Commun. Int. J.* **2020**. [CrossRef]

10.   Grebmer, C.; Diefenbach, S. The Challenges of Green Marketing Communication: Effective Communication to Environmentally Conscious but Skeptical Consumers. *Designs* **2020**, *4*, 25. [CrossRef]

11.   Popovic, I.; Bossink, B.; Van Der Sijde, P.; Fong, C.Y.M. Why Are Consumers Willing to Pay More for Liquid Foods in Environmentally Friendly Packaging? A Dual Attitudes Perspective. *Sustainability* **2020**, *12*, 2812. [CrossRef]

12.   Sanchez-Sabate, R.; Sabaté, J. Consumer Attitudes Towards Environmental Concerns of Meat Consumption: A Systematic Review. *Int. J. Environ. Res. Public Health* **2019**, *16*, 1220. [CrossRef] [PubMed]

13.   Tchorek, G.; Brzozowski, M.; Dziewanowska, K.; Allen, A.; Kozioł, W.; Kurtyka, M.; Targowski, F. Social Capital and Value Co-Creation: The Case of a Polish Car Sharing Company. *Sustainability* **2020**, *12*, 4713. [CrossRef]

14.   Iglesias, O.; Markovic, S.; Bagherzadeh, M.; Singh, J.J. Co-creation: A Key Link Between Corporate Social Responsibility, Customer Trust, and Customer Loyalty. *J. Bus. Ethics* **2018**, *163*, 151–166. [CrossRef]

15.   Luu, T.T. CSR and Customer Value Co-creation Behavior: The Moderation Mechanisms of Servant Leadership and Relationship Marketing Orientation. *J. Bus. Ethics* **2019**, *155*, 379–398. [CrossRef]

16. Kim, D.W.; Trimi, S.; Hong, S.; Lim, S. Effects of co-creation on organizational performance of small and medium manufacturers. *J. Bus. Res.* **2020**, *109*, 574–584. [CrossRef]

17. Fernando, Y.; Chukai, C. Value Co-Creation, Goods and Service Tax (GST) Impacts on Sustainable Logistic Performance. *Res. Transp. Bus. Manag.* **2018**, *28*, 92–102. [CrossRef]

18. Hajli, N.; Shanmugam, M.; Papagiannidis, S.; Zahay, D.; Richard, M.-O. Branding co-creation with members of online brand communities. *J. Bus. Res.* **2017**, *70*, 136–144. [CrossRef]

19. Cimbaljević, M.; Stankov, U.; Pavluković, V. Going beyond the traditional destination competitiveness—Reflections on a smart destination in the current research. *Curr. Issues Tour.* **2019**, *22*, 2472–2477. [CrossRef]

20. Chen, J.-S.; Kerr, D.; Chou, C.Y.; Ang, C. Business co-creation for service innovation in the hospitality and tourism industry. *Int. J. Contemp. Hosp. Manag.* **2017**, *29*, 1522–1540. [CrossRef]

21. Park, J.; Ha, S. Co-creation of service recovery: Utilitarian and hedonic value and post-recovery responses. *J. Retail. Consum. Serv.* **2016**, *28*, 310–316. [CrossRef]

22. Ahmed, I.; Nazir, M.S.; Ali, I.; Nurunnabi, M.; Khalid, A.; Shaukat, M.Z. Investing in CSR Pays You Back in Many Ways! The Case of Perceptual, Attitudinal and Behavioral Outcomes of Customers. *Sustainability* **2020**, *12*, 1158. [CrossRef]

23. Xu, H.; Wu, J.; Dao, M. Corporate social responsibility and trade credit. *Rev. Quant. Financ. Account.* **2019**, *54*, 1389–1416. [CrossRef]

24. Cuesta-Valiño, P.; Rodríguez, P.G.; Núñez-Barriopedro, E. The impact of corporate social responsibility on customer loyalty in hypermarkets: A new socially responsible strategy. *Corp. Soc. Responsib. Environ. Manag.* **2019**, *26*, 761–769. [CrossRef]

25. Kim, S.; Lee, H. The Effect of CSR Fit and CSR Authenticity on the Brand Attitude. *Sustainability* **2019**, *12*, 275. [CrossRef]

26. Julia, T.; Kassim, S. Exploring green banking performance of Islamic banks vs conventional banks in Bangladesh based on Maqasid Shariah framework. *J. Islam. Mark.* **2019**, *11*, 729–744. [CrossRef]

27. Hebbar, C.; Mahale, P. Impact of Demonetisation on Green Banking. *Glob. J. Manag. Bus. Res.* **2020**, *27*. [CrossRef]

28. Zhou, X.; Cui, Y. Green Bonds, Corporate Performance, and Corporate Social Responsibility. *Sustainability* **2019**, *11*, 6881. [CrossRef]

29. Da Luz, V.V.; Mantovani, D.; Nepomuceno, M.V. Matching green messages with brand positioning to improve brand evaluation. *J. Bus. Res.* **2020**, *119*, 25–40. [CrossRef]

30. De Mendonca, T.; Zhou, Y. Environmental Performance, Customer Satisfaction, and Profitability: A Study among Large U.S. Companies. *Sustainability* **2019**, *11*, 5418. [CrossRef]

31. Singh, S.K.; Chenb, J.; Giudicecd, M.; El-Kassar, A.-N. Environmental ethics, environmental performance, and competitive advantage: Role of environmental training. *Technol. Forecast. Soc. Chang.* **2019**, *146*, 203–211. [CrossRef]

32. Kautish, P.; Dash, G. Environmentally concerned consumer behavior: Evidence from consumers in Rajasthan. *J. Model. Manag.* **2017**, *12*, 712–738. [CrossRef]

33. Ibe-Enwo, G.; Igbudu, N.; Garanti, Z.; Popoola, T.; Enwo, I. Assessing the Relevance of Green Banking Practice on Bank Loyalty: The Mediating Effect of Green Image and Bank Trust. *Sustainability* **2019**, *11*, 4651. [CrossRef]

34. Igbudu, N.; Garanti, Z.; Popoola, T. Enhancing Bank Loyalty through Sustainable Banking Practices: The Mediating Effect of Corporate Image. *Sustainability* **2018**, *10*, 4050. [CrossRef]

35. Oliver, R.L. Whence consumer loyalty? *J. Mark.* **1999**, *63*, 33–44. [CrossRef]

36. Lyeonov, S.; Pimonenko, T.; Bilan, Y.; Streimikiene, D.; Mentel, G. Assessment of Green Investments' Impact on Sustainable Development: Linking Gross Domestic Product Per Capita, Greenhouse Gas Emissions and Renewable Energy. *Energies* **2019**, *12*, 3891. [CrossRef]

37. Amoako, G.K.; Dzogbenuku, R.K.; Abubakari, A. Do green knowledge and attitude influence the youth's green purchasing? Theory of planned behavior. *Int. J. Prod. Perform. Manag.* **2020**, *69*, 1609–1626. [CrossRef]

38. Herath, H.M.A.K.; Herath, H.M.S.P. Impact of Green Banking Initiatives on Customer Satisfaction: A Conceptual Model of Customer Satisfaction on Green Banking. *J. Bus. Manag.* **2019**, *21*, 24–35.

39. Manolas, E.; Tsantopoulos, G.; Dimoudi, K. Energy saving and the use of "green" bank products: The views of the citizens. *Manag. Environ. Qual. Int. J.* **2017**. [CrossRef]

40. Ott, I.; Soretz, S. Green Attitude and Economic Growth. *Environ. Resour. Econ.* **2016**, *70*, 757–779. [CrossRef]

41. Soumya, S. Green banking: A sustainable banking for environmental sustainability. *CLEAR Int. J. Res. Commer. Manag.* **2019**, *10*, 21–24.

42. Ghassim, B.; Bogers, M. Linking stakeholder engagement to profitability through sustainability-oriented innovation: A quantitative study of the minerals industry. *J. Clean. Prod.* **2019**, *224*, 905–919. [CrossRef]

43. Khalil, S.; O'Sullivan, P. Corporate social responsibility: Internet social and environmental reporting by banks. *Meditari Account. Res.* **2017**, *25*, 414–446. [CrossRef]

44. Emeseh, E.; Ako, R.; Okonmah, P.; Obokoh, O.L. Corporations, CSR and Self Regulation: What Lessons from the Global Financial Crisis? *Ger. Law J.* **2010**, *11*, 230–259. [CrossRef]

45. Issock, P.B.I.; Mpinganjira, M.; Roberts-Lombard, M. Modelling green customer loyalty and positive word of mouth. *Int. J. Emerg. Mark.* **2019**, *15*, 405–426. [CrossRef]

46. Wu, H.-C.; Cheng, C.-C. An Empirical Analysis of Green Experiential Loyalty: A Case Study. *J. Int. Food Agribus. Mark.* **2018**, *31*, 69–105. [CrossRef]

47. Chen, S.-Y. Using the sustainable modified TAM and TPB to analyze the effects of perceived green value on loyalty to a public bike system. *Transp. Res. Part A Policy Pract.* **2016**, *88*, 58–72. [CrossRef]

48. Skryhun, N.; Kapinus, L.; Petrovych, M. Consumer loyalty assessment as an important means of increasing company's profitability. *Sci. Educ.* **2020**, *5*, 3–8.

49. Maqbool, S.; Zameer, M.N. Corporate social responsibility and financial performance: An empirical analysis of Indian banks. *Future Bus. J.* **2018**, *4*, 84–93. [CrossRef]

50. Servera-Francés, D.; Piqueras-Tomás, L. The effects of corporate social responsibility on consumer loyalty through consumer perceived value. *Econ. Res.* **2019**, *32*, 66–84. [CrossRef]

51. Ashraf, S.; Ilyas, R.; Imtiaz, M.; Tahir, H.M. Impact of CSR on customer loyalty: Putting customer trust, customer identification, customer satisfaction and customer commitment into equation-a study on the banking sector of Pakistan. *Int. J. Multidiscip. Curr. Res.* **2017**, *5*, 1362–1372.

52. Chang, Y.-H.; Yeh, C.-H. Corporate social responsibility and customer loyalty in intercity bus services. *Transp. Policy* **2017**, *59*, 38–45. [CrossRef]

53. Ji, S.; Jan, I.U. The Impact of Perceived Corporate Social Responsibility on Frontline Employee's Emotional Labor Strategies. *Sustainability* **2019**, *11*, 1780. [CrossRef]

54. Ipsen, C.; Goe, R. Factors associated with consumer engagement and satisfaction with the Vocational Rehabilitation program. *J. Vocat. Rehabil.* **2016**, *44*, 85–96. [CrossRef]

55. Aramburu, I.A.; Pescador, I.G. The Effects of Corporate Social Responsibility on Customer Loyalty: The Mediating Effect of Reputation in Cooperative Banks Versus Commercial Banks in the Basque Country. *J. Bus. Ethics* **2019**, *154*, 701–719. [CrossRef]

56. Islam, T.; Islam, R.; Pitafi, A.H.; Xiaobei, L.; Rehmani, M.; Irfan, M.; Mubarik, M.S. The impact of corporate social responsibility on customer loyalty: The mediating role of corporate reputation, customer satisfaction, and trust. *Sustain. Prod. Consum.* **2021**, *25*, 123–135. [CrossRef]

57. Van Doorn, J.; Onrust, M.; Verhoef, P.C.; Bügel, M.S. The impact of corporate social responsibility on customer attitudes and retention—the moderating role of brand success indicators. *Mark. Lett.* **2017**, *28*, 607–619. [CrossRef]

58. Gürlek, M.; Düzgün, E.; Uygur, S.M. How does corporate social responsibility create customer loyalty? The role of corporate image. *Soc. Responsib. J.* **2017**, *13*, 409–427. [CrossRef]

59. Tajfel, H. *Intergroup Behavior. Introducing Social Psychology*; Penguin Books: New York, NY, USA, 1978; pp. 401–466.

60. Tajfel, H.; Turner, J.; Austin, C.; William, G.; Worchel, S. An Integrative Theory of Intergroup Conflict. In *Organizational Identity: A Reader*; Oxford University Press: Oxford, UK, 1979; pp. 56–65.

61. Farooq, O.; Rupp, D.E.; Farooq, M. The Multiple Pathways through which Internal and External Corporate Social Responsibility Influence Organizational Identification and Multifoci Outcomes: The Moderating Role of Cultural and Social Orientations. *Acad. Manag. J.* **2017**, *60*, 954–985. [CrossRef]

62. Abbas, M.; Gao, Y.; Shah, S.S.H. CSR and Customer Outcomes: The Mediating Role of Customer Engagement. *Sustainability* **2018**, *10*, 4243. [CrossRef]

63. Tuan, L.T.; Rajendran, D.; Rowley, C.; Khai, D.C. Customer value co-creation in the business-to-business tourism context: The roles of corporate social responsibility and customer empowering behaviors. *J. Hospit. Tour. Manag.* **2019**, *39*, 137–149. [CrossRef]

64. Rodriguez-Gomez, S.; Castro, M.L.A.; López, M.V.; Rodríguez-Ariza, L. Where Does CSR Come from and Where Does It Go? A Review of the State of the Art. *Adm. Sci.* **2020**, *10*, 60. [CrossRef]

65. Para-González, L.; Mascaraque-Ramírez, C.; Cubillas-Para, C. Maximizing performance through CSR: The mediator role of the CSR principles in the shipbuilding industry. *Corp. Soc. Responsib. Environ. Manag.* **2020**, *27*, 2804–2815. [CrossRef]

66. Palazzo, M.; Vollero, A.; Siano, A. From strategic corporate social responsibility to value creation: An analysis of corporate website communication in the banking sector. *Int. J. Bank Mark.* **2020**, *38*, 1529–1552. [CrossRef]

67. Kujala, J.; Korhonen, A. Value-Creating Stakeholder Relationships in the Context of CSR. In *Stakeholder Engagement: Clinical Research Cases*; Springer: Berlin/Heidelberg, Germany, 2017; pp. 63–85.

68. Salvioni, D.M.; Gennari, F. CSR, Sustainable Value Creation and Shareholder Relations. *Symph. Emerg. Issues Manag.* **2017**, *1*, 36–49. [CrossRef]

69. Mubushar, M.; Jaafar, N.B.; Ab Rahim, R. The influence of corporate social responsibility activities on customer value co-creation: The mediating role of relationship marketing orientation. *Span. J. Mark. ESIC* **2020**. [CrossRef]

70. Adamik, A.; Nowicki, M. Pathologies and Paradoxes of Co-Creation: A Contribution to the Discussion about Corporate Social Responsibility in Building a Competitive Advantage in the Age of Industry 4. *Sustainability* **2019**, *11*, 4954. [CrossRef]

71. Sheth, J.N. Customer value propositions: Value co-creation. *Ind. Mark. Manag.* **2020**, *87*, 312–315. [CrossRef]

72. Nurunnabi, M.; Esquer, J.; Munguia, N.; Zepeda, D.; Perez, R.; Velazquez, L. Reaching the sustainable development goals 2030: Energy efficiency as an approach to corporate social responsibility (CSR). *GeoJournal* **2020**, *85*, 363–374. [CrossRef]

73. Kiliç, M. Online corporate social responsibility (CSR) disclosure in the banking industry. *Int. J. Bank Mark.* **2016**. [CrossRef]

74. LeninKumar, V. The Relationship between Customer Satisfaction and Customer Trust on Customer Loyalty. *Int. J. Acad. Res. Bus. Soc. Sci.* **2017**, *7*, 450–465. [CrossRef]

75. Beirão, G.; Patrício, L.; Fisk, R.P. Value cocreation in service ecosystems. *J. Serv. Manag.* **2017**, *28*, 227–249. [CrossRef]

76. Buhalis, D.; Sinarta, Y. Real-time co-creation and nowness service: Lessons from tourism and hospitality. *J. Travel Tour. Mark.* **2019**, *36*, 563–582. [CrossRef]

77. Mainardes, E.W.; Teixeira, A.; Romano, P.C.D.S. Determinants of co-creation in banking services. *Int. J. Bank Mark.* **2017**, *35*, 187–204. [CrossRef]

78. Assiouras, I.; Skourtis, G.; Giannopoulos, A.; Buhalis, D.; Koniordos, M. Value co-creation and customer citizenship behavior. *Ann. Tour. Res.* **2019**, *78*, 102742. [CrossRef]

79. González-Mansilla, Ó.; Berenguer-Contrí, G.; Serra-Cantallops, A. The impact of value co-creation on hotel brand equity and customer satisfaction. *Tour. Manag.* **2019**, *75*, 51–65. [CrossRef]

80. Woratschek, H.; Horbel, C.; Popp, B. Determining customer satisfaction and loyalty from a value co-creation perspective. *Serv. Ind. J.* **2019**, *40*, 777–799. [CrossRef]

81. Cambra-Fierro, J.; Pérez, L.; Grott, E. Towards a co-creation framework in the retail banking services industry: Do demographics influence? *J. Retail. Consum. Serv.* **2017**, *34*, 219–228. [CrossRef]

82. Malik, M.I.; Ahsan, R. Towards innovation, co-creation and customers' satisfaction: A banking sector perspective. *Asia Pac. J. Innov. Entrep.* **2019**, *13*, 311–325. [CrossRef]

83. Izogo, E.E.; Elom, M.E.; Mpinganjira, M. Examining customer willingness to pay more for banking services: The role of employee commitment, customer involvement and customer value. *Int. J. Emerg. Mark.* **2020**. [CrossRef]

84. Wu, L.-W.; Wang, C.-Y.; Rouyer, E. The opportunity and challenge of trust and decision-making uncertainty: Managing co-production in value co-creation. *Int. J. Bank Mark.* **2019**, *38*, 199–218. [CrossRef]

85. Chadwick-Jones, J.K. *Social Exchange Theory: Its Structure and Influence in Social Psychology*; Academic Press: Cambridge, MA, USA, 1976.

86. Eisingerich, A.B.; Rubera, G.; Seifert, M.; Bhardwaj, G. Doing Good and Doing Better despite Negative Information?: The Role of Corporate Social Responsibility in Consumer Resistance to Negative Information. *J. Serv. Res.* **2010**, *14*, 60–75. [CrossRef]

87. Skarmeas, D.; Leonidou, C.N. When consumers doubt, Watch out! The role of CSR skepticism. *J. Bus. Res.* **2013**, *66*, 1831–1838. [CrossRef]

88. Zahller, K.A.; Arnold, V.; Roberts, R.W. Using CSR Disclosure Quality to Develop Social Resilience to Exogenous Shocks: A Test of Investor Perceptions. *Behav. Res. Account.* **2015**, *27*, 155–177. [CrossRef]

89. Ramlugun, V.G.; Raboute, W.G. Do CSR Practices Of Banks In Mauritius Lead To Satisfaction And Loyalty? *Stud. Bus. Econ.* **2015**, *10*, 128–144. [CrossRef]

90. Shabbir, M.S.; Shariff, M.N.M.; Yusof, M.S.B.; Salman, R.; Hafeez, S. Corporate social responsibility and customer loyalty in Islamic banks of Pakistan: A mediating role of brand image. *Acad. Account. Financ. Stud. J.* **2018**, *22*, 1–6.

91. Rivera, J.; Bigne, E.; Curras-Perez, R. Effects of Corporate Social Responsibility perception on consumer satisfaction with the brand. *Span. J. Mark. ESIC* **2016**, *20*, 104–114. [CrossRef]

92. Nyuur, R.B.; Ofori, D.F.; Amponsah, M.M. Corporate social responsibility and competitive advantage: A developing country perspective. *Thunderbird Int. Bus. Rev.* **2019**, *61*, 551–564. [CrossRef]

93. Nyame-Asiamah, F.; Ghulam, S. The relationship between CSR activity and sales growth in the UK retailing sector. *Soc. Responsib. J.* **2019**. [CrossRef]

94. Lu, J.; Ren, L.; Zhang, C.; Wang, C.; Shahid, Z.; Streimikis, J. The Influence of a Firm's CSR Initiatives on Brand Loyalty and Brand Image. *J. Compet.* **2020**, *12*, 106–124. [CrossRef]

95. Alkitbi, S.S.; Alshurideh, M.; Al Kurdi, B.; Salloum, S.A. Factors Affect Customer Retention: A Systematic Review. In Proceedings of the International Conference on Advanced Intelligent Systems and Informatics, Cairo, Egypt, 19–21 October 2020; pp. 656–667.

96. Arli, D.I.; Lasmono, H.K. Consumers' perception of corporate social responsibility in a developing country. *Int. J. Cons. Stud.* **2010**, *34*, 46–51. [CrossRef]

97. Saxton, G.D.; Gomez, L.; Ngoh, Z.; Lin, Y.-P.; Dietrich, S. Do CSR Messages Resonate? Examining Public Reactions to Firms' CSR Efforts on Social Media. *J. Bus. Ethics* **2019**, *155*, 359–377. [CrossRef]

98. Sanclemente-Téllez, J. Marketing and Corporate Social Responsibility (CSR). Moving between broadening the concept of marketing and social factors as a marketing strategy. *Span. J. Mark. ESIC* **2017**, *21*, 4–25. [CrossRef]

99. Bianchi, E.; Bruno, J.M.; Sarabia-Sanchez, F.J. The impact of perceived CSR on corporate reputation and purchase intention. *Eur. J. Manag. Bus. Econ.* **2019**, *28*, 206–221. [CrossRef]

100. Mostafa, R.B.; Elsahn, F. Exploring the mechanism of consumer responses to CSR activities of Islamic banks. *Int. J. Bank Mark.* **2016**, *34*, 940–962. [CrossRef]

101. Fatma, M.; Khan, I.; Rahman, Z. CSR and consumer behavioral responses: The role of customer-company identification. *Asia Pac. J. Mark. Logist.* **2018**, *30*, 460–477. [CrossRef]

102. Hameed, F.; Qayyum, A.; Awan, Y. Impact of Dimensions of CSR on Purchase Intention with Mediating Role of Customer Satisfaction, Commitment and Trust. *Pak. Bus. Rev.* **2018**, *20*, 13–30.

103. Bagh, T.; Khan, M.A.; Azad, T.; Saddique, S.; Khan, M.A. The Corporate Social Responsibility and Firms' Financial Performance: Evidence from Financial Sector of Pakistan. *Int. J. Econ. Financ. Issues* **2017**, *7*, 301–308.

104. Osakwe, C.N.; Yusuf, T.O. CSR: A roadmap towards customer loyalty. *Total. Qual. Manag. Bus. Excel.* **2020**, 1–17. [CrossRef]

105. Markovic, S.; Iglesias, O.; Singh, J.J.; Sierra, V. How does the Perceived Ethicality of Corporate Services Brands Influence Loyalty and Positive Word-of-Mouth? Analyzing the Roles of Empathy, Affective Commitment, and Perceived Quality. *J. Bus. Ethics* **2015**, *148*, 721–740. [CrossRef]

106. Cossío-Silva, F.-J.; Revilla-Camacho, M.-Á.; Vega-Vázquez, M.; Palacios-Florencio, B. Value co-creation and customer loyalty. *J. Bus. Res.* **2016**, *69*, 1621–1625. [CrossRef]

107. Chen, C.-F.; Wang, J.-P. Customer participation, value co-creation and customer loyalty—A case of airline online check-in system. *Comput. Hum. Behav.* **2016**, *62*, 346–352. [CrossRef]

108. Anouze, A.L.M.; AlAmro, A.S.; Awwad, A.S. Customer satisfaction and its measurement in Islamic banking sector: A revisit and update. *J. Islam. Mark.* **2019**, *10*, 565–588. [CrossRef]

109. Masud, A.K.; Bae, S.M.; Kim, J.D. Analysis of Environmental Accounting and Reporting Practices of Listed Banking Companies in Bangladesh. *Sustainability* **2017**, *9*, 1717. [CrossRef]

110. Bose, S.; Khan, H.Z.; Rashid, A.; Islam, S. What drives green banking disclosure? An institutional and corporate governance perspective. *Asia Pac. J. Manag.* **2018**, *35*, 501–527. [CrossRef]

111. Taghizadeh-Hesary, F.; Yoshino, N. Sustainable Solutions for Green Financing and Investment in Renewable Energy Projects. *Energies* **2020**, *13*, 788. [CrossRef]

112. Julia, T.; Kassim, S. How serious are Islamic banks in offering green financing?: An exploratory study on Bangladesh banking sector. *Int. J. Green Econ.* **2019**, *13*, 120–138. [CrossRef]

113. Rai, R.; Kharel, S.; Devkota, N.; Paudel, U.R. Customers perception on green banking practices: A desk. *J. Econ. Concerns* **2019**, *10*, 82–95.

114. Sachs, J.D.; Woo, W.T.; Yoshino, N.; Taghizadeh-Hesary, F. Importance of Green Finance for Achieving Sustainable Development Goals and Energy Security. *Handb. Green Financ.* **2019**, 3–12. [CrossRef]

115. Hameed, D.; Waris, I. Eco Labels and Eco Conscious Consumer Behavior: The Mediating Effect of Green Trust and Environmental Concern. Hameed, Irfan and Waris, Idrees (2018): Eco Labels and Eco Conscious Consumer Behavior: The Mediating Effect of Green Trust and Environmental Concern. *J. Manag. Sci.* **2018**, *5*, 86–105.

116. Shampa, T.S.; Jobaid, M.I. Factors Influencing Customers' Expectation Towards Green Banking Practices in Bangladesh. *Eur. J. Bus. Manag.* **2017**, *9*, 140–152.

117. Nwagwu, I. Driving sustainable banking in Nigeria through responsible management education: The case of Lagos Business School. *Int. J. Manag. Educ.* **2020**, *18*, 100332. [CrossRef]

118. Aruna, S.; Thirumaran, R. Consumers' perception, satisfaction and post purchase behaviour towards green convenience products in Chennai. *ZENITH Int. J. Multidiscip. Res.* **2017**, *7*, 1–13.

119. Khan, Z.; Ferguson, D.; Pérez, A. Customer responses to CSR in the Pakistani banking industry. *Int. J. Bank Mark.* **2015**, *33*, 471–493. [CrossRef]

120. Shah, S.S.A.; Khan, Z. Corporate social responsibility: A pathway to sustainable competitive advantage? *Int. J. Bank Mark.* **2019**, *38*, 159–174. [CrossRef]

121. Nysveen, H.; Pedersen, P.E. Influences of Cocreation on Brand Experience. *Int. J. Mark. Res.* **2014**, *56*, 807–832. [CrossRef]

122. Patterson, P.G.; Spreng, R.A. Modelling the relationship between perceived value, satisfaction and repurchase intentions in a business-to-business, services context: An empirical examination. *Int. J. Serv. Ind. Manag.* **1997**, *8*, 414–434. [CrossRef]

123. Khan, E.A.; Dewan, M.N.A.; Chowdhury, M.M.H. Development and validation of a scale for measuring sustainability construct of informal microenterprises. In Proceedings of the 5th Asia-Pacific Business Research Conference, Kuala Lumpur, Malaysia, 17–18 February 2014.

124. Podsakoff, P.M.; MacKenzie, S.B.; Lee, J.-Y.; Podsakoff, N.P. Common method biases in behavioral research: A critical review of the literature and recommended remedies. *J. Appl. Psychol.* **2003**, *88*, 879. [CrossRef]

125. Grimm, P. Social Desirability Bias. *Wiley Int. Enc. Market.* 2010. [CrossRef]

126. Gliner, J.A.; Morgan, G.A.; Harmon, R.J. Single-Factor Repeated-Measures Designs: Analysis and Interpretation. *J. Am. Acad. Child Adolesc. Psychiatry* **2002**, *41*, 1014–1016. [CrossRef]

127. Lindell, M.K.; Whitney, D.J. Accounting for common method variance in cross-sectional research designs. *J. Appl. Psychol.* **2001**, *86*, 114–121. [CrossRef] [PubMed]

128. Fornell, C.; Larcker, D.F. Evaluating structural equation models with unobservable variables and measurement error. *J. Mark. Res.* **1981**, *18*, 39–50. [CrossRef]

129. Preacher, K.J.; Hayes, A.F. SPSS and SAS procedures for estimating indirect effects in simple mediation models. *Behav. Res. Methods Instrum. Comput.* **2004**, *36*, 717–731. [CrossRef] [PubMed]

2

Parisian Time of Reflected Brownian Motion with Drift on Rays and its Application in Banking

Angelos Dassios * and Junyi Zhang *[ID]

Department of Statistics, London School of Economics, Houghton Street, London WC2A 2AE, UK
* Correspondence: A.Dassios@lse.ac.uk (A.D.); J.Zhang100@lse.ac.uk (J.Z.)

Abstract: In this paper, we study the Parisian time of a reflected Brownian motion with drift on a finite collection of rays. We derive the Laplace transform of the Parisian time using a recursive method, and provide an exact simulation algorithm to sample from the distribution of the Parisian time. The paper was motivated by the settlement delay in the real-time gross settlement (RTGS) system. Both the central bank and the participating banks in the system are concerned about the liquidity risk, and are interested in the first time that the duration of settlement delay exceeds a predefined limit. We reduce this problem to the calculation of the Parisian time. The Parisian time is also crucial in the pricing of Parisian type options; to this end, we will compare our results to the existing literature.

Keywords: Brownian motion; Parisian time; exact simulation; real-time gross settlement system

1. Introduction

Suppose we have a system of rays emanating from a common origin and a particle moving on this system. On each ray, the particle behaves as a reflected Brownian motion with drift; and once at the origin, it instantaneously chooses a ray for its next excursion randomly according to a given distribution. We are interested in the time length the particle spends on each ray, and the first time that the excursion time length on a ray exceeds a predefined threshold. We call this first exceeding time of threshold a Parisian time, as it generalizes the concept of Parisian time of standard Brownian motion in literature.

The study of excursion time length of Brownian motion goes back to Chung (1976). Other aspects of Brownian excursion have also been considered. Durrett et al. (1977) developed the relationships between the Brownian excursions, meanders and bridges using the limit processes of conditional functionals of Brownian motion. Imhof (1984) derived the joint density concerning the maximum of Brownian motion and 3-dimensional Bessel process. Kennedy (1976) derived the distribution of the maximum of excursion via the limiting processes and relates it to the standard Brownian motion. Getoor and Sharpe (1979) obtained a limiting result on the distribution of additive functionals over Brownian excursions. A literature review can be found in Zhang (2014).

More recently, Chesney et al. (1997) studied the Parisian time of Brownian motion, and used the result to price the Parisian type options. They are path-dependent options whose payoff depends not only on the final value of the underlying asset, but also on the path trajectory of the underlying above or below a predetermined barrier for a length of time. The two-sided Parisian option was considered in Dassios and Wu (2010), its pricing depends on the Parisian time of a drifted Brownian motion with a two-sided excursion time threshold. It turns out that the Parisian times derived in Chesney et al. (1997) and Dassios and Wu (2010) can be viewed as the special cases of our result. Moreover, the results in the current paper can be used to price more complicated Parisian type options. For more details about Parisian options, see Schröder (2003), Anderluh and van der Weide (2009) and Labart and Lelong (2009).

This paper is motivated by the real-time gross settlement system (RTGS, and known as CHAPS in the UK, see McDonough 1997; Padoa-Schioppa 2005). The participating banks in the RTGS system are concerned about liquidity risk and wish to prevent the excessive liquidity exposure between two banks. There is evidence suggesting that in CHAPS, banks usually set bilateral or multilateral limits on the exposed position with others (see Becher et al. 2008), this mechanism was studied by Che and Dassios (2013) using a Markov model. For a single bank, namely bank A, let a reflected Brownian motion be the net balance between bank A and bank i, and let u_i be the bilateral limit set up by bank A for bank i, Che and Dassios (2013) calculated the probability that the limit is exceeded in a finite time.

We consider another source of liquidity risk, the time-lag between the execution of the transaction and its final completion. As it is explained in McDonough (1997) and Padoa-Schioppa (2005), if a counterparty does not settle an obligation for the full value when due but at some unspecified time thereafter, the expected liquidity position of the payee could be affected. The settlement delay may force the payee to cover its cash-flow shortage by funding at short notice from other sources, which may result in a financial loss due to higher financing costs or to damage to its reputation. In more extreme cases, it may be unable to cover its cash-flow shortage at any price, in which case it may be unable to meet its obligation to others. As the settlement delay is the major source of liquidity risk in the RTGS system, both the central bank and the participating banks are interested in the length of the delay. Previous research in Che and Dassios (2013) has shown that the Markov-type models are adequate for CHAPS, we will extend this model here to study the settlement delay. For bank A and bank i in CHAPS, we view the net balance between them as a reflected Brownian motion with drift. Assume that bank A has set a time limit d_i on the duration of settlement delay for bank i, and they are interested in the first time that the limit is exceeded. In practice, an individual bank could set multiple limits or even remove the limit on different types of counterparties. We reduce this problem to the calculation of the Parisian time of a reflected Brownian motion with drift on rays. For more details about the CHAPS, see Che (2011) and Soramäki et al. (2007).

We construct the reflected Brownian motion with drift on rays in Section 2, then calculate the Laplace transform of the Parisian time in Section 3. An exact simulation algorithm to sample from the distribution of the Parisian time is provided in Section 4. We discuss the application of these results in Section 5.

2. Construction of the Underlying Process and the Parisian Time

In this section, we construct the reflected Brownian motion with drift on a finite collection of rays, and define the Parisian time we are interested in. Let n be a finite positive integer, we denote by S a system containing n rays emanating from the common origin, i.e., $S := \{S_1, \ldots, S_n\}$, and fix a distribution $P := \{P_i\}_{i=1,\ldots,n}$, so that $\sum_{i=1}^{n} P_i = 1$. We also define the functions $\mu(S_i) := \mu_i$ and $\sigma(S_i) := \sigma_i$ for $i = 1, \ldots, n$, where $\mu_i \in \mathbb{R}$ and $\sigma_i \in \mathbb{R}^+$ are constants (see Figure 1).

Consider a planar process $X(t)$ on the system of rays S. We represent the position of $X(t)$ by $(|X(t)|, \Theta(t))$, where $|X(t)|$ denotes the distance between $X(t)$ and the origin, and $\Theta(t) \in \{S_1, \ldots, S_n\}$ indicates the current ray of the process. Let $U(t) := \mu(\Theta(t))t + \sigma(\Theta(t))W_t$ be the "driving process", and $|X(t)|$ be the Skorokhod reflection of $U(t)$, i.e.,

$$|X(t)| = U(t) + \max_{0 \leq s \leq t}(-U(s))^+, \quad t \geq 0.$$

Then, $|X(t)|$ has the same distribution as a reflected Brownian motion with drift $\mu(\Theta(t))$ and dispersion $\sigma(\Theta(t))$. A proof of this can be seen in Jeanblanc et al. (2009) Section 4.1, Peskir (2006) and Graversen and Shiryaev (2000).

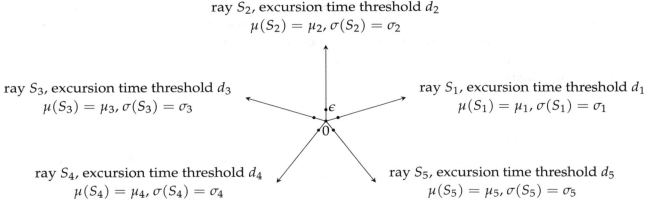

ray S_2, excursion time threshold d_2
$\mu(S_2) = \mu_2, \sigma(S_2) = \sigma_2$

ray S_3, excursion time threshold d_3
$\mu(S_3) = \mu_3, \sigma(S_3) = \sigma_3$

ray S_1, excursion time threshold d_1
$\mu(S_1) = \mu_1, \sigma(S_1) = \sigma_1$

ray S_4, excursion time threshold d_4
$\mu(S_4) = \mu_4, \sigma(S_4) = \sigma_4$

ray S_5, excursion time threshold d_5
$\mu(S_5) = \mu_5, \sigma(S_5) = \sigma_5$

Figure 1. A system of 5 rays emanating from a common origin.

We expect $\Theta(t)$ to be constant during each excursion of $X(t)$ away from the origin and has the same distribution as P when $X(t)$ returns to the origin. To this end, we initialize $\Theta(t)$ with $\mathbb{P}(\Theta(0) = S_i) = P_i, i = 1,\ldots,n$, and let $\Theta(t)$ remain constant whenever $|X(t)| \neq 0$. Once $|X(t)| = 0$, $\Theta(t)$ is randomized according to P, i.e.,

$$\mathbb{P}\left(\Theta(t) = S_i \mid |X(t^-)| = 0\right) = P_i, \quad i = 1,\ldots,n, \quad \forall t > 0.$$

This means the coefficients of $U(t)$ remain constant whenever $|X(t)| \neq 0$, and the Skorokhod reflection of $U(t)$ has the same distribution as a reflected Brownian motion with drift μ_i and dispersion σ_i on each ray S_i.

Therefore, we summarize the behaviour of $X(t)$ as follows. The initial state of $X(t)$ is distributed as $\mathbb{P}(X(0) = (0, S_i)) = P_i, i = 1,\ldots,n$. Then it behaves as a Brownian motion with drift μ_i and dispersion σ_i on ray S_i, as long as it does not return to the origin. Once at the origin, it instantaneously chooses a new ray according to P, independently of the past behaviour; that is,

$$\mathbb{P}(X(t) = (0, S_i) \mid |X(t^-)| = 0) = P_i, \quad i = 1,\ldots,n.$$

There are some special cases of $X(t)$. When $\mu_i = 0$ and $\sigma_i = 1$ for $i = 1,\ldots,n$, $X(t)$ becomes a Walsh Brownian motion. When $n = 2$, $P_1 = \alpha = 1 - P_2$, $\mu_1 = \mu_2 = 0$ and $\sigma_1 = \sigma_2 = 1$, $X(t)$ recovers the skew Brownian motion. We also obtain a Brownian motion with drift μ and dispersion σ by setting $n = 2$, $P_1 = P_2 = \frac{1}{2}$, $\mu_1 = \mu$, $\mu_2 = -\mu$ and $\sigma_1 = \sigma_2 = \sigma$; and a reflected Brownian motion by setting $n = 1$, $P_1 = 1$, $\mu = 0$ and $\sigma = 1$.

Next, we define the last zero time and excursion time length of $X(t)$ as $g(t) := \sup\{s \leq t \mid |X(s)| = 0\}$ and $U(t) := t - g(t)$. Then $U(t)$ represents the time length $X(t)$ has spent in the current ray since last time at the origin. On each ray S_i, there is a threshold $d_i > 0$ for the excursion time length, our target is to find the first time that the threshold is exceeded by $U(t)$. Thus, we are interested in the Parisian time τ defined as

$$\tau_i := \inf\{t \geq 0 \mid U(t) \geq d_i, \Theta(t^-) = S_i\}, \quad \text{for } i = 1,\ldots,n,$$
$$\tau := \min_{i=1,\ldots,n} \tau_i. \tag{1}$$

Note that $X(t)$ may make an excursion with infinite time length on a ray S_i if the drift μ_i on this ray is positive. Since our target is to study the Parisian time τ, we are only interested in the excursion time length up to d_i, even if the total length is infinite.

We need to calculate the excursion time length of $X(t)$, but the problem is there is no first excursion from zero; before any $t > 0$, the process has made an infinite number of small excursions away from the origin. To approximate the dynamic of a Brownian motion, Dassios and Wu (2010) introduced the "perturbed Brownian motion", we will extend this idea here.

For every $\epsilon > 0$, we define a perturbed process $X^\epsilon(t) = (|X^\epsilon(t)|, \Theta^\epsilon(t))$ on the system of rays S. On each ray S_i, $|X^\epsilon(t)|$ behaves as a reflected Brownian motion with drift μ_i, dispersion σ_i and starting from ϵ, as long as it does not return to the origin. Once at the origin, $X^\epsilon(t)$ not only chooses a new ray according to P, but also jumps to ϵ on the new ray. In other words, $X^\epsilon(t)$ has a perturbation of size ϵ at the origin which can be described as

$$\mathbb{P}\left(X^\epsilon(t) = (\epsilon, S_i) \mid |X^\epsilon(t^-)| = 0\right) = P_i, \quad i \in \{1, \ldots, n\}.$$

Hence, we describe the behaviour of $X^\epsilon(t)$ as follows. The initial state of $X^\epsilon(t)$ is distributed as $\mathbb{P}(X^\epsilon(0) = (\epsilon, S_i)) = P_i, i = 1, \ldots, n$. Then it behaves as a Brownian motion with drift μ_i, dispersion σ_i and starting from ϵ on ray S_i, as long as it does not return to the origin. Once at the origin, it instantaneously chooses a new ray according to P and jumps to ϵ on the new ray.

We define the Parisian time of $X^\epsilon(t)$ similarly as before. Let $g^\epsilon(t) := \sup\{s \leq t \mid |X^\epsilon(s)| = 0\}$ and $U^\epsilon(t) := t - g^\epsilon(t)$. We are interested in the Parisian time τ^ϵ defined as

$$\tau_i^\epsilon := \inf\{t \geq 0 \mid U^\epsilon(t) \geq d_i, \Theta^\epsilon(t^-) = S_i\}, \quad \text{for } i = 1, \ldots, n,$$
$$\tau^\epsilon := \min_{i=1,\ldots,n} \tau_i^\epsilon,$$

As $\epsilon \to 0$, the perturbation at origin vanishes, and $X^\epsilon(t) \to X(t)$ in a pathwise sense, then $\tau^\epsilon \to \tau$ in distribution. Hence, we will first derive the Laplace transform of τ^ϵ, then take the limit $\lim_{\epsilon \to 0} \mathbb{E}(e^{-\beta\tau^\epsilon})$ to calculate the Laplace transform of the Parisian time τ.

3. Laplace Transform of τ

We present the main result of the paper in this section. For simplicity, we denote the symmetric function

$$\Psi(x) := 2\sqrt{\pi}x\Phi(\sqrt{2}x) - \sqrt{\pi}x + e^{-x^2}, \quad x \in \mathbb{R},$$

where $\Phi(.)$ is the cumulative distribution function of standard normal distribution, and the constant

$$C_i := P_i\left(\frac{2}{\sqrt{2\pi\sigma_i^2 d_i}}\Psi\left(\frac{\mu_i\sqrt{d_i}}{\sqrt{2\sigma_i^2}}\right) + \frac{\mu_i}{\sigma_i^2}\right),$$

where μ_i, σ_i, P_i and d_i are defined in Section 2. For $\mu_i \in \mathbb{R}$, $\sigma_i \in \mathbb{R}^+$, $P_i \in (0,1]$ and $d_i > 0$, we deduce from the definition that $C_i > 0$.

Theorem 1. *Let $X(t)$ be a reflected Brownian motion with drift on a system of rays S, where $\mu_i \in \mathbb{R}$, $\sigma_i \in \mathbb{R}^+$, $P_i \in (0,1]$ and $d_i > 0$ are the drift, dispersion, entering probability and excursion time threshold of ray S_i, $i = 1, \ldots, n$. For $\beta \geq 0$, the Laplace transform of the Parisian time τ is*

$$\mathbb{E}\left(e^{-\beta\tau}\right) = \frac{\sum_{i=1}^n e^{-\beta d_i} C_i}{\sum_{i=1}^n C_i + \sum_{i=1}^n P_i \int_0^{d_i} (1 - e^{-\beta v}) e^{-\frac{\mu_i^2}{2\sigma_i^2}v} \frac{1}{\sqrt{2\pi\sigma_i^2 v^3}} dv}, \tag{2}$$

and the expectation of τ is

$$\mathbb{E}(\tau) = \frac{\sum_{i=1}^n d_i C_i + \sum_{i=1}^n P_i \int_0^{d_i} e^{-\frac{\mu_i^2}{2\sigma_i^2}v} \frac{1}{\sqrt{2\pi\sigma_i^2 v}} dv}{\sum_{i=1}^n C_i}. \tag{3}$$

Proof. We prepare some preliminary formulas for the proof. From Section 2, we know $X^\epsilon(t)$ starts from ϵ on ray S_i, and behaves as a Brownian motion with drift μ_i and dispersion σ_i as long as it does not return to the origin. Let $g_i(\epsilon, t)$ be the density of the first hitting time at 0 of such a Brownian motion, then

$$g_i(\epsilon, t) = \frac{\epsilon}{\sqrt{2\pi\sigma_i^2 t^3}} e^{-\frac{(\epsilon+\mu_i t)^2}{2\sigma_i^2 t}}, \quad \text{for } \mu_i \in \mathbb{R}, \ \sigma_i \in \mathbb{R}^+, \ \epsilon > 0, \ t > 0, \ i = 1, \dots, n.$$

We define the following functions in ϵ,

$$L_i(\epsilon) := \int_0^{d_i} e^{-\beta s} g_i(\epsilon, t) dt \quad \text{and} \quad U_i(\epsilon) := \int_{d_i}^{\infty} e^{-\beta d_i} g_i(\epsilon, t) dt,$$

and call them L_i and U_i for convenience. In their Laplace transforms respectively, L_i represents the excursion time length of $X^\epsilon(t)$ on ray S_i if it is shorter than the threshold d_i, and U_i represents the excursion time length if it is longer than d_i. In the latter case, we set the excursion time length to be d_i because we are only interested in the excursion up to the threshold.

These functions have the limits

$$\lim_{\epsilon \to 0} U_i(\epsilon) = 0 \quad \text{and} \quad \lim_{\epsilon \to 0} L_i(\epsilon) = 1.$$

Moreover, we calculate the limits of their derivatives to be

$$\lim_{\epsilon \to 0} \left(\frac{d}{d\epsilon} U_i(\epsilon) \right) = e^{-\beta d_i} \left(\frac{2}{\sqrt{2\pi\sigma_i^2 d_i}} \Psi\left(\frac{\mu_i \sqrt{d_i}}{\sqrt{2\sigma_i^2}} \right) + \frac{\mu_i}{\sigma_i^2} \right), \tag{4}$$

$$\begin{aligned}
\lim_{\epsilon \to 0} \left(\frac{d}{d\epsilon} L_i(\epsilon) \right) &= -\frac{2}{\sqrt{2\pi\sigma_i^2 d_i}} \Psi\left(\sqrt{\frac{\mu_i^2 d_i}{2\sigma_i^2} + \beta d_i} \right) - \frac{\mu_i}{\sigma_i^2} \\
&= -\left(\frac{2}{\sqrt{2\pi\sigma_i^2 d_i}} \Psi\left(\frac{\mu_i \sqrt{d_i}}{\sqrt{2\sigma_i^2}} \right) + \frac{\mu_i}{\sigma_i^2} \right) - \int_0^{d_i} (1 - e^{-\beta y}) e^{-\frac{\mu_i^2}{2\sigma_i^2} y} \frac{1}{\sqrt{2\pi\sigma_i^2 y^3}} dy,
\end{aligned} \tag{5}$$

the last equation can be checked using $\Psi(x) = 1 + \int_0^1 (1 - e^{-x^2 v}) \frac{1}{2v^{3/2}} dv$, which is obtained by a direct calculation from the definition of $\Psi(x)$.

Now we study the Parisian time τ^ϵ. Define the sequence of random times

$$\zeta_0 = 0, \ \zeta_{m+1} = \inf\{t > \zeta_m \mid |X^\epsilon(t)| = 0\}, \quad \text{for } m \in \mathbb{N}_0$$

recursively, and the mutually exclusive events

$$C_m := \{\zeta_m \le \tau^\epsilon < \zeta_{m+1}\}, \quad \text{for } m \in \mathbb{N}_0.$$

Then, C_m denotes the event that the exceeding of threshold occurs during the $(m+1)$-th excursion of $X^\epsilon(t)$ away from the origin. Next, we set $\{X^\epsilon(0) = (\epsilon, S_i)\}$ for an arbitrary but fixed i, and calculate the Laplace transforms $\mathbb{E}(e^{-\beta\tau^\epsilon} \mathbb{1}_{\{C_m\}} \mid X^\epsilon(0) = (\epsilon, S_i))$ for $m \in \mathbb{N}_0$.

For $m = 0$, we interpret C_0 as follows. Starting from ϵ on ray S_i, $X^\epsilon(t)$ spends more than d_i time before hitting the origin, hence the exceeding occurs during the first excursion. This is equivalent to the event that a Brownian motion with drift μ_i and dispersion σ_i spends more than d_i time to travel from ϵ to 0, which has probability $\int_{d_i}^{\infty} g_i(\epsilon, t)dt$. Thus $(\tau^\epsilon 1_{\{C_0\}} \mid X^\epsilon(0) = (\epsilon, S_i)) = d_i$, and

$$\mathbb{E}\left(e^{-\beta\tau^\epsilon} 1_{\{C_0\}} \mid X^\epsilon(0) = (\epsilon, S_i)\right) = \int_{d_i}^{\infty} e^{-\beta d_i} g_i(\epsilon, t)dt = U_i.$$

Next, we consider the event C_1. In this case, the duration of the first excursion of $X^\epsilon(t)$ is shorter than d_i, and the Laplace transform of the duration is $\int_0^{d_i} e^{-\beta s} g_i(\epsilon, t)dt$. After the first excursion, $X^\epsilon(t)$ returns to the origin and jumps to (ϵ, S_k) with probability P_k, then exceeds the excursion time threshold d_k before returning to the origin. The behaviour of $X^\epsilon(t)$ during the second excursion is similar to what we described for C_0, with the index i replaced by k. Thus, we have

$$\mathbb{E}\left(e^{-\beta\tau^\epsilon} 1_{\{C_1\}} \mid X^\epsilon(0) = (\epsilon, S_i)\right)$$
$$= \left(\int_0^{d_i} e^{-\beta s} g_i(\epsilon, t)dt\right)\left(\sum_{k=1}^{n} P_k \mathbb{E}\left(e^{-\beta\tau^\epsilon} 1_{\{C_0\}} \mid X^\epsilon(0) = (\epsilon, S_k)\right)\right) = L_i\left(\sum_{k=1}^{n} P_k U_k\right).$$

In the same way, we consider the event C_2. In this case, the duration of the first excursion of $X^\epsilon(t)$ is shorter than d_i, with the Laplace transform $\int_0^{d_i} e^{-\beta s} g_i(\epsilon, t)dt$. After the first excursion, $X^\epsilon(t)$ returns to the origin and jumps to (ϵ, S_k) with probability P_k. Restarting from (ϵ, S_k), $X^\epsilon(t)$ will exceed the excursion time threshold exactly during the second excursion (hence the third in total). The behaviour of $X^\epsilon(t)$ during the second and third excursions is similar to what we described for C_1, with the index i replaced by k. Hence,

$$\mathbb{E}\left(e^{-\beta\tau^\epsilon} 1_{\{C_2\}} \mid X^\epsilon(0) = (\epsilon, S_i)\right) = \left(\int_0^{d_i} e^{-\beta s} g_i(\epsilon, t)dt\right)\left(\sum_{k=1}^{n} P_k \mathbb{E}\left(e^{-\beta\tau^\epsilon} 1_{\{C_1\}} \mid X^\epsilon(0) = (\epsilon, S_k)\right)\right)$$
$$= L_i\left(\sum_{k=1}^{n} P_k L_k\left(\sum_{j=1}^{n} P_j U_j\right)\right) = L_i\left(\sum_{k=1}^{n} P_k L_k\right)\left(\sum_{j=1}^{n} P_j U_j\right).$$

The same explanation applies to C_m for any positive integer m, i.e., the duration of the first excursion of $X^\epsilon(t)$ is shorter than d_i, after that $X^\epsilon(t)$ restarts from (ϵ, S_k) and exceeds the threshold exactly during the m-th excursion. Hence, we deduce that

$$\mathbb{E}\left(e^{-\beta\tau^\epsilon} 1_{\{C_m\}} \mid X^\epsilon(0) = (\epsilon, S_i)\right) = L_i\left(\sum_{k=1}^{n} P_k \mathbb{E}\left(e^{-\beta\tau^\epsilon} 1_{\{C_{m-1}\}} \mid X^\epsilon(0) = (\epsilon, S_k)\right)\right).$$

This implies a recursive structure between the Laplace transforms of τ^ϵ conditioned on C_m and C_{m-1}, we solve for

$$\mathbb{E}\left(e^{-\beta\tau^\epsilon} 1_{\{C_m\}} \mid X^\epsilon(0) = (\epsilon, S_i)\right) = L_i\left(\sum_{k=1}^{n} P_k L_k\right)^{m-1}\left(\sum_{j=1}^{n} P_j U_j\right), \quad m = 1, 2, \ldots.$$

Since the exceeding of threshold may occur during any excursion of $X^\epsilon(t)$, we need to sum the result over $m \in \mathbb{N}_0$, this gives

$$\mathbb{E}\left(e^{-\beta\tau^\epsilon} \mid X^\epsilon(0) = (\epsilon, S_i)\right) = \sum_{m=0}^{\infty} \mathbb{E}\left(e^{-\beta\tau^\epsilon} 1_{\{C_m\}} \mid X^\epsilon(0) = (\epsilon, S_i)\right)$$
$$= U_i + \sum_{m=1}^{\infty}\left(L_i\left(\sum_{k=1}^{n} P_k L_k\right)^{m-1}\left(\sum_{j=1}^{n} P_j U_j\right)\right) = U_i + \frac{L_i\left(\sum_{j=1}^{n} P_j U_j\right)}{1 - \sum_{k=1}^{n} P_k L_k},$$

$$(6)$$

the last equation holds because for each k, $g_k(\epsilon, t)$ is a probability density function on $(0, \infty)$, so for any $\beta \geq 0$,

$$0 < \sum_{k=1}^n P_k L_k = \sum_{k=1}^n P_k \int_0^{d_k} e^{-\beta s} g_k(\epsilon, s) ds \leq \sum_{k=1}^n P_k \int_0^{d_k} g_k(\epsilon, s) ds < \sum_{k=1}^n P_k = 1.$$

Equation (6) boils down the Laplace transform of τ^ϵ to the initial state of $X^\epsilon(t)$, which is distributed as $\mathbb{P}(X^\epsilon(0) = (\epsilon, S_i)) = P_i$. Then we calculate the Laplace transform of τ^ϵ to be

$$\mathbb{E}\left(e^{-\beta \tau^\epsilon}\right) = \sum_{i=1}^n P_i \mathbb{E}\left(e^{-\beta \tau^\epsilon} \mid X^\epsilon(0) = (\epsilon, S_i)\right)$$
$$= \sum_{i=1}^n P_i \left(U_i + \frac{L_i(\sum_{j=1}^n P_j U_j)}{1 - \sum_{k=1}^n P_k L_k}\right) = \frac{\sum_{i=1}^n P_i U_i(\epsilon)}{1 - \sum_{k=1}^n P_k L_k(\epsilon)}. \tag{7}$$

As $\epsilon \to 0$, both numerator and denominator of the right hand side of (7) tend to 0, then we can calculate the limit $\lim_{\epsilon \to 0} \mathbb{E}(e^{-\beta \tau^\epsilon})$ using (4) and (5), and this gives $\mathbb{E}(e^{-\beta \tau})$. The expectation of τ is obtained by applying the moment generating function. $\quad\square$

As in Section 2, $X(t)$ can be reduced to a Brownian motion with drift or a standard Brownian motion by choosing the parameters accordingly, then we can compare Theorem 1 with the results in the existing literature.

Remark 1. *When $n = 2$, $\mu_1 = \mu \geq 0$, $\mu_2 = -\mu$, $\sigma_1 = \sigma_2 = 1$, $P_1 = P_2 = \frac{1}{2}$ and $d_1 > 0$, $d_2 > 0$, Equation (2) becomes the Laplace transform of the two-sided Parisian time of a Brownian motion with drift*

$$\mathbb{E}\left(e^{-\beta \tau}\right) = \frac{e^{-\beta d_1}\left(\sqrt{d_2}\Psi(\mu\sqrt{\frac{d_1}{2}}) + \mu\sqrt{\frac{d_1 d_2 \pi}{2}}\right) + e^{-\beta d_2}\left(\sqrt{d_1}\Psi(\mu\sqrt{\frac{d_2}{2}}) - \mu\sqrt{\frac{d_1 d_2 \pi}{2}}\right)}{\sqrt{d_2}\Psi\left(\sqrt{(\beta + \frac{\mu^2}{2})d_1}\right) + \sqrt{d_1}\Psi\left(\sqrt{(\beta + \frac{\mu^2}{2})d_2}\right)},$$

this is the main result of Dassios and Wu (2010). Moreover, for $n = 2$, $P_1 = P_2 = \frac{1}{2}$, $\mu_1 = \mu_2 = 0$, $\sigma_1 = \sigma_2 = 1$, we set $d_2 > 0$ and let $d_1 \to \infty$, then Equation (2) gives the Laplace transform of the one-sided Parisian time of a standard Brownian motion

$$\mathbb{E}(e^{-\beta \tau}) \to \frac{1}{1 + 2\sqrt{\pi \beta d_2}\exp(\beta d_2)\Phi(\sqrt{2\beta d_2})},$$

this was derived in Section 8.4.1 of Chesney et al. (1997).

4. Exact Simulation Algorithm of the Parisian Time

In this section, we provide an exact simulation algorithm to sample from the distribution of the Parisian time τ. Our algorithm is based on the exact simulation schemes of the truncated Lévy subordinator developed in Dassios et al. (2020). We refer to Algorithms 4.3 and 4.4 of Dassios et al. (2020) as AlgorithmI(.) and AlgorithmII(. , .), their full steps are attached in Appendix A.

Theorem 2. *Exact simulation algorithm of the Parisian time τ.*

1. *Initialize μ_i, σ_i, P_i, d_i and calculate C_i for $i = 1, \ldots, n$. Set $\lambda = \sum_{i=1}^n C_i$.*
2. *Generate a multinomial random variable I whose probability function is*

$$\mathbb{P}(I = i) = \frac{C_i}{\sum_{j=1}^n C_j} \text{ for } i = 1, \ldots, n,$$

via the following steps:

(a)   *Generate an uniform random variable $U_1 \sim U[0,1]$.*

(b)   *Set $\mathbb{P}(I=0) = 0$. For $i = 1, ..., n$, find the unique i such that*

$$\sum_{j=0}^{i-1} \mathbb{P}(I = j) < U_1 \leq \sum_{j=0}^{i} \mathbb{P}(I = j),$$

then return $I = i$.

3.   *Generate a random variable τ^* via the following steps:*

(a)   *Generate an exponential random variable $T \sim exp(\lambda)$ by setting $U_2 \sim U[0,1]$, then return $T = -\frac{1}{\lambda}\ln(1 - U_2)$.*

(b)   *For each $i = 1, ..., n$, generate the following subordinator:*

- *If $\mu_i = 0$, generate a subordinator X_i by setting $\alpha = \frac{1}{2}$ and*

$$X_i = AlgorithmI\left(\frac{TP_i}{\sqrt{2\pi\sigma_i^2 d_i}} \frac{\Gamma(1-\alpha)}{\alpha}\right);$$

- *If $\mu_i \neq 0$, generate a subordinator X_i by setting $\alpha = \frac{1}{2}$ and*

$$X_i = AlgorithmII\left(\frac{TP_i}{\sqrt{2\pi\sigma_i^2 d_i}} \frac{\Gamma(1-\alpha)}{\alpha}, \frac{\mu_i^2 d_i}{2\sigma_i^2}\right).$$

(c)   *Set $\tau^* = \sum_{i=1}^{n} d_i X_i$.*

4.   *Output $\tau = \tau^* + d_I$.*

Proof. For simplicity, we denote by $M := \sum_{i=1}^{n} e^{-\beta d_i} C_i$ and $\lambda := \sum_{i=1}^{n} C_i$, then the Laplace transform (2) can be written as

$$\mathbb{E}\left(e^{-\beta\tau}\right) = \frac{M}{\lambda + \sum_{i=1}^{n} P_i \int_0^{d_i}(1 - e^{-\beta v})e^{-\frac{\mu_i^2}{2\sigma_i^2}v}\frac{1}{\sqrt{2\pi\sigma_i^2 v^3}}dv}, \quad \text{for } \beta \geq 0.$$

Since $C_i > 0$ for $i = 1, ..., n$, we know $\lambda > 0$, and the denominator of $\mathbb{E}(e^{-\beta\tau})$ is positive. This enables us to rewrite the Laplace transform in an integration format using the exponential function

$$\begin{aligned}\mathbb{E}\left(e^{-\beta\tau}\right) &= M\int_0^\infty \exp\left(-t\left(\lambda + \sum_{i=1}^{n} P_i \int_0^{d_i}(1 - e^{-\beta v})e^{-\frac{\mu_i^2}{2\sigma_i^2}v}\frac{1}{\sqrt{2\pi\sigma_i^2 v^3}}dv\right)\right)dt \\ &= \frac{M}{\lambda}\int_0^\infty \lambda e^{-\lambda t}\exp\left(-\sum_{i=1}^{n}\frac{tP_i}{\sqrt{2\pi\sigma_i^2 d_i}}\int_0^1(1 - e^{-\beta d_i z})e^{-\frac{\mu_i^2 d_i}{2\sigma_i^2}z}\frac{1}{z^{3/2}}dz\right)dt.\end{aligned} \tag{8}$$

Equation (8) can be understood as a product of the Laplace transforms of two independent random variables, hence we can generate them separately, and view the Parisian time τ as their summation.

Denote by I a multinomial random variable with the probability function

$$\mathbb{P}(I = i) = \frac{C_i}{\sum_{j=1}^{n} C_j} \quad \text{for } i = 1, ..., n,$$

then we can generate I using the strip method, this becomes Step 2. Note that the random variable $d_I = \{d_1, ..., d_n\}$ has the Laplace transform

$$\mathbb{E}\left(e^{-\beta d_I}\right) = \sum_{i=1}^{n}\left(e^{-\beta d_i}\frac{C_i}{\sum_{j=1}^{n}C_j}\right) = \frac{M}{\lambda}.$$

Next, we denote by τ^* the random variable whose Laplace transform is

$$\mathbb{E}\left(e^{-\beta \tau^*}\right) = \int_0^\infty \lambda e^{-\lambda t}\exp\left(-\sum_{i=1}^{n}\frac{tP_i}{\sqrt{2\pi\sigma_i^2 d_i}}\int_0^1(1-e^{-\beta d_i z})e^{-\frac{\mu_i^2 d_i}{2\sigma_i^2}z}\frac{1}{z^{3/2}}dz\right)dt \qquad (9)$$

For each i, we interpret the expression

$$\exp\left(-\frac{tP_i}{\sqrt{2\pi\sigma_i^2 d_i}}\int_0^1(1-e^{-\beta d_i z})e^{-\frac{\mu_i^2 d_i}{2\sigma_i^2}z}\frac{1}{z^{3/2}}dz\right) \qquad (10)$$

as the Laplace transform of the random variable $d_i X_i(\frac{tP_i}{\sqrt{2\pi\sigma_i^2 d_i}})$, where $X_i(\frac{tP_i}{\sqrt{2\pi\sigma_i^2 d_i}})$ is a subordinator with truncated Lévy measure

$$e^{-\frac{\mu_i^2 d_i}{2\sigma_i^2}z}\frac{1}{z^{3/2}}\mathbb{1}_{\{0<z<1\}}dz$$

at time $\frac{tP_i}{\sqrt{2\pi\sigma_i^2 d_i}}$. Comparing (10) with (A1), we know $X_i(.)$ can be generated via Algorithms 4.3 and 4.4 in Appendix A.

Moreover, (9) implies that $\tau^* \overset{\text{law}}{=} \sum_{i=1}^{n} d_i X_i(\frac{TP_i}{\sqrt{2\pi\sigma_i^2 d_i}})$, where $T \sim \exp(\lambda)$ is an exponential random variable. Hence, we generate T in Step 3(a), sample from $X_i(\frac{TP_i}{\sqrt{2\pi\sigma_i^2 d_i}})$ in Step 3(b) and calculate τ^* via Step 3(c).

Finally, since $\mathbb{E}(e^{-\beta\tau}) = \mathbb{E}(e^{-\beta d_I})\mathbb{E}(e^{-\beta\tau^*})$, we have the representation $\tau \overset{\text{law}}{=} d_I + \tau^*$, where d_I and τ^* are independent, then τ can be generated via Step 4. □

Next, we illustrate the accuracy and performance of the exact simulation algorithm with a numerical example. We set $n = 7$, and

$$\mu_1 = 0, \ \mu_2 = 0.5, \ \mu_3 = -0.3, \ \mu_4 = 0, \ \mu_5 = 0.2, \ \mu_6 = 0, \ \mu_7 = -0.1;$$
$$\sigma_1 = 1.5, \ \sigma_2 = 2, \ \sigma_3 = 1.3, \ \sigma_4 = 1, \ \sigma_5 = 2, \ \sigma_6 = 1, \ \sigma_7 = 1;$$
$$P_1 = 0.1, \ P_2 = 0.2, \ P_3 = 0.1, \ P_4 = 0.2, \ P_5 = 0.2, \ P_6 = 0.1, \ P_7 = 0.1;$$
$$d_1 = 1, \ d_2 = 3, \ d_3 = 2.5, \ d_4 = 1.5, \ d_5 = 1.5, \ d_6 = 0.5, \ d_7 = 2.5.$$

Using the exact simulation algorithm, we generate samples from the Parisian time and calculate their average. On the other hand, we use Equation (3) to calculate the true expectation of τ to be 3.0534. Then we consider the following two standard measures for the associated error of the algorithm,

1. difference = sample average − true expectation
2. standard error = $\dfrac{\text{sample standard deviation}}{\sqrt{\text{number of samples}}}$

Table 1 reports the results, we see that the algorithm can achieve a high accuracy, and one has to generate more samples to decrease the standard error.

Table 1. Sample average and accuracy of the exact simulation algorithm.

Sample Size	Sample Average	Difference	Standard Error
1000	3.0666	0.0132	0.0616
4000	3.0302	−0.0232	0.0304
16,000	3.0470	−0.0065	0.0155
64,000	3.0509	−0.0025	0.0077
256,000	3.0520	−0.0014	0.0039
1,024,000	3.0538	0.0004	0.0019

In addition, we estimate the distribution function of the Parisian time. Using the exact simulation algorithm and the smoothing techniques (see Bowman and Azzalini 1997), we get the estimated curve for the distribution function. On the other hand, we apply the Gaver–Stehfest method (see Cohen 2007) to invert the Laplace transform $\frac{\mathbb{E}(e^{-\beta\tau})}{\beta}$ numerically and obtain the inverted curve for the distribution function. These curves are provided in Figure 2, they show that the exact simulation algorithm provides a good approximation for the distribution of the Parisian time.

We also illustrate the performance of the algorithm by recording the CPU time needed to generate these samples from the Parisian time. The experiment is implemented on an Intel Core i5-5200U CPU@2.20GHz processor, 8.00GB RAM, Windows 10, 64-bit Operating System and performed in Matlab R2019b. No parallel computing is used. Table 2 reports the results.

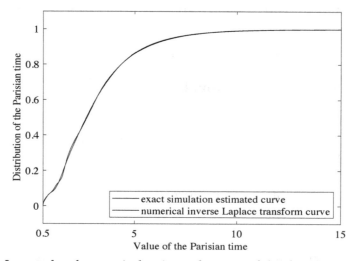

Figure 2. Inverted and numerical estimated curves of the distribution function.

Table 2. CPU time of the exact simulation algorithm.

Sample Size	CPU Time (in seconds)
1000	0.201831
4000	0.725738
16,000	3.080721
64,000	12.214876
256,000	52.715700
1,024,000	201.460605

5. Discussion

We can apply this model to study the settlement delay in CHAPS. For an individual bank A, we assume that there are n counterparties in the system, namely bank 1, bank 2, ..., bank n. We also assume that bank A uses an internal queue to manage its outgoing payments, and once the current payment is settled, it has probability P_i to make another payment to bank i, $i = 1, \ldots, n$. Let a reflected Brownian motion with drift μ_i and dispersion σ_i be the net balance between bank A and bank i.

To avoid the excessive exposure to liquidity risk, a time limit d_i has been set for the duration of settlement delay between bank A and bank i. Both the central bank and the participating banks are interested in the first time that the limit is exceeded.

We model the net balance between bank A and the counterparties by the planar process $X(t)$, and view the first exceeding time as the Parisian time of $X(t)$. Using the results in the current paper, we can sample from this first exceeding time and estimate its distribution function numerically. We remark that this approach can be adopted by both the policymaker in the central bank and the credit control departments of the participating banks to lay down decisive actions. For example, the central bank may use time-dependent transaction fees to provide incentives to earlier settlements. Alternatively, the participating banks may also learn to coordinate their payments over time, creating non-binding behavioural conventions or implicit contracts.

In particular, an empirical method has been developed in Denbee and Zimmerman (2012) to detect the apparent 'free-riding' in the RTGS system, referring to the behaviour that the banks wait for incoming payments to fund subsequent outgoing payments and not supply an amount of liquidity to the system commensurate with the share of payments they are responsible for. Suppose the banks are required to hold buffers of liquid assets in order that they can make payments in a stress scenario, and the buffers are continuously calculated based on past activity. Banks may have an incentive to delay their payments so that the regulatory buffer will be reduced at subsequent recalibrations. The method in Denbee and Zimmerman (2012) could help to detect this behaviour and calibrate buffers independent of strategic actions. The study in the current paper provides another point of view towards this method. We can estimate the distribution of the settlement delay and take this into consideration when calculating the buffers.

It is also possible to extend the model in the current paper to the settlement systems other than CHAPS. For example, the structure of settlement delay in Interbank Electronic Payment System (SPEI operated by Banco de México) has been specified in Alexandrova-Kabadjova and Solis (2012) with real transactions data from 7 April to 7 May 2010. We may assume that the Markov model is adequate for SPEI, and use these data to calibrate the parameters of the model. Moreover, the observations in Alexandrova-Kabadjova and Solis (2012) suggest that low value payments do not increase the settlement delay in the system. This is reasonable under the assumption that the net balance between two banks follows a reflected Brownian motion with drift, because the process will make an infinite number of small excursions at the origin.

This paper has focused on the model with one central bank (or agent) and several domestic participants, which is classified as a 'within border payment system' (see Bech et al. 2020). For a cross-border payment system, however, we need to consider a model containing two or more central banks, each with their own domestic participants. Assume that the system offers payment versus payment (PvP, see Bech et al. 2020) services, then the settlement delay may originate in any local system, and the first exceeding time of settlement delay of the whole system can be viewed as the joint distribution of the Parisian times of the local systems. With the technique developed in this paper, we are able to simulate the marginal distributions of the local exceeding time, but not the joint distribution. This is a topic for future research, and the result would be beneficial on a global scale.

In addition, our Brownian-type model reflects the random fluctuations of payments and delays, but the external events that can influence these are not taken into account. For example, the operational risks related to computer and telecommunication system breakdown may increase the settlement delay, see Rochet and Tirole (1996) for the impact of computer problem of the Bank of New York in 1985 and the San Francisco earthquake in 1989. More recently, many reports have suggested the impact of global pandemic in 2020 on the settlement systems. These might be interesting for a further study.

Author Contributions: Methodology, A.D. and J.Z.; software, J.Z.; formal analysis, A.D. and J.Z.; writing—original draft preparation, J.Z.; writing—review and editing, A.D.; supervision, A.D.; All authors have read and agreed to the published version of the manuscript.

Acknowledgments: The authors are grateful to the editor for handling this manuscript and both reviewers for giving us very helpful and inspiring comments, especially during the difficult time of pandemic.

Appendix A. Exact Simulation of Truncated Subordinator

In this appendix, we attach Algorithms 4.3 and 4.4 of Dassios et al. (2020). These algorithms exactly generate samples from the truncated subordinator $Z(t)$ with Laplace transform

$$\mathbb{E}\left(e^{-vZ(t)}\right) = \exp\left(-\frac{\alpha t}{\Gamma(1-\alpha)}\int_0^1 (1-e^{-vz})\frac{e^{-\eta z}}{z^{\alpha+1}}dz\right). \tag{A1}$$

We first present two ancillary algorithms, namely Algorithms 4.1 and 4.2 of Dassios et al. (2020).

Lemma A1 (Algorithm 4.1 of Dassios et al. 2020). *Exact simulation of (T, W).*

1. *Set $\xi = \Gamma(1-\alpha)^{-1}$; $A_0 = (1-\alpha)\alpha^{\frac{\alpha}{1-\alpha}}$.*
2. *minimise $C(\lambda) = A_0 e^{\xi^{\frac{1}{\alpha}}\lambda^{1-\frac{1}{\alpha}}\alpha(1-\alpha)^{\frac{1}{\alpha}-1}}(A_0 - \lambda)^{\alpha-2}$.*
3. *record critical value λ^*; set $C = C(\lambda^*)$.*
4. *repeat {*
5.   *sample $U \sim U[0, \pi]$; $U_1 \sim U[0, 1]$,*
6.   *set $Y = 1 - U_1^{\frac{1}{1-\alpha}}$; $A_U = [\sin^\alpha(\alpha U)\sin^{1-\alpha}((1-\alpha)U)/\sin(U)]^{\frac{1}{1-\alpha}}$,*
7.   *sample $R \sim \Gamma(2-\alpha, A_u - \lambda)$; $V \sim U[0, 1]$.*
8.   *if $(V \le A_U e^{\xi R^{1-\alpha}Y^\alpha}e^{-\lambda^* R}(A_U - \lambda^*)^{\alpha-2}Y^{\alpha-1}(1-(1-Y)^\alpha)/C)$, break.*
9. *}*
10. *sample $U_2 \sim U[0, 1]$,*
11. *set $T = R^{1-\alpha}Y^\alpha$; $W = Y - 1 + [(1-Y)^{-\alpha} - U_2((1-Y)^{-\alpha} - 1)]^{-\frac{1}{\alpha}}$.*
12. *return (T, W).*

Lemma A2 (Algorithm 4.2 of Dassios et al. 2020). *Exact simulation of $\{Z(t)|T > t\}$.*

1. *sample $U_1 \sim U[0, \pi]$; set $A_{U_1} = [\sin^\alpha(\alpha U_1)\sin^{1-\alpha}((1-\alpha)U_1)/\sin(U_1)]^{\frac{1}{1-\alpha}}$.*
2. *repeat {*
3.   *sample $U_2 \sim U[0, 1]$; set $Z = \left[-\frac{\log(U_2)}{A_{U_1}t^{\frac{1}{1-\alpha}}}\right]^{-\frac{1-\alpha}{\alpha}}$.*
4.   *if $(Z < 1)$, break.*
5. *}*
6. *return Z.*

Next we provide the Algorithm 4.3 and 4.4 of Dassios et al. (2020).

Theorem A1 (Algorithm 4.3 of Dassios et al. 2020). *Exact simulation of the subordinator $Z(t)$ when $\eta = 0$. The input is t.*

1. *set $Z = 0$; $S = 0$.*
2. *repeat {*
3.   *sample (T, W) via Algorithm 4.1; set $S = S + T$, $Z = Z + 1 + W$.*
4.   *if $(S > t)$, break.*
5. *}*
6. *set $Z_{S-T} = Z - 1 - W$; sample $Z_{t-(S-T)}$ via Algorithm 4.2.*
7. *return $Z_{S-T} + Z_{t-(S-T)}$.*

Theorem A2 (Algorithm 4.4 of Dassios et al. 2020). *Exact simulation of the subordinator $Z(t)$ when $\eta > 0$. The inputs are (t, η).*

1. *repeat {*
2.   *sample Z_t via Algorithm 4.3; $V \sim U[0,1]$.*
3.   *if ($V \le \exp(-\eta Z_t)$), break.*
4.   *}*
5. *return Z_t.*

Proof. For the proof as well as the motivation of the algorithms above, see Dassios et al. (2020). $\square$

References

1. Alexandrova-Kabadjova, Biliana, and Francisco Solis. 2012. The mexican experience in how the settlement of large payments is performed in the presence of a high volume of small payments. *Diagnostics for the Financial Markets–Computational Studies of Payment System*. Available online: https://ssrn.com/abstract=2191794 (accessed on 21 November 2020).
2. Anderluh, Jasper H. M., and Jan A. M. van der Weide. 2009. Double-sided Parisian option pricing. *Finance and Stochastics* 13: 205–38. [CrossRef]
3. Bech, Morten L., Umar Faruqui, and Takeshi Shirakami. 2020. Payments without borders. *BIS Quarterly Review*, March 1. Available online: https://ssrn.com/abstract=3561190 (accessed on 21 November 2020) .
4. Becher, Christopher, Marco Galbiati, and Merxe Tudela. 2008. The timing and funding of CHAPS Sterling payments. *Economic Policy Review* 14: 113–33. [CrossRef]
5. Bowman, Adrian W., and Adelchi Azzalini. 1997. *Applied Smoothing Techniques for Data Analysis: The Kernel Approach with S-Plus Illustrations*. Oxford: OUP, vol. 18.
6. Che, Xiaonan. 2011. Markov Type Models for Large-Valued Interbank Payment Systems. Ph. D. dissertation, The London School of Economics and Political Science (LSE), London, UK.
7. Che, Xiaonan, and Angelos Dassios. 2013. Stochastic boundary crossing probabilities for the Brownian motion. *Journal of Applied Probability* 50: 419–29. [CrossRef]
8. Chesney, Marc, Monique Jeanblanc-Picqué, and Marc Yor. 1997. Brownian excursions and Parisian barrier options. *Advances in Applied Probability* 29: 165–84. [CrossRef]
9. Chung, Kai Lai. 1976. Excursions in Brownian motion. *Arkiv för Matematik* 14: 155–77. [CrossRef] Cohen, Alan M. 2007. *Numerical Methods for Laplace Transform Inversion*. New York: Springer, vol. 5.
10. Dassios, Angelos, Jia Wei Lim, and Yan Qu. 2020. Exact simulation of a truncated Lévy subordinator. *ACM Transactions on Modeling and Computer Simulation* 30: 26. [CrossRef]
11. Dassios, Angelos, and Shanle Wu. 2010. Perturbed Brownian motion and its application to Parisian option pricing. *Finance and Stochastics* 14: 473–94. [CrossRef]
12. Denbee, Edward, and Rodney Garratt-Peter Zimmerman. 2012. Methods for evaluating liquidity provision in real-time gross settlement payment systems. *Diagnostics for the Financial Markets–Computational Studies of Payment System*. Available online: https://www.econstor.eu/bitstream/10419/212978/1/e45-bof-sci- monographs.pdf#page=55 (accessed on 21 November 2020).
13. Durrett, Richard T., Donald L. Iglehart, and Douglas R. Miller. 1977. Weak convergence to Brownian meander and Brownian excursion. *The Annals of Probability* 5: 117–29. [CrossRef]
14. Getoor, Ronald K., and Michael J. Sharpe. 1979. Excursions of Brownian motion and Bessel processes. *Zeitschrift für Wahrscheinlichkeitstheorie und Verwandte Gebiete* 47: 83–106. [CrossRef]
15. Graversen, Svend Erik, and Albert N. Shiryaev. 2000. An extension of P. Lévy's distributional properties to the case of a Brownian motion with drift. *Bernoulli* 6: 615–20. [CrossRef]
16. Imhof, Jan-Pierre. 1984. Density factorizations for Brownian motion, meander and the three-dimensional Bessel process, and applications. *Journal of Applied Probability* 21: 500–10. [CrossRef]
17. Jeanblanc, Monique, Marc Yor, and Marc Chesney. 2009. *Mathematical Methods for Financial Markets*. Springer Finance. London: Springer.
18. Kennedy, Douglas P. 1976. The distribution of the maximum Brownian excursion. *Journal of Applied Probability* 13: 371–76. [CrossRef]
19. Labart, Céline, and Jérôme Lelong. 2009. Pricing double barrier Parisian options using Laplace transforms. *International Journal of Theoretical and Applied Finance* 12: 19–44. [CrossRef]
20. McDonough, William J. 1997. *Real-Time Gross Settlement Systems*. Basel: Committee on Payment and Settlement Systems, Bank for International Settlements.

21. Padoa-Schioppa, Tommaso. 2005. *New Developments in Large-Value Payment Systems*. Basel: Committee on Payment and Settlement Systems, Bank for International Settlements.

22. Peskir, Goran. 2006. On reflecting Brownian motion with drift. Paper presented at 37th ISCIE International Symposium on Stochastic Systems Theory and Its Applications, Kyoto, Japan, pp. 1–5.

23. Rochet, Jean-Charles, and Jean Tirole. 1996. Controlling risk in payment systems. *Journal of Money, Credit and Banking* 28: 832–62. [CrossRef]

24. Schröder, Michael. 2003. Brownian excursions and Parisian barrier options: A note. *Journal of Applied Probability* 40: 855–64. [CrossRef]

25. Soramäki, Kimmo, Morten L. Bech, Jeffrey Arnold, Robert J. Glass, and Walter E. Beyeler. 2007. The topology of interbank payment flows. *Physica A: Statistical Mechanics and Its Applications* 379: 317–33. [CrossRef]

26. Zhang, Youyou. 2014. Brownian Excursions in Mathematical Finance. Ph. D. dissertation, The London School of Economics and Political Science, London, UK.

3

Valuation of FinTech Innovation based on Patent Applications

Jelena Kabulova * and Jelena Stankevičienė

Faculty of Business Management, Vilnius Gediminas Technical University, Saulėtekio al. 11, LT-10223 Vilnius, Lithuania; jelena.stankeviciene@vgtu.lt
* Correspondence: jelena.kabulova@vgtu.lt

Abstract: The financial services sector, perhaps more than any other, is being disrupted by advances in technology. The purpose of this study is to provide comprehensive data and evidence on value of the FinTech innovation event. First, a text-based filtering method for identifying FinTech patent applications is provided. Using machine learning applications, innovations are classified into major technology groups. The methodology for valuation of FinTech innovation is based on data of stock price changes. To assess the value impact, Poisson flow rates and stock price movements were combined. Further, to evaluate the effect of FinTech patents on the company's value, a combination of CAR of patent application and Poisson intensities were used. Research findings provide evidence that FinTech innovations bring significant value for innovators and Blockchain being especially valuable. Such innovations as blockchain, robo-advising and mobile transactions are the most valuable for the financial sector. On one side of the spectrum, the financial industry can be affected more negatively by the innovation of nonfinancial startups that carry disruptive technology at their core. However, on the other side of the spectrum, market leaders who make significant investments in their innovations can evade most of these negative effects. This helped to form an overall view of FinTech innovations.

Keywords: FinTech innovation; valuation; patent application

1. Introduction

Recent development of FinTech raised significant interest within the financial sector and beyond. This sudden evolution and development of financial technology was welcomed by many experts, claiming that FinTech has the potential to disrupt and transform the financial sector by making it more transparent, secure and less expensive [1–3]. For the past decade, sector leaders, represented by large financial institutions, have increased their interest along with investments in FinTech innovations [4,5]. The first two quarters of 2019 raised USD 37.9 billion of global investments in FinTech [6]. According to the Harvey Nash CIO Survey, in 2019, most competitive financial institutions considered FinTech to be their major investment [7].

Despite all of this, it is currently not entirely clear how this new and fast emerging technology can influence existing financial institutions and their business models; which emerging financial technologies will prove of bearing highest value to their creators. It is expected that with the help of FinTech innovations, financial institutions will be able to lower costs and increase customer inclusion that will lead to an increase in future profits [8]. At the moment, new sector entrants are already capitalizing on the growing demand for new, more customer-centric and digitally enabled services. With key technology continuing to evolve rapidly alongside changing consumer needs, industry leaders will be forced to compete with start-ups and tech companies for the new business models. It is difficult to properly asses the circumstances without systematic data analysis on FinTech innovations.

González, Gil, Cunill and Lindahl [9] state that financial innovations increase with increasing growth of volatility among sectors more dependent on external financing, as well as with higher non-stability (growth of instability) of banks, with higher volatility of bank incomes and higher losses of banks. Beck, Tao, Chen and Song [10] presented study based on data analysis of 32 countries over the period 1996–2010. Authors pioneer in assessing the relationship between financial innovation, at one end of the spectrum, and bank growth, as well as economic growth, on the other end. Minhua and Yu [11] use a well-established event study methodology to observe average positive market reactions to announcements of financial innovation regulations, thus implying positive impacts of regulations on company's operations and refer to such an impact as an 'innovation effect'. Lerner [12] studied patenting activities of investment banks and revealed a correlation with their size. Later, he tried to take into account the features of empirical research and the fact that granted patents were rarely used. Implemented analysis focused on organizations introducing financial innovations through the study of a number of hypotheses proposed in the literature. The results showed that the generation of innovation is inversely proportional to the size of the organization, emphasizing the failure of small companies to obtain their patent rights. Schmedders and Citanna [13], studied how the coefficient of incompleteness and structural changes in the financial market affect asset price volatility.

Summarizing the extensive theoretical literature on financial innovation and patenting, main areas of scientific research can be distinguished:

- Nature and design of financial innovation;
- Adoption of financial innovations and its motives;
- Conditions of the economic environment that stimulate financial innovation;
- Effects of financial innovation on profitability and economic well-being;
- Review of financial innovation.

However, key issues regarding the characteristics of financial innovations and their distribution remain unresolved. These issues relate to the nature of financial innovation, and the mathematical basis for assessing the impact of financial innovation in the financial market. In this regard, authors attempted to create a methodology for assessing the impact of financial innovations on the financial market. The proposed model is theoretical in nature and (since empirical studies for the totality of financial innovations are not possible) shows the relationship of the elements that affect the financial market.

The aim of study is to provide comprehensive data and evidence on the value of the FinTech innovation event. In search of a reliable set of innovative measures, some scholars show that researchers used various data collection tools, ranging from unstructured interviews, in which respondents were asked to list a number of measures (important for evaluating financial innovation), to structured interviews that required the respondent to list the list of measures affecting innovative strategies [14].

This paper builds upon a number of various articles and reports. Analysis of Fintech innovation value is based on the data of stock price changes linked with patent application disclosure. Results of the study can be used for further analysis of the reaction of financial sector to the innovation.

2. Literature Review

2.1. Analysis of Key FinTech Innovations

Financial technology or FinTech is a term used to describe the impact of new technologies on the financial services industry [15]. It covers a variety of products, processes, applications and business models that intend to transform the traditional understanding and way of providing financial services [16].

According to the Financial Stability Board FSB definition, "FinTech is technology-enabled innovation in financial services that could result in new business models, applications, processes or products with an associated material effect on the provision of financial services" [17].

From the point of view of procedures, FinTech refers to new applications, processes, products or business models in the field of financial services, consisting of one or more additional financial services, provided in whole or for the most part via the Internet. Services can be provided simultaneously by various independent service providers, typically including at least one licensed bank or insurance company [18].

Based on data analysis, different reports and scholars [15,17,19], the FinTech landscape can be mapped across four broad dimensions and technologies classified into major innovations groups that are ultimately developed for the purpose of application (present or future) in financial services (Table 1):

Table 1. Key FinTech innovations transforming financial services (source: elaborated by authors, based on articles, surveys and industry reports).

		Technology Innovation	Financial Services
Dimension	Artificial intelligence (AI) Big Data	Machine learning (ML) Predictive analytics Data analytics	Investment advice (robo-advising) Credit decisions Asset Trading
	Distributed computing	Distributed ledger (DLT) Blockchain	Digital currencies Back-office, recording Settle payments
	Cryptography	Smart contracts Biometrics Cybersecurity	Automatic transactions Identity protection Cybersecurity
	Mobile access internet	Digital wallets Application programming interfaces (APIs) Mobile transactions Internet of things (IoT)	Crowd funding person-to-person transactions (P2P) Smartphone wallets Inter-operability and expandability

Table 1 implies all the listed innovations should be considered FinTech as their implementation lies (or is intended for) in financial services.

The study presents how FinTech innovations in all four dimensions influence value from the point of view of individual traditional companies, i.e., market leaders and competitors. Theoretical discussion implies that disruptive innovations of potential market participants can be particularly unpleasant for industry leaders who struggle to adapt to changes and focus on customers. On the other hand, market leaders can benefit from disruption, because they have more financial resources and greater economies of scale for introducing new lines of business compared to competitors [20]. Empirical tests confirm the latest predictions that the amount of resources allocated to R&D&I can increase the agility of market leaders to damage from potential external disruptive innovations.

An analysis of the value of Fintech innovations requires reliable estimates (statistical data) of their value. Research on corporate innovation states that the reaction of stock prices to patent applications can be used to examine the valuation (value) of innovations [21]. However, it is less valuable that the reaction of price to a patent publication reflects an unexpected factor: market investors can anticipate a future event and partially include this expectation in the price of the firm's shares today. Without adjusting for the rational anticipation of the abnormal reaction of stock prices to a disclosed patent application, it will not give a rational assessment of innate value of financial innovation. Previously conducted research of stock price reactions to patent applications do not take into consideration the possible expectation of investors. However, in the study of Kogan, Papanikolaou, Seru, and Stoffman [22] the value of patents using pending adjusted price responses to patent grants was evaluated. Authors state that the market can expect several future financial innovations, but in this article, we focus on the Poisson distribution.

2.2. Classification of FinTech Innovations with Machine Learning

The application of a machine-learning method was used for the purpose of classifying patent applications based on textual data. Method was applied in three steps: 1—processing of textual data of applications; 2—building sample unit; 3—training algorithm to single out categories of innovations.

Table 2 presents the results of a machine-learning method performance—neural networks (out-of-sample). Such measures as "accuracy", "precision", "recall", and a combination of the last two called "F1 score" are used to determine classification performance [23]. Neural networks method carries three layers with neurons: 1.124 in first, 286 in second and 42 in third.

Table 2. Performance of machine-learning method (source: author, based on [24]).

	Neural Network (%)
Accuracy	94.7
Precision	98.8
Recall	97.4
F1 score	98.1

Table 3 reports performance scores of five main FinTech categories that were selected during text based filtering: (0) nonfinancial innovations, (1) blockchain, (2) cybersecurity, (3) mobile transactions, (4) robo-advising, (5) IoT.

Table 3. Performance of the neural network method for sample training (created by authors).

Category	Precision (%)	Recall (%)	No. of Applications in Category	No. of Applications in Predicted Category	No. of Applications
0	98.9	97.2	517	514	44.916
1	100.0	99.5	104	112	1.446
2	97.9	97.4	269	264	5.127
3	96.3	97.1	213	214	3.165
4	97.8	97.7	91	91	1.512
5	97.6	95.3	76	77	1.251
Total:	98.1	97.4	1.270	1.270	59.417

Performance of the used machine-learning method is summarized in Table 2. This algorithm has 98.8% precision and 97.4% of recall. Column of No. of Applications presents the text-filtered set of patent applications that were assigned into each of the five categories by the used algorithm. Created sample consists of 86% of nonfinancial innovations and 14% of FinTech patent applications

3. Methodology and Data

3.1. Methodology for Assessing Worth Based on Values with Reactions of Stock Market

The worth of FinTech innovations needs to be reliably estimated to be able to carry out empirical analysis. Lately, the research literature has acknowledged that new patent values can be studied on the basis of the fluctuations of the stock prices. However, there is a catch to it, as one must take into consideration the possibility of investors anticipation of the future patent case, that might correct the company's stock price prior the patent event itself. Consequently, to evade the biased estimation of the innovation value, a rational anticipation correction has to be implemented into the model. Most studies of the stock fluctuations do not take into consideration that possible future insight of the investors anticipating the possible patenting events.

Sometimes, more than one future innovation can be anticipated by the market. Thus, it is important to be able to evaluate the value of FinTech innovations, considering the possibility of multiple innovations. We created a method, that in itself was sufficiently general while giving a possibility to be used with a wide range of data count models (i.e., Poisson, negative binominal, etc.). To simplify the process, however, the focus was on the Poisson count distribution, which is used in many studies of patenting activity such as [25].

V_0 is the company value before the patent event, V^* is the value increase caused by one patent event. The count of the patents N that will happen over a period $(t, t + T)$ under our assumption is following a Poisson distribution:

$$Price(N = k | I_t) = \frac{\lambda^k e^{-\lambda}}{k!}, \; k = 0, 1, 2, \dots \tag{1}$$

Here the information set of the participants in the market is marked by I_t, at specific point in time marked by t. The time $t + T$ change value for the company is kV^* when the exact count of the patent events is k. We can express the value of the company before patent disclosure happens:

$$\overline{V}_{i,0} = V_{i,0} \sum_{k=1}^{\infty} \frac{\lambda^k e^{-\lambda}}{k!} (kAV_i) + \lambda AV_i \tag{2}$$

If we take independency of patent events as a constant, then the event of a patent produces a conditional distribution over further patents, which is a ZTP conditional Poisson distribution:

$$Pr(N = k | N \geq 1, I_t) = \frac{\lambda^k e^{-\lambda}}{(1 - e^{-\lambda}) k!}, \; k = 1, 2, \dots \tag{3}$$

So we can express the actual value of the company after the patent disclosure happens:

$$\overline{V}_{i,0} = V_{i,0} + \sum_{k=1}^{\infty} Pr(N = k | N \geq 1, I_t) kAV_i = V_{i,0} \sum_{k=1}^{\infty} \frac{\lambda^k e^{-\lambda}}{(1 - e^{-\lambda}) k!} kAV_i = V_{i,0} + \frac{\lambda}{1 - e^{-\lambda}} AV_i \tag{4}$$

Following Equations (2) and (4) we can express the value increase caused by one patent event as:

$$AV_i = \frac{\Delta \overline{V}}{\frac{\lambda}{1 - e^{-\lambda}} - \lambda} = \frac{e^\lambda - 1}{\lambda} \Delta \overline{V}_i \tag{5}$$

$\Delta \overline{V} \equiv \overline{V}_1 + \overline{V}_0$ correspond to the company value change after the patent application disclosure. In Equation (5) we made an uncomplicated calculation of the increasing value of a patent V^* using data of the observations. Mainly we could calculate the change of the market value $\Delta \overline{V}$ based on the irregular reactions of the stock prices. We could also calculate intensity parameter λ using empirical models of the patent counts, for example Hausman et al. [25].

3.2. Methodology of Assessing the Intensities of Innovations

The innovation intensity parameter λ has to be assessed as the time-variable value. To do that we used the innovator panel data from the patent filing counts and integrated it into the series of Poisson regressions. As there was a possibility of dependencies between the intensity of innovation and the specifics of the technology or the characteristics of the innovator, we constructed different combinations of the type of the technology and the innovator and we integrated them into the models separately. Total assessed count of the models was 18, which included 5 FinTech categories (15 models) and 3 models for benchmarking financial innovations that were not FinTech.

When evaluating public companies for a specific category of technology k, we used MLE (maximum likelihood estimation):

$$
\begin{aligned}
\log(\lambda_{i,k,t}) = \quad & a + \beta_1 Asset_{i,t} + \beta_2 R\&D\&I_{i,t} + \beta_3 R\&D\&I_{i,t-1} + \beta_4 R\&D\&I_{i,t-2} \\
& + \beta_5 R\&D\&I_{i,t-3} + \beta_5 Age_{i,t} + \beta_6 PreviousFinTech_{i,t} \\
& + \beta_6 PreviousOtherF_{i,t} + \beta_7 PreviousNonF_{i,t} + \gamma_i + \delta_t + \varepsilon_{i,k,t}
\end{aligned}
\tag{6}
$$

Here t and i are, respectively, year and innovating company. In this regression total assets are $Asset_{i,t}$; R&D&I spendings $n + 1$ years before the present year are $R\&D\&I_{i,t-n}$; total age of the company since the founding is Age; the stock of company's FinTech applications before the t year is $PriorFinTech_{it}$; the stock of the company's nonfinancial filings before the t year is $PriorNonF_{i,t}$; the stock of company's non-FinTech financial applications before t year is $PriorOtherF_{i,t}$. Indexes γ_i and δ_t are used to express the fixed effects of innovator and year and all other non-indicator controls are expressed in natural logarithm.

For private companies the following regression is assessed:

$$
\begin{aligned}
\log(\lambda_{i,k,t}) = \quad & a + \beta_1 PreviousFinTech_{i,t} + \beta_2 PreviousOtherF_{i,t} + \beta_3 PreviousNonF_{i,t} \\
& + \gamma_i + \delta_t + \varepsilon_{i,k,t}
\end{aligned}
\tag{7}
$$

Results of the Poisson regressions are represented in Table 6. As the table data suggests, more FinTech patent applications were completed by larger companies. Additionally, for the private companies, there were solid positive predictors of the innovations in FinTech in the form of company's age and amount of the prior non-FinTech applications. Further, for the individuals, the prior innovation experience in non-FinTech areas of finance was the most robust predictor of FinTech filing activity.

3.3. FinTech Innovation Patenting Data

Preparing data for the further analysis authors relied on various researches and data sources, such as open databases along with additional information processing and data matching. No commercial bulk data sources were used, therefore some limitations concerning data were necessary.

For the purpose of providing solid proof on the FinTech innovation event and value, a data set based on publically available patent applications was constructed. Patent applications were analyzed using publicly available data from World Intellectual Property Organization (WIPO) [26], European Patent Office (EPO) and Google Patents databases. This study was based on patent applications and not granted patents mainly for the reason that granting a patent takes years and FinTech is a relatively new field thus many of the patents were applied only recently.

We started by limiting the time span of patent application search to the period of 2015–2019. Which gave a search result of 1,511,546 applications. These applications were then limited to the International Patent Classification (IPC) classes "G" and "H", which were considered to potentially relate to FinTech [27]. It should be noted that not all developments relating to finance and business can be the subject of a patent [28].

Text in the abstract and description sections of patent application and information of assignees was used in order to distinguish assignees into groups of private/individual investors, private and public companies.

Due to the absence of clear and standard definitions of what explicit technologies FinTech covers, a list of terms related to finance was generated to pin down patent applications to those that represent financial services and products.

Table 4 shows main filtering (elimination) steps of applications to match specified criteria and the number of valid applications left for further analysis.

Table 4. Creating a sample for filtering patent applications (created by authors).

	Steps	Eliminated Applications	Valid Applications
1	Total number of patent applications from 2015 to [1] 2019		1,511,546
2	Eliminate applications that do not fall under the "G" or "H" classes of International Patent Classification (IPC)	790,631	720,915
3	Eliminate nonfinancial applications that do not meet the definition based on selected financial terms	731,214	59,417
4	Eliminate applications that fall under the category on "nonfinancial" after use of machine-learning algorithm	39,709	19,708
5	Eliminate applications with incomplete information	8867	10,841
6	Eliminate applications of universities, research institutes	128	10,713
7	Eliminate applications of companies that don't have public trading data	5801	4912
8	Patent applications left in the set:		4912
9	FinTech applications where the applicant is:		
	Public company		1159
	Private company		2974
	Individual		779

[1] Data from database was retrieved on November 2019. Therefore, not covering full year.

Total set of applications classified by machine learning method based on text filtering was 59,417, finance related was 19,708. From 19,708 applications, 8867 were eliminated as invalid, for the reason of missing necessary information (data). Finally, the data set was left with 4912 applications that were used for further analysis: 1159 on public companies; 2974 on private companies and 779 on individual innovators.

After application of machine learning algorithms to gathered data, the main innovations categories were distinguished: blockchain, mobile transactions, P2P, cybersecurity, IoT, data analytics and robo-advising.

In Table 5 applications are classified by different types of innovators. Data required for determining status, classification and dates were gathered from public sources. An interesting observation that can be drawn from this data is that private companies are most active and prevail in most of categories of

FinTech innovations. Public companies bring substantial contributions to innovations in robo-advising, while individuals contribute more in cybersecurity.

Table 5. FinTech patent applications by innovations applicants' type (created by authors).

Category	Individual	Public Company	Private Company
blockchain	5	94	109
cybersecurity	514	931	1.271
mobile transactions	162	88	993
robo-advising	89	17	347
IoT	9	29	254
Total:	779	1.159	2.974

It can be stated that public companies (as a group) stimulated (promoted) the introduction of only a small number of Fintech innovations.

In order to determine the value of a FinTech innovation patent application to several publicly traded companies new methodology was developed. Stock market reaction to the event of patent publication was used as basis for valuation. To understand intrinsic value of every innovation for the company, predicted count intensity and stock price change of company needed to be combined.

Such an approach gives an opportunity to determine how much companies operating in the sector of financial services tend to profit from their own FinTech innovations. Overall study shows that blockchain, robo-advisors and cybersecurity are among the innovations carrying the largest value to the companies. The developed method allowed us to determine how innovation's value impacts the financial industry using stock price data, which means it is limited to measure the effect of publicly traded companies.

Among the listed categories of FinTech, cybersecurity and mobile transactions had the largest number of innovations over the period of the historical sampling. Blockchain as a category secured its position as the fastest growing innovation in the field of FinTech. To study the consequences of introducing FinTech innovations, a methodology for evaluating financial technologies in the financial market (based on the cost of patent applications for one or more companies traded on the stock exchange) was developed.

The valuation was based on the observed reaction of the stock market to the disclosure of patent applications. It is important to note that this approach took into account market expectations regarding various types of patent applications filed by different categories of entities. Initially, the intensity of innovation was assessed using a Poisson regression model, which takes into account factors such as the type of technology, time effects and previous experience of the patent applicant. Then, for each patent application, the predicted counting intensity was combined with the movement of company stock prices to determine the implicit value of innovation for the company. Applying this approach of valuation, we analyzed the number of companies in the financial market that have benefited from their own innovations in the field of financial technology. Calculations showed that the value of FinTech innovations (i.e., the value received by innovator) in general is positive.

Further study presents how value is influenced by FinTech innovations from the viewpoint of traditional companies, i.e., market leaders and their competitors. In different studies, the presented theoretical discussions imply that disruptive innovations presented by potential market participants might be particularly unpleasant for industry leaders who find it difficult to adapt to changes and focus on customers. At the same time, industrial disruption can be potentially beneficial to market leaders, as they usually have greater economies of scale and more financial resources for introducing new lines of business, compared with competitors. Empirical tests confirm the latest predictions that market leaders' ability to evade damage from disruptive external innovations is closely related to the sum total of resources allocated for their own R&D&I.

This study complemented a significant number of studies that use patent data to study the innovative activities of companies [28,29]. Although the literature contains valuable information on innovation and corporate patenting in general, most of the previous research was based mostly on granted patent data and do not fully cover innovative activities in the field of FinTech, which actively has been carried out during recent years. Placing the main focus on patent applications in the field of FinTech innovation, we can mitigate problems of truncating data regarding patenting and provide more complete picture of the latest trends and models.

The developed model expanded on recognizing the nature of innovative events over time, which allowed us to more accurately assess the real value of such impact. In general, such approach of combining reactions of stock prices with predicted Poisson flow rates is helpful in exploring other different types of potentially recurring and to a certain extent expected phenomena, such as a reassessment of analyst estimates, the sequence of news releases by a company, or a wave of possible merges or bankruptcies.

Theoretical studies described in vast literature prove how external financial innovations can benefit or harm existing companies and how traditional companies can protect themselves from external threats by using their own innovations. It is rather difficult to test such theories because big samples of data about possible competitive threats from innovation are very difficult to obtain. This study used a new systematic data set in order to determine how innovations of potential participants can affect individual companies in the industry.

The approach presented in the article of FinTech patent applications identification and classification applying text analysis and machine learning contributes to literature that applies these methods to finance and economics. Machine learning algorithms that are used to classify texts are actually new to the financial field and can be used effectively to analyze a wide range of issues related to patent applications, legal documentation and other textual data.

3.4. Assessing the Value of Own Patent Filings

Further we evaluated the effect that owning FinTech patents has on the value of the publicly traded financial companies. To acquire this data, we used a combination of the cumulative (market-adjusted) abnormal returns (CAR) over the period of event of patent application with the Poisson intensities. We can use Equation (5)'s empirical analogue to assess the value of the innovation to the company:

$$V_{i,j,k,t}^{f\ IND} = \frac{e^{\lambda_{j,k,t}} - 1}{\lambda_{j,k,t} \times n_{k,t}} CAR_{i,t} M_{i,t} \tag{8}$$

Here the technology type of innovation is k, the company is i and the date of the publication of the innovation is t. $\lambda_{i,k,t}$ is the intensity of innovation from the Poisson regressions that was projected in Assessing the intensities of innovations Section; $n_{k,t}$ refers to a number of patents that have been disclosed on the date t by a company i; $CAR_{i,t}$ is a 4 day period calculation which starts 2 days prior the patent disclosure date t; $M_{i,t}$ refers to a company's market capitalization 5 days before the disclosure date t.

4. Results and Discussion

4.1. Results on Number of FinTech Innovation Events

This Table 6 presents Poisson regression models calculation on the number of FinTech innovation events that occur in a given time period (2015–2019). Regression is calculated for every technology category separately. Research and Development and Innovation are the company's expenditures that it spends on R&D&I before the year of patent application event. FinTech previous applications are the number of company's previous Fintech patent applications. Nonfinancial previous applications are the number of company's previous nonfinancial patent applications. All applications are counted in the same IPC "G" and "H" classes.

Table 6. Poisson count models calculated for FinTech innovations (created by authors).

Public Companies	Blockchain	Cybersecurity	Mobile Transactions	Robo-Advising	Internet of Things
Assets	0.943 **** (−0.193)	0.907 *** (−0.349)	−1.277 ** (−0.541)	−35.903 * (−20.399)	−0.355 (−0.486)
Research and Development and Innovation	0.073 (−0.304)	1.753 *** (−0.557)	−0.172 (−1.72)	59.590 ** (−29.945)	1.988 (−1.362)
Research and Development and Innovation 1	0.048 (−0.3)	−0.673 (−0.66)	1.908 (−2.245)	34.657 ** (−16.662)	3.738 (−2.336)
Research and Development and Innovation 2	−0.236 (−0.288)	0.364 (−0.662)	0.287 (−2.05)	−22.221 ** (−10.288)	−7.361 *** (−2.344)
Research and Development and Innovation 3	−0.273 (−0.248)	−0.935 * (−0.514)	−1.241 (−1.443)	29.204 ** (−14.246)	2.111 * (−1.129)
Age	−0.201 (−0.591)	−0.093 (−1.329)	−3.693 ** (−1.514)	37.648 (−139.437)	−0.295 (−2.107)
Fintech previous applications	0.111 (−0.11)	−0.092 * (−0.174)	0.244 (−0.309)	−5.566 (−3.711)	−1.126 *** (−0.339)
Nonfinancial previous applications	0.253 ** (−0.101)	0.197 (−0.176)	0.358 (−0.278)	27.971 ** (−12.487)	1.243 *** (−0.305)
Private Companies					
Age	1.145 *** (−0.166)	1.730 *** (−0.306)	3.399 *** (−0.628)	11.987 ** (−5.55)	3.547 *** (−0.725)
Fintech previous applications	−0.555 *** (−0.09)	−1.103 *** (−0.137)	−1.643 *** (−0.267)	−2.790 ** (−1.304)	−1.105 *** (−0.27)
Nonfinancial previous applications	0.619 *** (−0.101)	0.818 ** (−0.174)	0.966 *** (−0.281)	8.111 *** (−2.982)	0.867 ** (−0.369)

Data in parentheses represent robust standard errors. * $p < 0.10$; ** $p < 0.05$; *** $p < 0.01$.

In Table 7 we see a cumulative data for private innovation values across seven different categories and five major FinTech groups, FinTech innovations and non-FinTech financial innovations. CARs for each of the five categories are provided individually. The data prove that FinTech innovations lead to a notable value for the company. For the innovator value on average is 21.5 M USD and the median reaches 41 M USD. Comparing these values to innovations that fall under the category of non-FinTech financial, a substantially lower median value is created, that is USD 2.1 M, but the average value is still similar to the value FinTech innovations. In most of the innovation types the mean CAR values are positive. The fact that median and mean values in some innovation types have opposite signs, shows the degree of substantial asymmetry in the distributions. Mobile transactions have the only negative median value. Futher, the biggest values are seen in blockchain innovation, cybersecurity and robo-advising (USD 99.4 M, USD 56.3 M and USD 52.2 M, respectively).

We use bootstrapping to evaluate the importance of the median and mean values. Bootstrapped p values for medians and means are presented in the Table 7 in parentheses. We have received results that show statistical difference of zero of the positive medians for blockchain, cybersecurity, robo-advising and IoT. Additionally, the positive median for all FinTech innovations shows high statistical significance. Thus, the statement, that FinTech innovations bear significant value to their innovators is supported by the p values in Table 7.

Table 7 presents data on the value effect for the company of selected FinTech innovation categories. Values, that are expressed in millions USD, from public company's abnormal stock returns (CAR) linked to their patent application event, are calculated according to Equation (8). CARs are calculated over the period of 2 days: starting one day before the news of patent application. Data in parentheses represent p-values for means and medians, and a bootstrapping method was used to calculate p-values.

Table 7. FinTech innovation value for the company (created by authors).

Innovation Category	CAR (%)	Mean	Median	Standard Deviation
Blockchain	0.31	62.5 (0.431)	99.4 (<0.001)	1768.50
Cybersecurity	0.47	49.2 (0.456)	56.3 (0.083)	1021.73
Mobile transactions	−0.36	−89.7 (0.385)	−18.4 (0.089)	1792.64
Robo-advising	0.29	−104.6 (0.455)	52.2 (0.011)	964.1
IoT	−0.38	−31.4 (0.611)	2.2 (0.783)	817
All FinTech Innovations		21.5 (0.483)	41.0 (<0.001)	1548.80
Non FinTech Financial Innovations		19.6 (0.564)	2.1 (0.482)	3031.20

Further we evaluate the effect that underlying technologies have on the value of FinTech innovations. For this cause multivariate regressions are used. On the first stage the goal is a mitigation of skewness and outliers in the distribution of the value. For this cause, a logarithmic transformation is applied to the estimated values:

$$V = \begin{cases} \log(1 + V^*); & V^* > 0 \\ -\log(1 - V^*); & V^* < 0 \end{cases} \tag{9}$$

Here, V is a converted value that is later used in regressions as the dependent variable. V^* is the estimated in Equation (8) value. Further, following form regressions are estimated:

$$V_{i,k,t}^{f\ IND} = \alpha_i + \beta' TechD_k + \Gamma' X_{i,k,t} + \varepsilon_{i,k,t} \tag{10}$$

Here $V_i, {}^O{}_k, {}^W{}_t{}^N$ is the value (which is log transformed) of the patent application on a date t of technology type k to a company i. *TechD* are the binary variables and express categories of different FinTech. X contains controls of company size, company age before FinTech applications, before applications in other financial areas and before nonfinancial applications in IPC "G" and "H". Company and year fixed effects, patent breadth and quality controls are also included. Nonindicator controls are expressed in natural logarithm.

Table 8 presents regression results. According to the data, the most valuable innovation categories are blockchain followed by robo-advising. These types of innovation have much more significant value compared to mobile transactions baseline. However, it can be observed that other categories are not that significantly different from mobile transactions. These data show that, regarding future cost savings in financial services, there are big potential benefits offered by blockchain technology.

4.2. Discussion

In this analysis the value of FinTech innovation was presented through a patent lens. This is a tangible measure that proves that protecting the output of companies' investment can bear positive value effect. Being an essential source of competitive intelligence, patents can help companies to withstand introduction of disruptive innovation [30]. In this paper, the focus is put on patent applications rather than on granted patents which provides more of a complete analysis of recent trends in FinTech innovation.

Table 8. Innovation category and company value of FinTech (created by authors).

Innovation Category	Value
blockchain	2.022 **
	(0.652)
cybersecurity	0.245
	(0.533)
mobile transactions	1.341 *
	(0.731)
robo-advising	1.637 *
	(0.731)
IoT	0.704
	(0.947)

$* p < 0.10; ** p < 0.01.$

The method that was developed complements other researchers that used stock prices to determine the value of innovation. Presented study extends and combines reactions of stock prices with Poisson innovation intensities. It can be used to analyze different types of recurring and partially anticipated events. Approach used in this paper to identify and classify FinTech innovations using machine learning and text analysis can contribute to the economic literature. The study demonstrates a correlation between financial innovations and impact or value on the financial market.

Despite the current widespread of FinTech, the fundamental challenge that was faced analyzing FinTech innovations is that there is currently no official definition or consensus about what FinTech is and of what exact technologies or services it comprises [31].

4.3. Limitations

Patenting FinTech inventions has a number of challenges and one of the limitations is that it reflects only part of financial sectors' innovation activities as not all of them can be subject to patenting [32]. While previous researchers have focused more on the analysis of granted patents [33,34], trends on machine learning technologies and applications [35,36], the presented study is based on patent applications, mainly for the reason that granting a patent takes years and FinTech is a relatively new field, thus many of the patents were applied only recently.

The other limitation is related to the complexity of companies R&D&I expenditures that makes it hard to determine exact investments. Further research is needed for a broader understanding of FinTech innovation impact on financial sector and society.

5. Conclusions

Such an increase of interest in FinTech-powered innovation during recent years brings out the need for a deeper understanding of a potential value that these new emerging technologies can bear to their inventors. There is an increase in general understanding that patents play an important part in an organization's innovation strategy. Different sectors adopt different strategies for generating value from innovations. Currently there is an obvious difference between how financial services and technology companies perceive patents.

Analysis of valuation of financial innovation presented in this paper was based on stock price data. The developed model expanded on recognizing the nature of innovative events over time, which allowed to assess value impact more accurately. For this purpose, Poisson flow rates and stock price movements were combined, which proved to be useful exploring other partially anticipated recurring phenomena such as the sequence of company news releases and wave of mergers or bankruptcies.

The presented study provides evidence that FinTech innovations bring value to their inventors and generally are valuable to the whole financial sector. Most valuable FinTech innovations are blockchain innovation (USD 99.4 M), cybersecurity (USD 6.3 M) and robo-advising (USD 52.2 M).

On the other hand, some categories of FinTech innovation have a negative value effect on companies. Findings state that market leaders that invest in their own R&D&I, have tendency to avoid harm introduced by disruptive innovations.

For further research, the authors suggest to focus on a deeper analysis of the additional features of FinTech innovations and how they affect the value of companies in the financial sector. What is more, the conducted study can be used as basis for further research of social impact of FinTech innovation.

Author Contributions: Conceptualization, J.K.; data curation, J.K.; investigation, J.K.; resources, J.K.; writing—original draft preparation, J.K.; writing—review and editing, J.K. and J.S.; supervision, J.S. All authors have read and agreed to the published version of the manuscript.

References

1. Buehler, K.; Chiarella, D.; Heidegger, H.; Lemerle, M.; Lal, A.; Moon, J. *Beyond the Hype: Blockchains in Capital Markets*; McKinsey & Company: New York, NY, USA, 2015.
2. Harrist, M. How Fintech Is Powering The Global Economy. *Forbes.* 2017. Available online: https://www.forbes.com/sites/oracle/2017/03/14/how-fintech-is-powering-the-global-economy/ (accessed on 27 September 2020).
3. The Economist. The Fintech Revolution. A Wave of Startups Is Changing Finance for the Better. *The Economist.* 2015. Available online: https://www.economist.com/leaders/2015/05/09/the-fintech-revolution (accessed on 26 September 2020).
4. Nash, K.S. Big Banks Stake Fintech Claims with Patent Application Surge. *Wall Street Journal.* 2016. Available online: https://blogs.wsj.com/cio/2016/05/10/big-banks-stake-fintech-claims-with-patent-application-surge/ (accessed on 2 September 2020).
5. Russo, C. Goldman and Google are among the most Active Blockchain Investors. *Bloomberg.* 2017. Available online: https://www.bloomberg.com/news/articles/2017-10-17/goldman-google-make-list-of-most-active-blockchain-investors (accessed on 13 August 2020).
6. Pollari, I.; Ruddenklau, A. The Pulse of Fintech H1 2019. In *2019 bi-Annual Analysis of Global Investment Trends in the Fintech Sector*; KPMG Global: Zurich, Switzerland, 2019.
7. Bates, S.; Ellis, A. A Changing Perspective. Harvey Nash CIO Survey 2019. Available online: https://home.kpmg/xx/en/home/insights/2019/06/harvey-nash-kpmg-cio-survey-2019.html (accessed on 21 August 2020).
8. Casey, M.; Crane, J.; Gensler, G.; Johnson, S.; Narula, N. *The Impact of Blockchain Technology on Finance: A Catalyst for Change*; Geneva Reports on the World Economy 21; International Center for Monetary and Banking Studies (ICMB): Geneva, Switzerland, 2019.
9. González, L.O.; Gil, L.I.R.; Cunill, O.M.; Lindahl, J.M.M. The effect of financial innovation on European banks' risk. *J. Bus. Res.* **2016**, *69*, 4781–4786. [CrossRef]
10. Beck, T.; Chen, T.; Lin, C.; Song, F. Financial innovation: The bright and the dark sides. *J. Bank. Finance* **2016**, *72*, 28–51. [CrossRef]
11. Yang, M.; He, Y. How does the stock market react to financial innovation regulations? *Finance Res. Lett.* **2019**, *30*, 259–265. [CrossRef]
12. Lerner, J. Patent protection and innovation over 150 years. *Natl. Bur. Econ. Res.* **2002**, *97*, 1–40.
13. Citanna, A.; Schmedders, K. Excess price volatility and financial innovation. *Econ. Theory* **2005**, *26*, 559–587. [CrossRef]
14. Council of Canadian Academies. Innovation Impacts: Measurement and Assessment. The Expert Panel on the Socio-Eco-Nomic Impacts of Innovation Investments, 1–148. 2015. Available online: https://cca-reports.ca/wp-content/uploads/2018/10/roi_fullreporten.pdf (accessed on 19 July 2020).
15. European Commission. What Is FinTech? 2019. Available online: https://ec.europa.eu/info/business-economy-euro/banking-and-finance/fintech_en (accessed on 5 November 2019).
16. Chan, R. Asian Regulators Seek FinTech Balance. 2018. Available online: http://www.financeasia.com/News/401588,asian-regulators-seek-fintech-balance.aspx (accessed on 14 December 2019).
17. Financial Stability Board (FSB). *Decentralised Financial Technologies: Report on Financial Stability, Regulatory and Governance Implications*; Financial Stability Board: Basel, Switzerland, 2019.

18. European Commision. FinTech Action Plan: For a More Competitive and Innovative European Financial Sector. 2018. Available online: https://eur-lex.europa.eu/legal-content/EN/TXT/?uri=CELEX:52018DC0109 (accessed on 2 July 2020).

19. Lavender, J.; Pollari, I.; Raisbeck, M.; Hughes, B.; Speier, A. The Pulse of Fintech Q4 2017—Global Analysis of Investment in Fintech. Kpmg, (February), 1–80. 2017. Available online: https://assets.kpmg.com/content/dam/kpmg/xx/pdf/2017/02/pulse-of-fintech-q4-2016.pdf (accessed on 12 September 2020).

20. Christensen, C.; Raynor, M. *The Innovator's Solution: Creating and Sustaining Successful Growth*; Harvard Business Review Press: Brighton, MA, USA, 2013.

21. Nicholas, T. Does Innovation Cause Stock Market Runups? Evidence from the Great Crash. *Am. Econ. Rev.* **2008**, *98*, 1370–1396. [CrossRef]

22. Kogan, L.; Papanikolaou, D.; Seru, A.; Stoffman, N. Technological Innovation, Resource Allocation, and Growth. *Q. J. Econ.* **2017**, *132*, 665–712. [CrossRef]

23. MS Azure. Understand Automated Machine Learning Results. 2019. Available online: https://docs.microsoft.com/en-us/azure/machine-learning/ (accessed on 19 September 2020).

24. Czakon, J. 24 Evaluation Metrics for Binary Classification (And When to Use Them). 2019. Available online: https://neptune.ai/blog/evaluation-metrics-binary-classification (accessed on 7 June 2020).

25. Hausman, J.; Hall, B.H.; Griliches, Z. Econometric Models for Count Data with an Application to the Patents-R & D Relationship. *Econometrica* **1984**, *52*, 909–938. [CrossRef]

26. WIPO. PATENTSCOPE Database. 2019. Available online: https://www.wipo.int/patentscope/en/ (accessed on 17 October 2019).

27. European Patent Office (EPO). Espacenet Database. 2019. Available online: https://worldwide.espacenet.com/ (accessed on 17 October 2019).

28. Gardner, J.D. New Patent Office Guidelines and the Impact on the Patent Eligibility of Fintech Inventions. 2019. Available online: https://www.jdsupra.com/legalnews/new-patent-office-guidelines-and-the-34479/ (accessed on 19 May 2020).

29. Stankovic, M. Patentability of FinTech inventions. In *FinTech: Law and Regulation*; Madir, J., Ed.; Elgar Financial Law and Practice; Edward Elgar Publishing Ltd.: Geneva, Switzerland, 2019; p. 512.

30. Swycher, N.; Malek, M. Fintech-Understanding the Role of Patents. Available online: https://cipher.ai/wp-content/uploads/Fintech-understanding-the-role-of-patnets.pdf (accessed on 25 May 2020).

31. Georges, A.D.; Korenchan, J.L. The Patent Landscape of Cryptocurrency and Blockchain. SNIPPETS, 1–16. 2018. Available online: https://www.mbhb.com/intelligence/snippets/the-patent-landscape-of-cryptocurrency-and-blockchain (accessed on 14 August 2020).

32. Fatás, A. The Economics of Fintech and Digital Currencies. 2019. Available online: https://voxeu.org/article/economics-fintech-and-digital-currencies-new-ebook (accessed on 17 March 2020).

33. Bhatt, P.C.; Kumar, V.; Lu, T.-C.; Cho, R.L.-T.; Lai, K.K. Rise and Rise of Blockchain: A Patent Statistics Approach to Identify the Underlying Technologies. In Proceedings of the Intelligent Information and Database Systems, 12th Asian Conference, ACIIDS 2020, Phuket, Thailand, 23–26 March 2020. [CrossRef]

34. Unsal, O.; Rayfield, B. Trends in Financial Innovation: Evidence from Fintech Firms. Disruptive Innovation in Business and Finance in the Digital World. *Int. Financ. Rev.* **2019**, *20*, 15–25. [CrossRef]

35. Chae, S.; Gim, J. A Study on Trend Analysis of Applicants Based on Patent Classification Systems. *Information* **2019**, *10*, 364. [CrossRef]

36. Zambetti, M.; Sala, R.; Russo, D.; Pezzotta, G.; Pinto, R. A Patent Review on Machine Learning Techniques and Applications: Depicting Main Players, Relations and Technology Landscapes. In Proceedings of the XXIII Summer School Francesco Turco, Palermo, Italy, 12–14 September 2018.

4

Effects of the Type of CSR Discourse for Utilitarian and Hedonic Services

Andrea Pérez *, María del Mar García de los Salmones and Elisa Baraibar-Diez

Business Administration Department, University of Cantabria, 39005 Santander, Spain;
mariadelmar.garcia@unican.es (M.d.M.G.d.l.S.); elisa.baraibar@unican.es (E.B.-D.)
* Correspondence: andrea.perezruiz@unican.es

Abstract: In a context of corporate social responsibility (CSR) communication, we explore whether the use of expositive versus narrative discourses interacts with the type of service commercialized by the company (utilitarian vs. hedonic) to determine consumer perceptions and responses to corporate communication. Our main proposal is that, as representative examples of utilitarian services, banking companies would benefit significantly from communicating their CSR efforts with expositive discourses, whereas narrative discourses would be more adequate for hedonic services (e.g., catering). To test the research hypotheses, we use a 2 (expositive/narrative discourse) x 2 (utilitarian/hedonic service) between-subjects experimental design where we expose 302 consumers to different combinations of CSR messages and we evaluate changes in their message attributions and internal and external responses to them. The findings show that the interaction effect is significant and it works in the expected direction for issue importance, CSR fit, and CSR attributions. However, for CSR impact, attitude, trust, purchase, and advocacy intentions, the findings suggest that narrative discourses work better than expositive discourses both for utilitarian and hedonic services. No significant differences between types of discourses are observed for CSR motives, CSR commitment, and C-C identification and the interaction effect is also not significant for these variables.

Keywords: CSR; communication; discourse; exposition; narrative; storytelling; banking; catering; utilitarian service; hedonic service

1. Introduction

Since the 2008 Great Recession, increasing attention has been devoted to corporate social responsibility (CSR). Not only has the international community realized the importance of achieving sustainable economic, social, and environmental development for stability and progress in the world economy [1], but CSR has also become paramount for institutions and companies to recover credibility, trust, and reputation [2,3].

Nonetheless, it is noticeable that the business returns to CSR are contingent on stakeholders' awareness of a company's CSR activities [4]. However, studies frequently report that CSR awareness is typically low, while stakeholders also demonstrate to be highly skeptical of the CSR motives behind companies that engage in CSR efforts [5]. These ideas highlight the necessity that companies have nowadays to design better communication strategies to reap strategic benefits from its CSR activities [4]. The way companies design their CSR communication strategies is crucial for the success of CSR and research should focus on this issue to provide companies with useful insight to design CSR and communication strategies more adequately.

For instance, an interesting line of research has focused on exploring the effect that different discourse strategies have on audiences when exposed to communication [6–8]. Scholars have frequently discussed the advantages and disadvantages of designing messages based on expositive (semantic or rational) or narrative (i.e., storytelling) discourses [9,10]. Based on the premises of the narrative paradigm theory (NPT) [11], scholars have mostly defended that discourse will always tell a story and insofar as it invites an audience to believe it or to act on it, the narrative paradigm and its attendant logic, narrative rationality, are available for (better) interpretation and assessment. Therefore, narrative discourses are expected to report better outcomes for companies than expositive discourses [12–14]. Nonetheless, the empirical evidence along this line of research is largely inconclusive [15], with studies alternatively demonstrating the superior performance of expositive [16] or narrative [15] discourses, or even showing mixed results within the same experiments [17].

Some scholars have suggested that the inconclusiveness of previous findings may be due to the existence of an interaction effect between the type of discourse strategy and the type of product/service context of the company [17–19]. More precisely, scholars suggest that the type of discourse chosen by the company in its communications should match their product/service type to be successful [15]. For instance, banking services are utilitarian services that, based on the premises of the elaboration likelihood model (ELM), would benefit from applying rational nonnarrative appeals to their communications [20]. On the contrary, catering services are hedonic services, which are focused on pleasing consumers and, consequently, would benefit more from emotional narrative discourses [20]. Nevertheless, support for this matching principle is again contradictory and little consensus has been reached yet. As an example, in her qualitative study, Mortimer (2008) observed that narrative discourses could be useful for both hedonic and utilitarian services and that the matching of the discourse strategy to the type of service context was not necessarily an adequate communication approach for companies [15].

Along this line of research, we have observed that the lack of conclusive findings on the matching principle between the type of discourse and the type of service is especially evident in the CSR communication literature, where very few studies have tested this interaction effect [21]. All the papers discussed above have explored the role of the type of discourse and/or the service context in conventional commercial advertising (i.e., communication focused on presenting the products and services that can solve a consumer's problem), whereas very little research has been implemented so far in the CSR context. Nonetheless, CSR communication differs from commercial advertising significantly because its main goal is not to "sell" products/services but to promote corporate sustainable development endeavors and define corporate values and personality [22]. It also differs from commercial advertising because of its normative or moralistic character. Therefore, the few conclusions (if any) that could be extracted from previous literature on the interaction effect between the type of discourse and the type of service could not be translated into the CSR literature straightforwardly and, as so, further research is needed in the context of CSR communication.

Based on these ideas, the research goal of the present paper is to explore whether the use of expositive versus narrative discourses interacts with the type of service (utilitarian vs. hedonic) to determine consumer perceptions and responses to CSR communication. To propose our research hypotheses, we base on the ELM [23] and the distinction between functional and self-congruity types of message processing [15,18] to propose that utilitarian (banking) services would benefit significantly from communicating their CSR efforts with expositive discourses, whereas narrative discourses should be left for hedonic (catering) services that would achieve better results with them. To measure the consequences of the interaction effect, we evaluate changes in consumer message attributions and internal and external responses to a CSR message [4] in a 2 × 2 experimental context where consumers are exposed to different combinations of expositive vs. narrative messages in utilitarian vs. hedonic service contexts. In testing this proposal, the paper will contribute to previous literature in two ways. First, the paper will provide further insight into the discourse by service interaction effect that has reported inconclusive findings in previous literature. Second, it will do so in the context of CSR communication, where previous literature has largely neglected the possibility of an interaction effect between both conditions.

We structure the paper as follows. First, we revise literature on discourse and communication strategies and types of services to propose the research hypotheses of the study. Second, we describe the research method, paying special attention to its design, sample, and measurement scales. Third, we describe the main findings of the paper and we discuss them in the light of previous literature. We conclude by presenting the most relevant implications, limitations, and future lines of research derived from the study.

2. Literature Review

2.1. Expositive and Narrative Discourses in Corporate Communication

An extensive line of research in marketing and communication literature suggests that the success of corporate communication largely depends on the type of discourse used by companies in their public messages [6,8]. In this regard, designing a message that will be perceived as rational, emotional, or mixed in its discourse is a primary strategic consideration in corporate communication [24].

Along this line, companies have traditionally applied two opposite types of discourses to their corporate communications; they present messages that are mostly expositive or narrative in character [9,10]. Expositive (semantic, rational, or nonnarrative) perspectives on communication include "self-evident propositions, demonstrations, proofs, and verbal expressions of certain and probable knowing" [7]. Thus, exposition mainly bases on the description of rational arguments, statistics, numbers, names, and facts [12]. Expositive messages do not go any deeper into the reality behind those numbers and they avoid emotional connotations as much as possible [9]. In numerous occasions, this approach has been referred to as informational communication [15]. On the contrary, the narrative (storytelling) rationality implies that "facts need some narrative to bind them together to enhance their intelligibility" [7]. In narrative messages, companies may use storytelling, which refers to the art of telling emotional stories to engage with the audience. Corporate storytelling is the "practice of using narration from within the organization relating to its people, practices, policies and visions to effectively engage with staff (and external stakeholders)" [25]. Thus, narrative messages are aimed at generating emotional connections between stakeholders and companies [26,27] by adding favorable and unique associations to companies through messages that can better embrace the core corporate values [27].

Based on the narrative paradigm theory (NPT) [11], previous research has mostly defended that people tend to think narratively more than paradigmatically or in an expositive way [20]. Therefore, narrative discourses are expected to lead to better audience responses than expositive discourses [12–14]. Consisting of a sequence of story—understanding—shared meaning, storytelling, materialized in a compelling story, gains access to the mind and sensations of those who are listening or watching, enriched in their learning and feelings. This connection provokes empathy and, therefore, it allows the audience to understand and be sensitive to the experience that they are being told about, which derives into better attitudes and allows the formation of stronger relationships and engagement [28].

Nonetheless, empirical evidence is inconclusive when it comes to corroborating the role of expositive and narrative discourses on consumers' message attributions and responses to corporate communication. For instance, Mortimer (2008) examined a sample of service advertisements that had been recognized for their success and she found that the majority of advertisements utilized emotional discourses [15]. On the contrary, in a study that explored retail services advertising, Stafford and Day (1995) found the main effect for discourse across industries, in which rational discourses led to more positive levels of attitude towards the ad than emotional discourses [16]. Hill et al. (2004) tested the hypothesis that a successful visualization advertising strategy (i.e., an ad based on a narrative discourse) evoked clear and vivid mental images of the service on consumers, thus making CSR communication more successful [17]. However, their findings only supported this hypothesis for some outcomes such as perceived informativity, service quality, and likelihood to use, but it was not supported for perceived uniqueness.

2.2. Interaction Effect between Discourse Strategy and Type of Service

A plausible explanation for the inconclusiveness of previous literature is that responses to corporate communication do not only depend on the type of discourse adopted by the company, but also on the type of service context where the company operates [15–17,21]. Generally, in service literature, scholars differentiate between utilitarian and hedonic services [16,20]. For instance, banking services are utilitarian services that provide functional utilities, deliver cognitive benefits, and are characterized by low employee contact, moderate customization, an equipment-orientation, and direction toward things [16,20]. On the contrary, catering services are hedonic services that are consumed primarily for affective or sensory gratification purposes, provide consumers with emotions, and are characterized by high employee contact, considerable customization, and an orientation toward people, not things (i.e., they are more personal) [16,20].

Based on the elaboration likelihood model (ELM) [23] and the functional congruity and self-congruity types of message processing [15,18], we propose that an expositive discourse is especially adequate for communicating about the CSR of banking (utilitarian) services, whereas narrative approaches would be more suitable for the CSR communication of catering (hedonic) services.

In this regard, banking services are high-involvement services for consumers [29] and, as such, the amount this audience type would think about a message coming from a banking company would be high. Um (2008) shows that elaboration is higher when the argument is relevant to the person (i.e., high involvement), and lower when the argument is irrelevant [30]. Therefore, in the case of a banking company, persuasion is most commonly achieved through central and functional processing routes [15,24], which occur when the person who receives the information is likely to focus and process the finer points in the message (e.g., the quality of the argument) [18,24]. Therefore, for banking services, communicating CSR facts with a rational, expositive discourse would be more adequate than using a narrative, storytelling discourse because, as utilitarian services, the functional aspects of consumption are more important and rational decision is dominant over emotional responses [31]. Consumers evaluate utilitarian services using cognitive criteria [20]. This rationale matches the use of expositive discourses, which assume that consumers make rational decisions and, therefore, they prefer nonnarrative messages [21].

On the contrary, in catering services, the hedonic aspect of consumption is highly important and affective responses may overwhelm cognitive responses [31]. Catering services are value-expressive, which means that consumers will generally make their decisions to use the service based on the image that is associated to the company and the association that will be created between the company's image and his/her image [18]. Consumers are expected to be influenced by this type of hedonic service more at a personal level, making it difficult for them to disassociate themselves from the service and perceiving it as an extension of themselves [19]. Therefore, when the service is value-expressive, audience persuasion is influenced through an affective, peripheral, and self-congruity processing route [18], which occurs when the person focuses more lightly on source cues to form their attitudes [18] because these cues require little mental effort [24]. In this context, narrative discourses will be more adequate than expositive discourses. In this regard, "well-designed, well-told stories convey both information and emotion, both the explicit and the tacit, both the core and context" [32]. CSR stories have an ameliorative effect, enhancing the ability of audiences to exist more meaningfully and improve their mental models of others and themselves [33]. Thus, corporate storytelling generates an emotional connection between consumers and companies [26,27] and, consequently, it is expected to intensify consumer positive responses to CSR messages when they evaluate hedonic services.

2.3. Message Attributions in CSR Communication

To explore how the interaction between type of discourse and type of service affects consumer perceptions and responses to CSR communication, we test the differentiated effect of CSR messages on the prominent framework of CSR communication developed by Du et al. (2010) [4]. According to these authors, one key aspect to create stakeholder awareness and managing stakeholder perceptions of a company's CSR activities is the message content (i.e., the "what to communicate" question). Du et al. (2010) and subsequent researchers who have tested their conceptual framework empirically [34], defend that the content of a CSR message should emphasize: (a) the importance of the social issue, (b) the impact the company has on the cause, (c) the motives why it engages in the social cause, (d) the fit (i.e., congruence, similarity, compatibility) between the cause and the company, and (e) the company's long-term commitment to the cause.

Issue importance refers to the relevance of the social cause on a global scale. When companies include information about issue importance in the CSR message, they increase stakeholders' awareness of the cause, which will improve message diagnosticity, allow stakeholders to effectively process CSR appeals and, consequently, improve responses to the CSR message [35,36].

CSR impact reflects the results of the collaboration between the company and the social cause, that is, the impact the company has achieved on the social cause over the time they have collaborated. Mentioning CSR impact gives the message an objective charge, it enhances its credibility, and it let stakeholders evaluate the true level of a company's CSR involvement and commitment to the social cause, which can lead to positive communication outcomes [4,37].

As for CSR motives, it is generally agreed that the perception of a company's intrinsic (altruistic) motives to collaborate with a social cause increases perceived sincerity and positive emotions, whereas a behavior attributed only to extrinsic (egoistic) motives is perceived as dishonest, opportunistic, and misleading for stakeholders, arousing negative feelings [38,39]. Literature also defends that perceptions of corporate altruistic motives lead stakeholders to understand the company's commitment to the social cause as more lasting and stable over time [40] because it derives from the company's value system directly [41].

CSR fit refers to the congruence between the social cause and the company, which can be functional (i.e., the congruence of the type of product/service marketed by the company, and the type of social cause supported) or based on image cues (i.e., the holistic, symbolic, and peripheral judgement of company identity and its relatedness and similarity to the cause identity) [42–44]. A good cause–company fit may minimize negative judgments about the company's motives to collaborate with the cause [45] and, therefore, it leads to better communication outcomes [4,46]. On the contrary, a low perceived fit is likely to increase cognitive elaboration and make egoistic motives more salient, arousing negative feelings toward CSR messages [44].

Finally, CSR commitment relates to the company's long-term commitment to the social cause. CSR commitment improves stakeholders' responses because a long-term commitment (versus a reactive, shorter-term CSR action) provides more time to learn about a company-cause collaboration [4]. It also reflects a genuine concern for increasing community welfare and, consequently, it improves attitudes towards the company [35].

As reported in the previous section of this paper, we expect that these consumer perceptions of the message content are dependent upon the interaction between type of discourse (expositive vs. narrative) and type of service (utilitarian vs. hedonic) [15,16,18,21]. Thus, we hypothesize that consumers will perceive the different components of the CSR message discussed by Du et al. (2010) differently in each industry depending on the type of CSR discourse used by companies. Based on this idea, this study tests the following research hypotheses:

H1: In a utilitarian service context, an expositive CSR discourse generates statistically significant higher perceptions of (a) issue importance, (b) CSR impact, (c) CSR motives, (d) CSR fit, and (e) CSR commitment than a narrative CSR discourse.

H2: In a hedonic service context, a narrative CSR discourse generates statistically significant higher perceptions of (a) issue importance, (b) CSR impact, (c) CSR motives, (d) CSR fit, and (e) CSR commitment than an expositive CSR discourse.

2.4. Consumer Responses to CSR Communication

Then, message attributions generate internal and external outcomes among stakeholders, which refer respectively to their attitudinal and behavioral responses to the company's CSR communication strategy [4,34]. As stated by Du et al. (2010), when analyzing consumer responses specifically, internal outcomes mainly include CSR attributions, service brand attitude, consumer-company (C-C) identification, and trust, whereas external outcomes refer to purchase and advocacy intentions [4].

CSR communication makes consumers aware of such initiatives, then, it derives in positive CSR attributions [21]. Therefore, corporate communications are important in raising CSR attributions among consumers to induce positive attitudes and behavioral intentions. Without this sort of communication, consumers will purchase a similar service that does not have such CSR attributes [21].

Along with CSR awareness (i.e., associations), Keller (1998) considers that to gain consumer-based brand equity, the consumer should also hold brand associations that are strong, favorable, and unique in comparison to other brands offered in the same category [47]. These brand associations refer to service brand attitude as described by Du et al. (2010) [4]. A large component of Keller's (1998) model depicts various types of brand associations in the form of service-related and non-service-related attributes, such as CSR [48]. Improving brand attitude is important for companies because it is linked to the consumer intention to use the service directly [49].

C-C identification refers to the cognitive and affective state of connection that a consumer perceives between him/herself and a company because of the identification of substantial overlap between the consumer's perceptions of his/her identity and the perceptions of the company's identity [50]. A company that is skilled in meeting the consumer's needs for self-definition is also a company the consumer is satisfied with because C-C identification provides a more favorable context for consumers to respond to corporate performance experiences as against to prior expectations. In addition, the higher C-C identification, the higher consumer loyalty and the wish to establish long-term relationships with the company [51].

Trust is understood as the existence of a bidirectional relationship where one exchange partner (consumer) believes in the other's (company) reliability and integrity [52]. Achieving consumer trust is especially important for companies because it serves as a key driver of consumer retention strategies, especially in retail service markets. Along this line, in numerous occasions, research has confirmed the link between trust and other relevant outcomes of corporate strategies such as perceived value, purchase, advocacy, and loyalty [53,54].

Purchase intentions refer to consumer commitment to buy goods or use services from a company over time [55]. Therefore, it reflects a deeply held commitment of consumers to repurchase from the company [56]. Purchase intentions have always been defended as the primary criteria used by companies to assess the adequacy of their consumer retention strategies [57].

Finally, advocacy intentions refer to consumer positive word-of-mouth, that is, informal communication directed at other consumers about products, services, and companies [58]. Advocacy has a large influence on people close to the consumer because it may encourage them to also show interest in the company and buy its products or services [55].

Based on the interaction effect suggested in this study, the following research hypotheses are proposed:

H3: In a utilitarian service context, an expositive CSR discourse generates a statistically significant higher level of (a) CSR attributions, (b) service brand attitude, (c) C-C identification, (d) trust, (e) purchase intentions, and (f) advocacy intentions than a narrative CSR discourse.

H4: In a hedonic service context, a narrative CSR discourse generates a statistically significant higher level of (a) CSR attributions, (b) service brand attitude, (c) C-C identification, (d) trust, (e) purchase intentions, and (f) advocacy intentions than an expositive CSR discourse.

3. Method

3.1. Research Design

To test the research hypotheses, we used a 2 (expositive/narrative discourse) x 2 (utilitarian/hedonic service) between-subjects experimental design.

We collected data in a northern city in Spain (i.e., Santander, Cantabria) between April and July 2018, after we had properly trained research assistants for the task. Each research assistant was assigned randomly to collect data in one of the four experimental conditions. We used a convenience sampling procedure based on gender and age to select respondents and assign them to each scenario. In total, 302 participants took place in the experiment and they were distributed across scenarios as shown in Table 1. The sample comprised 49.7% women and 50.3% men. Participants' age ranged from 19 to 90. More precisely, 22.2% of the participants were younger than 35, 38.7% were between 35 and 55, and 39.1% were older than 55. Sampling quotas were very similar in the four scenarios and they were representative of the population in the Spanish region where data was collected.

Table 1. Sample sizes.

Service Type	Discourse Strategy	n
Utilitarian (bank)	Expositive	75
	Narrative	75
Hedonic (restaurant)	Expositive	76
	Narrative	76

For each scenario, research assistants gave short explanations to the participants before the procedure started. The explanations did not convey the real purpose of the study. Instead, participants were told that the purpose was to understand their level of interest in CSR activities. Participants became aware of a fictitious company and its CSR program by evaluating website content (Appendix A, Figures A1 and A2). The experiment contained stimuli from fictitious websites portraying information on the CSR activities implemented by the company over the last year, which were focused especially on the fight against childhood leukemia in two service contexts: a bank (utilitarian) and a restaurant (hedonic).

We purposely used fictitious stimuli to control for participants' knowledge, attitudes, and behavioral intentions concerning real companies, therefore avoiding their influence on the conceptual model proposed in this study [59]. We focused on the website for several reasons. First, website audiences generally perceive home pages primarily as an advertisement designed to entice them to experience the site [24]. Thus, communication theory matches this online context well. Second, a website is the most frequent medium used to engage in CSR communication because it provides a highly accessible but inexpensive medium to avoid accusations of spending more on communication than on the CSR activities themselves [38]. Third, websites are a preferred medium to communicate CSR commitment because of the richness of argumentation and opportunities for interactivity they provide [38]. We chose childhood leukemia as the social cause of our study based on previous studies that had considered health as a critical issue for CSR assessment [60].

To avoid potential confounding effects, all experimental website content used the same images and structure so that the only difference between them was the company itself and the discourse strategy used to present the information [61]. In the four treatments, information about key characteristics of the focal company and its CSR activities (e.g., numbers, figures) were kept constant. The website content conveyed that "Your Bank" (bank, utilitarian service) or "Ecofood" (restaurant, hedonic service) had invested "x" amount of money to collaborate with the childhood leukemia cause and it had achieved "x" results because of the collaboration during the last year. In the narrative treatments, the company's CSR activities were described through an emotional story that involved the son of a company's employee who suffered from childhood leukemia. In the expositive treatments, the same information was described, although this time it was presented objectively and in a rational way, with bullet points, only using facts, figures, and statistics, and without referring to the employee's son who suffered from the disease.

Participants were asked to read the fictitious information about the company and its CSR website at their own pace. After reading it, they had to complete a questionnaire that included manipulation and post-test measures. The experiment included a manipulation check to test for perceived differences between utilitarian and hedonic services in terms of competence (*expert* vs. *inexperienced/competent* vs. *incompetent*) [62] and attractiveness (*attractive* vs. *unattractive/pleasant* vs. *unpleasant*) [62]. Utilitarian services usually rate higher in functional components than emotional components of customer experience and companies offering this type of services tend to be perceived as more competent and experienced than companies providing hedonic services [63]. On the contrary, participants were expected to perceive hedonic services as more delightful, enjoyable, and attractive than utilitarian services [21]. A manipulation check to evaluate message authenticity (*The information presented in the website seems able to occur in the real world/is authentic/provides an abundance of facts so that I believe it is authentic*) [64] and participants' skepticism towards the information presented in the websites (*Claims are exaggerated/are intended to mislead/are not believable/are not true*) [65] tested for perceived differences between expositive and narrative discourses. Expositive discourses do not go deep into the reality behind the rational arguments, statistics, numbers, names, and facts that they provide [12]. On the contrary, CSR stories make social causes much more real to the audience and they make the messages more convincing and memorable [26]. Therefore, they are expected to be more authentic and elicit less skepticism than expositive discourses. Measurement of all items took place on seven-point Likert-type and semantic differential scales.

3.2. Measurement Scales

Seven-point Likert-type and semantic differential scales were used to evaluate post-test measures. We measured issue importance with the three-item scale proposed by Russell and Russell (2010) [66]. To measure CSR impact, we applied the five-item scale proposed by Connors et al. [67]. CSR motives were evaluated by adopting the three-item scale originally proposed by Becker-Olsen et al. [68]. The five-item scale used to measure CSR fit was adapted from Speed and Thompson (2000) and Skard and Thorbjornsen (2014) [69,70]. We measured CSR commitment using a five-item scale taken from Walton (2014) [71]. CSR attributions were measured with a three-item scale taken from Wagner et al. (2009) [72]. We evaluated service brand attitude with the four-item scale also proposed by Wagner et al. (2009) [72]. To measure C-C identification, we applied the five-item scale proposed by Currás (2007) [62]. To measure trust, we used the three-item scale proposed by Morgan and Hunt (1994) [52]. Finally, we evaluated purchase and advocacy intentions with two three-item scales adapted from the original proposals of Groza et al. (2011) and Romani et al. (2013), respectively [73,74]. Table 2 presents all the items.

When building the questionnaire, we also discussed sources of common method variance (CMV), such as social desirability bias, to refine the gathering of empirical data [75]. To avoid the transient mood state of the participants, we aimed at reducing evaluation apprehension by guaranteeing anonymity. For this purpose, we instructed the research assistants to assure the participants that their answers were anonymous and that there were no right or wrong answers. In doing so, the participants were encouraged to answer questions as honestly as possible [75]. After collecting data, we also applied statistical analyses to control for CMV. More precisely, we conducted Harman's single-factor test, which corroborated that all the scales items loaded on more than one single factor. Therefore, they were not concentrated in any one general factor, which corroborated that the correlation among variables was not influenced by their common source [75]. Thus, CMV did not influence the findings of our quantitative research significantly.

Table 2. Measurement scales.

Message Attributions	
Factors	**Items**
Issue importance	IMPO1) The company transmits that this is an important cause; IMPO2) The company transmits it is vital to tackle this cause; IMPO3) The company transmits that companies have a responsibility to address this cause
Impact	*The information presented on the website is ...* IMPA1) Abstract/Concrete; IMPA2) Ambiguous/Clear; IMPA3) Not descriptive/Descriptive; IMPA4) Not vivid/Vivid; IMPA5) Not easy to imagine/Easy to imagine
Motives	*The motivations of the company to support the cause are ...* MOTI1) Self-interested/Community interested; MOTI2) Firm-focused/Customer-focused; MOTI3) Profit-motivated/Socially-motivated
Fit	FIT1) The image of the cause and the image of the company are similar; FIT2) The company and the cause fit together well; FIT3) The company and the cause stand for similar things; FIT4) It makes sense to me that the company sponsors this cause; FIT5) There is a logical connection between the cause and the company
Commitment	COMM1) The company seems to feel strongly about helping the cause; COMM2) The company demonstrates a real interest in making an impact to help the cause; COMM3) The company is capable of long-lasting beneficial effects towards the cause; COMM4) The company seems like they will support the cause for a long period; COMM5) The company will more than likely make a large impact toward helping the cause
Consumer Responses	
Attributions	ATTR1) The company is socially responsible; ATTR2) The company is concerned to improve the well-being of society; ATTR3) The company follows high ethical standards
Attitude	*My general feeling towards the company is ...* ATTI1) Unfavorable/Favorable; ATTI2) Bad/Good; ATTI3) Unpleasant/Pleasant; ATTI4) Negative/Positive
Identification	IDEN1) My way of being sticks with what I perceive from the company; IDEN2) I look like what I think the company represents; IDEN3) I am similar to how I perceive the company; IDEN4) The image I have of the company matches the image I have of myself; IDEN5) The company's identity resembles my identity
Trust	TRUS1) The company can be trusted; TRUS2) The company can be counted on to do what is right; TRUS3) The company has high integrity
Purchase	*If the company existed, how likely would it be that you purchased its services?* ?PURC1) Very unlikely/Very likely; PURC2) Improbable/Probable; PURC3) Impossible/Possible
Advocacy	ADVO1) I intend to say positive things about the company to friends, relatives and other people; ADVO2) I intend to mention favorable things about the company with my friends, relatives, or other people; ADVO3) I intend to recommend to purchase services of the company to my friends, relatives, and other people

4. Findings

4.1. Manipulation Checks

We performed two independent-samples t-tests on the manipulation check questions to verify if the participants rated corporate competence and attractiveness and message authenticity and skepticism differently in the alternative experimental conditions. As per expectations, the participants perceived the hedonic service to be more attractive (meanU = 5.090, meanH = 5.880; t = 4.983, $p < 0.050$) and pleasant (meanU = 5.190, meanH = 5.970; t = 5.369, $p < 0.050$) than the utilitarian service, whereas there were no significant differences in the competence dimension (meanU = 5.050, meanH = 5.303; t = 1.953, $p > 0.050$), where both types of services were perceived equally expert (meanU = 5.010, meanH = 5.180; t = 1.268, $p > 0.050$). Although the test did not report significant differences concerning skepticism towards the message (meanE = 3.171, meanN = 2.901; t = 1.808, $p > 0.050$), the narrative discourse was perceived to be more realistic (meanE = 5.170, meanN = 5.480; t = 2.210, $p < 0.050$) and authentic (meanE = 4.890, meanN = 5.300; t = 2.822, $p < 0.050$) and to provide more abundance of authentic facts (meanE = 4.900, meanN = 5.330; t = 2.894, p < 0.050) than the expositive message. Therefore, the results indicated that the experimental manipulation was successful because the different scenarios were perceived differently by the participants.

4.2. Evaluation of the Measurement Scales

We implemented a first-order confirmatory factor analysis (CFA) to analyze the psychometric properties of the measurement scales. To evaluate the quality of all the indicators that are explained in this section, we followed the recommendations of Hair et al. (2014) [76].

Table 3 shows the results of the analysis implemented with the scales that measured message attributions. The findings corroborated that all the comparative fit indexes were very close or exceeded the recommended value of 0.900, thus corroborating the goodness of the model fit (NFI = 0.897, NNFI = 0.932, CFI = 0.943, IFI = 0.943). The root mean square error of approximation (RMSEA) value was also below the maximum limit of 0.080 recommended in the literature (RMSEA = 0.060). Additionally, scales yielded acceptable psychometric properties: factor loadings were greater than 0.500, composite reliability (CR) indicators were greater than 0.700, average variance extracted (AVE) indicators were greater than 0.500, and these AVE indicators were also greater than the squared correlation with any other construct.

Table 3. Confirmatory factor analysis (CFA) message attributions (n = 302).

Factors	Items	Mean	s.d.	λ	R2	CR	AVE
Issue importance	IMPO1	5.680	1.239	0.804	0.647		
	IMPO2	5.520	1.296	0.904	0.817	0.869	0.690
	IMPO3	5.330	1.539	0.778	0.606		
CSR impact	IMPA1	5.320	1.245	0.816	0.666		
	IMPA2	5.420	1.306	0.846	0.716		
	IMPA3	4.940	1.376	0.757	0.573	0.875	0.584
	IMPA4	4.310	1.438	0.701	0.491		
	IMPA5	5.010	1.396	0.689	0.475		
CSR motives	MOTI1	4.550	1.585	0.836	0.698		
	MOTI2	4.640	1.548	0.812	0.659	0.895	0.740
	MOTI3	4.880	1.565	0.929	0.864		
CSR fit	FIT1	5.120	1.422	0.865	0.749		
	FIT2	5.160	1.465	0.895	0.802		
	FIT3	5.140	1.562	0.911	0.831	0.938	0.753
	FIT4	5.440	1.481	0.790	0.624		
	FIT5	5.530	1.550	0.874	0.764		
CSR commitment	COMM1	5.350	1.285	0.633	0.400		
	COMM2	5.240	1.295	0.705	0.497		
	COMM3	4.830	1.309	0.763	0.582	0.869	0.574
	COMM4	4.800	1.404	0.830	0.689		
	COMM5	5.070	1.370	0.836	0.699		

Model fit: S-Bχ2(d.f. = 176) = 368.745 (p < 0.010); NFI = 0.897; NNFI = 0.932; CFI = 0.943; IFI = 0.943; RMSEA = 0.060.

Similarly, Table 4 shows the results of the analysis implemented with the scales that measured consumer internal and external responses to CSR communication. These scales also reported acceptable psychometric properties in the analysis.

Table 4. CFA consumer responses (n = 302).

Factors	Items	Mean	s.d.	λ	R2	CR	AVE
Attributions	ATTR1	5.250	1.319	0.855	0.731	0.857	0.667
	ATTR2	5.340	1.244	0.819	0.671		
	ATTR3	5.180	1.300	0.775	0.600		
Attitude	ATTI1	5.360	1.246	0.880	0.774	0.951	0.828
	ATTI2	5.540	1.331	0.910	0.828		
	ATTI3	5.530	1.375	0.946	0.894		
	ATTI4	5.590	1.348	0.902	0.814		
Identification	IDEN1	4.750	1.375	0.802	0.643	0.945	0.777
	IDEN2	4.620	1.373	0.892	0.795		
	IDEN3	4.540	1.475	0.934	0.873		
	IDEN4	4.420	1.502	0.903	0.815		
	IDEN5	4.380	1.509	0.870	0.758		
Trust	TRUS1	4.630	1.318	0.852	0.726	0.894	0.739
	TRUS2	4.900	1.210	0.875	0.766		
	TRUS3	4.940	1.242	0.851	0.724		
Purchase	PURC1	4.750	1.412	0.859	0.738	0.937	0.832
	PURC2	4.670	1.599	0.963	0.928		
	PURC3	4.770	1.613	0.912	0.832		
Advocacy	ADVO1	5.030	1.579	0.952	0.906	0.957	0.882
	ADVO2	5.070	1.573	0.968	0.937		
	ADVO3	4.880	1.624	0.896	0.803		

Model fit: S-Bχ2(d.f. = 173) = 353.142(p < 0.010); NFI = 0.928; NNFI = 0.953; CFI = 0.962; IFI = 0.962; RMSEA = 0.059.

4.3. Hypotheses Testing

We contrasted the hypotheses applying multivariate ANOVA (Table 5).

Table 5. Multivariate ANOVA.

Factors	Type of Service (S)			Discourse Strategy (D)			Interaction (S x D)
	Mean (U)	Mean (H)	F (p)	Mean (E)	Mean (N)	F (p)	
Issue importance	5.202	5.809	21.258 (0.000)	5.351	5.665	5.579 (0.019)	8.228 (0.004)
CSR impact	4.845	5.155	6.337 (0.012)	4.744	5.258	17.419 (0.000)	0.003 (0.953)
CSR motives	4.331	5.050	20.861 (0.000)	4.539	4.848	3.884 (0.059)	1.624 (0.203)
CSR fit	4.785	5.758	47.898 (0.000)	5.099	5.450	6.113 (0.014)	14.590 (0.000)
CSR commitment	4.812	5.303	16.215 (0.000)	4.958	5.160	2.762 (0.098)	0.038 (0.845)
Attributions	4.896	5.614	34.802 (0.000)	5.108	5.406	5.903 (0.016)	6.823 (0.009)
Attitude	4.970	6.026	68.856 (0.000)	5.328	5.676	7.414 (0.007)	1.579 (0.210)
Identification	4.311	4.766	9.217 (0.003)	4.522	4.558	0.054 (0.817)	1.140 (0.287)
Trust	4.471	5.171	33.888 (0.000)	4.532	5.115	23.363 (0.000)	4.098 (0.044)
Purchase	4.396	5.061	16.998 (0.000)	4.528	4.934	6.313 (0.013)	0.134 (0.715)
Advocacy	4.433	5.548	50.338 (0.000)	4.620	5.369	22.534 (0.000)	5.228 (0.023)

F-value (d.f. = 1), p-values in parentheses, type of service (utilitarian vs. hedonic), CSR discourse (expositive vs. narrative).

As shown in Table 5, the findings indicated that the type of service (S) had a significant influence over all message attributions and consumer responses to CSR, whereas the discourse strategy (D) also had some significant influence over issue importance, CSR impact, CSR fit, CSR attributions, service brand attitudes, trust, purchase intentions, and advocacy intentions, but not over CSR motives, CSR commitment, or C-C identification. These three variables had similar means in the expositive and the narrative scenarios.

As for the interaction effect between the type of discourse and the type of service over message attributions, multivariate ANOVA detected a significant interaction for issue importance (F = 8.228, $p < 0.050$) (Figure 1): the expositive discourse outperformed the narrative discourse in the bank context, whereas the narrative discourse outperformed the expositive discourse in the restaurant context. These results supported the hypotheses H1a and H2a. Similarly, results revealed a significant interaction, in the expected direction, for CSR fit (F = 14.590, $p < 0.050$) (Figure 2). Therefore, the hypotheses H1d and H2d were supported. For CSR impact, CSR motives, and CSR commitment, multivariate ANOVA did not detect any significant interaction effect. However, as seen in Table 5, the discourse strategy had a significant effect over CSR impact, which was statistically higher for the narrative (vs. expositive) discourse (meanE = 4.744, meanN = 5.258; F = 17.419, $p < 0.050$). Therefore, the hypothesis H2b was supported by the findings, whereas the hypotheses H1b, H1c, H1e, H2c, and H2e were not supported.

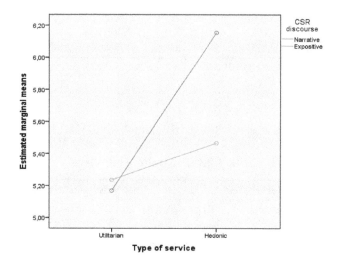

Figure 1. Effects of service type and discourse strategy on issue importance.

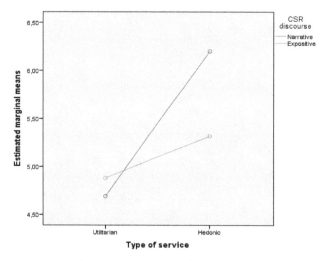

Figure 2. Effects of service type and discourse strategy on CSR fit.

Concerning the interaction effect of discourse strategy and type of service over consumer responses to CSR, multivariate ANOVA results showed that a significant interaction existed for CSR attributions ($F = 6.823$, $p < 0.050$) (Figure 3): the expositive discourse outperformed the narrative discourse in the bank context, whereas the narrative discourse outperformed the expositive discourse in the restaurant context. These results supported the hypotheses H3a and H4a.

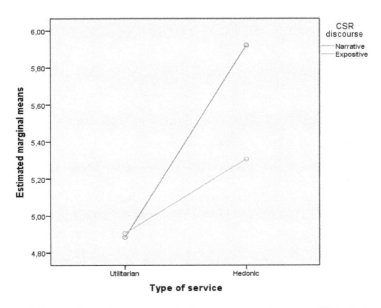

Figure 3. Effects of service type and discourse strategy on CSR attributions.

The analysis also detected interaction effects for trust ($F = 4.098$, $p < 0.050$) (Figure 4) and advocacy intentions ($F = 5.228$, $p < 0.050$) (Figure 5). Nonetheless, in these two cases, the narrative discourse reported higher responses for both the utilitarian and the hedonic service. In these cases, the interaction effects highlighted that the difference in trust and advocacy intentions reported by the participants when exposed to the narrative (vs. expositive) discourse was statistically higher in the hedonic (vs. utilitarian) scenarios. Based on these results, then, the hypotheses H3d and H3f were not supported by the findings of the study, whereas the hypotheses H4d and H4f were supported.

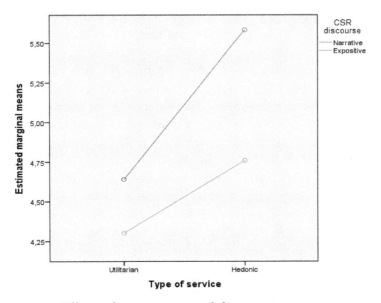

Figure 4. Effects of service type and discourse strategy on trust.

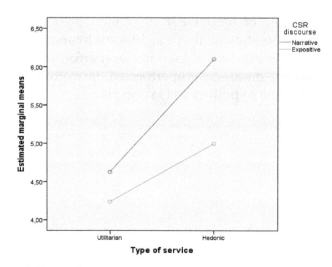

Figure 5. Effects of service type and discourse strategy on advocacy.

For service brand attitude, C-C identification and purchase intentions, multivariate ANOVA did not detect any significant interaction effect. However, as seen in Table 5, the discourse strategy had a significant effect over service brand attitude (meanE = 5.328, meanN = 5.676; F = 7.414, $p < 0.050$) and purchase intentions (meanE = 4.528, meanN = 4.934; F = 6.313, $p < 0.050$), which were statistically higher for the narrative (vs. expositive) discourse. Therefore, the hypotheses H4b and H4e were supported by the findings, whereas the hypotheses H3b, H3c, H3e, and H4c were not supported.

5. Discussion

As a first interesting finding of this paper, the research shows that there were significant differences in message attributions and consumer responses across different types of services. In this regard, the catering service reported statistically significant higher valuations than the banking service for all the dependent variables in our conceptual model. This finding is not surprising as previous empirical literature in the services sector has already proved that hedonic services receive better outcomes from their communication strategies than utilitarian services [16,17,77,78]. Along this line, scholars have proposed that affect may provide a richer understanding of the experiential aspects of service consumption and such consumption emotion may even serve as a stronger motivator for purchase than utilitarian attributes [31]. Additionally, scholars also defend that experiential services are inherently more interesting to consumers than utilitarian services and, then, consumers are more involved with the category domain and more motivated to process promotional information [16,77]. Based on these ideas, research has mostly defended the superior role of hedonic services to generate more positive consumer responses [20], even to the point that several studies have demonstrated that, roughly speaking, any sort of corporate communication is frequently more effective for hedonic than utilitarian services [16,17,77,78]. Although this idea has been tested mostly in the context of conventional commercial communication, our paper contributes to this line of thought by corroborating the same finding in the context of CSR communication.

As for the effect of the type of discourse strategy on message attributions and consumer responses to CSR communication, our findings suggest that this is not as clear as the effect of the service type. On the contrary, here it is important to analyze the interaction effect between discourse strategy and type of service to get a better picture of the implications of choosing between an expositive and a narrative discourse when designing CSR communications. In this regard, our findings align with previous results in academic literature, as some empirical studies have also observed the difficulty to ascertain clear general conclusions derived from the application of different discourses [17].

For instance, there were no significant differences according to the type of discourse strategy for CSR motives, CSR commitment, and C-C identification. A possible explanation is that these three variables were among the lowest-rated attributes of CSR communication in the diverse scenarios explored in the study. Even though the two types of discourses evaluated in the study elicited positive outcomes in most of the message attributions and consumer responses, they were not able to transmit enough altruism nor enough long-term commitment on the part of the company to collaborate in the specific leukemia cause. This finding reinforces the arguments of previous scholars who have defended that consumers are highly skeptical of companies and their CSR activities [79], which undermines the power of CSR communication to transmit altruistic motives and long-term commitment for the company-cause collaboration, even if the company relies on narrative messages to communicate its CSR activities through storytelling. Similarly, C-C identification was the lowest-rated consumer response in both the expositive and narrative scenarios. This result may be explained by the utilization of fictitious information (companies and social cause) for the experiment. As it has happened in other studies, to feel identified with a company and its CSR efforts, consumers must cognitively categorize themselves as members of the company (i.e., actual customers). Awareness of belonging and connection to a company is a way for consumers to achieve a positive social identity and, as a consequence of this sense of connection, the company is psychologically accepted as part of that personal identity and the consumer feels identified with it [80]. However, when analyzing fictitious companies in experiments, participants do not have the time to develop a strong connection to the company and, as so, C-C identification ranks low.

The superiority of expositive (vs. narrative) discourses for utilitarian services was confirmed only for issue importance, CSR fit, and CSR attributions, whereas the superiority of narrative (vs. expositive) discourses for hedonic services was proved for issue importance, CSR impact, CSR fit, CSR attributions, service brand attitude, trust, purchase, and advocacy intentions. Indeed, in most cases, the results showed that, in both the banking and restaurant contexts, message attributions and responses to CSR communication were significantly higher when consumers were exposed to the narrative discourse. This was especially the case for CSR impact, service brand attitude, and purchase intentions, for which no interaction effect between discourse strategy and service type was observed. For the three variables, the narrative discourse always reported better results than the expositive discourse for both the utilitarian and the hedonic services. This finding was also corroborated for trust and advocacy intentions and the findings in these cases are especially worth mentioning. For trust and advocacy intentions, the interaction effect between discourse strategy and service type was significant but it worked in a different direction than our previous expectations. Consumers reported higher trust and advocacy intentions when exposed to the narrative discourse in banking and restaurant scenarios. Nonetheless, in these two cases, the difference between using an expositive and a narrative discourse was notably higher in the hedonic condition than in the utilitarian condition. This finding suggests that making a wrong decision when choosing the discourse strategy (i.e, selecting an expositive message instead of a narrative one) would be more damaging to a company commercializing hedonic services than utilitarian services. In doing so, hedonic services face the risk of losing a greater amount of trust and advocacy intentions than a company commercializing utilitarian services taking the same decision.

Although these findings do not fully align with the principles of the ELM defended in previous literature, an interesting explanation for them may be found in the arguments provided by Stafford (1996) concerning the use of documentation strategies for corporate communication [77]. A documentation strategy refers to the provision of facts and figures within corporate messages that explain or demonstrate the benefits, value, quality, or advantages of the information provided [17]. As reported in her study, using a documentation strategy has positive effects on consumer responses in hedonic settings, whereas it has no significant effects in terms of informativeness, uniqueness, perceived quality, or likelihood to use the service in utilitarian service contexts [77]. In our experiment, the expositive and narrative scenarios used the same documentation strategy (i.e., the same facts, numbers, etc.), while the findings reported that the matching principle fitted the narrative–hedonic combination much better than the expositive–utilitarian combination. More precisely, while 8 sub hypotheses of the 11 initially proposed were supported by our findings for the restaurant context, only 3 out of 11 sub hypotheses were supported for the banking service. Therefore, the findings seem to corroborate the more positive effect of documentation in the hedonic context. In this regard, Singh and Dalal (1999) defend that, regardless of their nature, all corporate messages 'inform' because they create awareness, impressions, knowledge, and beliefs about services, companies, and messages [24]. Thus, the difference in corporate communication depends largely on the emotional connection that it establishes between the company and consumers.

Under these premises, it is also easy to understand why the narrative discourse outperformed the expositive discourse in our study, even in the utilitarian conditions. It seems that, along with documentation features, adding visualization elements (e.g., narrative discourses based on storytelling) to corporate communication [17] generates a favorable general context for communication, which aligns with the principles of the NPT [11]. According to this theory, corporate stories activate narrative rationality, making the information contained in the message more salient, accessible, and intelligible for consumers to interpret and assess the message [7]. This theory suggests that well-designed and well-told stories not only convey information but they also convey emotion [32], which enhances the potential of the message to make its information more real to consumers, easier to remember and more convincing [12,81]. Not in vain, Mortimer (2008) showed how the majority of successful advertisements utilize emotional appeals for not only experiential but also utilitarian services [15]. Therefore, our findings align with those of Mortimer (2008), as she also detects that narrative discourses can be adequate for both utilitarian and hedonic services.

The superior performance of narrative over expositive discourses in our paper can also be justified by the communication context explored in the study. More precisely, we analyzed consumer responses to CSR communication that, in itself, is more affective and emotional than conventional commercial communications such as advertising. As opposed to commercial advertising, CSR communication does not directly seek to "sell" a product/service. CSR communication is institutional communication that mostly seeks to improve corporate image. Therefore, emotional elements in the message may be more important to the consumer than the functional, objective elements when evaluating CSR communication. This idea is supported by the insights provided by previous scholars such as Batra and Ahtola (1990) or Kempf (1999) [20,82]. More precisely, Batra and Ahtola (1990) showed that consumer attitudes are compounded of two distinct dimensions, hedonic and utilitarian attitudes, and that different service attributes contribute to each dimension differently [82]. For instance, experiential sensory attributes are closely associated with the hedonic component of attitude, whereas more functional attributes are associated with the utilitarian part of attitude [20]. Along this line, it can be argued that CSR is a hedonic attribute of the company, which especially affects the hedonic component of consumer responses and, as so, fits into the narrative–hedonic matching principle proposed in this paper much better than functional, rational attributes.

6. Conclusions, Implications, Limitations, and Future Lines of Research

The main goal of this paper has been to determine whether the use of expositive versus narrative discourses interacts with the type of service commercialized by a company to determine consumer perceptions and responses to CSR communication. For this purpose, we have developed a conceptual model based on the theoretical framework of CSR communication of Du et al. (2010) that we have tested empirically with a sample of consumers who have evaluated a fictitious CSR message coming from a banking and a catering company, respectively. In this regard, although research from diverse disciplines has defended an interaction effect between the discourse strategy and the service context, scholars have scarcely explored this idea in the CSR context, where a significant gap exists between the theory and practice of CSR communication. This scarcity of previous literature highlights the contribution of our paper.

The findings of the paper demonstrate that the matching principle suggested by the ELM does not apply as clearly to the context of CSR communication as it does to conventional commercial communication (e.g., advertising). As expected, it is confirmed that for hedonic services, narrative discourses outperform expositive discourses in terms of message attributions and consumer attitudinal (i.e., internal) and behavioral (i.e., external) responses to CSR communication. Nonetheless, and in accordance with the NPT, the use of narrative discourses can also be useful for utilitarian services as they also generate some better message attributions (i.e., CSR impact) and consumer responses (i.e., service brand attitude, trust, purchase, and advocacy intentions) than expositive discourses. Unfortunately, the findings also show that companies that commercialize utilitarian services, such as banking companies, do not profit from CSR communication as much as companies in the context of hedonic services. In our study, the bank reaped more modest responses to its CSR efforts than the restaurant. Along this line, the findings demonstrate that the choice between expositive and narrative discourses has a noticeably higher effect on consumer responses in hedonic than utilitarian contexts, indicating that the decision of the type of discourse strategy to follow is more strategic for hedonic than utilitarian services.

Based on these findings, we highlight some managerial implications that could help companies improve their CSR communication.

In this regard, the most significant implication of the study relates to the benefits that companies can gain by presenting CSR through attractive and compelling stories, especially in the context of hedonic services. CSR stories make social causes real to the audience, they reframe arguments in an easy-to-grasp and easy-to-remember format and they make messages memorable in multiple ways (visually, factually, and emotionally) [26]. In doing so, CSR storytelling generates an emotional connection between the audience and the company [26,27] and, consequently, it intensifies consumer positive attitudes and responses to CSR messages [64,83]. This way of presenting CSR information matches the characteristics of hedonic services especially well as hedonic services are characterized by affective gratification purposes [20] and they mostly provide consumers with emotions [31]. Therefore, we recommend that companies that commercialize hedonic services design CSR messages based on storytelling instead of using expositive discourses that lack emotional bases to engage consumers. Nonetheless, recent studies have identified that companies are missing opportunities to maximize the impact of narrative discourse strategies, especially in the online context [15,81]. More precisely, storytelling is a relatively unpopular form of communication in companies' websites, as very few companies and brands use it [81,84,85]. The scarcity of stories in corporate communication is especially evident in the context of CSR communication, where companies have only recently started to transmit messages through storytelling [86].

In the case of utilitarian services, companies should first decide the communication objectives they want to prioritize and, based on that, select the best discourse strategy to achieve those goals. If the objective is to improve the overall CSR image of the company (i.e., CSR attributions), or improve the visibility of the social cause (i.e., issue importance), companies such as banks should better use an expositive discourse. On the contrary, if they want to focus on consumer behavioral responses (i.e., purchase, advocacy), it is best to use a narrative discourse.

One additional implication, which can benefit both utilitarian and hedonic services, relates to the messages attributions that companies should try to improve in their future CSR communication. On the one hand, the findings of the present study demonstrate that CSR motives are the most poorly rated attributions in CSR communication. Consumers have demonstrated to be highly skeptical of corporate motives to relate to social causes; they have a natural tendency to perceive egoism behind company–cause connections [87]. Nonetheless, avoiding skepticism and improving motives attribution is key to success in CSR communication, as this variable relates closely to consumer behavior such as purchase, advocacy, and loyalty intentions [88]. Therefore, companies must focus their CSR messages on providing convincing reasoning for their motives to engage with social causes, which should be as altruistic as possible to reduce consumer skepticism and improve their support responses. On the other hand, companies should also focus on improving C-C identification, which rated notably low in all the conditions of our experiment. C-C identification has been proved to be an essential attitudinal response to CSR communication that derives in positive outcomes for companies, including trust, satisfaction and loyalty [50].

Finally, this study is not without limitations and future research should consider them to improve our knowledge of CSR communication. First, the use of fictitious companies and fictitious CSR messages can limit the generalization of our findings. Future studies should explore consumer responses to the CSR communication of real companies to determine whether our research findings also apply to CSR messages and consumers in real contexts. Second, future research should also focus on studying additional interaction effects between discourse strategy and other variables that may affect message attributions and consumer responses to CSR communication more intensively than the discourse–service match tested in this paper. For instance, an interesting interaction effect could emerge between discourse strategy and the CSR stimulus (i.e., social cause) chosen by the company as the focus of its CSR efforts [21]. Then, we suggest that future authors test our conceptual model for diverse social causes to corroborate (or not) our findings. In addition, previous research has suggested that the type of CSR support provided by companies (i.e., monetary vs. in-kind support) may affect consumer responses to CSR messages in CSR communication [89]. Consumers tend to react to in-kind support more favorably than to monetary support [89] and this fact may determine the effect of different discourse strategies. In testing these ideas, we suggest that scholars delve further into CSR literature to build their arguments. Given the differences between conventional commercial communication and CSR communication, we believe that scholars can develop hypotheses that are more accurate if they base their arguments on CSR theories instead of grounding them solely on communication and advertising literature.

Author Contributions: Conceptualization, A.P. and E.B.-D.; methodology, A.P. and M.d.M.G.d.l.S.; software, A.P.; validation, A.P., M.d.M.G.d.l.S. and E.B.-D.; writing—original draft preparation, A.P., M.d.M.G.d.l.S. and E.B.-D.; writing—review and editing, A.P., M.d.M.G.d.l.S. and E.B.-D. All authors have read and agreed to the published version of the manuscript.

Appendix A. Website Stimuli Evaluated by the Participants

 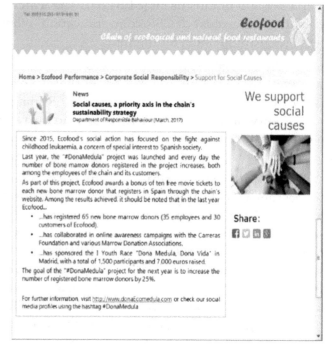

Figure A1. Expositive discourse strategy. Website A (utilitarian service), Website B (hedonic service).

Figure A2. Narrative discourse strategy. Website C (utilitarian service), Website D (hedonic service).

References

1. Mason, C.; Simmons, J. Forward looking or looking unaffordable? Utilising academic perspectives on corporate social responsibility to assess the factors influencing its adoption by business. *Bus. Ethics A Eur. Rev.* **2011**, *20*, 159–176. [CrossRef]

2. Liang, X.; Hu, X.; Meng, H. Truly sustainability or hypocrisy: The effects of corporate sustainable orientation on consumers' quality perception and trust based on evidence from China. *Sustainability* **2020**, *12*, 2735. [CrossRef]

3. Ahmed, I.; Nazir, M.S.; Ali, I.; Nurunnabi, M.; Khalid, A.; Shaukat, M.Z. Investing in CSR pays you back in many ways! The case of perceptual, attitudinal and behavioral outcomes of customers. *Sustainability* **2020**, *12*, 1158. [CrossRef]

4. Du, S.; Bhattacharya, C.B.; Sen, S. Maximizing business returns to corporate social responsibility (CSR): The role of CSR communication. *Int. J. Manag. Rev.* **2010**, *12*, 8–19. [CrossRef]

5. Skarmeas, D.; Leonidou, C.N. When consumers doubt, watch out! The role of CSR skepticism. *J. Bus. Res.* **2012**, *66*, 1831–1838. [CrossRef]

6. Martin, J.; Powers, M. Organizational stories: More vivid and persuasive than quantitative data. In *Psychological Foundations of Organizational Behavior*; Foresman: Glenview, IL, USA, 1983; pp. 162–168.

7. Weick, K.E.; Browning, L.D. Argument and narration in organizational communication. *J. Manag.* **1986**, *12*, 243–259. [CrossRef]

8. Martin, J. Stories and scripts in organizational settings. In *Cognitive Social Psychology*; Elsevier: New York, NY, USA, 1982; pp. 255–305.

9. Lewis, N.; Sznitman, S.R. You brought it on yourself: The joint effects of message type, stigma, and responsibility attribution on attitudes toward medical cannabis. *J. Commun.* **2017**, *67*, 181–202. [CrossRef]

10. Murphy, S.T.; Frank, L.B.; Chatterjee, J.S.; Baezconde-Garbanati, L. Narrative versus nonnarrative: The role of identification, transportation and emotion in reducing health disparities. *J. Commun.* **2013**, *63*, 116–137. [CrossRef] [PubMed]

11. Fisher, W.R. The narrative paradigm: An elaboration. *Commun. Monogr.* **1985**, *52*, 347–367. [CrossRef]

12. Kaufman, B. Stories that sell, stories that tell. *J. Bus. Strategy* **2003**, *24*, 11–15. [CrossRef]

13. Woodside, A.G. Brand-consumer storytelling theory and research: Introduction to a Psychology & Marketing speciall issue. *Psychol. Mark.* **2010**, *27*, 531–540.

14. Lundqvist, A.; Liljander, V.; Gummerus, J.; van Riel, A. The impact of storytelling on the consumer brand experience: The case of a firm-originated story. *J. Brand Manag.* **2013**, *20*, 283–297. [CrossRef]

15. Mortimer, K. Identifying the components of effective service advertisements. *J. Serv. Mark.* **2008**, *22*, 104–113. [CrossRef]

16. Stafford, M.R.; Day, E. Retail services advertising: The effects of appeal, medium, and service. *J. Advert.* **1995**, *24*, 37–41. [CrossRef]

17. Hill, D.J.; Blodgett, J.; Baer, R.; Wakefield, K. An investigation of visualization and documentation strategies in services advertising. *J. Serv. Res.* **2004**, *7*, 155–166. [CrossRef]

18. Johar, J.S.; Sirgy, M.J. Value-expressive versus utilitarian advertising appeals: When and why to use which appeal. *J. Advert.* **1991**, *20*, 23–33. [CrossRef]

19. Albers-Miller, N.D.; Stafford, M.R. International services advertising: An examination of variation in appeal use for experiential and utilitarian services. *J. Serv. Mark.* **1999**, *13*, 390–406. [CrossRef]

20. Kempf, D.S. Attitude formation from product trial: Distinct roles of cognition and affect for hedonic and functional products. *Psychol. Mark.* **1999**, *16*, 35–50. [CrossRef]

21. Andreu, L.; Casado-Díaz, A.B.; Mattila, A.S. Effects of message appeal and service type in CSR communication strategies. *J. Bus. Res.* **2015**, *68*, 1488–1495. [CrossRef]

22. Yang, C.-M.; Hsu, T.-F. Effects of skepticism about corporate social responsibility advertising on consumer attitude. *Soc. Behav. Pers.* **2017**, *45*, 453–468. [CrossRef]

23. Petty, R.E.; Cacioppo, J.T. *Attitudes and Persuasion: Classic and Contemporary Approaches*; William C. Brown: Dubuque, IO, USA, 1981.

24. Singh, S.N.; Dalal, N.P. Web home pages as advertisements. *Commun. ACM* **1999**, *42*, 91–98. [CrossRef]

25. Gill, R. An integrative review of storytelling: Using corporate stories to strengthen employee engagement and internal and external reputation. *Prism* **2011**, *8*, 1–16.

26. Escalas, J.E. Narrative processing: Building consumer connections to brands. *J. Consum. Psychol.* **2004**, *14*, 168–180.

27. Herskovitz, S.; Crystal, M. The essential brand persona: Storytelling and branding. *J. Bus. Strategy* **2010**, *31*, 21–28. [CrossRef]

28. Zak, P.J. Why your brain loves good storytelling. *Harv. Bus. Rev.* **2014**, *28*, 1–5.

29. Pérez, A.; del Mar García de los Salmones, M.; López-Gutiérrez, C. Corporate reputation in the Spanish context: An interaction between reporting to stakeholders and industry. *J. Bus. Ethics* **2015**, *129*, 733–746.

30. Um, N.H. Revisit elaboration likelihood model: How advertising appeals work on attitudinal and behavioural brand loyalty centering around low vs. high involvement product. *Eur. J. Soc. Sci.* **2008**, *7*, 126–139.

31. Jiang, Y.; Lu Wang, C. The impact of affect on service quality and satisfaction: The moderation of service contexts. *J. Serv. Mark.* **2006**, *20*, 211–218. [CrossRef]

32. Sole, D.; Wilson, D.G. *Storytelling in Organizations: The Power and Traps of Using Stories to Share Knowledge in Organizations*; Harvard Graduate School of Education: Cambridge, MA, USA, 2002.

33. Aldama, F.L. The Science of storytelling: Perspectives from cognitive science, neuroscience, and the humanities. *Projections* **2015**, *9*, 80–95. [CrossRef]

34. Pérez, A.; del Mar García de los Salmones, M.; Liu, M.T. Maximising business returns to corporate social responsibility communication: An empirical test. *Bus. Ethics A Eur. Rev.* **2019**, *28*, 275–289.

35. Pomering, A.; Johnson, L.W. Advertising corporate social responsibility initiatives to communicate corporate image: Inhibiting scepticism to enhance persuasion. *Corp. Commun. An Int. J.* **2009**, *14*, 420–439. [CrossRef]

36. Menon, S.; Kahn, B. Corporate sponsorships of philanthropic activities: When do they impact perception of sponsor brand? *J. Consum. Psychol.* **2003**, *13*, 316–327. [CrossRef]

37. Bhattacharya, C.B.; Korschun, D.; Sen, S. Strengthening stakeholder-company relationships through mutually beneficial corporate social responsibility initiatives. *J. Bus. Ethics* **2009**, *85*, 257–272. [CrossRef]

38. Parguel, B.; Benoit-Moreau, F.; Larceneux, F. How sustainability ratings might deter "greenwashing": A closer look at ethical corporate communication. *J. Bus. Ethics* **2011**, *102*, 15–28. [CrossRef]

39. García de los Salmones, M.M.; Pérez, A. Effectiveness of CSR advertising: The role of reputation, consumer attributions, and emotions. *Corp. Soc. Responsib. Environ. Manag.* **2018**, *25*, 194–208. [CrossRef]

40. van Rekom, J.; van Riel, C.B.M.; Wierenga, B. A methodology for assessing organizational core values. *J. Manag. Stud.* **2006**, *43*, 175–201. [CrossRef]

41. Maignan, I.; Ralston, D.A. Corporate social responsibility in Europe and the U.S.: Insights from businesses' self-presentations. *J. Int. Bus. Stud.* **2002**, *33*, 497–514. [CrossRef]

42. Lafferty, B.A.; Goldsmith, R.E.; Hult, G.T.M. The impact of the alliance on the partners: A look at cause-brand alliances. *Psychol. Mark.* **2004**, *21*, 509–531. [CrossRef]

43. Trimble, C.S.; Rifon, N.J. Consumer perceptions of compatibility in cause-related marketing messages. *Int. J. Nonprofit Volunt. Sect. Mark.* **2006**, *11*, 29–47. [CrossRef]

44. Bigné, E.; Chumpitaz, R.; Currás, R. Alliances between brands and social causes: The influence of company credibility on social responsibility image. *J. Bus. Ethics* **2010**, *96*, 169–186.
45. Rifon, N.J.; Choi, S.M.; Trimble, C.S.; Li, H. Congruence effect in sponsorship: The mediating role of sponsor credibility and consumer attributions of sponsor motive. *J. Advert.* **2004**, *33*, 29–42. [CrossRef]
46. Benoit-Moreau, F.; Parguel, B. Building brand equity with environmental communication: An empirical investigation in France. *EuroMed J. Bus.* **2011**, *6*, 100–116. [CrossRef]
47. Keller, K.L. *Strategic Brand Management*; Prentice-Hall: Upper Saddle River, NJ, USA, 1998.
48. O'Cass, A.; Grace, D. Exploring consumer experiences with a service brand. *J. Prod. Brand Manag.* **2004**, *13*, 257–268. [CrossRef]
49. Bravo, R.; Matute, J.; Pina, J.M. Corporate social responsibility as a vehicle to reveal the corporate identity: A study focused on the websites of Spanish financial entities. *J. Bus. Ethics* **2012**, *107*, 129–146. [CrossRef]
50. Pérez, A.; del Mar García de los Salmones, M.; Rodríguez del Bosque, I. The effect of corporate associations on consumer behaviour. *Eur. J. Mark.* **2013**, *47*, 218–238.
51. Garcia de los Salmones, M.M.; Perez, A.; Rodriguez del Bosque, I. The social role of financial companies as a determinant of consumer behaviour. *Int. J. Bank Mark.* **2009**, *27*. [CrossRef]
52. Morgan, R.M.; Hunt, S.D. The commitment-trust theory of relationship marketing. *J. Mark.* **1994**, *58*, 20–38. [CrossRef]
53. Chiou, J.-S.; Droge, C. Service quality, trust, specific asset investment, and expertise: Direct and indirect effects in a satisfaction-loyalty framework. *J. Acad. Mark. Sci.* **2006**, *34*, 613–627. [CrossRef]
54. Lewis, B.R.; Soureli, M. The antecedents of consumer loyalty in retail banking. *J. Consum. Behav.* **2006**, *5*, 15–31. [CrossRef]
55. Oliver, R.L. *Satisfaction: A Behavioral Perspective on the Consumer*; McGraw-Hill: New York, NY, USA, 1997.
56. Oliver, R.L. Whence consumer loyalty? *J. Mark.* **1999**, *63*, 33–44. [CrossRef]
57. Khan, Z.; Ferguson, D.; Pérez, A. Customer responses to CSR in the Pakistani banking industry. *Mark. Intell. Plan.* **2015**, *33*. [CrossRef]
58. Westbrook, R.A. Product/consumption-based affective responses and postpurchase processes. *J. Mark. Res.* **1987**, *24*, 258–270. [CrossRef]
59. Kim, Y. Strategic communication of corporate social responsibility (CSR): Effects of stated motives and corporate reputation on stakeholder responses. *Public Relat. Rev.* **2014**, *40*, 838–840. [CrossRef]
60. Nan, X.; Heo, K. Consumer responses to Corporate Social Responsibility (CSR) initiatives: Examining the role of brand-cause fit in cause-related marketing. *J. Advert.* **2007**, *36*, 63–74. [CrossRef]
61. Alniacik, U.; Alniacik, E.; Genc, N. How corporate social responsibility information influences stakeholders' intentions. *Corp. Soc. Responsib. Environ. Manag.* **2011**, *18*, 234–245. [CrossRef]
62. Currás, R. *Comunicación de la Responsabilidad Social Corporativa: Imagen e Identificación con la Empresa como Antecedentes del Comportamiento del Consumidor*; Universitat de València: Valencia, Spain, 2007.
63. Ladhari, R.; Souiden, N.; Dufour, B. The role of emotions in utilitarian service settings: The effects of emotional satisfaction on product perception and behavioral intentions. *J. Retail. Consum. Serv.* **2017**, *34*, 10–18. [CrossRef]
64. Chiu, H.-C.; Hsieh, Y.-C.; Kuo, Y.-C. How to align your brand stories with your products. *J. Retail.* **2012**, *88*, 262–275. [CrossRef]
65. Mohr, L.A.; Eroğlu, D.; Ellen, P.S. The development and testing of a measure of skepticism toward environmental claims in marketers' communications. *J. Consum. Aff.* **1998**, *32*, 30–55. [CrossRef]
66. Russell, D.W.; Russell, C.A. Here or there? Consumer reactions to corporate social responsibility initiatives: Egocentric tendencies and their moderators. *Mark. Lett.* **2010**, *21*, 65–81. [CrossRef]
67. Connors, S.; Anderson-MacDonald, S.; Thomson, M. Overcoming the 'window dressing' effect: Mitigating the negative effects of inherent skepticism towards corporate social responsibility. *J. Bus. Ethics* **2017**, *145*, 599–621. [CrossRef]
68. Becker-Olsen, K.L.; Cudmore, B.A.; Hill, R.P. The impact of perceived corporate social responsibility on consumer behavior. *J. Bus. Res.* **2006**, *59*, 46–53. [CrossRef]
69. Speed, R.; Thompson, P. Determinants of sport sponsorship response. *J. Acad. Mark. Sci.* **2000**, *28*, 226–238. [CrossRef]
70. Skard, S.; Thorbjørnsen, H. Is publicity always better than advertising? The role of brand reputation in communicating corporate social responsibility. *J. Bus. Ethics* **2014**, *124*, 149–160. [CrossRef]

71. Walton, M.R. *The PR in CSR: Assessing Perceptions of Partnerships Versus Donations in Corporate Social Responsibility Initiatives*; Texas A&M University: Canyon, TX, USA, 2014.

72. Wagner, T.; Lutz, R.J.; Weitz, B.A. Corporate hypocrisy: Overcoming the threat of inconsistent corporate social responsibility perceptions. *J. Mark.* **2009**, *73*, 77–91. [CrossRef]

73. Groza, M.D.; Pronschinske, M.R.; Walker, M. Perceived organizational motives and consumer responses to proactive and reactive CSR. *J. Bus. Ethics* **2011**, *102*, 639–652. [CrossRef]

74. Romani, S.; Grappi, S.; Bagozzi, R.P. Explaining consumer reactions to corporate social responsibility: The role of gratitude and altruistic values. *J. Bus. Ethics* **2013**, *114*, 193–206. [CrossRef]

75. Podsakoff, P.M.; MacKenzie, S.B.; Lee, J.Y.; Podsakoff, N.P. Common method biases in behavioral research: A critical review of the literature and recommended remedies. *J. Appl. Psychol.* **2003**, *88*, 879–903. [CrossRef]

76. Hair, J.F.; Black, W.C.; Babin, B.J.; Anderson, R.E. *Multivariate Data Analysis*, 7th ed.; Pearson Education Limited: Harlow, UK, 2014.

77. Stafford, M.R. Tangibility in services advertising: An investigation of verbal versus visual cues. *J. Advert.* **1996**, *25*, 13–28. [CrossRef]

78. Wakefield, K.L.; Inman, J.J. Situational price sensitivity: The role of consumption occasion, social context and income. *J. Retail.* **2003**, *79*, 199–212. [CrossRef]

79. Forehand, M.R.; Grier, S. When is honesty the best policy? The effect of stated company intent on consumer skepticism. *J. Consum. Psychol.* **2003**, *13*, 349–356.

80. Currás, R.; Bigné, E.; Alvarado, A. The role of self-definitional principles in consumer identification with a socially responsible company. *J. Bus. Ethics* **2009**, *89*, 547–564. [CrossRef]

81. Delgado-Ballester, E.; Fernández-Sabiote, E. Once upon a brand: Storytelling practices by Spanish brands. *Spanish J. Mark.-ESIC* **2016**, *20*, 115–131. [CrossRef]

82. Batra, R.; Ahtola, O.T. Measuring the hedonic and utilitarian sources of consumer attitudes. *Mark. Lett.* **1990**, *2*, 159–170. [CrossRef]

83. van Laer, T.; de Ruyter, K.; Visconti, L.M.; Wetzels, M. The extended transportation-imagery model: A meta-analysis of the antecedents and consequences of consumers' narrative transportation. *J. Consum. Res.* **2014**, *40*, 797–817. [CrossRef]

84. Spear, S.; Roper, S. Using corporate stories to build the corporate brand: An impression management perspective. *J. Prod. Brand Manag.* **2013**, *22*, 491–501. [CrossRef]

85. Du, S.; Vieira, E.T. Striving for legitimacy through corporate social responsibility: Insights from oil companies. *J. Bus. Ethics* **2012**, *110*, 413–427. [CrossRef]

86. Gill, R. Why the PR strategy of storytelling improves employee engagement and adds value to CSR: An integrated literature review. *Public Relat. Rev.* **2015**, *41*, 662–674. [CrossRef]

87. Bigné, E.; Currás, R.; Sánchez, I. Brand credibility in cause-related marketing: The moderating role of consumer values. *J. Prod. Brand Manag.* **2009**, *18*, 437–447. [CrossRef]

88. Pérez, A.; del Bosque, I.R. How customer support for corporate social responsibility influences the image of companies: Evidence from the banking industry. *Corp. Soc. Responsib. Environ. Manag.* **2015**, *22*. [CrossRef]

89. Hildebrand, D.; Demotta, Y.; Sen, S.; Valenzuela, A. Consumer responses to corporate social responsibility (CSR) contribution type. *J. Consum. Res.* **2017**, *44*, 738–758. [CrossRef]

5

Non-Parametric Model for Evaluating the Performance of Chinese Commercial Banks' Product Innovation

Luning Shao, Jianxin You, Tao Xu * and Yilei Shao

School of Economics and Management, Tongji University, Shanghai 200092, China;
shaoluning@tongji.edu.cn (L.S.); yjx2256@vip.sina.com (J.Y.); 2014shaoyl@tongji.edu.cn (Y.S.)
* Correspondence: xutao0709@yeah.net.

Abstract: A thorough analysis of commercial banks' product innovation performance is essential to promoting bank product innovation capabilities and sustainable development. In this paper, the product innovation performance of commercial banks is defined as the conversion efficiency of input and output factors. The credit risk of product innovation of banks is considered as an undesirable output and incorporated in the performance evaluation system. Depending on whether there is a synchronous relationship between innovation income and risks, a Fixed Correlation model (FCM) and a Variable Correlation model (VCM) are then constructed based on Data Envelopment Analysis (DEA) method for the evaluation of commercial bank product innovation performance. In addition, an output optimization model of the objective function is also constructed to estimate the target income of commercial banks' product innovation in the FCM and VCM. Finally, the proposed model is applied to Chinese listed commercial banks for estimating the performance and target income of product innovation.

Keywords: data envelopment analysis; commercial banks; product innovation; performance evaluation; innovation risk

1. Introduction

In recent years, Chinese commercial banks continue to strengthen their capability of innovation and risk management through product innovation, which is also regarded as an important strategy for the improvement of their core competitiveness [1,2]. A thorough analysis of commercial banks' product innovation performance is essential to promoting the banks' competitiveness and sustainable development [3]. Regarding the definition of bank product innovation, Roberts and Amit [4] divide the innovative activities of banks into product innovation, service innovation, process innovation and channel innovation, where product innovation mainly refers to the innovation of corporate and personal banking business; Lerner and Tufano [5] hold that financial innovation of banks includes product and process innovation. Based on the Guidelines for the Financial Innovation of Commercial Banks, issued by the China Banking Regulatory Commission, this paper defines the product innovation of commercial banks as innovations in business and products carried out to meet the demand of customers.

To our best knowledge, the performance of a certain commercial bank product innovation depends on various factors in the innovation process, as examples, R&D personnel, expenses and income obtained from innovative products [6]. R&D personnel and expenses could be regarded as input factors in the process of bank product innovation, while income is an output factor. Thus, the product innovation performance of commercial banks could be defined as the conversion efficiency of input and output factors. The DEA method is introduced in this paper to evaluate the performance of Chinese commercial banks' product innovation, since it is a total factor efficiency evaluation method that can evaluate the efficiency of decision making units (DMU) with multiple inputs into multiple outputs [7]. As a non-parametric total factor productivity evaluation method, the DEA method can effectively avoid model misspecification. As such, it has been widely used in estimating total-factor efficiencies [8,9].

Although banks can generate more revenue through innovative products [2], it is noted that different from other industries' innovation, financial product innovation also creates potential risks for bank operations. Calmès and Théoret [10], Aktan et al. [11] analyzed the statistics of commercial banks in Canada and Istanbul, respectively, and found that the growth of the innovative products may lead to an increase of risks for commercial banks. Therefore, it is of great significance to consider the impact of product innovation risks when analyzing the performance of commercial banks' product innovation. According to the Core Indicators for the Risk Management of Commercial Banks released by the China Banking Regulatory Commission, risks faced by commercial banks mainly include the liquidity risk, the credit risk, the market risk and the operational risk. Considering the reality of product innovation in Chinese commercial banks, it could be discovered that commission revenue related to loans and quasi-loans are the main source of banks' handling charge income [12], the credit risk can be seen as the major risk involved in the process of product innovation. As such, in this paper, the credit risk is considered as an undesirable output and is incorporated in the performance evaluation system.

As a research on the evaluation of bank product innovation performance, the main contribution of this article lies in the fact that the FCM and VCM are constructed based on DEA for evaluating commercial banks' product innovation performance. To be specific, it assigns a weak disposability setting and a strong disposability setting to undesirable output, according to the relationship between the innovation income and risk. In addition, an output optimization model of the objective function is also constructed to estimate the target income of commercial banks' product innovation in the FCM and VCM. Finally, the proposed model is applied to Chinese listed commercial banks for estimating the performance and target income of product innovation.

The remaining parts of this paper are as follows. Section 2 is a literature review. In Section 3, the DEA-based methodology is introduced to calculate the performance of Chinese commercial banks' product innovation and estimate the target income of product innovation. Section 4 illustrates sampling and data sources, corresponding empirical results, further discussion and suggestions. Conclusion follows in Section 5.

2. Literature Review

Performance evaluation is a well-studied subject in the existing literature. In particular, the non-parametric DEA method has been widely used. For example, Vlontzos et al. [13] used DEA to evaluate energy performance and environmental performance. Cai et al. [14] used DEA to analyze the efficiency of China's photovoltaic industry. DEA is also broadly used in studies related to commercial banks. Wang et al. [15] analyzed the efficiency of 16 major Chinese commercial banks during the period 2003–2011 using DEA approach; Liu et al. [16] constructed production possibility sets using the free-disposal axioms and utilized the corresponding DEA model with undesirable intermediate variables to evaluate the efficiency of listed Chinese banks; Ohsato and Takahashi [17] applied a slack-based measure DEA model to evaluate the management efficiency of regional banks in Japan. Undesirable outputs have attracted growing attention from scholars in research on performance evaluation and other bank-related issues. For instance, Wang et al. [15] proposed a DEA model considering undesirable outputs and applied it to the performance evaluation of 26 Chinese commercial banks.

In addition, DEA can also be utilized to discuss the improvement objectives of inputs and outputs while evaluating performance. In existing research, three methodologies are most frequently used. This first involves the investigation of slack variables associated with outputs and is now widely applied in studies where DEA is utilized to evaluate performance [18]; the second estimates potential optimization using an inverse DEA model [19]. Inverse DEA was first developed by Wei et al. [20], which estimates inputs/outputs with a given proficiency; the third uses objective functions with specific directions to calculate optimal variables [21].

In studies concerning banks' product innovation, Wenqiang et al. [22] used stochastic frontier analysis to evaluate the efficiency of bank innovation and analyzed the main driving factors for bank product innovation. Lyu [23] investigated the overall innovation and managerial innovation capabilities of listed Chinese banks. There are also scholars who analyze the factors that affect the innovation performance of commercial products. As examples, Rossignoli and Arnaboldi [24] studied relations between innovation, performance and risks of commercial banks in financial crisis. Wen [25] studied the relationship between internet finance and commercial banks' innovation performance; Zeng et al. [26] investigated the impact of financial supervision on product innovation of commercial banks.

It could be found that, in the existing literature, quantitative research on commercial banks' product innovation performance is still scarce and rarely touches on the impact of risks. The current research related to commercial banks' product innovation and risks is mostly built upon the discussion of relations between income structure, non-interest income and commercial banks' profit-making ability. Few studies so far have incorporated risks associated with product innovation into performance evaluation. Thus, this paper proposes a DEA-based non-parametric model to evaluate and analyze commercial banks' product innovation performance, which including the credit risk associated with product innovation.

3. Methodology

This section first introduces the input–output process of commercial bank product innovation. Subsequently, a bank product innovation performance evaluation model based on the DEA is constructed. Finally, an optimization model is also established to estimate the target income of bank product innovation.

3.1. Input and Output Variables

Before using DEA to evaluate the performance, input and output variables should be determined. There is a wide variety of input/output variables used for the evaluation of commercial banks' performance, which differs according to the objective of the evaluation. It is generally agreed that commercial banks' product innovation income is realized through the input of innovation-related personnel and funds [22].

Considering the reality of Chinese commercial banks' product innovation, Lyu [23] and Wenqiang, Jihui and Hua [22] note that input factors related to commercial banks' product innovation include fixed assets, the number of employees, as well as the handling charge and commission expense, while output factors include the handling charge and commission income. Different from commercial banks' traditional interest income, the handling charge and commission income refer to earnings generated by intermediary services such as consultation, guarantee, escrow services, etc. They can reflect the output of commercial banks' product innovation activity [27]. Similarly, the handling charge and commission expense can reflect the financial input related to commercial banks' product innovation. Given the fact that better-educated employees make a greater contribution to innovation [28,29], employees holding a bachelor's degree or above (educated personnel) are selected to constitute the innovation personnel. Commercial banks' fixed assets, as the basis for bank operation, are treated as another input factor in this study.

Through analyzing the structure of the handling charge and commission income, this study has found that loan-related commissions revenue is the main component of the banks' product innovation income [12]. The related credit risk is therefore included in this study as a major risk. According to the Notice of the China Banking Regulatory Commission on Further Strengthening Credit Risk Management, released in 2016, commercial banks' off-balance-sheet loans should be convertible into risk assets with a conversion coefficient of 100%, which can be regarded as normal commercial loans. According to the Administrative Measures for the Loan Loss Reserves of Commercial Banks, issued by the China Banking Regulatory Commission in 2012, commercial banks should create a credit provision tantamount to 1% of normal quasi-loans. Thus, this paper sets 1% of commercial banks' off-balance-sheet loans as the anticipated non-performing loans to measure the product innovation risk. Figure 1 shows the process of commercial banks' product innovation factoring in risk impact, where fixed assets (F), product educated personnel (L) and product innovation funds (K) generate product innovation income (Rt) and product innovation credit risk (B).

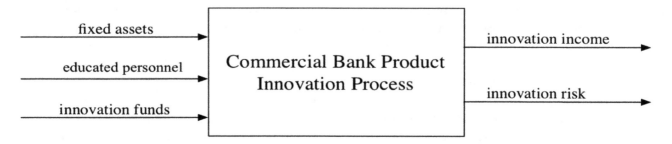

Figure 1. Commercial Bank Product Innovation Process Considering Risk Impact.

3.2. Models for the Evaluation of Commercial Banks' Product Innovation Performance

Based on the input and output variables discussed in Section 3.1, commercial banks' product innovation performance is defined as the input–output conversion efficiency, and the DEA model is introduced to evaluate the product innovation performance. Suppose there are n DMUs, noted as DMU_j $(j = 1, 2, \ldots, n)$, a performance evaluation model can be constructed as follows.

$$
\begin{aligned}
&\text{Max } \theta_i \\
\text{s.t.} \quad &\sum_{j=1}^{n} \lambda_j L_j \leq L_i, \\
&\sum_{j=1}^{n} \lambda_j K_j \leq K_i, \\
&\sum_{j=1}^{n} \lambda_j F_j \leq F_i, \\
&\sum_{j=1}^{n} \lambda_j B_j = B_i, \\
&\sum_{j=1}^{n} \lambda_j R_{tj} \geq \theta_i R_{ti}, \\
&\lambda_j \geq 0, j = 1, 2, \ldots, n.
\end{aligned}
\tag{1}
$$

In Model (1), λ is the intensity variable of each DMU, and the objective function represents the proxy of each DMU's efficiency. Since Model (1) is an output-oriented DEA method, the range of θ_i is set to be $[1, +\infty]$. In this paper, $\frac{1}{\theta_i}$ is used to represent the performance. The value of 1 indicates that the DMU is in DEA efficient, otherwise, the DMU is inefficient.

Additionally, different from the traditional DEA model, Model (1) places an equality constraint on B_i, the product innovation risk. The equation indicates that undesirable and desirable outputs are correlated [30], which could be regarded as a model with a weak disposability setting [31]. Based on such a setting, it could be understood that the product innovation income of commercial banks and the corresponding credit risk reflect the same trends. The risk will increase with the expansion of product innovation.

On the other hand, as commercial banks' risk management techniques and capability improve, the product innovation risk can be lowered without reducing income. In that case, no synchronous relationship exists between commercial banks' product innovation income and related risk. Based on this assumption, Model (2) is constructed.

Different from Model (1), Model (2) places an inequality constraint on B_i and can be regarded as a DEA model with a strong disposability setting [30]. With this setting, changes of the undesirable output do not affect the desirable output. In other words, the fact that commercial banks' product innovation income and related credit risk change in the same trend is neglected. Therefore, the weak disposability and strong disposability settings represent a product innovation with and without risk management technique optimization, respectively.

$$
\begin{aligned}
&\text{Max } \theta_i \\
\text{s.t.} \quad & \sum_{j=1}^{n} \lambda_j L_j \le L_i, \\
& \sum_{j=1}^{n} \lambda_j K_j \le K_i, \\
& \sum_{j=1}^{n} \lambda_j F_j \le F_i, \\
& \sum_{j=1}^{n} \lambda_j B_j \le B_i, \\
& \sum_{j=1}^{n} \lambda_j R_{tj} \ge \theta_i R_{ti}, \\
& \lambda_j \ge 0, j = 1, 2, \ldots, n.
\end{aligned}
\tag{2}
$$

A strong disposability setting implies that commercial banks manage credit risk through the improvement of risk management techniques and capability. In fact, relevant government agencies in China have already developed policies and carried out reforms to better control risks in the banking sector and maintain financial stability. Major commercial banks have also taken various measures to strengthen their risk management ability. Policy support, together with the development of technologies such as the Internet and big data, has made it possible to build a model based on the strong disposability of credit risk. On the other hand, when a weak disposability setting applies, it can be understood that even with policy support and cooperation between banks and companies, it is still difficult to optimize risk management ability in the short term. With this setting, commercial banks' risk management techniques cannot be optimized within a short period of time, potential credit risk and product innovation income remain in a synchronous relationship.

In this paper, the model that features a synchronous relationship between commercial banks' product innovation income and associated risks is defined as the FCM. In addition, if commercial banks can improve their risk management techniques without any restraint, potential credit risk may also be subject to the influence of these techniques. Therefore, this study also proposes a model with a strong disposability setting, which defined as the VCM.

3.3. Models for the Estimation of Product Innovation Target Income

Analyzing the target output of DMUs is crucial for DEA-based performance evaluation. Considering the existence of both desirable and undesirable outputs in this study, an output optimization model of the objective function can be constructed to independently estimate the target income of commercial banks' product innovation. According to the relationship between commercial banks' product innovation income and associated risks, two models—Model (3) and Model (4)—are proposed for the estimation of product innovation target income.

In Model (3), the optimal target can be obtained by calculating the optimal η_i^* and λ_i^*. η_i is the rate of change of product innovation income and non-performing loans. In this study, the values of product innovation income and potential credit risk cannot be negative (i.e., η_i must be a positive number). The optimal output obtained through Model (3) can represent the anticipated goals of bank operations. In this study, it can be seen as the target income of commercial banks' product innovation.

$$\text{Max } R_{wi} = R_{ti}\eta_i$$

$$\text{s.t.} \quad \sum_{j=1}^{n} \lambda_j L_j \leq L_i,$$

$$\sum_{j=1}^{n} \lambda_j K_j \leq K_i,$$

$$\sum_{j=1}^{n} \lambda_j F \leq F_i, \tag{3}$$

$$\sum_{j=1}^{n} \lambda_j B_j = \eta_i B_i,$$

$$\sum_{j=1}^{n} \lambda_j R_{tj} \geq \eta_i R_{ti},$$

$$\eta_i, \lambda_j \geq 0, j = 1, 2, \ldots, n.$$

$$\text{Max } R_{si} = \hat{R}_{ti}$$

$$\text{s.t.} \quad \sum_{j=1}^{n} \lambda_j L_j \leq L_i,$$

$$\sum_{j=1}^{n} \lambda_j K_j \leq K_i,$$

$$\sum_{j=1}^{n} \lambda_j F \leq F_i, \tag{4}$$

$$\sum_{j=1}^{n} \lambda_j B_j \leq \hat{B}_i,$$

$$\sum_{j=1}^{n} \lambda_j R_{tj} \geq \hat{R}_{ti},$$

$$\hat{B}_i \leq \delta_i \hat{R}_{ti}$$

$$\hat{R}_{ti}, \hat{B}_i, \lambda_j \geq 0, j = 1, 2, \ldots n.$$

Model (4) ignores the synchronous relationship between product innovation income and risks. In other words, the growth of commercial banks' product innovation income could also be realized by optimizing risk management techniques. Since credit risk control is an important instrument for commercial banks to realize anticipated goals, the ratio of potential credit risk to product innovation income optimization should be less than the actual rate of risk management technique optimization (δ_i). The constraint $\hat{B}_i \leq \delta_i \hat{R}_{ti}$ is therefore placed on Model (4). Other variables and constraints in Model (4) are the same as those in Model (3).

As discussed above, in the VCM, the added value of commercial banks' product innovation income is mainly influenced by risk management techniques and the scale of product innovation; while in the FCM, the latter is the only influential factor. Therefore, the gap between the added values of product innovation income in the VCM and FCM can reflect the profit generated by the optimization of risk management techniques. This is shown by Formulas (5)–(7).

$$\Delta R_{ti}^{s} = R_{ti}^{s*} - R_{ti}, \tag{5}$$

$$\Delta R_{ti}^{w} = R_{ti}^{w*} - R_{ti}, \tag{6}$$

$$\Delta R_{ti}^{c} = \Delta R_{ti}^{s} - \Delta R_{ti}^{w}. \tag{7}$$

In the Formulas (5)–(7), R_{ti}^{s*} is the product innovation target income in the VCM; and R_{ti}^{w*} means the target income in the FCM. ΔR_{ti}^{w} and ΔR_{ti}^{s} represent the added values of product innovation income in the FCM and VCM, respectively. As mentioned above, $\Delta R_{ti}^{c} = \Delta R_{ti}^{s} - \Delta R_{ti}^{w}$ could be regarded as the innovation income brought about by optimizing risk management techniques. The ratio $(R_{ti}^{*} - R_{ti})/R_{ti}$ in this paper is defined as RII, which means the ratio of product innovation target income increase to actual income.

To make a clear description, all the acronyms mentioned in this paper are listed in the following nomenclatures.

Nomenclatures
CNY   Chinese Yuan
DEA   Data Envelopment Analysis
DMU   Decision-Making Unit
FCM   Fixed Correlation Model
VCM   Variable Correlation Model
RII   The Ratio of Product Innovation Target Income Increase to Actual Income

4. Empirical Analysis

4.1. Sampling and Data Source

In this paper, 25 commercial banks listed in China's stock market were selected as samples. According to the categorization of China's commercial banks, these samples were divided into four groups—state-owned commercial banks, joint-stock commercial banks, urban commercial banks and rural commercial banks—as shown in Table 1. All data were obtained from the annual reports released by these listed commercial banks. Related descriptive statistics are shown in Table 2.

Table 1. Sample Commercial Banks and Categorization.

Bank Type	Bank Name
State-Owned	Industrial and Commercial Bank of China (ICBC), Agricultural Bank of China (ABC), Bank of China (BC), China Construction Bank (CBC), Bank of Communications (BCM)
Joint-Stock	China Merchants Bank (CMB), Shanghai Pudong Development Bank (SPDB), China CITIC Bank (CITIC), China Everbright Bank (CEB), Huaxia Bank (HXB), China Minsheng Bank (CMBC), China Guangfa Bank (CGB), Industrial Bank (IB), Ping An Bank (PAB), China Zheshang Bank (CZB), Evergrowing Bank Bank (EB), China Bohai Bank (CBB)
Urban	Bank of Ningbo (NBCB), Bank of Jiangsu (JSB), Bank of Hangzhou (HCCB), Bank of Nanjing (NJCN), Bank of Beijing (BOB), Bank of Shanghai (BOSC), Bank of Guiyang (GYCB)
Rural	Jiangyin Rural Commercial Bank (JYRB), Rural Commercial Bank of Zhangjiagang (ZJGRB), Wuxi Rural Commercial Bank (WXRB), Changshu Rural Commercial Bank (CSRB), Wujiang Rural Commercial Bank (WJRB)

Table 2. Descriptive Statistics.

Year	Parameter	Fixed Assets	No. of Employees Holding Bachelor's Degree and above	Handling Charge and Commission Expense	Handling Charge and Commission Income	Anticipated Non-Performing Loans
	Unit	10^9 CNY	10^3	10^9 CNY	10^9 CNY	10^9 CNY
2013	Minimum	0.335	0.703	0.001	0.050	0.019
	Maximum	158.968	221.393	12.224	134.550	24.998
	Average	29.937	49.639	1.769	24.815	6.815
	Standard Deviation	52.467	74.346	2.879	38.035	7.932
2015	Minimum	0.418	0.772	0.010	0.067	0.043
	Maximum	195.401	249.961	18.279	161.670	32.100
	Average	37.834	55.985	2.628	32.851	7.700
	Standard Deviation	62.940	82.489	4.182	43.414	8.611
2017	Minimum	0.626	1.080	0.023	0.077	0.079
	Maximum	216.156	276.062	19.041	158.666	38.706
	Average	44.253	61.245	3.930	36.659	8.656
	Standard Deviation	69.497	88.953	5.175	43.816	11.065

4.2. Product Innovation Performance Analysis

Based on the data of the 25 commercial banks in 2013, 2015 and 2017, their product innovation performance values in specific years can be obtained through Models (1) and (2). The results are shown in Figure 2. The efficiency change of the four types of commercial banks during the observation period can be found in Figure 3.

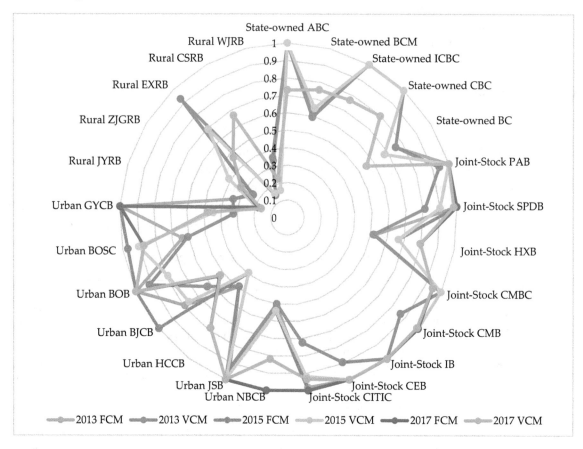

Figure 2. Product Innovation Performance in 2013, 2015 and 2017.

It can be discovered that the average efficiency of the 25 banks was 0.7665 in 2013 in the FCM. The efficiency of joint-stock banks was at the highest level, followed by state-owned banks. Their efficiency values, 0.9218 and 0.8722, respectively, were higher than those of urban commercial banks (0.7755) and rural commercial banks (0.3996). Among joint-stock banks, five (PAB, SPDB, CMBC, IB and CEB) were efficient in the DEA model; while HXB was the only one in the group that had an efficiency value (0.5248) lower than the yearly average. During the period, the efficiency value of HXB was the lowest among all joint-stock banks, indicating that its product innovation performance was not yet on par with its counterparts in this group. Among state-owned banks, the BCM and the BC had efficiency values of 0.6067 and 0.7545 respectively. The other banks in this group all had an efficiency value of 1.

The efficiency values of joint-stock and urban commercial banks were consistently on the rise during the observed period, while those of state-owned banks took on an opposite trend. The efficiency values of the four groups of banks during the observed period in the FCM are shown in Figure 3a. In 2017, the efficiency value of joint-stock banks was 0.9681 and their innovation performance remained in the leading position; whereas urban commercial banks' product innovation efficiency value had been rising for all three years under observation, overtaking that of state-owned banks (0.7215) to reach 0.8836 in 2017. In the VCM, the same conclusions apply. The efficiency value of state-owned banks under this model was slightly higher than that of their joint-stock counterparts in 2013, but assuming a trend similar to the FCM. This can be seen in Figure 3b.

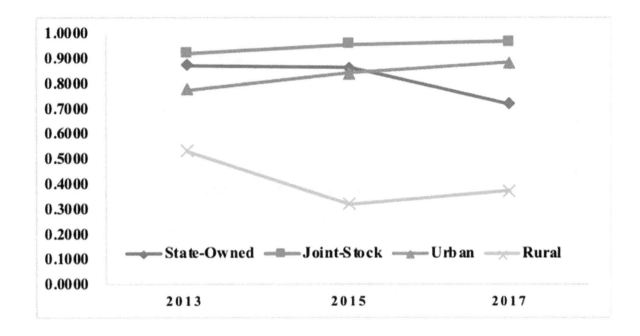

(a)

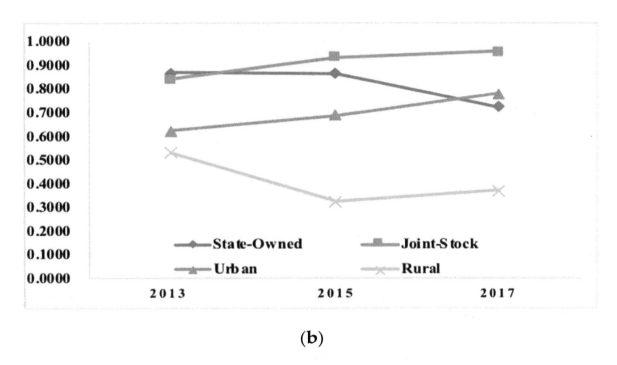

(b)

Figure 3. Innovation Performance changes in the FCM (**a**) and VCM (**b**) in 2013, 2015 and 2017.

As mentioned in this article, the difference between the FCM and the VCM is whether to consider the synchronous relationship between credit risk and product innovation income. In order to analyze this relationship, this article presents the scatter plots of commercial bank product innovation revenue and risk in 2013, 2015 and 2017, as shown in Figure 4. The data on the ordinate axis represent product innovation revenue, and the data on the abscissa axis represent anticipated non-performing loans. Obvious linear relationships are observed in the scatter plots below. Therefore, the rationality of the assumptions in the FCM model proposed in this paper is also verified.

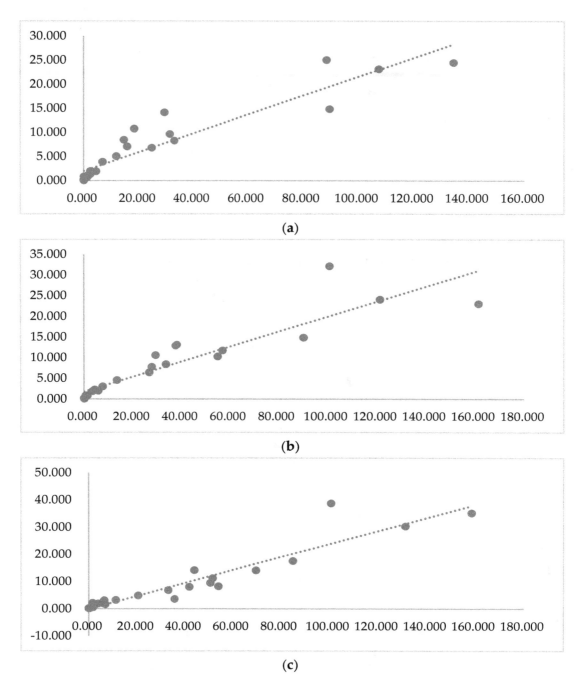

Figure 4. Relationship between product innovation target income and risk of commercial banks in 2013 (**a**), 2015 (**b**), and 2017 (**c**).

4.3. Analyzing the Target Income of Commercial Banks' Product Innovation

Analyzing the target output of DMUs is crucial for DEA-based performance evaluation. In this paper commercial banks' product innovation target income in the FCM and VCM can be obtained by using Model (3), Model (4). Added values of income in the FCM and VCM can be calculated using Formulas (5) and (6), respectively. The results are shown in Table 3.

In Table 3, the 25 selected commercial banks differ significantly in the added value of product innovation income. Since product innovation income changes in the same trend with the associated credit risk, it is found that the optimized product innovation income is lower than the actual income. In terms of income changes, although the values of most state-owned banks were positive, a few still saw a decline in income, e.g., the BCM (−5.300, −16.441, −2.966). This is different from what was observed in joint-stock and urban commercial banks. In the VCM, the values of the 25 selected banks' income change were all above 0, implying that enhancing commercial banks' risk management ability can effectively raise their product innovation income.

Table 3. Added values of income in the FCM and VCM in 2013, 2015 and 2017.

Type	DMU	2013		2015		2017	
		ΔR_{ti}^w	ΔR_{ti}^s	ΔR_{ti}^w	ΔR_{ti}^s	ΔR_{ti}^w	ΔR_{ti}^s
State-Owned	ICBC	10.618	29.982	108.126	130.000	39.200	74.244
	CBC	−18.387	0.000	43.102	69.999	71.054	84.468
	BCM	−5.300	20.112	−16.441	17.588	−2.966	23.977
	ABC	37.603	50.003	90.386	100.001	116.235	126.221
	BC	19.887	42.935	−10.462	42.791	22.661	59.785
Joint-Stock	CEB	−9.070	1.907	0.000	0.000	−13.895	0.000
	HXB	−0.946	6.422	−3.479	10.308	−1.333	8.886
	CMBC	−12.470	0.002	−38.745	0.000	−12.337	5.689
	PAB	0.000	0.737	0.000	0.000	−17.763	0.000
	SPDB	0.000	3.366	0.000	3.201	−22.272	0.886
	IB	−22.065	0.004	−30.398	0.000	−23.944	0.002
	CMB	−8.156	4.895	−27.989	0.000	−30.845	0.563
	CITIC	−14.538	7.005	0.000	3.292	−27.074	3.566
Urban	BOB	−3.125	0.434	0.000	0.918	−5.661	0.000
	GYCB	0.000	0.246	−0.713	2.881	0.000	1.771
	HCCB	−0.088	1.333	0.000	0.000	−0.062	0.579
	JSB	−0.803	0.188	0.000	1.078	−2.571	0.000
	NJCB	−0.567	0.755	−4.055	3.737	−0.245	3.646
	NBCB	−0.253	1.797	−4.837	0.617	−4.450	1.415
	BOSC	−0.670	1.642	0.000	2.022	−0.886	1.403
Rural	CSRB	0.050	0.226	0.228	0.522	0.367	0.560
	JYRB	0.170	0.241	−0.028	0.121	−0.032	0.092
	WXRB	0.276	0.312	0.356	0.413	0.294	0.464
	WJRB	−0.016	0.002	0.016	0.089	0.112	0.355
	ZJGRB	0.046	0.157	0.034	0.215	0.120	0.410

Figure 5a,b show the RII values in the FCM and VCM, respectively, and Figure 6 shows the average RII values of different types of banks during the observed period. Average RII of four types of commercial banks in 2013, 2015 and 2017 can be found in Table 4. According to Figure 5a, in the FCM, the average rates of change of joint-stock and urban commercial banks' product innovation income were all below 0, indicating that reducing the scale of product innovation may lead to the reduction of both the income and the credit risk associated with innovation. During the observed period, rural commercial banks had the highest RII. Although the average RII of state-owned banks was lower than that of rural banks, the former was apparently on an upward trajectory. Among rural commercial banks, the RII of WXRB was the highest, standing at 200.27%, followed by CSRB's 122.20%. Among state-owned banks, ABC had the greatest RII increase. This indicates that commercial banks can scale up product innovation by strengthening their product innovation capability.

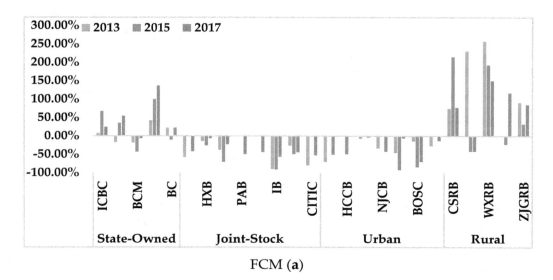

FCM (**a**)

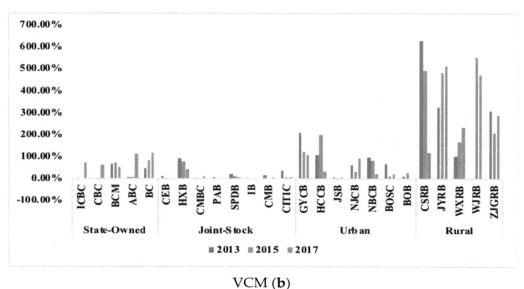

VCM (**b**)

Figure 5. RII of each bank in the FCM (**a**) and VCM (**b**) in 2013, 2015 and 2017.

Table 4. Average RII of Four Types of Commercial Banks in 2013, 2015 and 2017.

	Type	2013	2015	2017	Average
F C M	State-Owned	7.43%	29.78%	46.18%	27.79%
	Joint-Stock	−37.95%	−29.46%	−39.81%	−35.74%
	Urban	−28.03%	−32.09%	−26.52%	−28.88%
	Rural	130.76%	75.47%	77.46%	94.57%
V C M	State-Owned	23.37%	30.84%	84.49%	46.23%
	Joint-Stock	23.61%	12.05%	7.93%	14.53%
	Urban	80.15%	67.96%	39.76%	62.62%
	Rural	274.52%	381.80%	326.43%	327.58%

In the VCM, the RIIs of the four groups of banks were all above 0, mainly because the impact of banks' risk management ability was not considered. Rural commercial banks had an average RII of 327.58% during the observed period, the highest among all four groups, while the average RIIs of urban, state-owned and joint-stock commercial banks were 62.62%, 46.23% and 14.53%, respectively. Therefore, banks with an RII above 0 can increase the scale of product innovation to generate more income, while those with an RII below 0 should properly control the scale of product innovation.

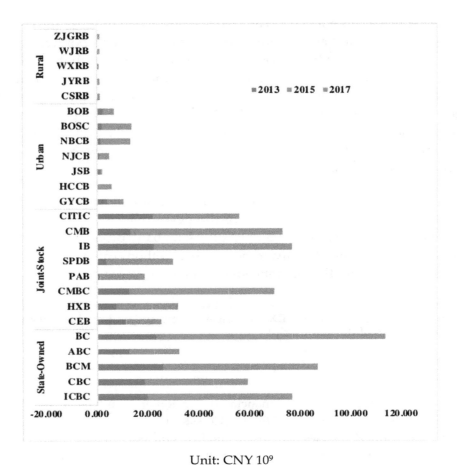

Unit: CNY 10^9

Figure 6. Added-Value of Product Innovation Income after Risk Management Ability Optimization.

4.4. Findings and Discussions

This section analyzed the data of 25 selected listed Chinese commercial banks between 2013 and 2017 and discussed their product innovation performance using the proposed DEA-based model. Findings of the empirical analysis are as follows: (1) the four groups of commercial banks differed significantly in their product innovation performance between 2013 and 2017. Among them, joint-stock commercial banks had the best innovation performance, while rural commercial banks had the lowest performance value. (2) During the observed period, the efficiency values of joint-stock and urban commercial banks were consistently on the rise, while those of state-owned banks were on a downward trajectory. (3) Restrained by the existing risk management ability, joint-stock and urban commercial banks need to control the scale of product innovation and subsequently reduce related income to boost performance. Upgrading the risk management ability can effectively lift product innovation income.

According to the research conclusions, the following management suggestions are proposed for the innovation and development of commercial banks: (1) Rural commercial banks should further increase the importance and investment of product innovation, optimize resource allocation, expand the scale of innovative product business, and enhance product innovation capabilities; (2) under the current level of risk, joint-stock commercial banks and city commercial banks need to properly control the scale of product innovation to control product innovation risks; (3) all types of commercial banks should increase their risk management capabilities and use platforms and tools such as the Internet and big data to strengthen their risk management capabilities.

5. Conclusions

This study proposes a DEA-based non-parametric model to estimate the performance and target income of Chinese commercial banks' product innovation. The product innovation performance of commercial banks is defined as the conversion efficiency of input and output. The credit risk of product innovation of banks is considered as an undesirable output and incorporated in the performance evaluation system. The main contribution of this article lies in the fact that the FCM and VCM are constructed for evaluating commercial banks' product innovation performance. In addition, an output optimization model of the objective function is also constructed to estimate the target income of commercial banks' product innovation in the FCM and VCM. Finally, the proposed model is applied to Chinese listed commercial banks for estimating the performance and target income of product innovation. Some management suggestions have also been put forward to help the sustainable development of commercial banks.

Generally, three further research directions can be drawn from this research. Firstly, the Malmquist index can be introduced in a dynamic analysis of the performance of banks' product innovation. Secondly, it will be interesting to discuss the impact of risk on bank product innovation performance if product innovation risk is uncertain. Thirdly, some suitable methods can be proposed to select data for estimating the performance under the big data environment.

Author Contributions: Conceptualization, L.S. and T.X.; data curation, Y.S.; funding acquisition, J.Y.; methodology, T.X.; supervision, J.Y.; writing—original draft, T.X.; writing—review and editing, L.S. All authors have read and agreed to the published version of the manuscript.

References

1.   Norden, L.; Silva Buston, C.; Wagner, W. Financial innovation and bank behavior: Evidence from credit markets. *Soc. Sci. Electron. Publ.* **2014**, *43*, 130–145. [CrossRef]
2.   Wang, F.; Huang, M.; Shou, Z. Business expansion and firm efficiency in the commercial banking industry: Evidence from the US and China. *Asia Pac. J. Manag.* **2015**, *32*, 551–569. [CrossRef]
3.   Zhao, J.H.; Min, D.; Mathematics, D.O.; University, L.N. Empirical analysis on the influence factors of commerical bank's intermediary business Innovation—A case of CCB. *Technol. Dev. Enterp.* **2015**, *22*, 27.
4.   Roberts, P.W.; Amit, R. The Dynamics of Innovative Activity and Competitive Advantage: The Case of Australian Retail Banking, 1981 to 1995. *Organ. Sci.* **2003**, *14*, 107–122. [CrossRef]
5.   Lerner, J.; Tufano, P. The Consequences of Financial Innovation: A Counterfactual Research Agenda. *NBER Work. Pap.* **2011**, *3*, 41–85.
6.   Lepetit, L.; Nys, E.; Rous, P.; Tarazi, A. The Provision of Services, Interest Margins and Loan Pricing in European Banking. *Ssrn Electron. J.* **2006**. [CrossRef]
7.   Zhu, J.; Price, C.C.; Zhu, J.; Hillier, F.S. *Data Envelopment Analysis: A Handbook of empirical Studies and Applications*; Springer: Berlin, Germany, 2015; Volume 238, pp. 267–280.
8.   Xie, L.; Chen, C.L.; Yu, Y.H. Dynamic Assessment of Environmental Efficiency in Chinese Industry: A Multiple DEA Model with a Gini Criterion Approach. *Sustainability* **2019**, *11*, 2294. [CrossRef]
9.   Yang, W.X.; Li, L.G. Analysis of Total Factor Efficiency of Water Resource and Energy in China: A Study Based on DEA-SBM Model. *Sustainability* **2017**, *9*, 1316. [CrossRef]
10. Calmès, C.; Théoret, R. The impact of off-balance-sheet activities on banks returns: An application of the ARCH-M to Canadian data. *J. Bank. Financ.* **2010**, *34*, 1719–1728. [CrossRef]
11. Aktan, B.; Chan, S.-G.; Zikovic, S.; Evrim-Mandaci, P. Off-Balance Sheet Activities Impact on Commercial Banks Performance: An Emerging Market Perspective. *Econ. Res.* **2013**, *26*, 117–132. [CrossRef]
12. Chateau, J.P.D. Marking-to-model credit and operational risks of loan commitments: A Basel-2 advanced internal ratings-based approach. *Int. Rev. Financ. Anal.* **2009**, *18*, 260–270. [CrossRef]
13. Vlontzos, G.; Niavis, S.; Manos, B. A DEA approach for estimating the agricultural energy and environmental efficiency of EU countries. *Renew. Sustain. Energy Rev.* **2014**, *40*, 91–96. [CrossRef]
14. Cai, H.; Liang, L.; Tang, J.; Wang, Q.; Wei, L.; Xie, J. An Empirical Study on the Efficiency and Influencing Factors of the Photovoltaic Industry in China and an Analysis of Its Influencing Factors. *Sustainability* **2019**, *11*, 6693. [CrossRef]
15. Wang, K.; Huang, W.; Wu, J.; Liu, Y.-N. Efficiency measures of the Chinese commercial banking system using an additive two-stage DEA. *Omega* **2014**, *44*, 5–20. [CrossRef]

16. Liu, W.; Zhou, Z.; Ma, C.; Liu, D.; Shen, W. Two-stage DEA models with undesirable input-intermediate-outputs. *Omega* **2015**, *56*, 74–87. [CrossRef]
17. Ohsato, S.; Takahashi, M. Management Efficiency in Japanese Regional Banks: A Network DEA. *Procedia Soc. Behav. Sci.* **2015**, *172*, 511–518. [CrossRef]
18. Bian, Y.; He, P.; Xu, H. Estimation of potential energy saving and carbon dioxide emission reduction in China based on an extended non-radial DEA approach. *Energy Policy* **2013**, *63*, 962–971. [CrossRef]
19. Gattoufi, S.; Amin, G.R.; Emrouznejad, A. A new inverse DEA method for merging banks. *IMA J. Manag. Math.* **2014**, *25*, 73–87. [CrossRef]
20. Wei, Q.; Zhang, J.; Zhang, X. An inverse DEA model for inputs/outputs estimate. *Eur. J. Oper. Res.* **2000**, *121*, 151–163. [CrossRef]
21. Fukuyama, H.; Matousek, R. Modelling bank performance: A network DEA approach. *Eur. J. Oper. Res.* **2017**, *259*, 721–732. [CrossRef]
22. Wenqiang, Y.; Jihui, G.; Hua, L. The Internal Driving Force of Commercial Bank Transformation and Upgrading—Based on the Perspective of Innovation Efficiency. *Financ. Forum* **2017**, *22*, 13.
23. Lyu, X. The Evaluation of the Innovation Capability of A-Share Listed Banks under the Impact of Internet Banking: Based on Generalized DEA Model of Panel Data. *J. Account. Econ.* **2016**, *23*, 253–271.
24. Rossignoli, B.; Arnaboldi, F. Financial innovation: Theoretical issues and empirical evidence in Italy and in the UK. *Int. Rev. Econ.* **2009**, *56*, 275–301. [CrossRef]
25. Wen, L. Research on the Relationship between Internet Finance and Commercial Bank's Innovation Performance—Based on the Analysis of MOA Theory. *Financ. Theory Pract.* **2017**, *38*, 6.
26. Zeng, W.; Chen, S.; Zhou, Z.B. The Impact of Financial Supervision on Commercial Bank's Product Innovation-the Research Based on Two-stage DEA Model. *Chin. J. Manag. Sci.* **2016**, *24*, 1–7.
27. Linyun, C.; Sitai, Y. Research on Intermediary Business and Business Performance of Commercial Banks. *Times Financ.* **2017**, *38*, 2.
28. Mottaleb, K.A.; Sonobe, T. What determines the performance of small enterprises in developing countries? Evidence from the handloom industry in Bangladesh. *Int. J. Bus. Glob.* **2013**, *10*, 39–55. [CrossRef]
29. Heffernan, S.A.; Fu, X.; Fu, M. The Determinants of Financial Innovation. *Soc. Sci. Electron. Publ.* **2009**. [CrossRef]
30. Yang, H.L.; Pollitt, M. The necessity of distinguishing weak and strong disposability among undesirable outputs in DEA: Environmental performance of Chinese coal-fired power plants. *Energy Policy* **2010**, *38*, 4440–4444. [CrossRef]
31. Fare, R.; Grosskopf, S.; Pasurka, C. Effects on relative efficiency in electric power generation due to environmental controls. *Resour. Energy* **1986**, *8*, 167–184. [CrossRef]

6

Multi-Attribute Decision Making based on Stochastic DEA Cross-Efficiency with Ordinal Variable and its Application to Evaluation of Banks' Sustainable Development

Jinpei Liu [1,2], Mengdi Fang [1], Feifei Jin [1,*], Chengsong Wu [1] and Huayou Chen [3]

[1]   School of Business, Anhui University, Hefei 230601, China; liujinpei@ahu.edu.cn (J.L.); m18201053@stu.ahu.edu.cn (M.F.); 91027@ahu.edu.cn (C.W.)

[2]   Department of Industrial and Systems Engineering, North Carolina State University, Raleigh, NC 27695, USA

[3]   School of Mathematical Sciences, Anhui University, Hefei 230601, China; huayouc@ahu.edu.cn

*   Correspondence: jinfeifei@ahu.edu.cn.

Abstract: Multi-attribute decision making (MADM) is a cognitive process for evaluating data with different attributes in order to select the optimal alternative from a finite number of alternatives. In the real world, a lot of MADM problems involve some random and ordinal variables. Therefore, in this paper, a MADM method based on stochastic data envelopment analysis (DEA) cross-efficiency with ordinal variable is proposed. First, we develop a stochastic DEA model with ordinal variable, which can derive self-efficiency and the optimal weight of each attribute for all decision making units (DMUs). To further improve its discrimination power, cross-efficiency as a significant extension is proposed, which utilizes peer DMUs' optimal weight to evaluate the relative efficiency of each alternative. Then, based on self-efficiency and cross-efficiency of all DMUs, we construct corresponding fuzzy preference relations (FPRs) and consistent fuzzy preference relations (FPRs). In addition, we obtain the priority weight vector of all DMUs by utilizing the row wise summation technique according to the consistent FPRs. Finally, we provide a numerical example for evaluating operation performance of sustainable development of 15 listed banks in China, which illustrates the feasibility and applicability of the proposed MADM method based on stochastic DEA cross-efficiency with ordinal variable.

Keywords: stochastic DEA; multi-attribute decision making; ordinal variable; cross-efficiency

1. Introduction

Sustainable development (SD) is a widely used phrase and idea, which firstly emerged in the context of environmental concerns [1–3]. However, with the development of society and economy, we gradually realized the significance of sustainable development of economy. To some extent, the operation performance of banks can reflect economic trends. Therefore, it is important to maintain the sustainable development of banks. Recently, sustainable development of banks has become a hotspot. Munir and Gallagher [4] proposed that optimizing the benefits and costs can improve sustainable development of banks. Xue et al. [5] considered that adjusting and optimizing the layout of the physical branches of commercial banks is crucial to its sustainable development. Jiang and Han [6] suggested that adopting diversification strategy is beneficial to achieving sustainable development of banks.

Multi-attribute decision making (MADM) is one of the most common and popular research fields in the theory of decision science [7]. It assumes that there exists a set of alternatives with multiple attributes which decision makers (DMs) need to evaluate. The purpose of MADM is to select the optimal one from a finite number of alternatives. Generally speaking, each MADM problem includes two parts: classifying and ranking. Classifying can be considered as the grouping of the alternatives based on the similarities of attributes. Ranking is defined as the rank of alternatives from the optimal to the worst [8]. In recent years, some methods have been proposed to handle MADM problems, such as total sum (TS) method [9], simple additive weighting (SAW) method [10], the analytic hierarchy process (AHP) method [11], multiplicative analytic hierarchy process (MAHP) method [12], the technique for order preference by similarity to ideal solution (TOPSIS) method [13], and data envelopment analysis (DEA) method [14].

In MADM problems, we need some decision making information including attribute values and attribute weights, which denote the characteristics of alternatives and relative importance of attributes, respectively [7]. Nevertheless, attribute values are known, so we have to obtain attribute weights by the aforementioned approaches. However, DEA is a nonparametric programming efficiency rating technique for evaluating the relative efficiency of DMUs with multiple inputs and outputs, whose evaluation results come from input and output data [15–17]. Compared with other methods, attribute weights derived by DEA is relatively objective. Therefore, DEA has been widely applied in many fields for different purposes [18–20], such as assessment of environmental sustainability [21,22], supplier selection [23–25], and evaluation of the influence of E-marketing on hotel performance [26].

Due to the inherent complexity and competition of the real world, MADM problems often involve some random and ordinal variables. However, previous DEA studies have been undertaken in a deterministic environment, which cannot solve the above situation. Therefore, it is necessary to incorporate the stochastic variable into DEA. Then, we propose the stochastic DEA model with ordinal variable. Recently, stochastic DEA has become the research hotspot. A well-known method to extend DEA to the case of random inputs and outputs is to utilize chance constrained programming (CCP) [27], which was proposed by Charnes and Cooper [28]. The CCP admits random data variations and permits constraint violations up to the specified probability limit. Khodabakhshi et al. [29] extended the super-efficiency DEA model to an input-oriented super-efficiency stochastic DEA model by CCP. The major contributions on the stochastic DEA may be attributed to the work of Sengupta [30]. A prominent characteristic of his study is that stochastic DEA is transformed into a deterministic equivalent [31]. In addition to Sengupta's work, Sueyoshi [31] proposed a DEA future analysis method that considered how to integrate future information into DEA, and then applied it to restructure strategy of a Japanese petroleum company. Wu et al. [32] followed the Cooper's approach to develop stochastic DEA model by considering undesirable outputs with weak disposability.

However, although stochastic DEA model can evaluate MADM problems with random and ordinal variables, the following disadvantages also exist. One is that DEA identifies many efficient alternatives where efficiency score is equivalent to one, and cannot further discriminate them. Another is that the ranking order of all alternatives cannot involve appraisal of peer DMUs and influences the accuracy and persuasion of evaluation results in MADM problems. Faced with these drawbacks, many researchers have taken efforts to modify DEA methods, including weight restriction, super-efficiency, cross-efficiency and so on [33]. The weight restriction methods commonly attach additional constrains to relative weights, including absolute weight restriction [34], common weights [35], and cone ratio restriction [36]. Nevertheless, all weight restriction approaches use priority information or predefined parameters, thus they are subjective to some extent. Andersen and Petersen [37] proposed a super efficiency method for ranking DMUs. The cross-efficiency evaluation method is an important extension, which is invented to utilize peer DMUs' optimal weights to appraise relative efficiency of each DMU [38–41]. Compared with the traditional DEA approach concentrating on self-efficiency evaluation, cross-efficiency evaluation method has the following main characteristics: (1) taking peer-evaluation of all alternatives into account and guaranteeing a unique ranking order for whole DMUs, (2) eliminating unrealistic weight schemes without predetermining any weight restrictions, and (3) effectively distinguishing better DMUs and poor DMUs [42]. Owing to these superiorities, cross-efficiency evaluation results can be more reasonable and acceptable. Therefore, cross-efficiency has been widely applied to diverse fields, including R&D project selections and the ranking of universities' comprehensive ability. However, there are few DEA methods to handle the issue that

MADM problems involve some random and ordinal variables. To further extend the application of DEA on aforementioned MADM problems, we develop a MADM method based on stochastic DEA cross-efficiency with ordinal variable.

The main purpose of this paper is to address the MADM problems with random and ordinal variables. Therefore, we propose a MADM method based on stochastic DEA cross-efficiency with ordinal variable. The major characteristics of this method are presented as follows. One is that both stochastic variable and ordinal variable are incorporated into DEA model, which is considerably consistent with the actual circumstance. The other is that it simultaneously considers the self-efficiency and cross-efficiency in evaluation process of MADM problems, and then constructs corresponding consistent FPRs. Subsequently, we calculate the priority weight vector of all alternatives by utilizing the row wise summation technique and derive the full ranking order of them.

The rest of this paper is organized as follows. In Section 2, we briefly introduce the traditional CCR model and its correlative properties. In Section 3, we develop a MADM method based on stochastic DEA cross-efficiency with ordinal variable. Section 4 gives a numerical example for evaluating operation performance of sustainable development of 15 listed banks in China, which illustrates the applicability of this proposed approach. Finally, some conclusions and future research work are presented in Section 5.

2. Preliminaries

In this section, we briefly review some basic concepts of DEA model. DEA is a data-oriented methodology for identifying efficiency production frontiers and evaluating the relative efficiency of DMUs that multiple inputs of production factors produce certain amount outputs [43]. Suppose that there are n DMUs to be evaluated, where each DMU is characterized by its production process of consuming m inputs to generate s outputs. For convenience, the inputs and outputs of $DMU_j(j = 1, 2, \cdots, n)$ are denoted as $x_{ij}(i = 1, 2, \cdots, m)$ and $y_{rj}(r = 1, 2, \cdots, s)$, respectively. To evaluate performance of specific DMU_k, Charnes et al. [44] proposed the following model to calculate its relative efficiency under the assumption of constant returns to scale (CRS).

$$
\begin{aligned}
& \min \theta_k \\
& S.t \ \sum_{j=1}^{n} \lambda_j y_{rj} \geq y_{rk}, r = 1, 2, \cdots, s, \\
& \quad \sum_{j=1}^{n} \lambda_j x_{ij} \leq \theta_k x_{ik}, i = 1, 2, \cdots, m, \\
& \quad \lambda_j \geq 0, j = 1, 2, \cdots, n.
\end{aligned}
\tag{1}
$$

The above model is called input-oriented CCR model, where λ_j are the nonnegative multipliers used to aggregate existing DMUs into a virtual one [45], θ_k is the relative efficiency score of DMU_k. To understand the CCR model clearly, we give the dual form of the CCR model:

$$
\begin{aligned}
& \max z = \sum_{r=1}^{s} \omega_r y_{rk} \\
& S.t \ \sum_{r=1}^{s} \omega_r y_{rj} - \sum_{i=1}^{m} \mu_i x_{ij} \leq 0, j = 1, 2, \cdots, n, \\
& \quad \sum_{i=1}^{m} \mu_i x_{ik} = 1, \\
& \quad \omega_r \geq 0, r = 1, 2, \cdots, s; \mu_i \geq 0, i = 1, 2, \cdots, m.
\end{aligned}
\tag{2}
$$

where x_{ij} and y_{rj} are the inputs and outputs of $DMU_j(j = 1, 2, \cdots, n)$, μ_i and ω_r are the input and output weights. x_{ik} and y_{rk} are the inputs and outputs of specific DMU_k, respectively. The optimal solution of the objective function is the relative efficiency of DMU_k. If the efficiency score of DMU_k is less than one, the DMU_k is defined as DEA inefficient. Conversely, if the efficiency score is equal to one, the DMU_k is considered as DEA efficient. In the following, we extend the CCR model by incorporating discretionary variable, ordinal variable and stochastic variable. Then, we develop a MADM method.

3. Multi-Attribute Decision Making Method

Generally speaking, MADM is an evaluation process where the optimal alternative needs to be chosen from a finite number of feasible alternatives based on a set of attributes [8]. Owing to the inherent complexity and competition of real world, MADM problems often involve some random and ordinal variables. However, the traditional DEA approach assumes that all inputs and outputs are discretionary where they are under the control of management, thus it insufficiently addresses the above situation. Therefore, we propose a stochastic DEA model with ordinal variable, which constructs production frontiers that incorporate inefficiency and stochastic error [45].

3.1. Stochastic DEA Model with Ordinal Variable

The basic CCR model supposes that all inputs and outputs are deterministic. In other words, they are under the control of management [45]. However, in the real world, there are many situations where some inputs and outputs are out of the control of management. Hence, the aforementioned models need to be modified to adapt to these circumstances. First, we assume that I denotes the set including all input variables, and then divide them into two categories: a set of discretionary inputs $I_D(i = 1, 2, \cdots, p)$, and a set of ordinal inputs $I_O(i = p + 1, p + 2, \cdots, m)$. We rewrite model (3) in a new form as follows:

$$\max z = \sum_{r=1}^{s} \omega_r y_{rk}$$
$$S.t \sum_{r=1}^{s} \omega_r y_{rj} - \sum_{i=1}^{p} \mu_i^1 x_{ij}^1 - \sum_{i=p+1}^{m} \mu_i^2 x_{ij}^2 \leq 0,$$
$$\sum_{i=1}^{p} \mu_i^1 x_{ik}^1 + \sum_{i=p+1}^{m} \mu_i^2 x_{ik}^2 = 1,$$
$$\omega_r \geq 0, \mu_i^1 \geq 0, \mu_i^2 \geq 0, j = 1, 2, \cdots, n.$$

(3)

The above model simultaneously considers discretionary and ordinal inputs. The model (3) is an output-oriented model in which we find the optimal output value on the condition that the input values are fixed. The optimal solution of the objective function of model (3) is the self-efficiency of the specific DMU_k. The symbols μ_i^1 and μ_i^2 represent weight multipliers of the discretionary inputs and ordinal inputs, respectively.

It is notable that this study pays attention to real situations where we can control the quantity of inputs, while being unable to control the outputs. The reason is that the quantity of outputs relies on many external factors such as economic factors, political factors and other social factors. Therefore, the output is commonly considered as stochastic variable. The traditional DEA model for performance evaluation is deterministic type, which does not take the random errors of output variable into account in production process. However, stochastic DEA constructs production frontiers that incorporate both inefficiency and stochastic error, which moves the frontiers closer to the bulk of the producing units [45]. Therefore, the measured technical efficiency of DMUs is improved comparing to the deterministic model. In this subsection, we introduce the stochastic outputs into model (3). Suppose that all stochastic outputs are denoted by $\widetilde{y}_{rj}(r = 1, 2, \cdots, s)$, and each $\widetilde{y}_{rj}$ has a certain probability distribution. The following model (4) is developed:

$$\max E\left(\sum_{r=1}^{s} \omega_r \widetilde{y}_{rk}\right)$$

$$S.t \ \sum_{i=1}^{p} \mu_i^1 x_{ik}^1 + \sum_{i=p+1}^{m} \mu_i^2 x_{ik}^2 = 1,$$

$$\Pr\left(\frac{\sum_{r=1}^{s} \omega_r \widetilde{y}_{rj}}{\sum_{i=1}^{p} \mu_i^1 x_{ij}^1 + \sum_{i=p+1}^{m} \mu_i^2 x_{ij}^2} \leq \beta_j\right) \geq 1 - \alpha_j,$$

$$\omega_r \geq 0, \mu_i^1 \geq 0, \mu_i^2 \geq 0, j = 1, 2, \cdots, n. \tag{4}$$

The above model is designed to evaluate the expected efficiency of the specific DMU_k. The inequality constraint guarantees that the probability of the efficiency score of DMU_j less than or equal to β_j should be higher than $1 - \alpha_j$. The symbols $(\omega_r, \mu_i^1, \mu_i^2)$ represent weight multipliers of stochastic outputs, discretionary inputs and ordinal inputs, respectively. Pr denotes a probability and the superscript "~" expresses that $\widetilde{y}_{rj}$ is a stochastic variable. The other symbol β_j is a predefined value whose range is between 0 and 1. β_j stands for a desirable level of efficiency of DMU_j, which is determined by outside conditions including decision level of management or market circumstances [31]. Meanwhile, α_j is also a prescribed value whose range is between 0 and 1. It is considered as an allowable risk level that violates the related constraints.

To obtain the computational feasibility, the stochastic DEA model should convert into the deterministic DEA model. In this paper, we utilize the CCP technique to transform the second constraint of model (4) into the following form.

$$\Pr\left(\frac{\sum_{r=1}^{s} \omega_r \widetilde{y}_{rj} - \sum_{r=1}^{s} \omega_r \overline{y}_{rj}}{\sqrt{U_j}} \leq \frac{\beta_j\left(\sum_{i=1}^{p} \mu_i^1 x_{ij}^1 + \sum_{i=p+1}^{m} \mu_i^2 x_{ij}^2\right) - \sum_{r=1}^{s} \omega_r \overline{y}_{rj}}{\sqrt{U_j}}\right) \geq 1 - \alpha_j, j = 1, 2, \cdots, n, \tag{5}$$

where $\overline{y}_{rj}$ is the expected value of $\widetilde{y}_{rj}$ and

$$U_j = \left(\begin{array}{cccc} \omega_1 & \omega_2 & \cdots & \omega_s \end{array}\right) \times \left(\begin{array}{cccc} V(\widetilde{y}_{1j}) & Cov(\widetilde{y}_{1j}, \widetilde{y}_{2j}) & \cdots & Cov(\widetilde{y}_{1j}, \widetilde{y}_{sj}) \\ Cov(\widetilde{y}_{2j}, \widetilde{y}_{1j}) & V(\widetilde{y}_{2j}) & \cdots & Cov(\widetilde{y}_{2j}, \widetilde{y}_{sj}) \\ \vdots & \vdots & \ddots & \vdots \\ Cov(\widetilde{y}_{sj}, \widetilde{y}_{1j}) & Cov(\widetilde{y}_{sj}, \widetilde{y}_{2j}) & \cdots & V(\widetilde{y}_{sj}) \end{array}\right) \times \left(\begin{array}{c} \omega_1 \\ \omega_2 \\ \vdots \\ \omega_s \end{array}\right), j = 1, 2, \cdots, n. \tag{6}$$

$U_j (j = 1, 2, \cdots, n)$ represents the variance-covariance matrix of the DMU_j where the symbol "V" stands for a variance and the symbol "Cov" denotes a covariance. To follow the CCP technique, this subsection introduces a new variable which follows the standard normal distribution with zero mean and unity variance.

$$\widetilde{Z}_j = \frac{\sum_{r=1}^{s} \omega_r \widetilde{y}_{rj} - \sum_{r=1}^{s} \omega_r \overline{y}_{rj}}{\sqrt{U_j}}, j = 1, 2, \cdots, n. \tag{7}$$

Therefore, the Formula (5) can be rewritten as follows:

$$\Pr\left(\widetilde{Z}_j \leq \frac{\beta_j\left(\sum_{i=1}^{p} \mu_i^1 x_{ij}^1 + \sum_{i=p+1}^{m} \mu_i^2 x_{ij}^2\right) - \sum_{r=1}^{s} \omega_r \overline{y}_{rj}}{\sqrt{U_j}}\right) \geq 1 - \alpha_j, j = 1, 2, \cdots, n. \tag{8}$$

After a simple transformation, we can obtain the following formula.

$$\frac{\beta_j\left(\sum\limits_{i=1}^{p}\mu_i^1 x_{ij}^1 + \sum\limits_{i=p+1}^{m}\mu_i^2 x_{ij}^2\right) - \sum\limits_{r=1}^{s}\omega_r \overline{y}_{rj}}{\sqrt{U_j}} \geq \Phi^{-1}(1-\alpha_j), j = 1, 2, \cdots, n. \tag{9}$$

where Φ represents a cumulative normal distribution function and Φ^{-1} denotes its inverse function. Based on Equation (9), the model (4) can be rewritten as follows:

$$\begin{aligned}
&\max E\left(\sum\limits_{r=1}^{s}\omega_r \widetilde{y}_{rk}\right) \\
&S.t \; \sum\limits_{i=1}^{p}\mu_i^1 x_{ik}^1 + \sum\limits_{i=p+1}^{m}\mu_i^2 x_{ik}^2 = 1, \\
&\frac{\beta_j\left(\sum\limits_{i=1}^{p}\mu_i^1 x_{ij}^1 + \sum\limits_{i=p+1}^{m}\mu_i^2 x_{ij}^2\right) - \sum\limits_{r=1}^{s}\omega_r \overline{y}_{rj}}{\sqrt{U_j}} \geq \Phi^{-1}(1-\alpha_j), \\
&\omega_r \geq 0, \mu_i^1 \geq 0, \mu_i^2 \geq 0, j = 1, 2, \cdots, n.
\end{aligned} \tag{10}$$

The second inequality constraint of model (10) includes quadratic expression and brings computational difficulty. To further simplify the computational process, we suppose that each stochastic output is denoted by $\widetilde{y}_{rj} = \overline{y}_{rj} + h_{rj}\delta$ $(r = 1, 2, \cdots, s; j = 1, 2, \cdots, n)$, where $\overline{y}_{rj}$ is the expected value of $\widetilde{y}_{rj}$ and h_{rj} is its standard deviation. δ is assumed to follow a standard normal distribution $N(0,1)$. B_j represents the covariance matrix of DMU_j. Under such an assumption, B_j can be defined as follows:

$$B_j = \begin{pmatrix}
h_{1j}^2 & h_{1j}h_{2j} & \cdots & h_{1j}h_{sj} \\
h_{2j}h_{1j} & h_{2j}^2 & \cdots & h_{2j}h_{sj} \\
\vdots & \vdots & \ddots & \vdots \\
h_{sj}h_{1j} & h_{sj}h_{2j} & \cdots & h_{sj}^2
\end{pmatrix}. \tag{11}$$

Hence, U_j can be rewritten as the following form,

$$U_j = \begin{pmatrix} \omega_1 & \omega_2 & \cdots & \omega_s \end{pmatrix} \times \begin{pmatrix}
h_{1j}^2 & h_{1j}h_{2j} & \cdots & h_{1j}h_{sj} \\
h_{2j}h_{1j} & h_{2j}^2 & \cdots & h_{2j}h_{sj} \\
\vdots & \vdots & \ddots & \vdots \\
h_{sj}h_{1j} & h_{sj}h_{2j} & \cdots & h_{sj}^2
\end{pmatrix} \times \begin{pmatrix} \omega_1 \\ \omega_2 \\ \vdots \\ \omega_s \end{pmatrix} = \left(\sum\limits_{r=1}^{s}\omega_r h_{rj}\right)^2, \forall r = 1, 2, \cdots, s; j = 1, 2, \cdots, n. \tag{12}$$

By incorporating Equation (12) into model (10), then the stochastic DEA model with ordinal variable can be transformed into the following equivalent linear programming:

$$\begin{aligned}
&\max \sum\limits_{r=1}^{s}\omega_r \overline{y}_{rk} \\
&S.t \; \sum\limits_{i=1}^{p}\mu_i^1 x_{ik}^1 + \sum\limits_{i=p+1}^{m}\mu_i^2 x_{ik}^2 = 1, \\
&\beta_j\left(\sum\limits_{i=1}^{p}\mu_i^1 x_{ij}^1 + \sum\limits_{i=p+1}^{m}\mu_i^2 x_{ij}^2\right) - \sum\limits_{r=1}^{s}\omega_r \overline{y}_{rj} \geq \sum\limits_{r=1}^{s}\omega_r h_{rj}\Phi^{-1}(1-\alpha_j), \\
&\omega_r \geq 0, \mu_i^1 \geq 0, \mu_i^2 \geq 0, j = 1, 2, \cdots, n.
\end{aligned} \tag{13}$$

Here, the dual form of model (13) is presented as follows:

$$
\begin{aligned}
& \min \theta_k \\
& S.t \ \sum_{j=1}^{n} \lambda_j \left(\beta_j x_{ij}^1 \right) \leq \theta_k x_{ik}^1, i = 1, 2, \cdots, p, \\
& \quad \sum_{j=1}^{n} \lambda_j \left(\beta_j x_{ij}^2 \right) \leq \theta_k x_{ik}^2, i = p+1, p+2, \cdots, m, \\
& \quad \sum_{j=1}^{n} \lambda_j \left[\overline{y}_{rj} + h_{rj} \Phi^{-1} \left(1 - \alpha_j \right) \right] \geq \overline{y}_{rk}, r = 1, 2, \cdots, s, \\
& \quad \lambda_j \geq 0, 0 \leq \alpha_j \leq 1, 0 \leq \beta_j \leq 1, j = 1, 2, \cdots, n.
\end{aligned}
\tag{14}
$$

We can derive the optimal weights ($\omega_r, \mu_i^1, \mu_i^2$) of outputs and inputs by solving model (13). Based on the optimal weights of DMU_k, the cross-efficiency of DMU_j is calculated by the following formula:

$$
E_{kj} = \frac{\sum_{r=1}^{s} \omega_{rk} \widetilde{y}_{rj}}{\sum_{i=1}^{p} \mu_{ik}^1 x_{ij}^1 + \sum_{i=p+1}^{m} \mu_{ik}^2 x_{ij}^2}, k, j = 1, 2, \cdots, n, k \neq j.
\tag{15}
$$

which is the peer evaluation of DMU_k to DMU_j. Then, we obtain the cross-efficiency matrix.

$$
E = \begin{pmatrix}
E_{11} & E_{12} & \cdots & E_{1n} \\
E_{21} & E_{22} & \cdots & E_{2n} \\
\vdots & \vdots & \ddots & \vdots \\
E_{n1} & E_{n2} & \cdots & E_{nn}
\end{pmatrix}
\tag{16}
$$

However, we cannot derive priority weight vector of all DMUs by cross-efficiency matrix E. Therefore, we need to construct corresponding preference relations to yield the priority weight vector of whole alternatives.

3.2. Constructing the Consistent Fuzzy Preference Relations for Ranking DMUs

It is known that traditional ways to construct a preference relation are based on experts' subjective evaluation involving their professional knowledge and ideas, which lead to different preference information for different experts [46]. However, compared with traditional approaches, using the pairwise efficiency derived by DEA method to construct a preference relation is more objective. In this subsection, we present the following specific procedures of construction process. First, we can obtain the efficiency scores $E_{kk}, E_{kj}, E_{jk}, E_{jj}(k, j = 1, 2, \cdots, n)$ by solving model (13) and calculating Equation (15). Then, we construct corresponding fuzzy preference relations (FPRs)$R = \left(r_{kj} \right)_{n \times n}$, the element of R is defined as follows:

$$
r_{kj} = \frac{E_{kk} + E_{jk}}{E_{kk} + E_{kj} + E_{jk} + E_{jj}}, r_{jj} = 0.5, j = 1, 2, \cdots, n.
\tag{17}
$$

where $R = \left(r_{kj} \right)_{n \times n}$ is characterized by $r_{kj} + r_{jk} = 1$ and $r_{jj} = 0.5$. r_{kj} represents the evaluation of unit k over unit j. If $r_{kj} > 0.5$, it denotes that unit k is superior to unit j. Conversely, if $r_{kj} < 0.5$, it stands for that unit j is superior to unit k. Based on FPRs $R = \left(r_{kj} \right)_{n \times n}$, we can construct corresponding consistent FPRs $A = \left(a_{kj} \right)_{n \times n}$ by utilizing the following formulas.

$$
c_k = \sum_{j=1}^{n} r_{kj} = \sum_{j=1}^{n} \frac{E_{kk} + E_{jk}}{E_{kk} + E_{jk} + E_{jj} + E_{kj}}, k = 1, 2, \cdots, n.
\tag{18}
$$

$$a_{kj} = \frac{c_k - c_j}{2(n-1)} + 0.5. \tag{19}$$

Based on the consistent FPRs $A = \left(a_{kj}\right)_{n \times n}$, we can derive the priority weight vector of all alternatives by using the row wise summation technique and obtain the whole ranking order. The priority weight vector $v_k (k = 1, 2, \cdots, n)$ of DMU_k is calculated by the following equation,

$$v_k = \frac{\displaystyle\sum_{j=1}^{n} a_{kj}}{\displaystyle\sum_{k=1}^{n}\sum_{j=1}^{n} a_{kj}} = \frac{\displaystyle\sum_{j=1}^{n} a_{kj} + \frac{n}{2} - 1}{n(n-1)}. \tag{20}$$

In summary, we show the detailed procedures of MADM method based on stochastic DEA cross-efficiency with ordinal variable.

Step 1: Solve model (13); we obtain the self-efficiency $E_{kk} (k = 1, 2, \cdots, n)$ and the optimal weights $\mu_i^{1*} (i = 1, 2, \cdots, p)$, $\mu_i^{2*} (i = p+1, p+2, \cdots, m)$, $\omega_r^* (r = 1, 2, \cdots, s)$.

Step 2: Utilize Formula (15) to calculate the cross-efficiency $E_{kj} (k \neq j, k, j = 1, 2, \cdots, n)$ by the optimal weights of other peer DMUs.

Step 3: Use Equation (17) to calculate the value of $r_{kj} (k, j = 1, 2, \cdots, n)$ and construct the FPRs $R = \left(r_{kj}\right)_{n \times n}$.

Step 4: Construct corresponding consistent FPRs $A = \left(a_{kj}\right)_{n \times n}$ based on the FPRs $R = \left(r_{kj}\right)_{n \times n}$ by utilizing Equations (18) and (19).

Step 5: Obtain the priority weight vector $v_k (k = 1, 2, \cdots, n)$ of DMU_k by calculating the Formula (20).

Step 6: Rank all alternatives in accordance with the descending order of priority weight vector $v_k (k = 1, 2, \cdots, n)$ and select the optimal one.

4. Example and Discussion

With the development of society, we gradually realize the significance of sustainable development of economy. To some extent, the operation performance of banks can reflect the economic trend. Therefore, it is important to maintain sustainable development of banks. In this section, we provide a numerical example for evaluating operation performance of sustainable development of 15 listed banks in China, which illustrates practicability and validity of the proposed MADM method based on stochastic DEA cross-efficiency with ordinal variable. The 15 listed banks are Bank of China (DMU_1), Construction Bank of China (DMU_2), Industrial and Commercial Bank of China (DMU_3), Agricultural Bank of China (DMU_4), Industrial Bank Co., Ltd. (DMU_5), Bank of Communications (DMU_6), Shanghai Pudong Development Bank (DMU_7), Ping An Bank Co., Ltd. (DMU_8), China Minsheng Bank (DMU_9), China Merchants Bank (DMU_{10}), China Citic Bank (DMU_{11}), China Everbright Bank (DMU_{12}), Huaxia Bank (DMU_{13}), Beijing Bank (DMU_{14}) and Shanghai Bank (DMU_{15}), respectively. Owing to operating similar business, these banks compete with each other. Then, we want to know the bank with the best performance under the same conditions. Therefore, we have to evaluate the relative performance of all listed banks by aforementioned method and obtain a full ranking of them. Here, we employ the intermediation approach to determine input and output factors of these banks. Compared with other approaches, this method is more suitable for evaluating the whole bank and superior in evaluating efficiency of bank's profitability. Then, it also reduces heavy computation and is considerably consistent with bank's daily operation. Therefore, based on the intermediation approach, we determine four input factors (m = 4) and two output factors (s = 2). The input factors consist of (i) fixed assets (x_1), which stand for the capital value of tangible assets; (ii) labor costs (x_2), which refer to the costs of the full-time employees; (iii) interest expense (x_3) and the number of branches (x_4). The output factors include the amount of the loan (y_1) and the amount of deposit (y_2). Among these six attributes, x_1, x_2 and x_3 are considered as the discretionary variables, x_4 is the ordinal variable, y_1 and y_2 are assumed as the stochastic variables. Our data come from the national Tai'an database. Table 1 gives a summary of the inputs and outputs. Table 2 gives order ranking for branches' number of all listed banks. Table 3 gives descriptive statistics of raw data.

Table 1. Input and output variables.

Index	Sym	Item	Unit
Input 1	X_1	Fixed assets	100-million CNY
Input 2	X_2	Labor costs	100-million CNY
Input 3	X_3	Interest expense	10-billion CNY
Input 4	X_4	The number of branches	
Output 1	Y_1	Loan	100-billion CNY
Output 2	Y_2	Deposit	100-billion CNY

Table 2. Order ranking for branches' number of all listed banks.

Banks	Rank	Banks	Rank
Bank of China	4	China Minsheng Bank	9
Construction Bank of China	3	China Merchants Bank	5
Industrial and Commercial Bank of China	2	China Citic Bank	7
Agricultural Bank of China	1	China Everbright Bank	9
Industrial Bank Co., Ltd.	6	Huaxia Bank	10
Bank of Communications	5	Beijing Bank	11
Shanghai Pudong Development Bank	7	Shanghai Bank	11
Ping An Bank Co., Ltd.	8		

Table 3. Descriptive statistics of raw data.

Attribute	Fixed Assets	Labor Costs	Interest Expense	Ranking of Branches' Number	Loan	Deposit
Average	715.51	152.35	17.66	6.53	70.51	86.29
Min	43.95	27.62	4.59	1	6.43	9.24
Max	2161.56	402.22	37.56	11	198.93	232.26

There are two parameters which are not part of the given database: α and β. We run the stochastic DEA model (13) in Matlab software with different values for these parameters to see the sensitivity of the result. Table 4 shows self-efficiency scores of 15 listed banks which are calculated with diverse combinations between $\alpha = \{0.05, 0.1, 0.2\}$ and $\beta = \{0.8, 0.85, 0.9, 0.95, 1\}$. It presents the values of three statistics of self-efficiency, including the minimum, maximum and the mean. As suggested by Sueyoshi [31], regular trends are found in Table 4. It is notable that the mean, the maximum and the minimum of the self-efficiency increase as α or β increases. However, there are two cases that exist in Table 4 and cannot be viewed as exceptions. One is that an increase in β from 0.95 to 1 decreases the maximum of self-efficiency from 1 to 0.9754 when $\alpha = 0.1$. The other is that the maximum of self-efficiency has no variation between $\beta = 0.95$ and $\beta = 1$ under the condition of $\alpha = 0.2$. It is obvious that there is smaller difference among self-efficiency scores under the condition that α or β chooses diverse values. Therefore, we choose $\alpha = 0.1$ and $\beta = 0.95$ for the rest of the paper.

With the original data, we complete Step 1 of the developed method. In the following, we will accomplish Step 2 to 6. In Step 2, we use the optimal attribute weights of each bank to calculate the cross-efficiency of the 15 listed banks by utilizing Formula (15) and the results are presented in Table 5. In Table 5, $E_{kj}(k = 1, 2, \cdots, 15)$ denotes the peer evaluation of DMU_k to DMU_j. In Step 3, we utilize the Formula (17) to calculate the value of $r_{kj}(k, j = 1, 2, \cdots, 15)$ and construct corresponding FPRs $R = (r_{kj})_{15 \times 15}$. Table 6 shows the values of the FPRs R. In Step 4, we construct the consistent FPRs $A = (a_{kj})_{15 \times 15}$ by using Equations (18) and (19). Table 7 presents the values of the consistent FPRs A. In Step 5, we obtain the priority weight vector of each listed bank by utilizing Equation (20). In Step 6, we can select the optimal one by ranking all listed banks in accordance with the descending order of priority weight vector $v_k (k = 1, 2, \cdots, 15)$ and the result is documented in Table 8.

Table 4. Self-efficiency under different α and β.

β	α	min	max	mean
0.8	0.05	0.4142	0.7649	0.6470
	0.1	0.4528	0.8435	0.6791
	0.2	0.5171	0.8716	0.7064
0.85	0.05	0.4401	0.8127	0.6874
	0.1	0.4811	0.8963	0.7215
	0.2	0.5494	0.9205	0.7502
0.9	0.05	0.4660	0.8605	0.7278
	0.1	0.5094	0.9312	0.7576
	0.2	0.5817	0.9593	0.7933
0.95	0.05	0.4919	0.9283	0.7696
	0.1	0.5377	1.0000	0.8212
	0.2	0.6141	1.0000	0.8365
1	0.05	0.5178	0.9561	0.8087
	0.1	0.5660	0.9754	0.8434
	0.2	0.6464	1.0000	0.8770

Table 5. Cross-efficiency and self-efficiency score.

	$E_{1,j}$	$E_{2,j}$	$E_{3,j}$	$E_{4,j}$	$E_{5,j}$	$E_{6,j}$	$E_{7,j}$	$E_{8,j}$
$E_{k,1}$	0.9010	0.9493	0.9498	0.9507	0.9059	0.6197	0.8449	0.6523
$E_{k,2}$	0.8762	1.0000	0.8815	0.8851	0.8317	0.5170	0.7675	0.6071
$E_{k,3}$	0.9005	0.9246	0.9016	0.9259	0.8458	0.5912	0.7884	0.6076
$E_{k,4}$	0.8961	0.9374	0.9272	0.8707	0.8361	0.4318	0.7651	0.6326
$E_{k,5}$	0.7182	0.5316	0.5085	0.5325	0.8379	0.2974	0.7553	0.8421
$E_{k,6}$	0.8000	0.7858	0.7684	0.7870	0.7827	1.0000	0.7508	0.6226
$E_{k,7}$	0.6880	0.4986	0.5146	0.4992	0.8108	0.4244	0.8102	0.5327
$E_{k,8}$	0.5317	0.3765	0.3377	0.3772	0.7480	0.3673	0.6536	0.8627
$E_{k,9}$	0.5940	0.4900	0.4691	0.4908	0.6672	0.5191	0.6298	0.6017
$E_{k,10}$	0.8565	0.8067	0.7437	0.8082	0.8942	0.9491	0.8380	0.9062
$E_{k,11}$	0.7483	0.5406	0.5460	0.5413	0.9022	0.4473	0.8256	0.6656
$E_{k,12}$	0.4792	0.3245	0.3215	0.3250	0.6325	0.3444	0.5905	0.5295
$E_{k,13}$	0.3340	0.2141	0.2176	0.2144	0.4578	0.2772	0.4225	0.3466
$E_{k,14}$	0.2555	0.1648	0.1631	0.1650	0.3608	0.4986	0.3379	0.3115
$E_{k,15}$	0.2065	0.1279	0.1230	0.1281	0.3217	0.4377	0.2799	0.3316

	$E_{9,j}$	$E_{10,j}$	$E_{11,j}$	$E_{12,j}$	$E_{13,j}$	$E_{14,j}$	$E_{15,j}$
$E_{k,1}$	0.8543	0.6192	0.8056	0.7620	0.6979	0.7845	0.6618
$E_{k,2}$	0.7839	0.5166	0.7338	0.6950	0.6278	0.6723	0.5966
$E_{k,3}$	0.7981	0.5907	0.7465	0.7081	0.6484	0.7363	0.6161
$E_{k,4}$	0.8015	0.4315	0.7223	0.6923	0.6017	0.5903	0.5718
$E_{k,5}$	0.8082	0.2972	0.8971	0.8132	0.6871	0.4417	0.6563
$E_{k,6}$	0.7322	0.9484	0.7443	0.7046	0.7071	0.8947	0.6888
$E_{k,7}$	0.7309	0.4241	0.8104	0.7341	0.7082	0.7067	0.6541
$E_{k,8}$	0.6590	0.3670	0.9505	0.8461	0.8474	0.4468	0.8502
$E_{k,9}$	0.7477	0.5186	0.6937	0.6462	0.6509	0.6153	0.6363
$E_{k,10}$	0.8242	1.0000	0.9245	0.8610	0.8855	0.8809	0.8901
$E_{k,11}$	0.8133	0.4470	0.8555	0.8408	0.8092	0.7158	0.7597
$E_{k,12}$	0.5678	0.3441	0.7268	0.6991	0.6749	0.5365	0.6391
$E_{k,13}$	0.3933	0.2770	0.5495	0.4752	0.5377	0.4546	0.5040
$E_{k,14}$	0.2976	0.4982	0.4880	0.4076	0.5828	0.5987	0.5709
$E_{k,15}$	0.2401	0.4374	0.5198	0.3980	0.7339	0.5277	0.6945

Table 6. Fuzzy preference relations R.

	$r_{1,j}$	$r_{1,j}$	$r_{3,j}$	$r_{4,j}$	$r_{5,j}$	$r_{6,j}$	$r_{7,j}$	$r_{8,j}$
$r_{k,1}$	0.5000	0.5035	0.4933	0.4883	0.4627	0.5421	0.4618	0.4730
$r_{k,2}$	0.4965	0.5000	0.4925	0.4896	0.4278	0.5407	0.4254	0.4354
$r_{k,3}$	0.5067	0.5075	0.5000	0.4959	0.4352	0.5423	0.4394	0.4430
$r_{k,4}$	0.5117	0.5104	0.5041	0.5000	0.4453	0.5784	0.4446	0.4520
$r_{k,5}$	0.5373	0.5722	0.5648	0.5547	0.5000	0.6109	0.5043	0.4895
$r_{k,6}$	0.4579	0.4593	0.4577	0.4216	0.3891	0.5000	0.4135	0.4312
$r_{k,7}$	0.5382	0.5746	0.5606	0.5554	0.4957	0.5865	0.5000	0.5303
$r_{k,8}$	0.5270	0.5646	0.5570	0.5480	0.5105	0.5688	0.4697	0.5000
$r_{k,9}$	0.5668	0.5904	0.5828	0.5745	0.5378	0.5776	0.5280	0.5300
$r_{k,10}$	0.4502	0.4564	0.4612	0.4187	0.3747	0.4999	0.4018	0.3921
$r_{k,11}$	0.5155	0.5539	0.5404	0.5328	0.4968	0.5724	0.4908	0.5438
$r_{k,12}$	0.5853	0.6235	0.6120	0.6042	0.5536	0.6203	0.5449	0.5817
$r_{k,13}$	0.6472	0.6841	0.6724	0.6619	0.6050	0.6769	0.6126	0.6592
$r_{k,14}$	0.6637	0.6866	0.6825	0.6567	0.5715	0.6333	0.6183	0.5899
$r_{k,15}$	0.6343	0.6600	0.6499	0.6368	0.5952	0.5987	0.6004	0.6254

	$r_{9,j}$	$r_{10,j}$	$r_{11,j}$	$r_{12,j}$	$r_{13,j}$	$r_{14,j}$	$r_{15,j}$
$r_{k,1}$	0.4332	0.5498	0.4845	0.4147	0.3528	0.3363	0.3657
$r_{k,2}$	0.4096	0.5436	0.4461	0.3765	0.3159	0.3134	0.3400
$r_{k,3}$	0.4172	0.5388	0.4478	0.3880	0.3276	0.3175	0.3501
$r_{k,4}$	0.4255	0.5813	0.4463	0.3958	0.3381	0.3433	0.3632
$r_{k,5}$	0.4622	0.6253	0.5032	0.4464	0.3950	0.4285	0.4048
$r_{k,6}$	0.4224	0.5001	0.4276	0.3797	0.3231	0.3667	0.4013
$r_{k,7}$	0.4720	0.5982	0.5092	0.4551	0.3874	0.3817	0.3996
$r_{k,8}$	0.4700	0.6079	0.4562	0.4183	0.3408	0.4101	0.3746
$r_{k,9}$	0.5000	0.5903	0.5366	0.4761	0.3996	0.1792	0.4031
$r_{k,10}$	0.4097	0.5000	0.4036	0.3592	0.3017	0.3684	0.3746
$r_{k,11}$	0.4634	0.5964	0.5000	0.4567	0.3951	0.4088	0.4292
$r_{k,12}$	0.5239	0.6408	0.5433	0.5000	0.4244	0.4489	0.4495
$r_{k,13}$	0.6004	0.6983	0.6049	0.5756	0.5000	0.5435	0.5783
$r_{k,14}$	0.8208	0.6316	0.5912	0.5511	0.4565	0.5000	0.9109
$r_{k,15}$	0.5969	0.6254	0.5708	0.5505	0.4217	0.8717	0.5000

Table 7. Consistent fuzzy preference relations A.

	$a_{1,j}$	$a_{2,j}$	$a_{3,j}$	$a_{4,j}$	$a_{5,j}$	$a_{6,j}$	$a_{7,j}$	$a_{8,j}$
$a_{k,1}$	0.5000	0.5110	0.5069	0.5000	0.4737	0.5182	0.4756	0.4835
$a_{k,2}$	0.4890	0.5000	0.4959	0.4890	0.4626	0.5072	0.4646	0.4725
$a_{k,3}$	0.4931	0.5041	0.5000	0.4931	0.4668	0.5113	0.4687	0.4766
$a_{k,4}$	0.5000	0.5110	0.5069	0.5000	0.4736	0.5182	0.4756	0.4835
$a_{k,5}$	0.5263	0.5374	0.5332	0.5264	0.5000	0.5446	0.5020	0.5099
$a_{k,6}$	0.4818	0.4928	0.4887	0.4818	0.4554	0.5000	0.4574	0.4653
$a_{k,7}$	0.5244	0.5354	0.5313	0.5244	0.4980	0.5426	0.5000	0.5079
$a_{k,8}$	0.5165	0.5275	0.5234	0.5165	0.4902	0.5347	0.4921	0.5000
$a_{k,9}$	0.5254	0.5364	0.5323	0.5254	0.4991	0.5436	0.5010	0.5089
$a_{k,10}$	0.4754	0.4864	0.4823	0.4754	0.4490	0.4936	0.4510	0.4589
$a_{k,11}$	0.5238	0.5348	0.5307	0.5239	0.4975	0.5421	0.4994	0.5073
$a_{k,12}$	0.5498	0.5608	0.5567	0.5498	0.5235	0.5680	0.5254	0.5333
$a_{k,13}$	0.5878	0.5988	0.5947	0.5878	0.5615	0.6060	0.5634	0.5713
$a_{k,14}$	0.5686	0.5796	0.5755	0.5686	0.5422	0.5868	0.5442	0.5521
$a_{k,15}$	0.5533	0.5644	0.5602	0.5534	0.5270	0.5716	0.5290	0.5369

Table 7. *Cont.*

	$a_{9,j}$	$a_{10,j}$	$a_{11,j}$	$a_{12,j}$	$a_{13,j}$	$a_{14,j}$	$a_{15,j}$
$a_{k,1}$	0.4746	0.5246	0.4762	0.4502	0.4122	0.4314	0.4467
$a_{k,2}$	0.4636	0.5136	0.4652	0.4392	0.4012	0.4204	0.4356
$a_{k,3}$	0.4677	0.5177	0.4693	0.4433	0.4053	0.4245	0.4398
$a_{k,4}$	0.4746	0.5246	0.4762	0.4502	0.4122	0.4314	0.4466
$a_{k,5}$	0.5009	0.5510	0.5025	0.4765	0.4385	0.4578	0.4730
$a_{k,6}$	0.4564	0.5064	0.4579	0.4320	0.3940	0.4132	0.4284
$a_{k,7}$	0.4990	0.5490	0.5006	0.4746	0.4366	0.4558	0.4710
$a_{k,8}$	0.4911	0.5411	0.4927	0.4667	0.4287	0.4479	0.4631
$a_{k,9}$	0.5000	0.5500	0.5016	0.4756	0.4376	0.4568	0.4721
$a_{k,10}$	0.4500	0.5000	0.4515	0.4256	0.3876	0.4068	0.4220
$a_{k,11}$	0.4984	0.5485	0.5000	0.4740	0.4360	0.4552	0.4705
$a_{k,12}$	0.5244	0.5744	0.5260	0.5000	0.4620	0.4812	0.4965
$a_{k,13}$	0.5624	0.6124	0.5640	0.5380	0.5000	0.5192	0.5345
$a_{k,14}$	0.5432	0.5932	0.5448	0.5188	0.4808	0.5000	0.5152
$a_{k,15}$	0.5280	0.5780	0.5295	0.5035	0.4655	0.4848	0.5000

Table 8. Ranking of 15 listed banks.

Banks	Weight	Rank
Bank of China	0.0694683	6
Construction Bank of China	0.0709367	3
Industrial and Commercial Bank of China	0.0703883	4
Agricultural Bank of China	0.0694709	5
Industrial Bank Co., Ltd	0.0659563	11
Bank of Communications	0.0718976	2
Shanghai Pudong Development Bank	0.0662167	9
Ping An Bank Co., Ltd	0.0672700	7
China Minsheng Bank	0.0660825	10
China Merchants Bank	0.0727509	1
China Citic Bank	0.0662932	8
China Everbright Bank	0.0628283	12
Huaxia Bank	0.0577616	15
Beijing Bank	0.0603234	14
Shanghai Bank	0.0623554	13

We can obtain the ranking of all listed banks:

$$DMU_{10} > DMU_6 > DMU_2 > DMU_3 > DMU_4 > DMU_1 > DMU_8 > DMU_{11}$$
$$> DMU_7 > DMU_9 > DMU_5 > DMU_{12} > DMU_{15} > DMU_{14} > DMU_{13}. \tag{21}$$

From the ranking in Table 7, we find that the optimal DMU is selected as DMU_{10}. It is obvious that China Merchants Bank is the listed bank with the best operation performance. However, according to self-efficiency of all listed banks, we derive the following ranking:

$$DMU_{10} = DMU_6 = DMU_2 > DMU_3 > DMU_1 > DMU_4 > DMU_8 > DMU_{11}$$
$$> DMU_5 > DMU_7 > DMU_9 > DMU_{12} > DMU_{15} > DMU_{14} > DMU_{13}. \tag{22}$$

We cannot select the best bank in accordance with the above ranking result. In addition, the ranking result obtained from the developed method is different from that derived by traditional DEA approach. The stochastic DEA cross-efficiency with ordinal variable method effectively distinguishes all listed banks and yields the whole ranking. Meanwhile, it can greatly avoid impact of subjectivity of experts and strengthen the discrimination power. Therefore, our proposed method is reliable and valid compared with the traditional DEA method.

5. Conclusions

In this article, we proposed MADM method based on stochastic DEA cross-efficiency with ordinal variable and applied it to evaluating operation performance of sustainable development of 15 listed banks in China. First, we obtained self-efficiency scores of each bank and optimal attribute weights by solving stochastic DEA model. Then, we calculated cross-efficiency of all listed banks by utilizing the optimal attribute weights. Subsequently, according to self-efficiency and cross-efficiency of whole banks, we constructed corresponding FPRs and consistent FPRs. Finally, we used the row wise summation technique to derive the priority weight vector of all listed banks. Based on the unique ranking order of whole banks, we selected the best one.

In summary, the developed MADM method based on stochastic DEA cross-efficiency with ordinal variable is proved effective for evaluating MADM problems. The advantages of this approach are presented as follows. One is that it simultaneously incorporates stochastic variable and ordinal variable, which is considerably consistent with actual circumstances. The other is that it takes cross-efficiency into account in evaluation process of MADM problems and constructs corresponding FPRs, which guarantee the objectivity and persuasion of evaluation results. Furthermore, it requires no assumption of the functional relationships between multiple inputs and multiple outputs of alternatives, and all evaluation results come from original data. However, our method exists some limitations. One is that the stochastic output variable is assumed to follow standard normal distribution and directly applied to the stochastic DEA model. Standard normal distribution is one of the many probability distributions, we need to examine whether other distributions can be used for stochastic DEA model. Another is that the value of parameters α and β is predefined. We have no mature approach to find the optimal value of parameters α and β.

In the future research, we intend to design an integrated method that combines DEA with multiplicative FPRs to handle performance evaluation of MADM problems. Another is that we need to consider the relation among different types of variables in MADM problems and extend existing DEA methods to address it.

Author Contributions: All of the authors contributed to this research. F.J. and J.L. provided case and idea. H.C. and M.F. were responsible for data collection and analysis. J.L. and C.W. provided revised advice. M.F. wrote the first draft of the article. All authors have read and agreed to the published version of the manuscript.

Funding: The work was supported by the National Natural Science Foundation of China (Nos. 71901001, 71501002, 71871001, 71771001), the Construction Fund for Scientific Research Conditions of Introducing Talents in Anhui University (No. S020118002/085), the Key Research Project of Humanities and Social Sciences in Colleges and Universities of Anhui Province (Nos. SK2019A0013, SK2018A0605), the Humanities and Social Sciences Planning Project of the Ministry of Education (No. 20YJAZH066), Project of Anhui Ecological and Economic Development Research Center, the Natural Science Foundation of Hefei University (No. 17ZR06ZDA), and the Natural Science Foundation for Distinguished Young Scholars of Anhui Province (No. 1908085J03).

References

1. Hak, T.; Janoušková, S.; Moldan, B. Sustainable Development Goals: A need for relevant indicators. *Ecol. Indic.* **2016**, *60*, 565–573. [CrossRef]
2. Aleksic, A.; Braje, I.N.; Jelavić, S.R. Creating Sustainable Work Environments by Developing Cultures that Diminish Deviance. *Sustain.* **2019**, *11*, 7031. [CrossRef]
3. Goodland, R. Environmental sustainability in agriculture: Diet matters. *Ecol. Econ.* **1997**, *23*, 189–200. [CrossRef]
4. Munir, W.; Gallagher, K.P. Scaling Up for Sustainable Development: Benefits and Costs of Expanding and Optimizing Balance Sheet in the Multilateral Development Banks. *J. Int. Dev.* **2020**, *32*, 222–243. [CrossRef]
5. Xue, J.; Zhu, D.; Zhao, L.; Wang, C.; Li, H. Redundancy Identification and Optimization Scheme of Branches for Sustainable Operation of Commercial Banks. *Sustain.* **2019**, *11*, 4111. [CrossRef]
6. Jiang, H.; Han, L. Does Income Diversification Benefit the Sustainable Development of Chinese Listed Banks? Analysis Based on Entropy and the Herfindahl–Hirschman Index. *Entropy* **2018**, *20*, 255. [CrossRef]

7. Xiao, P.; Wu, Q.; Li, H.; Zhou, L.; Tao, Z.; Liu, J. Novel Hesitant Fuzzy Linguistic Multi-Attribute Group Decision Making Method Based on Improved Supplementary Regulation and Operational Laws. *IEEE Access* **2019**, *7*, 32922–32940. [CrossRef]

8. Khameneh, A.Z.; Kılıçman, A.; Kılıçman, A. Multi-attribute decision-making based on soft set theory: A systematic review. *Soft Comput.* **2018**, *23*, 6899–6920. [CrossRef]

9. Bernroider, E.; Stix, V. A method using weight restrictions in data envelopment analysis for ranking and validity issues in decision making. *Comput. Oper. Res.* **2007**, *34*, 2637–2647. [CrossRef]

10. Yeh, C.H. The selection of multi-attribute decision making methods for scholarship student selection. *Int. J. Sel. Assess.* **2003**, *11*, 289–296. [CrossRef]

11. Kulak, O.; Kahraman, C. Fuzzy multi-attribute selection among transportation companies using axiomatic design and analytic hierarchy process. *Inf. Sci.* **2005**, *170*, 191–210. [CrossRef]

12. Barzilai, J.; Lootsma, F.A. Power relations and group aggregation in the multiplicative AHP and SMART. *J. Multi-Criteria Decis. Anal.* **1997**, *6*, 155–165. [CrossRef]

13. Xu, Z.; Zhang, X. Hesitant fuzzy multi-attribute decision making based on TOPSIS with incomplete weight information. *Knowl.-Based Syst.* **2013**, *52*, 53–64. [CrossRef]

14. Ho, W.; Xu, X.; Dey, P. Multi-criteria decision making approaches for supplier evaluation and selection: A literature review. *Eur. J. Oper. Res.* **2010**, *202*, 16–24. [CrossRef]

15. Liu, X.; Chu, J.; Yin, P.; Sun, J. DEA cross-efficiency evaluation considering undesirable output and ranking priority: A case study of eco-efficiency analysis of coal-fired power plants. *J. Clean. Prod.* **2017**, *142*, 877–885. [CrossRef]

16. Hatami-Marbini, A.; Tavana, M.; Agrell, P.J.; Lotfi, F.H.; Beigi, Z.G. A common-weights DEA model for centralized resource reduction and target setting. *Comput. Ind. Eng.* **2015**, *79*, 195–203. [CrossRef]

17. Li, Y.; Lei, X.; Dai, Q.; Liang, L. Performance evaluation of participating nations at the 2012 London Summer Olympics by a two-stage data envelopment analysis. *Eur. J. Oper. Res.* **2015**, *243*, 964–973. [CrossRef]

18. An, Q.; Chen, H.; Xiong, B.; Wu, J.; Liang, L. Target intermediate products setting in a two-stage system with fairness concern. *Omega* **2017**, *73*, 49–59. [CrossRef]

19. Emrouznejad, A.; Parker, B.R.; Tavares, G. Evaluation of research in efficiency and productivity: A survey and analysis of the first 30 years of scholarly literature in DEA. *Socio-Econ. Plan. Sci.* **2008**, *42*, 151–157. [CrossRef]

20. Karsak, E.E.; Dursun, M. An integrated supplier selection methodology incorporating QFD and DEA with imprecise data. *Expert Syst. Appl.* **2014**, *41*, 6995–7004. [CrossRef]

21. Jin, J.; Zhou, D.; Zhou, P. Measuring environmental performance with stochastic environmental DEA: The case of APEC economies. *Econ. Model.* **2014**, *38*, 80–86. [CrossRef]

22. Chen, L.; Lai, F.; Wang, Y.-M.; Huang, Y.; Wu, F.-M. A two-stage network data envelopment analysis approach for measuring and decomposing environmental efficiency. *Comput. Ind. Eng.* **2018**, *119*, 388–403. [CrossRef]

23. Toloo, M.; Nalchigar, S. A new DEA method for supplier selection in presence of both cardinal and ordinal data. *Expert Syst. Appl.* **2011**, *38*, 14726–14731. [CrossRef]

24. Dobos, I.; Vörösmarty, G. Inventory-related costs in green supplier selection problems with Data Envelopment Analysis (DEA). *Int. J. Prod. Econ.* **2019**, *209*, 374–380. [CrossRef]

25. Wu, M.-Q.; Zhang, C.-H.; Liu, X.-N.; Fan, J.-P. Green Supplier Selection Based on DEA Model in Interval-Valued Pythagorean Fuzzy Environment. *IEEE Access* **2019**, *7*, 108001–108013. [CrossRef]

26. Shuai, J.-J.; Wu, W.-W. Evaluating the influence of E-marketing on hotel performance by DEA and grey entropy. *Expert Syst. Appl.* **2011**, *38*, 8763–8769. [CrossRef]

27. Liu, W.; Wang, Y.-M.; Lyu, S. The upper and lower bound evaluation based on the quantile efficiency in stochastic data envelopment analysis. *Expert Syst. Appl.* **2017**, *85*, 14–24. [CrossRef]

28. Charnes, A.; Cooper, W.W. Deterministic Equivalents for Optimizing and Satisficing under Chance Constraints. *Oper. Res.* **1963**, *11*, 18–39. [CrossRef]

29. Khodabakhshi, M.; Asgharian, M.; Gregoriou, G.N. An input-oriented super-efficiency measure in stochastic data envelopment analysis: Evaluating chief executive officers of US public banks and thrifts. *Expert Syst. Appl.* **2010**, *37*, 2092–2097. [CrossRef]

30. Sengupta, J.K. Data envelopment analysis for efficiency measurement in the stochastic case. *Comput. Oper. Res.* **1987**, *14*, 117–129. [CrossRef]

31. Sueyoshi, T. Stochastic DEA for restructure strategy: An application to a Japanese petroleum company. *Omega* **2000**, *28*, 385–398. [CrossRef]

32. Wu, C.; Li, Y.; Liu, Q.; Wang, K. A stochastic DEA model considering undesirable outputs with weak disposability. *Math. Comput. Model.* **2013**, *58*, 980–989. [CrossRef]

33. Li, F.; Zhu, Q.; Chen, Z.; Xue, H. A balanced data envelopment analysis cross-efficiency evaluation approach. *Expert Syst. Appl.* **2018**, *106*, 154–168. [CrossRef]

34. Roll, Y.; Cook, W.D.; Golany, B. Controlling Factor Weights in Data Envelopment Analysis. *IIE Trans.* **1991**, *23*, 2–9. [CrossRef]

35. Kao, C.; Hung, H.-T. Data envelopment analysis with common weights: The compromise solution approach. *J. Oper. Res. Soc.* **2005**, *56*, 1196–1203. [CrossRef]

36. Charnes, A.; Cooper, W.; Huang, Z.; Sun, D. Polyhedral Cone-Ratio DEA Models with an illustrative application to large commercial banks. *J. Econ.* **1990**, *46*, 73–91. [CrossRef]

37. Andersen, P.; Petersen, N.C. A Procedure for Ranking Efficient Units in Data Envelopment Analysis. *Manag. Sci.* **1993**, *39*, 1261–1264. [CrossRef]

38. Sexton, T.R.; Silkman, R.H.; Hogan, A.J. Data envelopment analysis: Critique and extensions. *New Dir. Program Eval.* **1986**, *1986*, 73–105. [CrossRef]

39. Doyle, J.; Green, R. Efficiency and cross-efficiency in DEA: Derivations, meanings and uses. *J. Oper. Res. Soc.* **1994**, *45*, 567–578. [CrossRef]

40. Liu, J.P.; Fang, S.C.; Chen, H.Y. Multiplicative data envelopment analysis cross-efficiency and stochastic weight space acceptability analysis for group decision making with interval multiplicative preference relations. *Inf. Sci.* **2020**, *514*, 319–332. [CrossRef]

41. Liu, J.; Song, J.; Xu, Q.; Tao, Z.; Chen, H. Group decision making based on DEA cross-efficiency with intuitionistic fuzzy preference relations. *Fuzzy Optim. Decis. Mak.* **2018**, *18*, 345–370. [CrossRef]

42. Liu, H.-H.; Song, Y.-Y.; Yang, G.-L. Cross-efficiency evaluation in data envelopment analysis based on prospect theory. *Eur. J. Oper. Res.* **2019**, *273*, 364–375. [CrossRef]

43. Jradi, S.; Ruggiero, J. Stochastic data envelopment analysis: A quantile regression approach to estimate the production frontier. *Eur. J. Oper. Res.* **2019**, *278*, 385–393. [CrossRef]

44. Charnes, A.; Cooper, W.; Rhodes, E. Measuring the efficiency of decision making units. *Eur. J. Oper. Res.* **1978**, *2*, 429–444. [CrossRef]

45. Wu, D.; Lee, C.-G. Stochastic DEA with ordinal data applied to a multi-attribute pricing problem. *Eur. J. Oper. Res.* **2010**, *207*, 1679–1688. [CrossRef]

46. Wu, D. Performance evaluation: An integrated method using data envelopment analysis and fuzzy preference relations. *Eur. J. Oper. Res.* **2009**, *194*, 227–235. [CrossRef]

7

Toward a Quadruple Bottom Line: Social Disclosure and Financial Performance in the Banking Sector

Francesco Manta [1,*]**, Annunziata Tarulli** [1]**, Domenico Morrone** [1] **and Pierluigi Toma** [2]

[1]   Faculty of Economics and Management, LUM Jean Monnet University, 70010 Casamassima (Ba), Italy; Tarulli.phdstudent@lum.it (A.T.); morrone@lum.it (D.M.)

[2]   Department of Economics and Management, University of Salento, 73100 Lecce, Italy; pierluigi.toma@unisalento.it

*   Correspondence: manta.phdstudent@lum.it

Abstract: The present study aims to analyze the existence of a possible significant relationship between social disclosure and financial performance in banking institutions. This phenomenon was analyzed by considering the percentage of female executives on boards, and the implementation of the equal opportunity policy when it was applied. We used a sample of 61 banks from European Union countries (between 2015–2017), and sampling was environmental, social, or governance (ESG)-driven in order to capture the effect of non-financial disclosure provided by Bloomberg. A cross-section econometric model was built in order to examine the relationship between the percentage of female directors on boards and the equal opportunity policy. Both the independent variables of banks and performance indicators were adopted as dependent variables. Our study provides empirical evidence that while there is a lack of efficiency and performance when boards are fragmented, the enactments of equal opportunity policies create a good reputation for the firm and the positive performance of staff. The study aims to contribute to the ongoing debate on social sustainability and on the phenomenon of the glass ceiling, and provides political and entrepreneurial implications.

Keywords: CSP–CFP relationship; banking sustainability; glass ceiling; board composition; equal opportunity policy

---

1. Introduction

Banking institutions play a crucial role in the accomplishment of the United Nations' Sustainable Development Goals (SDGs) [1]. Their activity goes beyond a mere matter of ecological impact tout-court, being a zero-emission industrial sector—as is considered in several empirical analyses on corporate sustainability [2,3]. Their indirect impact on sustainable activities is, instead, noticeable: for example, they can boost clean energy projects, invest in green bonds, offer green credit funds, and finance virtuous social initiatives [4]. All these practices, as discussed in the literature, enhance the corporate social performance (CSP) of the banking institutions, which has a positive impact on their corporate financial performance (CFP) [5]. Other relevant outcomes are attributed to the increased corporate social responsibility (CSR) practices [6] as an instrument to improve both corporate reputation and firm performance [7].

The impact of banking activity on external stakeholders is significantly positive when CSR commitment occurs, and it is increased by continuous social reporting through the years [8,9]. The current literature contains several studies on how banks incentivize sustainable development [10,11]. This field of study outlines, in particular, the efforts carried out by financial institutions, as well as concentrating on the single area of action, such as environmental credit risk management, sustainable project finance, impact investing, and banking loans activities [12,13]. Recent studies have focused on how banks implement their strategies to promote sustainability in an enlarged perspective, while assessing internal operations, too [14].

This is quite an unexplored field, which opens a wide range of questions that ought to be answered. An interesting dimension is provided by the role of environmental, social, or governance (ESG) disclosure, which is the clarification of sustainability strategies carried on by firms—even banking institutions.

In the last few years, new literature in the field of corporate sustainability has emerged, introducing the field of study to new issues regarding the inclusion of corporate governance sustainability. This includes research on the Triple Bottom Line (TBL) concept [15] in the new framework of the Quadruple Bottom Line [16–20]. The long perpetrated financial crisis that occurred in 2007—the consequences of which are still felt in the current economy—showcased several issues, especially regarding social and governance problems [21]. This is because, while banks might only have an indirect effect on the environment, as the financial industry is a zero-emission sector, social and governance issues are critical concerns regarding corporate sustainability in the banking sector. The global financial crisis (GFC) sparked a debate on the role of corporate governance strategies because they had a crucial impact on the catastrophic outcome of the GFC [22,23]. One of the most recently debated issues on corporate governance improvement is gender diversity on boards. As a result, many financial firms have recently begun to adopt gender balance strategies. The EU Commission has approved several directives to satisfy the gender balance for non-executive directors, which should come into force in 2020 for listed companies [24]. The European Parliament has also approved a regulation recommendation for large firms to increase the number of under-represented gender members (usually women) in non-executive roles to at least 40% of the total directors in order to reduce the existing gender gap. While these are positive examples, such as the Norwegian model [25], the results are far from being satisfactory. This is due to an ongoing debate regarding the real effects of board diversity on corporate governance issues and on operative results. Jensen and Anderson, among others, have stated that more visible diversity is a positive outcome of efficient resource utilization and better innovative product and strategy development, which includes a cross-sectional mix of competences and backgrounds [26,27]. Furthermore, regarding social and corporate governance issues, Farag and Mallin argue that a larger presence of women on boards is helpful in the reduction of the phenomenon of the "glass ceiling" [21] and provides higher incomes for women in high directive positions. Moreover, Putnam takes a different position, arguing that the costs of communication and coordination due to diversity could overcome the benefits [28].

The aim of the paper is to investigate the impact of two dimensions of ESG disclosure—specifically, the governance and the social components—by analyzing variables of gender diversity in board composition and the effort of the firm in actively adopting non-discrimination policies on financial performance. We do this using a sample of 61 banks from the 28 countries of the European Union between 2015 and 2017. The result of the empirical analysis shows a negative relationship between diverse board composition and operative result measures, and a positive relationship between equal opportunity policies and return on equity.

The choice of banking sector is related to the strategical importance of the latter in financing sustainable economic development [1–4]. Therefore, it is crucial to investigate whether the banking sector has sought more environmentally sustainable goals since the GFC. The current literature shows that gender diversity in board composition and the adoption of non-discrimination policies are a clear example in this perspective [29,30]. Therefore, this contribution could be a further observation regarding the sustainable path of a strategic area.

The theoretical contribution of this paper is consistent with other studies that argue that the cohesion and homogeneity of boards have a positive impact on financial performance in the presence of highly profitable activities. The reason for this is the reduction of assertiveness in the decision-making process. Moreover, it suggests that, according to the results, the social component related to non-discrimination policies has a positive impact on market capitalization, implying a positive reaction from the market towards adequate social policies for inclusion.

The paper is composed as follows: in Section 2, we explore the current literature on sustainability strategies in banking and the gender and inclusion policies related to corporate governance strategies. Then, in Section 3, we discuss the methodology and sampling used, matching them with the hypothesis formulation. The final sections, Sections 4–6, consist of an in-depth examination of results, a discussion on the results, the political implications, and the conclusions.

2. Theoretical Background and Hypotheses Development

The goal of the present work is to contribute to the analysis of the social and governance dimensions of sustainability, focusing on the bank sector. The intent is to observe if the two aforementioned performances could affect the CFP of banking institutions. Gender diversity and non-discrimination policies are present in the ESG disclosure, indicating the sustainable commitment inside the CSP framework.

The following literature review was developed by taking the main contributions present in the scientific context into account, starting with an overview of the research area from a firm perspective, notwithstanding the industrial sector. Indeed, a specific focus on banks, which has only recently gained much interest [29,30], could not prospect the whole phenomenon in its entirety.

With regard to the CSP, it is important to underline the presence of a full-bodied literature from different decades and, until now, there has not been a convergent definition that can define precise borders [31]. Surely, this difficulty is connected with the different contexts where CSP could be addressed but, taking into account some of the last definitions, it could be represented as a snapshot of a firm's overall social performance at a particular point in time—a summary of the firm's aggregate social posture [32]. In addition, evaluating the strong relationship with CSR, CSP could also be a firm's overall social performance at a specific point in time, which can be ascribed to its investments in CSR over time [33,34]. Following the strong debate about CSP, it is simple to comprehend the absence of a univocal perspective on the relationship between Corporate Social Performance (CSP) and Corporate Financial Performance (CFP), too [35,36]. In regards to the two concepts, surely, CSP deserves more attention, having more intangible borders. However, even if there is a lack of a common definition/vision, scholars, considering the growing importance of this topic, are concretely involved in this field of research, aiming to highlight all possible dynamics.

Some authors represented the difficult work to make the contributions provided by previous researches comparable [37,38], as well as the theoretical problems in the empirical analysis [39], since it is difficult, for example, to define a standard metric to measure the corporate social performance [40]. Therefore, the need to redefine this topic in accordance with a common outlook is clear [41] when identifying a wide approved methodology [42]. Recent papers have still tried to update this framework, introducing new points of view as the difference among developed and emerging market firms [43], the results coming from different industry contexts [44] or the mediation role of national institutions [45]. The aim of this work is to further contribute to the exploration of the growing dimensions in terms of attention, social performances, indicating gender representation—that is, the percentage of female directors on boards—and the equal opportunity polices provided in the bank sector. This perspective, related to gender composition on the boards, was recently opened to highlight a specific aspect of CSP [46,47]. This is applied to the Corporate Sustainability theory regarding all firms. Thus, there are four main hypotheses regarding the relationship between Corporate Social Performance (CSP) and Corporate Financial Performance (CFP):

- Negative relationship: in line with what Milton Friedman asserted, "a company that opts to invest in Social Responsibility would produce significantly higher costs than the profits that can be generated" [48]. Consequently, such "wrong" investments would cause a deterioration in the level of economic and financial indicators;

- Positive relationship: according to this hypothesis, there would be a direct and growing relationship between CSP and CFP, even if their causal relationship seemed doubtful. It can be argued that good financial performances generate good social performances: in fact, more profitable companies, when allocating profits, would have more resources for programs focused on social responsibility than less profitable enterprises. On the other hand, investing socially also affects the level of reputation, which indirectly generates a return in terms of cash flow. This is confirmed by the work of Barnett and Salomon [49], which suggests that companies with a higher CSR index perform better than those with a lower score [50];

- Mixed relationship: the connection between CSP and CFP may not always be constant over time and can take the form of a "U" or a "U-inverted" depending on the commitment undertaken. The "U" relationship can be explained by the hypothesis that, for a company, the implementation of a Corporate Social Responsibility program could initially generate an increase in costs compared to revenues (and, therefore, a decrease in terms of economic performance–financial), a trend that reverses in the medium to long term. On the contrary, the U-inverted relationship would suggest the existence of an "excellent" level, beyond which, being socially responsible in the long term would not produce any economic advantage; for instance, Wu and Shen and Farag and Mallin stated the existence of a mixed relationship between CSP and CFP in the financial sector [5,21];

- No relationship: according to the latter hypothesis, CSP and CFP should be assumed as two separate variables that are unrelated to each other and, consequently, corporate social responsibility would have no impact on the profitability of companies [51].

Focusing on the bank industry, there is a need to prioritize social and governance dimensions since, as is commonly known, banks are zero-emission firms themselves, so the environmental disclosures might have an indirect impact on the bank's performance by enhancing reputation, social engagement, and green credit line access [4,5]. Governance and social measures, such as diversity and inclusion, are reported to have an impact on the financial performance of banks [52,53]. The importance given to the board composition of banks is justified and proven by several studies: De Andres, for example, underlines some features, such as size and independence, compared to boards in non-financial institutions [54]. Another relevant issue in the field deals with the importance of bank governance strategies and their accountability to other stakeholders: it is argued that bank performance trends have a spillover effect on other banks worldwide [55].

The different composition of boards, carrying various peculiar experiences and backgrounds, has increased in importance among scholars [21,55–58]. In this field, a famous definition by Ingley and Van der Valt describes diversity in boards as the complex of different values, backgrounds, and expertise owned by each member, and this affects the very decision-making process of the board itself [59]. Earlier, Kosnik provided a relevant distinction between board membership and outside board members, arguing that diversity in board members helps to reduce narrow-mindedness on the board's executive proposals: i.e., the decision making process may result in easing the cross-section of different backgrounds [56].

A relevant aspect concerns gender diversity and the existence of a possible effect of the presence of women within the boards of banks. Research on social psychology stresses the relevance of diversity in regard to the existing differences between male and female directors in better applying their skills in some specific fields: women, for example, are likely to have a legal, HR, or public relations background in respect to their male counterparts, who are more focused on operations and marketing [60].

Research in this field focuses on the concept of "value in diversity" and states that the presence of women on boards shall have a positive effect in representing the various interest of shareholders, enhancing discussion [61] and transparency [62].

The phenomenon of the "glass ceiling" is a crucial issue when speaking about female employment, which, of course, reflects its effects at all levels. Women, therefore, are pushed to invest more effort into their work and to gain more capabilities in order to reach higher positions, as they are supposed to be more industrious and talented [63].

The empirical testing of board diversity when profiling, in particular, gender diversity has been investigated in several studies [21,55,64–66]. A comprehensive analysis of the literature operated by Terjesen et al. recognizes more than 400 publications on this subject, showing that the degree of the presence of women as directors and its impact on performance has no clear or univocal results [67]. Some of them have a positive relationship, while others show negative effects, giving an undetermined conclusion of the issue.

The diversity–performance nexus has spare and ambiguous outcomes, and a real postulation of the phenomenon has not occurred. This could be due to the discrepancies in sample sizes, periods of time, and industries, in addition to the econometrics problems—e.g., endogeneity [21]. Most of the studies are empirical and depend on a series of variables that might radically influence the results in each specific case. Indeed, very few studies rely on the empirical results obtained by the analysis of financial firms [21,55], and most of them count on the outcomes of studies made on non-financial firms, proving both positive [68,69] and negative effects [70,71].

Indeed, there is not unanimous consent about the positive or negative effects of board gender diversity on financial performance, which turns out to be impacted by several conditions that are arbitrary and country-specific [72]. Therefore, the first hypothesis can be formulated either as affirmative or null. We opted for an affirmative form:

Hypothesis 1 (H1). *The percentage of female executives generates a positive effect on the single variables of corporate financial performance.*

A parallel but similar approach might be followed when we speak about diversity in terms of ethnicity and disability. Inclusion and non-discrimination policies have become a central topic for many countries, so that regulatory frameworks have been introduced by the government in order to guarantee equal opportunities for every demographic category. Beyond the legal and ethical context, the managerial one must also deal with this relevant issue. There is a massive literature review that applies the concept of inclusion, examining, from different aspects, firms and their performance [73]. Most of the analyses focus on corporate non-financial disclosure, since CSR reporting has a strong relevance for what regards the company's reputation and its corporate social performance [74–77].

Literature has only recently focused on non-financial reporting over the last fifteen years [78,79], and CSR has become a relevant aspect in firm reputation and strategic asset [64]. Moreover, a few studies have focused on the relation between CSP and CFP as result of voluntary non-financial reporting, subordinating reporting to a positive financial performance [78]. The reason for considering the literature on non-financial reporting is due to the nature of the considered variable, since the equal opportunity policy is a parameter that is voluntarily adopted by firms. Beyond the gender diversity aspect, as already disclosed in the previous paragraph, some studies focus on the composition of boards, considering various demographic groups, including nationality [55] and ethnic groups [80,81]. To the best of our knowledge, there is no specific literature on the effect of the adoption of equal opportunity and non-discrimination policies on corporate financial performance. Erhardt et al. argue of the existence of a positive relationship between cultural diversity (as a complex of observable and non-observable features) and organizational performance in US firms [80]. Therefore, our second hypothesis aims to capture the effect of the adoption of equal opportunity policies voluntarily disclosed by banks on the variables of corporate financial performance, so we formulated it as follows:

Hypothesis 2 (H2). *The equal opportunity policy generates a positive effect on the single variables of corporate financial performance.*

3. Materials and Methods

3.1. Sampling and Variable Definition

The methodology adopted to build the analyzed sample can be defined "ESGs-driven"—i.e., driven by the bank's environmental, social, and governance disclosure score presence provided by Bloomberg LP. In fact, the increasing interest in non-financial disclosure by society, the government, and NGOs led companies to shed light on their sustainable practices. However, even though ESG variables have been adopted for more than a decade, the Bloomberg LP database presents missing data for several banks and years. Nevertheless, this study offers new insights into researching the effects of female boardroom participation and the adoption of the equal opportunity policy on the financial performance of banks engaged in non-financial disclosure. The sample identification followed several passages, and data was collected from different databases, using new variables. Therefore, the sample was unique. Using the BankFocus database [82], a first database was set up by looking for all the banks active in the time period of 2011–2017 that belonged to the European Union geographic region. This first database had 5251 active banks. However, it was almost useless for the purpose of the study, because there were no indicators on the BankFocus database that could express the commitment of the banks in terms of sustainability. To address this shortcoming, these indicators were found on the Bloomberg database, obtaining—after eliminating the banks without ESG data—a database made up of 152 active banks that presented ESG data over the reference as a final output [83].

As mentioned above, the dataset, characterized by such a large time period (2011–2017), was missing some data, which proved it, therefore, to be unbalanced. It was concluded that a shorter time period, ranging from 2015 to 2017, could be more significant for the purposes of the analysis. Considering all these facts, the final database was obtained, which appeared to be composed of 61 active banks belonging to the European Union geographic area (28 countries). The distribution of the sample was totally unbiased and not proportional to the total number of banks in each country, and it was interesting to observe the matter of communication of CSR activities.

At this point, some considerations of the sample size were necessary. The sample had the maximum size available for the databases from which the data were extracted [82,83]. In addition, there were two factors that made the sample homogeneous: first, although the European Union geographic area did not have a banking union, it certainly had common rules and exchanges; second, in a fragmented dataset, the two largest shares (i.e., Italy and the United Kingdom) did not exceed 10%–15% of the total. Therefore, they were to be considered low shares. In addition, Italy and the United Kingdom had diametrically opposed behaviours, equilibrating their effects. Lastly, statistical tests were carried out with dummy variables for both countries: the dummy was not significant.

The variables present in the database could be divided into three main categories:

- Corporate Financial Performance variables (i.e., return on average assets (ROAA), return on average equity (ROAE), ln Market Capitalization, Tobin's Q, and ln Net Interest Income), taken as dependent variables;
- Corporate Social Performance variables (percentage of female executives and the equal opportunity policy), taken as independent variables;
- Control variables (e.g., Leverage, Net Interest Margin, Loan Dept, Cost to Income ratio, Coverage, and ln Total Assets).

Dependent variables were described as follows:

The ROAA (acronym for Return on Average Assets) is an indicator to assess the profitability of a company's assets and is used by banks and financial institutions as a tool to estimate financial performance [5,51,53,71,84–89]. ROAA indicates the efficiency of a company in using its resources and is very useful for analyzing similar companies belonging to the same sector. This accounting-based performance measure is able to record the ability of banks to generate income based on the total capital employed: that is, returns generated from the assets financed by the banks [84,88].

ROAE (acronym for Return on Average Equity), on the other hand, is a profitability indicator aimed at measuring the performance of a company by evaluating the profit obtained on the basis of the money invested in the capital. A high ROAE identifies a favourable situation, in which the company generates more income for each unit of equity [5,51,53,71,84,88].

Market Capitalization represents the assessment made by the market on the value of a company. The capitalization is estimated by multiplying the number of existing shares by the market price of a specific trading day (Schroders). The variable was used in its logarithmic value [53].

For testing the market value of the firm, we used Tobin's Q, which is intended as the ratio between current market value and the rate of replacement of the value of the firm [53,72,86,87,90–93]. The market value of the firm is the sum of common shareholders' investment in a company, the stocks, and the sum of long and short-term debt. The replacement value of firm assets is the sum of gross property and short-term assets [2]. Tobin's Q reflects the market's expectations for future performances rather than accounting-based measures; thus, it represents a good proxy for the firm's competitive advantages [69,94,95].

The Net Interest Income is calculated as the difference between the revenues generated by the company assets and the charges related to the liabilities. Based on a bank's specific assets and liabilities (i.e., whether at a fixed or variable rate), the Net Interest Income may be more or less sensitive to changes in interest rates [5,88]. The variable was used in its logarithmic value.

The independent variables were extracted from the Bloomberg database, and were described as follows:

The Percentage of Female Executives (field ID: ES291, mnemonic: PERCENTAGE_OF_FEMALE_EXECUTIVES) provides the number of female managers as a percentage of the total managers [53,69,72,85,87,93], starting from the end of the tax year where available, or, otherwise, to the last financial year to date. Executives are defined by the company or the individuals who make up the executive committee or management committee/board or equivalent. The field is part of the group of ESG fields (environmental, social, or governance).

The Equal Opportunity Policy (field ID: ES058, mnemonic: EQUAL_OPPORTUNITY_POLICY) variable relates to equal treatment legislation and indicates whether the company has actively committed itself to guarantee the non-discrimination of any demographic group. This may be in the form of an equal opportunity policy as described by the company. The field is part of the group of ESG fields (environmental, social, or governance). Being a dichotomous dummy variable, the field reported '1' for Yes or '0' for No [83]. As far as we know, there is no use of this variable in the current literature.

The control variables referred to the financial characteristics of the banks:

Leverage refers to the ratio between the book value of the equity and total liabilities [53,84], detecting the capital adequacy of the bank [5,96].

Net Interest Margin (NIM) refers to the ratio of net interest income to earning assets, which is the sum of total investment earning interest or dividends and net loans [53,71,97], expressed as a percentage. The net interest margin reflects the business the bank engages in. For example, higher margins are associated with banks with more lending operations instead of those that engage in advising and mediating. Hence, this variable is not reflecting performance, but merely revealing the source of the bank's revenues [97].

The Total Asset variable identifies the size of the company and represents a determinant of social and financial performance [98]. The variable is expressed in its logarithmic value (ln Total Asset) [5,53,84–86].

Further control variables were the ones proposed by Wu and Shen among the bank's main characteristics [5]: Loan Dept—that is, the ratio between net loans and deposits and short-term funding [86,99]; Cost to Income ratio, expressed as a percentage of the ratio of total operating expenses to operating revenues [51]; and, lastly, Coverage, calculated as the ratio between loan loss reserves to gross loans [53,84].

All the variables are resumed as follows in Table 1.

Table 1. Variable description (own elaboration).

Variables	Description	Source
DEPENDENT VARIABLES		
CFP Variables		
ROAA	Return on Average Assets %	BankFocus
	(Profit or loss after tax/Total assets) × 100	
ROAE	Return on Average Equity %	BankFocus
	(Profit or loss after tax/Total equity) × 100	
ln Market Capitalization	log (Market Capitalization)	BankFocus *
Tobin's Q	(Market capitalization/Total assets)	BankFocus
ln Net Interest Income (expense)	log (Net Interest income)	BankFocus *
	(Total interest income—Total interest expense)	
INDEPENDENT VARIABLES		
CSP Variables		
Percentage of female executives	Number of female directors, as percentage of the total board members	Bloomberg
Equal opportunity policy	States if firms are involved in equal opportunity policies, such as inclusion and non-discrimination	Bloomberg
CONTROL VARIABLES		
Leverage	(Equity/Liabilities)	BankFocus
Net Interest Margin (NIM) %	(Net interest income (expense)/Total earning assets) × 100	BankFocus
Loan Dept	(Net Loans/Deposits & Short-Term Funding)	BankFocus *
Cost to Income (efficiency) ratio	(Total operating expenses/Operating revenues) × 100	BankFocus
Coverage	(Loan loss reserves/Gross Loans)	BankFocus *
ln Total Asset	log (Total Assets)	BankFocus *

* Own elaboration from BankFocus data.

3.2. Econometric Model

Once we defined the considered variables, we built our econometric models. Even if the study included a timeline of three years, we considered the average value of each variable, being the time period short enough not to register sensible variations during the period. The model, therefore, has been identified as a cross-section analysis, split into five different regression analyses per each hypothesis, resulting in ten different analyses. The model adopted is validated by previous work [53,86,100]. A linear regression model was used to test our hypotheses with some modifications (i.e., introducing new variables and different combinations between the independent and control ones).

The first hypothesis ought to be studied according to the following econometric models:

- $ROAA_i = \beta_0 + \beta_1 LEVERAGE_i + \beta_2 \text{ NET INTEREST MARGIN}_i + \beta_3 \text{ LOAN DEPT}_i + \beta_4 \text{ COST TO INCOME}_i + \beta_5 COVERAGE_i + \beta_6 \text{ ln TOTAL ASSET}_i + \beta_7 \text{ Percentage of Female Executives}_i + \varepsilon_i$

- $ROAE_i = \beta_0 + \beta_1 LEVERAGE_i + \beta_2 \text{ NET INTEREST MARGIN}_i + \beta_3 \text{ LOAN DEPT}_i + \beta_4 \text{ COST TO INCOME}_i + \beta_5 COVERAGE_i + \beta_6 \text{ ln TOTAL ASSET}_i + \beta_7 \text{ Percentage of Female Executives}_i + \varepsilon_i$

- $\text{ln MarketCapitalisation}_i = \beta_0 + \beta_1 LEVERAGE_i + \beta_2 \text{ NET INTEREST MARGIN}_i + \beta_3 \text{ LOAN DEPT}_i + \beta_4 \text{ COST TO INCOME}_i + \beta_5 COVERAGE_i + \beta_6 \text{ ln TOTAL ASSET}_i + \beta_7 \text{ Percentage of Female Executives}_i + \varepsilon_i$

- $\text{Tobin's Q}_i = \beta_0 + \beta_1 LEVERAGE_i + \beta_2 \text{ NET INTEREST MARGIN}_i + \beta_3 \text{ LOAN DEPT}_i + \beta_4 \text{ COST TO INCOME}_i + \beta_5 COVERAGE_i + \beta_6 \text{ ln TOTAL ASSET}_i + \beta_7 \text{ Percentage of Female Executives}_i + \varepsilon_i$

- $\text{ln Net Interest Income}_i = \beta_0 + \beta_1 LEVERAGE_i + \beta_2 \text{ NET INTEREST MARGIN}_i + \beta_3 \text{ LOAN DEPT}_i + \beta_4 \text{ COST TO INCOME}_i + \beta_5 COVERAGE_i + \beta_6 \text{ ln TOTAL ASSET}_i + \beta_7 \text{ Percentage of Female Executives}_i + \varepsilon_i$

So as the following ones, built in order to verify Hypothesis 2:

- $ROAA_i = \beta_0 + \beta_1 \text{ LEVERAGE}_i + \beta_2 \text{ NET INTEREST MARGIN}_i + \beta_3 \text{ LOAN DEPT}_i + \beta_4 \text{ COST TO INCOME}_i + \beta_5 COVERAGE_i + \beta_6 \text{ ln TOTAL ASSET}_i + \beta_7 \text{ Equal Opportunity Policy}_i + \varepsilon_i$

- $ROAE_i = \beta_0 + \beta_1 LEVERAGE_i + \beta_2$ NET INTEREST MARGIN$_i$ + β_3 LOAN DEPT$_i$ + β_4 COST TO INCOME$_i$ + $\beta_5 COVERAGE_i$ + β_6 ln TOTAL ASSET$_i$ + β_7 Equal Opportunity Policy$_i$ + ε_i
- ln MarketCapitalisation$_i$ = $\beta_0 + \beta_1 LEVERAGE_i + \beta_2$ NET INTEREST MARGIN$_i$ + β_3 LOAN DEPT$_i$ + β_4 COST TO INCOME$_i$ + $\beta_5 COVERAGE_i$ + β_6 ln TOTAL ASSET$_i$ + β_7 Equal Opportunity Policy$_i$ + ε_i
- Tobin's Q$_i$ = $\beta_0 + \beta_1 LEVERAGE_i + \beta_2$ NET INTEREST MARGIN$_i$ + β_3 LOAN DEPT$_i$ + β_4 COST TO INCOME$_i$ + $\beta_5 COVERAGE_i$ + β_6 ln TOTAL ASSET$_i$ + β_7 Equal Opportunity Policy$_i$ + ε_i
- ln Net Interest Income$_i$ = $\beta_0 + \beta_1 LEVERAGE_i + \beta_2$ NET INTEREST MARGIN$_i$ + β_3 LOAN DEPT$_i$ + β_4 COST TO INCOME$_i$ + $\beta_5 COVERAGE_i$ + β_6 ln TOTAL ASSET$_i$ + β_7 Equal Opportunity Policy$_i$ + ε_i

3.3. Correlation Matrix

Table A1 (Appendix A) illustrates the correlation matrix of the variables under study. Overall, the analysis highlighted good direct linear correlations between independent social performance variables and dependent variables in Market Capitalization and Net Interest Income. Furthermore, the independent variable Percentage of Female Executives had a medium/low correlation with the dependent variable ROAE. In detail:

- The independent variable Percentage of Female Executives, on the one hand, was the only one with a direct, albeit modest (0.25) linear correlation with the dependent variable ROAE.
- The independent variable Equity Opportunity Policy, on the other hand, was characterized by small correlations, which were not significant for the purposes of the analysis.

Considering the other dependent variables, there were no relevant significant values.

4. Results

Table 2 reports the results relating to Hypothesis 1, which investigated the possible existence of a positive relationship between the independent variable Percentage of Female Executives and the dependent variables relating to financial performance.

Table 2. Hypothesis 1 (H1) test (own elaboration).

	ROAA	ROAE	ln Market Capitalization	Tobin's Q	ln Net Interest Income
Intercept	2.9760 ***	61.5837 ***	−6.1653 ***	0.4262 ***	−6.1960 ***
	(0.7370)	(11.1582)	(0.8540)	(0.1164)	(0.8842)
Percentage of Female Executives	−0.0074 *	−0.0116	−0.0025	−0.0013 **	0.0059
	(0.0041)	(0.0619)	(0.0047)	(0.0006)	(0.0049)
Leverage	0.0728 ***	−0.3016	0.0971 ***	0.0068 **	0.0976 ***
	(0.0203)	(0.3074)	(0.0235)	(0.0032)	(0.0244)
Net Interest Margin (NIM)	0.1322 ***	1.5963 ***	0.0641 **	0.0288 ***	0.0439
	(0.0234)	(0.3538)	(0.0271)	(0.0037)	(0.0280)
Loan Dept	−0.0038 ***	−0.0698 ***	−0.0034 ***	−0.0003 *	−0.0004
	(0.0011)	(0.0159)	(0.0012)	(0.0002)	(0.0013)
Cost to Income	−0.0186 ***	−0.3548 ***	−0.0119 ***	0.0002	−0.0102 **
	(0.0035)	(0.0531)	(0.0041)	(0.0006)	(0.0042)
Coverage	−0.1074 ***	−1.1165 ***	−0.0869 ***	−0.0078 ***	0.0088
	(0.0092)	(0.1390)	(0.0106)	(0.0015)	(0.0110)
ln Total Assets	−0.0678 *	−1.1635 **	0.8395 ***	−0.0208 ***	1.0844 ***
	(0.0346)	(0.5240)	(0.0401)	(0.0055)	(0.0415)
Observ.	61	61	61	61	61
R-square	0.8660	0.7528	0.9140	0.8950	0.9376
Adj. R-square	0.8483	0.7202	0.9027	0.8811	0.9293

Significance: * $p < 0.10$; ** $p < 0.05$; *** $p < 0.01$; standard error value is in brackets.

The output of the regressions carried out on the sample identified a negative and significant relationship between the percentage of women holding top positions and two variables of financial performance: ROAA (characterized by low significance with p-value less than 10% and with $\beta = -0.0074$) and Tobin's Q (characterized by an average significance with the p-value less than 5% and with $\beta = -0.0013$). No further significant relationships emerged with the other dependent variables.

These results showed that H1 was not confirmed and differed from other contributions in literature. In fact, Carter, Simkins, and Simpson (2003) documented a positive relationship between the gender and ethnic diversity of the board and corporate performance, as proxied by Tobin's Q [85]. In addition, other studies validate this positive relationship [69,84,93,101], finding evidence that is consistent with the idea that the market values workplace diversity. However, the model results did not allow us to foster the major literature in the field, but made us reflect on the reasons behind it. In fact, some explanations of the negative influence of females on ROAA and Tobin's Q may be down to differences in country and organizational culture, family dynamics (that might constrain the board's active participation), gender pay gaps, obstacles in hiring or reaching top management charge for women, etc. These are some suggestions for further investigation.

Moreover, Table 3 reports the results relating to the second hypothesis, in which we investigated the possible existence of a positive relationship between the independent variable Equal Opportunity Policy and the dependent variables relating to financial performance. The use of the dichotomous dummy variable, relating to the adoption of equal opportunity policies, gave a positive outcome for the dependent variable ROAE (characterized by a high significance with a p-value lower than 1% and with $\beta = 9.4735$). Therefore, equal opportunity policies only influence profitability on invested capital.

Table 3. Hypothesis 2 (H2) test (own elaboration).

	ROAA	ROAE	ln Market Capitalization	Tobin's Q	ln Net Interest Income
Intercept	2.1768 ***	53.9355 ***	−6.2132 ***	0.3058 **	−5.7088 ***
	(0.7290)	(10.4717)	(0.8402)	(0.1176)	(0.8787)
Equal Opportunity Policy	0.4687	9.4735 **	−0.1397	0.0521	−0.1744
	(0.2895)	(4.1591)	(0.3337)	(0.0467)	(0.3490)
Leverage	0.0825 ***	−0.2162	0.0980 ***	0.0083 **	0.0914 ***
	(0.0202)	(0.2915)	(0.0234)	(0.0033)	(0.0245)
Net Interest Margin (NIM)	0.1251 ***	1.4877 ***	0.0651 **	0.0279 ***	0.0474
	(0.0237)	(0.3406)	(0.0273)	(0.0038)	(0.0286)
Loan Dept	−0.0036 ***	−0.0673 ***	−0.0035 ***	−0.0003	−0.0005
	(0.0011)	(0.0152)	(0.0012)	(0.0002)	(0.0013)
Cost to Income	−0.0174 ***	−0.3417 ***	−0.0119 ***	0.0004	−0.0109 **
	(0.0035)	(0.0508)	(0.0040)	(0.0006)	(0.0043)
Coverage	−0.1045 ***	−1.1246 ***	−0.0855 ***	−0.0073 ***	0.0062
	(0.0090)	(0.1297)	(0.0104)	(0.0015)	(0.0109)
ln Total Assets	−0.0635 *	−1.3281 ***	0.8466 ***	−0.0193 ***	1.0772 ***
	(0.0345)	(0.4955)	(0.0398)	(0.0056)	(0.0416)
Observ.	61	61	61	61	61
R-square	0.8643	0.7747	0.9139	0.8890	0.9362
Adj. R-square	0.8464	0.7450	0.9025	0.8743	0.9277

Significance: * $p < 0.10$; ** $p < 0.05$; *** $p < 0.01$; standard error value is in brackets.

According to the results that were previously shown, H2 was confirmed. To the best of our knowledge, to date, no contribution in literature has used this variable, so there are no previous works capable of validating our study. This makes our results so unique that they will certainly be the subject of future research.

5. Discussion

The debate on diversity has dramatically risen in the last two decades, focusing on both institutional and entrepreneurial concern on social issues. Some disruptive events, such as the financial crisis, have contributed to the boost of policies and strategic decisions regarding these aspects.

This paper aimed to investigate the relationship between gender diversity and financial performance, and the influence of the possible existence of equal opportunity policies within banking institutions in a relatively recent period. The choice, besides the necessity to compose a balanced dataset, was strategic to observe the differences and possible comparisons with previous periods that were temporally closer to the financial crisis. This choice gave the opportunity to settle the consequences of social policies adopted after 2007.

As the analyses conducted show, the impact of the percentage of female executives on boards had a slightly negative effect on ROAA and the Tobin's Q. These were the only two variables in which the relationship was significant. It did not have any significant relationship with the others. This result is consistent with the analysis of Farag and Mallin, who observed a decrease in the financial performance of banks when the composition of boards started to have a diffused fragmentation [21]. This is justified as a lack of efficiency in decisional processes, which, of course, condition the pace of the firm (financial or non-financial), impacting negatively on the financial performance. This is particularly evident in the relationship with Tobin's Q, which is a measure of the replacement of assets. A decrease or, worse, a lack in efficiency obviously impacts the rate of replacement and the market value of the firm. This is even more evident when dealing with banking institutions, in which the replacement of financial assets happens at a faster pace than any other firm.

The second step of the analysis revealed a very positive relationship between the equal opportunity policy variable and the ROAE. This was a very interesting result, which, of course, had a twofold consideration: on one hand, we observed internally a possible positive effect on operations, as the productivity of employees and their positive effect on process in terms of cross-section decisional processes and strategy composition increased; on the other hand, we observed the possible improvement of the bank's reputation in the market, increasing their return on equity. This is a novelty in literature, according to the extant literature, which qualifies as a relevant contribution to the present study.

The non-significance of the other relationships with the two considered variables gives an interesting perspective: the indicators used in the analyses are probably not the ones influenced by the social dimension of sustainability in financial firms. There are, indeed, numerous indicators that contribute to the debate of non-financial disclosure in all the production sectors in a precious way.

6. Conclusions

The aim of the study was to find a relationship between CSP—namely, social and governance sustainability components and CFP in the banking sector. According to the results obtained, H1 has been rejected, as negative significant relationships were found between the percentage of females on boards and ROAA and Tobin's Q, while H2 has been confirmed as a significant positive relationship between the adoption of equal opportunity policies and the ROAE was found. The research contributed to the study of sustainable behaviour in the banking sector, aiming for the pursuit of the SDGs of the United Nations, with a specific focus on the social and governance disclosure, which is often underestimated in comparison with the conventional aspect of the TBL scheme. Social sustainability has numerous implications both in the firm's theory and governmental political action. The most discussed topic regards the popular "glass ceiling," a wage gap between men and women that, nowadays, must be overcome. Some scholars proved the need for women to make more effort to reach higher positions, so a further step in policy ought to be made in this way, allowing equal salaries between sexes. The impact on the financial performance is crucial for the firm's activity, both on decisional and operative levels. The values collected show, first of all, that many institutions are still far from being involved in equal opportunity policies, so an effort from governments in boosting the adoption of social policies is still needed. Based on the results, our study has obtained suggestive results, but a lot could still be done.

Of course, the study has some limitations that might be overcome. First, the study, for lack of data, ought to be completed on a larger sample by selecting other variables from other databases. ESG disclosure is, actually, not a very spread practice, yet, with regard to the banking sector, as observed through the sampling strategy. This, of course, implies different possible outcomes. The sampling strategy may be conducted notwithstanding the existence of the interest of banks in ESG reporting activities, which is itself a relevant deduction. Contrarily, we based our sampling starting from the Bloomberg assessment of ESG disclosure in financial firms. Another limitation is given by the short time interval, which is also linked to the lack of data. Future studies might consider the opportunity to enlarge the sample gradually on both the population and time interval aspects, as the information disclosure on the sustainability aspect improves itself as a good practice on the firm side. Possible future analyses may consider the time effect on the variables.

Author Contributions: Conceptualization, F.M. and A.T.; methodology, P.T.; software, P.T.; validation, P.T., A.T., and F.M.; formal analysis, D.M.; investigation, F.M.; resources, A.T.; data curation, A.T.; writing—original draft preparation, F.M.; writing—review and editing, A.T. and P.T; visualization, F.M.; supervision, D.M.; project administration, F.M. All authors have read and agreed to the published version of the manuscript.

Acknowledgments: The authors thank Andrea Santaloia for the proof-reading activity.

Appendix A

Table A1. Correlation matrix (own elaboration).

	ROAA	ROAE	Ln NII	Ln Total Assets	NIM	Leverage	Ln MktCapitalisation	Tobin's q	Coverage	Percentage of Female Executives	Equal Opportunity Policy
ROAA	1										
ROAE	0.777	1									
Ln NII	−0.263	−0.302	1								
Ln Total Assets	−0.445	−0.310	0.911	1							
NIM	0.597	0.127	−0.038	−0.321	1						
Leverage	0.512	0.004	−0.184	−0.494	0.761	1					
Ln MktCapitalization	−0.036	0.033	0.836	0.864	−0.111	−0.281	1				
Tobin's q	0.774	0.338	−0.295	−0.494	0.884	0.749	−0.162	1			
Coverage	−0.412	−0.593	0.058	−0.076	0.190	0.399	−0.305	−0.010	1		
Percentage of Female Executives	0.044	0.253	−0.163	−0.131	−0.113	−0.194	−0.097	−0.110	−0.312	1	
Equal Opportunity Policy	0.036	0.143	0.173	0.193	0.004	−0.105	0.160	−0.004	−0.002	−0.077	1

References

1. Avrampou, A.; Skouloudis, A.; Iliopoulos, G.; Khan, N. Advancing the sustainable development goals: Evidence from leading European banks. *Sustain. Dev.* **2019**, *27*, 743–757. [CrossRef]
2. Russo, A.; Pogutz, S. Eco-efficiency vs Eco-effectiveness. Exploring the link between GHG emissions and firm performance. In *Academy of Management Proceedings*; Academy of Management: Briarcliff Manor, NY, USA, 2009; Volume 2009, pp. 1–6. [CrossRef]
3. Perrini, F.; Russo, A.; Tencati, A.; Vurro, C. Going beyond a long-lasting debate: What is behind the relationship between corporate social and financial performance. *EABIS Res. Proj. Work. Pap.* **2009**. Available online: http://citeseerx.ist.psu.edu/viewdoc/download?doi=10.1.1.542.519&rep=rep1&type=pdf (accessed on 28 November 2019).
4. Zimmermann, S. Same but Different: How and Why Banks Approach Sustainability. *Sustainability* **2019**, *11*, 2267. [CrossRef]
5. Wu, M.W.; Shen, C.H. Corporate social responsibility in the banking industry: Motives and financial performance. *J. Bank. Financ.* **2013**, *37*, 3529–3547. [CrossRef]
6. Dell'Atti, S.; Trotta, A.; Iannuzzi, A.P.; Demaria, F. Corporate social responsibility engagement as a determinant of bank reputation: An empirical analysis. *Corp. Soc. Responsib. Environ. Manag.* **2017**, *24*, 589–605. [CrossRef]
7. Forcadell, F.J.; Aracil, E. European banks' reputation for corporate social responsibility. *Corp. Soc. Responsib. Environ. Manag.* **2017**, *24*, 1–14. [CrossRef]
8. Buallay, A. Is sustainability reporting (ESG) associated with performance? Evidence from the European banking sector. *Manag. Environ. Qual. Int. J.* **2019**, *30*, 98–115. [CrossRef]
9. Nobanee, H.; Ellili, N. Corporate sustainability disclosure in annual reports: Evidence from UAE banks: Islamic versus conventional. *Renew. Sustain. Energy Rev.* **2016**, *55*, 1336–1341. [CrossRef]
10. Weber, O.; Remer, S. *Social Banks and the Future of Sustainable Finance*; Taylor & Francis: Abingdon, UK, 2011; Volume 64.
11. EFB. Available online: https://www.ebf.eu/priorities/financing-growth/sustainable-finance/ (accessed on 7 April 2020).
12. Meena, R. Green banking: As initiative for sustainable development. *Glob. J. Manag. Bus. Stud.* **2013**, *3*, 1181–1186.
13. Biswas, N. Sustainable green banking approach: The need of the hour. *Bus. Spectr.* **2011**, *1*, 32–38.
14. Özçelik, F.; Öztürk, B.A. Evaluation of banks' sustainability performance in Turkey with grey relational analysis. *Muhasebe Ve Finansman Dergisi* **2014**. Available online: http://mufad.org.tr/journal-/attachments/article/743/11.pdf (accessed on 28 November 2019).
15. Elkington, J. Partnerships from cannibals with forks: The triple bottom line of 21st-century business. *Environ. Qual. Manag.* **1998**, *8*, 37–51. [CrossRef]
16. Hawkes, J. *The Fourth Pillar of Sustainability: Culture's Essential Role in Public Planning*; Common Ground: Melbourne, Australia, 2001.
17. Caust, J. Putting the "art" back into arts policy-making: How arts policy has been "captured" by the economists and the marketers. *Int. J. Cult. Policy* **2003**, *9*, 51–63. [CrossRef]
18. Lawler III, E.E. Sustainable effectiveness and organization development: Beyond the triple bottom line. *OD Pract.* **2014**, *46*, 65–67.
19. Alibašić, H. Measuring the sustainability impact in local governments using the quadruple bottom line. *Int. J. Sustain. Policy Pract.* **2017**, *13*, 37–45. [CrossRef]
20. Budsaratragoon, P.; Jitmaneeroj, B. Measuring causal relations and identifying critical drivers for corporate sustainability: The quadruple bottom line approach. *Meas. Bus. Excell.* **2019**, *23*, 292–316. [CrossRef]
21. Farag, H.; Mallin, C. Board diversity and financial fragility: Evidence from European banks. *Int. Rev. Financ. Anal.* **2017**, *49*, 98–112. [CrossRef]
22. Kirkpatrick, G. The corporate governance lessons from the financial crisis. *OECD J. Financ. Mark. Trends* **2009**, *1*, 61–87. [CrossRef]
23. Erkens, D.H.; Hung, M.; Matos, P. Corporate governance in the 2007–2008 financial crisis: Evidence from financial institutions worldwide. *J. Corp. Financ.* **2012**, *18*, 389–411. [CrossRef]
24. European Commission. Proposal for a Directive of the European Parliament and of the Council on Improving the Gender Balance among Non-Executive Directors of Companies Listed on Stock Exchanges

and Related Measures. Brussels, 14.11.2012; COM 2012 614 final, 2012/0299 (COD). Available online: https://eur-lex.europa.eu/legal-content/EN/TXT/?uri=CELEX%3A52012PC0614 (accessed on 12 December 2019).

25. Mateos de Cabo, R.M.; Gimeno, R.; Nieto, M.J. Gender Diversity on European Banks' Board of Directors. *J. Bus. Ethics* **2012**, *109*, 145–162. [CrossRef]

26. Jensen, M.C. The Modern Industrial Revolution, Exit, and the Failure of Internal Control Systems. *J. Financ.* **1993**, *48*, 831–880. [CrossRef]

27. Anderson, C.; Reeb, D.M.; Upadhyay, A.; Zhao, W. The Economics of Director Heterogeneity. *Financ. Manag.* **2011**, *40*, 5–38. [CrossRef]

28. Putnam, R.D. Pluribus Unum: Heterogeneity and Community in the Twenty-First Century-The 2006 Johan Skytte Prize Lecture. *Scand. Political Stud.* **2007**, *30*, 137–174. [CrossRef]

29. Birindelli, G.; Iannuzzi, A.P.; Savioli, M. The impact of women leaders on environmental performance: Evidence on gender diversity in banks. *Corp. Soc. Responsib. Environ. Manag.* **2019**, *26*, 1485–1499. [CrossRef]

30. Birindelli, G.; Dell'Atti, S.; Iannuzzi, A.P.; Savioli, M. Composition and activity of the board of directors: Impact on ESG performance in the banking system. *Sustainability* **2018**, *10*, 4699. [CrossRef]

31. Wood, D.J. Corporate social performance revisited. *Acad. Manag. Rev.* **1991**, *16*, 691–718. [CrossRef]

32. Barnett, M.L. Stakeholder influence capacity and the variability of financial returns to corporate social responsibility. *Acad. Manag. Rev.* **2007**, *32*, 794–816. [CrossRef]

33. Orlitzky, M.; Siegel, D.S.; Waldman, D.A. Strategic corporate social responsibility and environmental sustainability. *Bus. Soc.* **2011**, *50*, 6–27. [CrossRef]

34. Sila, I. Investigating changes in TQM's effects on corporate social performance and financial performance over time. *Total Qual. Manag. Bus. Excell.* **2020**, *31*, 210–229. [CrossRef]

35. Marom, I.Y. Toward a unified theory of the CSP–CFP link. *J. Bus. Ethics* **2006**, *67*, 191–200. [CrossRef]

36. Kong, Y.; Antwi-Adjei, A.; Bawuah, J. A systematic review of the business case for corporate social responsibility and firm performance. *Corp. Soc. Responsib. Environ. Manag.* **2020**, *27*, 444–454. [CrossRef]

37. Griffin, J.J.; Mahon, J.F. The corporate social performance and corporate financial performance debate: Twenty-five years of incomparable research. *Bus. Soc.* **1997**, *36*, 5–31. [CrossRef]

38. Perrini, F.; Russo, A.; Tencati, A.; Vurro, C. Deconstructing the relationship between corporate social and financial performance. *J. Bus. Ethics* **2011**, *102*, 59–76. [CrossRef]

39. Wood, D.J.; Jones, R.E. Stakeholder mismatching: A theoretical problem in empirical research on corporate social performance. *Int. J. Organ. Anal.* **1995**, *3*, 229–267. [CrossRef]

40. Masip, M. Desperately Seeking a Standard Metric for Corporate Social Performance. In *Non-Financial Disclosure and Integrated Reporting: Practices and Critical Issues*; Emerald Publishing Limited: Bingley, UK, 2020.

41. Roman, R.M.; Hayibor, S.; Agle, B.R. The relationship between social and financial performance: Repainting a portrait. *Bus. Soc.* **1999**, *38*, 109–125. [CrossRef]

42. Callan, S.J.; Thomas, J.M. Corporate financial performance and corporate social performance: An update and reinvestigation. *Corp. Soc. Responsib. Environ. Manag.* **2009**, *16*, 61–78. [CrossRef]

43. Ting, I.W.K.; Azizan, N.A.; Bhaskaran, R.K.; Sukumaran, S.K. Corporate Social Performance and Firm Performance: Comparative Study among Developed and Emerging Market Firms. *Sustainability* **2020**, *12*, 26. [CrossRef]

44. Tuppura, A.; Arminen, H.; Pätäri, S.; Jantunen, A. Corporate social and financial performance in different industry contexts: The chicken or the egg? *Soc. Responsib. J.* **2016**, *12*, 672–686. [CrossRef]

45. Shin, J.Y.; Moon, J.J.; Kang, J. How Do National Institutions Moderate the Relationship between CSP and CFP? In *Academy of Management Proceedings*; Academy of Management: Briarcliff Manor, NY, USA, 2015; Volume 2015, p. 10995. [CrossRef]

46. Dunn, P.; Sainty, B. The relationship among board of director characteristics, corporate social performance and corporate financial performance. *Int. J. Manag. Financ.* **2009**, *5*, 407–423. [CrossRef]

47. Boulouta, I. Hidden connections: The link between board gender diversity and corporate social performance. *J. Bus. Ethics* **2013**, *113*, 185–197. [CrossRef]

48. Friedman, M. The Social Responsibility of Business is to Increase its Profits. *N. Y. Time Mag.* **1970**, *13*, 173–178.

49. Barnett, M.L.; Salomon, R.M. Does it pay to be really good? Addressing the shape of the relationship between social and financial performance. *Strateg. Manag. J.* **2012**, *33*, 1304–1320. [CrossRef]

50. Han, J.J.; Kim, H.J.; Yu, J. Empirical study on relationship between corporate social responsibility and financial performance in Korea. *Asian J. Sustain. Soc. Responsib.* **2016**, *1*, 61–76. [CrossRef]

51. Soana, M.G. The relationship between corporate social performance and corporate financial performance in the banking sector. *J. Bus. Ethics* **2011**, *104*, 133. [CrossRef]

52. Carter, D.A.; D'Souza, F.; Simkins, B.J.; Simpson, W.G. The gender and ethnic diversity of US boards and board committees and firm financial performance. *Corp. Gov. Int. Rev.* **2010**, *18*, 396–414. [CrossRef]

53. Bussoli, C.; Conte, D.; Letorri, G.; Barone, M. Does It Pay to Be Sustainable? Evidence from European Banks. *Int. J. Bus. Manag.* **2019**, *14*, 128–146. [CrossRef]

54. De Andres, P.; Vallelado, E. Corporate governance in banking: The role of the board of directors. *J. Bank. Financ.* **2008**, *32*, 2570–2580. [CrossRef]

55. García-Meca, E.; García-Sánchez, I.M.; Martínez-Ferrero, J. Board diversity and its effects on bank performance: An international analysis. *J. Bank. Financ.* **2015**, *53*, 202–214. [CrossRef]

56. Kosnik, R.D. Effects of board demography and directors' incentives on corporate greenmail decisions. *Acad. Manag. J.* **1990**, *33*, 129–150.

57. Hillman, A.J.; Cannella, A.A.; Paetzold, R.L. The resource dependence role of corporate directors: Strategic adaptation of board composition in response to environmental change. *J. Manag. Stud.* **2000**, *37*, 235–256. [CrossRef]

58. Hillman, A.J.; Cannella, A.A.; Harris, I.C. Women and racial minorities in the boardroom: How do directors differ? *J. Manag.* **2002**, *28*, 747–763. [CrossRef]

59. Ingley, C.B.; Van der Walt, N.T. Board configuration: Building better boards. *Corp. Gov.* **2003**, *3*, 5–17. [CrossRef]

60. Zelechowski, D.D.; Bilimoria, D. Characteristics of women and men corporate inside directors in the US. *Corp. Gov. Int. Rev.* **2004**, *12*, 337–342. [CrossRef]

61. Letendre, L. The dynamics of the boardroom. *Acad. Manag. Exec.* **2004**, *18*, 101–104. [CrossRef]

62. Upadhyay, A.; Zeng, H. Gender and ethnic diversity on board and corporate information environment. *J. Bus. Res.* **2014**, *67*, 2456–2463. [CrossRef]

63. Eagly, A.H.; Carli, L.L. The female leadership advantage: An evaluation of the evidence. *Leadersh. Q.* **2003**, *14*, 807–834. [CrossRef]

64. Farrell, K.A.; Hersch, P.L. Additions to corporate boards: The effect of gender. *J. Corp. Financ.* **2005**, *11*, 85–106. [CrossRef]

65. Matsa, D.; Miller, A. A female style in corporate leadership? Evidence from quotas. *Am. Econ. J. Appl. Econ.* **2013**, *5*, 136–169. [CrossRef]

66. Goergen, M.; Renneboog, L. Inside the board room. *J. Corp. Financ.* **2014**, *28*, 1–5. [CrossRef]

67. Terjesen, S.; Sealy, R.; Singh, V. Women Directors on Corporate Boards: A Review and Research Agenda. *Corp. Gov. Int. Rev.* **2009**, *17*, 320–337. [CrossRef]

68. Carter, D.A.; Simkins, B.J.; Simpson, W.G. Corporate governance, board diversity, and firm value. *Financ. Rev.* **2003**, *38*, 33–53. [CrossRef]

69. Campbell, K.; Vera, A.M. Gender Diversity in the Boardroom and Firm Financial Performance. *J. Bus. Ethics* **2008**, *83*, 435–451. [CrossRef]

70. Ryan, M.K.; Haslam, A.S. The Glass Cliff: Evidence that Women are Over-Represented in Precarious Leadership Positions. *Br. J. Manag.* **2005**, *16*, 81–90. [CrossRef]

71. Pathan, S.; Faff, R. Does Board Structure in Banks Really Affect their Performance? *J. Bank. Financ.* **2013**, *37*, 1573–1589. [CrossRef]

72. Ferreira, D. Board Diversity: Should We Trust Research to Inform Policy? *Corp. Gov. Int. Rev.* **2015**, *23*, 108–111. [CrossRef]

73. Arvidsson, S. Disclosure of non-financial information in the annual report: A management-team perspective. *J. Intellect. Cap.* **2011**, *12*, 277–300. [CrossRef]

74. Bonsón, E.; Bednárová, M. CSR reporting practices of Eurozone companies. *Revista De Contabilidad.* **2015**, *18*, 182–193. [CrossRef]

75. Ellerup Nielsen, A.; Thomsen, C. Reporting CSR—What and how to say it? *Corp. Commun. Int. J.* **2007**, *12*, 25–40. [CrossRef]

76. Perrini, F. The practitioner's perspective on non-financial reporting. *Calif. Manag. Rev.* **2006**, *48*, 73–103. [CrossRef]

77. Tschopp, D.; Huefner, R.J. Comparing the evolution of CSR reporting to that of financial reporting. *J. Bus. Ethics* **2015**, *127*, 565–577. [CrossRef]

78. Carnevale, C.; Mazzuca, M.; Venturini, S. Corporate social reporting in European banks: The effects on a firm's market value. *Corp. Soc. Responsib. Environ. Manag.* **2012**, *19*, 159–177. [CrossRef]

79. Stolowy, H.; Paugam, L. The expansion of non-financial reporting: An exploratory study. *Account. Bus. Res.* **2018**, *48*, 525–548. [CrossRef]

80. Erhardt, N.L.; Werbel, J.D.; Shrader, C.B. Board of director diversity and firm financial performance. *Corp. Gov. Int. Rev.* **2003**, *11*, 102–111. [CrossRef]

81. Brammer, S.; Millington, A.; Pavelin, S. Gender and Ethnic Diversity among UK Corporate Boards. *Corp. Gov. Int. Rev.* **2007**, *15*, 393–403. [CrossRef]

82. BankFocus Database. Available online: https://banks.bvdinfo.com (accessed on 21 June 2019).

83. Bloomberg Database on ESG. Available online: https://www.bloomberg.com/impact/products/esg-data (accessed on 30 June 2019).

84. Bussoli, C.; Conte, D. The "Virtuous Circle" Between Corporate Social Performance and Corporate Financial Performance in the European Banking Sector. *Int. J. Bus. Adm.* **2018**, *9*, 80–92. [CrossRef]

85. Bukar, M.; Ahmed, A. Effect of board of directors' gender diversity on financial performance of deposit money banks in Nigeria. *Glob. J. Appl. Manag. Soc. Sci.* **2020**, *18*, 9–19.

86. Adams, R.B.; Ferreira, D. Gender diversity in the boardroom. European Corporate Governance Institute. *Financ. Work. Pap.* **2004**, *57*, 30.

87. Ali, S.; Zhang, J.; Naseem, M.A.; Ahmad, F. Moderating Role of Ownership in Relationship between CSRD And Firm Performance. *J. Dev. Areas.* **2019**, *53*. [CrossRef]

88. de Koning, C. Reputation, Corporate Social Responsibility, and Financial Performance of Banks. *MaRBLe* **2018**, *1*. [CrossRef]

89. Simpson, W.G.; Kohers, T. The link between corporate social and financial performance: Evidence from the banking industry. *J. Bus. Ethics* **2002**, *35*, 97–109. [CrossRef]

90. Dowell, G.; Hart, S.; Yeung, B. Do Corporate Global Environmental Standards Create or Destroy Market Value? *Manag. Sci.* **2000**, *46*, 1059–1074. [CrossRef]

91. King, A.; Lenox, M.J. Does It Really Pay to Be Green? An Empirical Study of Firm Environmental and Financial Performance. *J. Ind. Ecol.* **2001**, *50*, 105–116. [CrossRef]

92. Konar, S.; Cohen, M.A. Does the Market Value Environmental Performance? *Rev. Econ. Stat.* **2001**, *83*, 281–289. [CrossRef]

93. Cardillo, G.; Onali, E.; Torluccio, G. Does gender diversity on banks' boards matter? Evidence from public bailouts. *J. Corp. Financ.* **2020**, 101560. [CrossRef]

94. Demsetz, H.; Villalonga, B. Ownership structure and corporate performance. *J. Corp. Financ.* **2001**, *7*, 209–233. [CrossRef]

95. Wernerfelt, B.; Montgomery, C.A. Tobin's q and the importance of focus in firm performance. *Am. Econ. Rev.* **1988**, 246–250.

96. Waddock, S.A.; Graves, S.B. The corporate social performance–financial performance link. *Strateg. Manag. J.* **1997**, *18*, 303–319. [CrossRef]

97. Gonenc, H.; Scholtens, B. Responsibility and Performance Relationship in the Banking Industry. *Sustainability* **2019**, *11*, 3329. [CrossRef]

98. Ullmann, A.A. Data in search of a theory: A critical examination of the relationships among social performance, social disclosure, and economic performance of US firms. *Acad. Manag. Rev.* **1985**, *10*, 540–557.

99. Gangi, F.; Mustilli, M.; Varrone, N.; Daniele, L.M. Corporate Social Responsibility and Banks' Financial Performance. *Int. Bus. Res.* **2018**, *11*, 42–58. [CrossRef]

100. Carnevale, C.; Mazzuca, M. Sustainability report and bank valuation: Evidence from European stock markets. *Bus. Ethics A Eur. Rev.* **2014**, *23*, 69–90. [CrossRef]

101. Ellis, K.M.; Keys, P.Y. Stock returns and the promotion of workforce diversity. *J. Financ. Econ.* **2003**, *18*, 17–34.

8

Industry-Specific and Macroeconomic Determinants of Non-Performing Loans: A Comparative Analysis of ARDL and VECM

Changjun Zheng [1], Probir Kumar Bhowmik [1,*] and Niluthpaul Sarker [2]

[1] School of Management, Huazhong University of Science and Technology, Wuhan 430074, China;
zhchjun@hust.edu.cn

[2] Department of Accounting and Information Systems, Jagannath University, Dhaka 1100, Bangladesh;
niluthpaul@yahoo.com

* Correspondence: probir9012@gmail.com

Abstract: With the growth of an economy, the banking industry expands and the competitiveness becomes intense with the increased number of banks in the economy. The objective of this research was to discover the influence of industry-specific and macroeconomic determinants of non-performing loans (NPLs) in the entire banking system of Bangladesh. We performed an analysis for the period from 1979 to 2018 by an autoregressive distributed lag (ARDL) model and checked the robustness of the results in the vector error correction (VEC) model. The outcomes of this research suggest that both industry-specific and macroeconomic factors influence NPLs significantly. Among the industry-specific determinants, bank loan growth, net operating profit, and deposit rates negatively impact NPLs with statistical significance while bank liquidity and lending rates have a significant positive affiliation with NPLs. Gross domestic product (GDP) growth and unemployment, among the macroeconomic variables, have a negative connection with NPLs. Whereas, domestic credit and exchange rates have a significant positive association with NPLs. The contribution of this research is that the outcomes found by means of econometric models can be used for predicting and measuring NPLs in upcoming years, not only for Bangladesh but also for developing and emerging economies. Individual banks, as well as the banking sector, by and large, can get a guideline from this research.

Keywords: loan expansion; GDP; NPL; ARDL; VECM; Johansen test of co-integration; unit root

JEL Classification: C58; G21; E60

---

1. Introduction

Non-performing loans (NPLs) are a threat to sustainable development for developing countries. NPLs are considered as the major indicator of the financial stability of the banking sector. In developing economies, banks usually take greater risks to increase their market shares. With the chance of higher profit, risk increases, which ultimately results in non-performing loans [1]. NPLs have become a matter of concern for all countries in the world, and as a prerequisite to reinstate the functionality of financial markets, NPLs and its determinants should be addressed carefully [2]. Ex-post credit risk as an element of non-performing loans is one of the key features of the banking system and economic downturn [3,4]. Banks at risk of failing have significant proportions of NPLs in their portfolios of loans before collapse or financial distress [5].

Banks are intertwined and operate with other banks in a competitive industry. Hence, the bad performance of a bank can affect the entire sector and cause performance variability and create fear. Degraded loan quality creates threats of systemic risk, fear and causes drainage of deposits, a hindrance to financial intermediation, and finally, slows down the pace of economic growth and development. Non-performing loans play a crucial part in creating a poor performance of banks [6,7]. Banks are restrained from an intermediation role to the real economy and economic growth by NPLs [8,9]. NPLs have been termed "financial pollution" for their negative impacts on the economy [10,11]. If regulatory authorities implement any policy, the underlying determinants of NPLs should be taken care of first. As per Basel II, a loan unpaid for more than 90 days is considered as uncollectible.

After the global financial crunch of 2007 and 2008 followed by the share market scam in 2010 and 2011 in Bangladesh, the country faced financial turbulence in the economy, and the banking sector went through a transition time. Fifteen new banks have received licenses to operate in the economy in the last 10 years, and 11 banks in the last 5 years. At present, a total of 59 banks are operating in the economy. Hence, there is acute competitiveness in the industry.

After 2010, non-performing loans started to increase rapidly (Figure 1). In 2011, they were 2.70 billion US dollars; in 2012, they were 5.09 billion US dollars, and in 2018, breaking all records, they soared up to 13.20 billion US dollars. For a developing country like Bangladesh, it is a matter of concern and a threat to sustainable development.

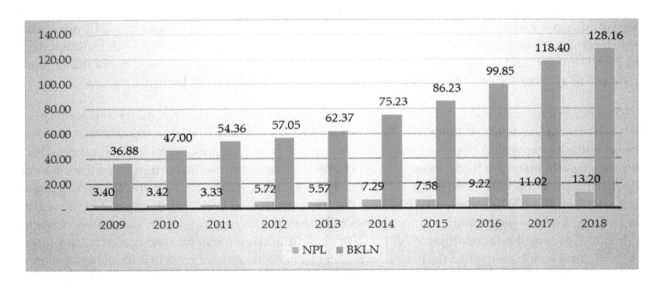

Figure 1. Non-performing loan (NPL) and bank loan (BKLN) growth in Bangladesh (in billion USD); Source: Bangladesh Bank.

The Non-Performing Loan Ratio (NPLR) reached 40.65% in 1998, which is the highest ever in the history of Bangladesh. Although it gradually came down, this was not enough as it had been 10.30% in 2018 (Figure 2). Total banking sector NPLs were around 4% of the total GDP in 2018. This current research examines both industry-specific and macroeconomic components of NPLs of all 59 banks in the economy for the period from 1979 to 2018. In our study, we used data from the whole banking sector using a time series dataset with an annual frequency. This study can be considered as a reference to understand and measure the determinants of NPLs in Bangladesh and for developing countries like Bangladesh. To analyze our dataset, we first used the ARDL model and then by finding co-integration with the variables through the Johansen test of co-integration, we conducted a VEC model. Results found in both the models are analogous, indicating the robustness of the study. To know the stability of the models used in the study, we performed some diagnostic tests.

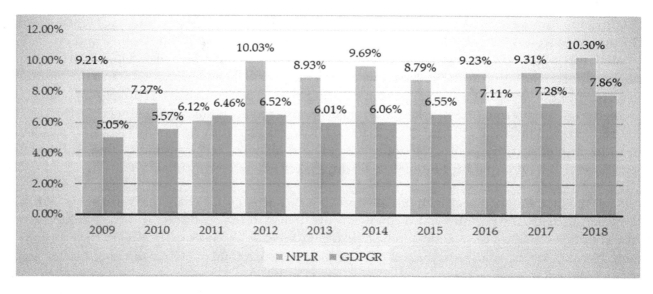

Figure 2. Non-performing loan ratio (NPLR) and gross domestic product growth rate (GDPGR) in Bangladesh; Source(s): Fred and WDI Database.

2. Theoretical Background

During our study, we went through many literary works to know the variables, models, and backgrounds on which research was conducted already. We found that factors of NPLs are broadly categorized into two major sources. The macroeconomic sources are GDP and inflation [2,12], unemployment [8], and real interest rates [13,14] and the industry-specific factors are management efficacy [4,15] and bank size [3,5], which may impact the ability to repay loans.

Researchers have found an affiliation between macroeconomic determinants and loan quality, which is a crucial yardstick of the banking sector's health. Previous findings suggest that bad loans decrease with the expansion of the economy. Borrowers have enough income to repay on time. During economic growth, loans are likely to be approved irrespective of the creditworthiness of the customers while during the economic downturn, NPLs tend to increase (Messai and Jouini 2013). Keeton and Morris (1987) studied 2470 commercial banks in the US from 1979 to 1985, which suggested the regional economy and inferior performance of industries had been the key factors for in loan losses. Espinoza and Prasad [16] found relationships of NPLs with economic advancement, risk aversion, and interest rates. NPL used to increase when there is a decreasing trend in economic growth and an increase in risk aversion and interest rates. Louzis, Vouldis et al. [3] looked into types of loans, i.e., consumer, business, mortgage, etc., to find determinants impelling NPLs. They found that macroeconomic variables, such as gross domestic product, interest rates, unemployment, and public debts, can impact the growth of NPLs.

Skarica [17] found that prime sources of NPLs are the economic (GDP) downturn, lack of employment, and the rate of inflation. In a study in France and Germany, it was found that macroeconomic variables influence NPLs [18]. Researchers also found the French economy to be vulnerable to bank-specific factors compared to Germany. Economic expansion and unemployment is positively associated with the reduction of NPLs. Macroeconomic variables, including unemployment and economic development, significantly influence NPLs while industry-specific variables, such as management skill and risk preferences, have consequences on future NPLs [19].

As our quest for literature went on, we found a good number of industry-specific determinants impacting NPLs, i.e., profitability expressed as return on asset (ROA) or return on equity (ROE), capital size expressed as the capital adequacy ratio (CAR), and performance as managerial efficiency. Of these aspects, ROE and ROA have been used as variables to explain managerial efficiency. Weak credit monitoring and poor control over operating expenses led to decreased cost efficiency, which supports the bad management theorem [5]. The bad management theory is also found by [20] while applying NPL as technical efficiency. Shreds of evidence were found on the "too big to fail" syndrome in the US banking sector and it was also argued that an increase in income negatively impacts NPLs [21]. Cost efficiency also impacts NPLs. Poor management and moral hazards have been positively associated with variations in NPLs. Managerial efficiency as a proxy to ROA has negative connections with NPLs [22]. Podpiera and Weill [4] used cost efficiency to describe management quality to find an underlying relationship with NPLs. They performed Granger causality tests to show the unconditional connection of inefficiency to NPLs. Louzis, Vouldis et al. [3] using dynamic panel data found management quality along with GDP, unemployment, interest rate, and public debt are the determinants of NPLs. In a very recent study (2019) on the banking system structure of Bangladesh, Barun Kumar Dey [23] found that poor follow-up of loans after disbursement and lack of willingness to write off bad loans are the root causes that cause NPLs to increase. He also argued that NPLs limit lending capacity, the trickle-down effect of which slows down economic growth in the long run. Also, a high level of NPLs leads to higher requirements of loan loss provisioning, which in turn affects ROA and ROE and creates a threat for solvency and liquidity. Finally, NPLs change the nature risk preferences of the managers that leads to a higher cost of funds and less efficiency.

Vardar and Özgüler [24] found the presence of a steady and long-run affiliation between non-performing loans, macroeconomic variables, and bank-specific factors. Inflation and unemployment were found to be positively and significantly associated with NPLs. Bardhan and Mukherjee [25] found results supporting the 'bad management hypothesis' predicting negative future relationships with NPAs (non-performing assets). They used performance as a proxy for managerial efficiency. They also found capital adequacy ratio (CAR) requirements had an impact on the NPAs of banks. According to their research, large banks have more default rates compared to smaller ones.

Rajan, Bardhan, and Mukherjee [25,26] identified that future NPLs are related to past earnings and increases in profit can reduce NPLs. They also explained that managers could manipulate their power to alter credit policies to inflate current earnings, change the terms of the loan, and relax the conditions, which may lead to bad loans. Using the data of 129 Spanish banks from 1993 to 2003 García-Marco and Robles-Fernández [27] found that higher ROEs had been the key reason to boost risk and higher default rates. ROE has positive associations with elevated NPLs [28].

Changes in credit management policy, loan interest rates, fees, and commissions are also other determinants of NPLs. GDP and ROA have a negative impact while unemployment and interest rates have a positive impact on NPLs [14]. In a study in the United States, it was found that elevated interest rates and superfluous lending as internal aspects and economic conditions as external aspects have a significant positive connection to NPLs [29]. Structural differences between countries can create differences in the efficiency of banks as well [30].

Kjosevski [31] conducted sector-wise research and found NPLs of both the enterprise and household were negatively sensitive to profitability, loan growth, and better economic conditions while banks' solvency and unemployment were positively correlated. The authors of [19] examined NPLs determinants in the Eurozone and, like past examinations, found bank-specific and macroeconomic elements had a remarkable impact clarifying variations in NPLs [32,33].

We found researches on Bangladesh covering a research period of 5 to 20 years. A synopsis is given in Table 1.

Table 1. Empirical studies related to Bangladesh.

Author(s)	Data and Methodology	Findings
[34]	Panel data: 2003 to 2014 of NBFI; Regression and correlation;	Loan growth, firm size, and broad money have statistical significance with NPLs. The researcher found NPL ratio has significant relationships neither with GDP nor with Inflation. The study has been conducted on Non-Banking Financial Intuitions (NBFI).
[35]	Panel data: 2010–2014 Simple linear regression	NPLs have positive connections to Net Interest Margin (NIM), inefficiency ratio and aggregate deposit while CAR, solvency ratio, and aggregate credit have a negative relationship with NPLs.
[36]	Primary data: 50 respondents; Secondary data: 2011 to 2015 five commercial banks; Linear regression	Non-performing loan ratio negatively influences return on assets (ROA) and return on equity (ROE) with statistical significance.
[37]	Data: 2012 to 2016; Linear regression	Excess liquidity can moderately impact non-performing loans.
[38]	Data: 2009 to 2017; Least Square Multiple Regression	Loan loss provision (LLP) has a significant negative relationship with profitability.
[39]	Primary data: 150 respondents; Descriptive statistics.	Researchers found aggressive credit expansion, the willingness of borrowers are the determinants that help increase NPLs.
[40]	Data: 2010 to 2015 for 20 banks; Linear regression	Researchers found a positive relationship of NPLs with Credit-deposit ratio, net interest margin. While the capital adequacy ratio and return on assets negatively impact NPLs. NPLs are also influenced by the sensitive sector's loan and priority sector's loan. Unsecured loans, investment deposit ratio, capital adequacy ratio, return on assets, profit per employee, have a negative control on NPLs.
[41]	Data: 2000 to 2017, ARDL Method	The researcher of this study disagrees with the point that NPLs are impacted by GDP or inflation. Rather he found no statistical relationship using the ARDL method in his research.
[42]	Primary Data: 30 managers and Secondary Data: 1999 to 2008; Linear regression	From survey research, researchers found political influence and economic condition directly cause non-performing loans. In the quantitative analysis, they found that collection efforts by banks also play a significant role in a loan to become bad.
[43]	Data: 2011 to 2015; 8 Islamic banks; Descriptive Statistics; Varimax rotation	This research put light on the Islamic banking system in Bangladesh and found a significant negative liaison with non-performing investments (NPIs) and profitability. Researchers also argued that creditworthiness, employed ethics, and bureaucracy influence NPIs.
[44]	Data: 2008 to 2017 40 banks; Linear Regression	A significant negative relationship between ROA and NPLs has been established by this study.
[45]	Data: 2008 to 2017; 40 banks; Regression	This research suggests that capital adequacy is negatively impacted by the level of non-performing loans in banks of Bangladesh. The researchers also argued that variations in CAR could significantly influence profitability, deposit rates, liquidity, and overall corporate governance of the banks.
[46]	Penal Data: 2004 to 2013; 18 banks; Pearson correlation test, Unit root test, Granger causality test	Researchers in this study found the theoretical establishment of the concept that GDP and inflation impact true in empirical findings. GDP impacts NPLs negatively, while inflation impacts NPLs positively. They also found that interest spread of the banks is inversely related to NPLs.
[47]	Time Series Data: 2008 to 2013; 30 banks; Regression	NPLs have a significant negative relation with the Net profit margin (NPM).
[48]	Panel Data: 1997 to 2012; 259 South Asian banks; Multiple regression, Unit root, GMM	Modal hazard type II and adverse selection problems, poor management of the banks can cause non-performing loans. Researchers also found that the global financial crisis had been another reason for NPLs.
[49]	Data: 2005 to 2014; 22 banks; ADF unit root test, Pearson Correlation Matrix, Granger Causality Test	Through econometric analysis, researchers reached the conclusion that NPLs are negatively associated with inflation rate and interest rate spread. Again, NPLs are positively analogous to GDP and the unemployment rate.
[49]	Data: 2013 to 2017; 30 banks; Pooled OLS Regression	The research findings of this study are that return on assets (ROA) is influenced by the capital adequacy ratio (CAR) and non-performing loans. The suggestion from researchers is that banks should go for timely legal action to collect the bad loans.

3. Research Objective, Methodology, and Data

3.1. Research Objective

The purpose of this study was to identify the significance of industry-specific and macroeconomic determinants of non-performing loans (NPLs) of the banking sector. We conducted our study on a developing country and compared the results in autoregressive distributed lag (ARDL) and vector error correction (VEC) model. The findings of this study will help to understand the underlying causes of NPLs in developing economies and help individual banks to take measures to sustain in the competitive industry.

3.2. Methodology

3.2.1. Model Specification

This paper suggests that NPLs in the economy of Bangladesh depend both on macroeconomic and industry-specific elements. We discuss the functional relationship of the determinants as follows:

$$NPLR_t = f(IS_t, ME_t) \tag{1}$$

where '$NPLR_t$' (non-performing loan ratio) is the dependent determinants of time t; 'IS_t,' comprises the industry-specific determinants for time t; and 'ME_t' contains the macroeconomic determinants causing the banking sector for time t.

To evade the hidden multi-collinearity problem, which can ascend from correlated independent variables, we made two different models. Log was used for all variables, and two regression models were developed as:

Model: 1

$$
\begin{aligned}
InNPLR_t = \beta_0 + {} & \beta_1(InGDPGR)_t \\
& + \beta_2(InCPI)_t + \beta_3(InDOCR)_t + \beta_4(InUNEM)_t + \beta_5(InEXR)_t \\
& + \varepsilon_t
\end{aligned}
\tag{2}
$$

Model: 2

$$
\begin{aligned}
InNPLR_t = \alpha_0 + {} & \alpha_1(InBKLN)_t \\
& + \alpha_2(InLIQ)_t + \alpha_3(InNOP)_t + \alpha_4(InLDR)_t + \alpha_5(InDPR)_t + \varepsilon_t
\end{aligned}
\tag{3}
$$

where "In" indicates the logarithmic form of the variables under investigation. β_0 and α_0 are the coefficients of the constant. $\beta_1, \beta_2, \beta_3, \beta_4, \beta_5, \alpha_1, \alpha_2, \alpha_3, \alpha_4$, and α_5 represent the partial coefficients of the independent variables. Lastly, ε_t represents the stochastic term.

3.2.2. Unit Root Tests

We checked the unit root of the series used in this study using the ADF (Augmented Dickey-Fuller) and PP (Philip and Perron). The null hypothesis indicates that the series have a unit root, whereas the alternative hypothesis suggests stationarity. At $\phi = 1$, variables have a unit root, and at $\phi < 1$, it becomes stationary (Equation (4)). The regression for the ADF test is given below:

$$\Delta Y_t = \Phi Y_{t-1} + \sum_{i=1}^{p} \alpha_i Y_{t-1} + \mu_t. \tag{4}$$

3.2.3. ARDL (Autoregressive Distributed Lag) Model

An autoregressive distributed lag (ARDL) model is an ordinary least square (OLS) used for the time series dataset. ARDL is widely accepted for the co-integration of non-stationary variables corresponding to error-correction (EC) dynamics and it also finds a parametric equation in the EC form [50,51]. An important benefit related to the ARDL modeling approach is that it is useful regardless of regressors being (0) or I (1). Again, ARDL permits a large number of lags. Finally, it accepts the development of a dynamic error correction (EC) model that coordinates short-run elements with the long-run stability, thus losing no long-run data [52–54]. The following equation explains the ARDL model:

$$\Delta Y_t = \beta_0 + \sum_{(i-1)}^{p} \beta_i \Delta Y_{(t_{-i})} + \sum_{(i-1)}^{p} \beta_j \Delta X_{(t-1)} + \lambda_1 Y_{(t-1)} + \lambda_2 X_{(t-1)} + \varepsilon_t \tag{5}$$

3.2.4. Co-Integration Test

As all series were stationary at the first differentiation I (1), Johansen co-integration analysis was used to persuade the convergence in the long run (Johansen and Juselius 1990). The Johansen test recommends the existence of co-integration for at least one co-integrating vector.

3.2.5. Vector Error Correction (Vec) Model

When there are co-integrations among the variables, VECM can be applied to find long-run equilibrium associations. Co-integration is confirmed by Johansen tests for co-integration. We developed the following models to assess the short-run and long-run coefficients of the variables:

$$\begin{aligned}
\Delta lnNPLR_t &= \beta_0 + \sum_{(i-1)}^{n} \beta_1 lnNPLR_{(t_{-j})} + \beta_2 (\Delta lnGDPGR)_{(t-j)} \\
&+ \beta_3 (\Delta lnCPI)_{(t-j)} \\
&+ \beta_4 (\Delta lnDOCR)_{(t-j)} + \beta_5 (\Delta lnUNEM)_{(t-j)} + \beta_6 (\Delta lnEXR)_{(t-j)} + \beta_7 \varepsilon_{(t-1)} + \mu_t
\end{aligned} \tag{6}$$

$$\begin{aligned}
\Delta lnNPLR_t &= \alpha_0 + \sum_{(i-1)}^{n} \alpha_1 lnNPLR_{(t_{-j})} + \alpha_2 (\Delta lnBKLN)_{(t-j)} \\
&+ \alpha_3 (\Delta lnLIQ)_{(t-j)} \\
&+ \alpha_4 (\Delta lnNOP)_{(t-j)} + \alpha_5 (\Delta lnLDR)_{(t-j)} + \alpha_6 (\Delta lnDPR)_{(t-j)} + \beta_7 \varepsilon_{(t-1)} + \mu_t
\end{aligned} \tag{7}$$

The variation in the independent variables is demonstrated by 'Δ', and the error correction term is expressed by '$\varepsilon_{(t-1)}$'. β_1 and α_1 are the speed of adjustment by which short and long-run disequilibrium is adjusted. 'μ_t' is the error term.

3.3. Data

Time series data were tested in this paper. We collected data from the Civil, Environmental, and Infrastructure Engineering (CEIE) databases, the World Development Indicators (WDI) databases, and the Bangladesh Bank (the central bank of Bangladesh) databases. We collected data for 40 years, from 1979 to 2018, of all 59 commercial banks for the last 40 years (Table 2).

Table 2. Variable Definition.

Variables		Interpretation
	lnNPLR	Non-performing loan ratio: Doubtful and bad loans to total loan ratio
Macroeconomic Variables	lnGDPGR	Gross domestic product growth rate: The annual gross domestic product growth rates of Bangladesh.
	lnCPI	Consumer price index: The weighted average prices of consumer goods and services. The year 2006 has been considered a base year.

Table 2. *Cont.*

Variables		Interpretation
	lnDOCR	Domestic Credit: The aggregate of net dues on the central government and dues on other segments of the national economy.
	lnUNEM	Rate of unemployment: The annual unemployment rate in Bangladesh.
	lnEXR	Exchange rates: The annual exchange rates of BDT (currency of Bangladesh) against USD.
	lnBKLN	Banking sector gross loan: The annual aggregate loan disbursement by the entire banking sector of Bangladesh
	lnLIQ	Bank liquidity: The annual liquid asset ratio provided by Bangladesh Bank. Liquid assets include cash and government securities. It measures the capacity of banks to meet their obligations.
Industry-specific Variables	lnNOP	Net operating profit: The annual net operating profit of the entire banking sector.
	lnLDR	Bank lending rate: The rate at which banks lend to their customers. Bangladesh bank provides weighted average lending interest rates of all sorts of loans including short term and long term loans.
	lnDPR	Bank deposit rate: Deposit rates are the weighted average interest rates banks at which collect funds from its customers for investment.

4. Results and Discussion

4.1. Unit Root Test

Unit root tests (Table 3) for macroeconomic variables with ADF found two macroeconomic variables of lnGDPGR and lnEXR found to be stationary at the level I (0) while lnCPI, indoor, and lnUNEM became stationary at first differentiation as indicated by I (1) at the 5% level of confidence. On the other hand, in PP, only lnGDPGR was stationary at the level I (0); all other variables became stationary, except lnCPI, after first differentiation I (1) at a 5% confidence level. lnCPI became stationary at first differentiation I (1) with 10% at the confidence level. Unit root tests (Table 3) for industry-specific variables with ADF found two macroeconomic variables, lnNOP (at 10% confidence level) and lnDPR, to be stationary at the level I (0) while lnBNLN, lnLIQ, and lnLDR became stationary at first differentiation as indicated by I (1) at the 5% level of confidence. On the other hand, in PP, all the variables became stationary after first differentiation I (0).

Table 3. Augmented Dickey-Fuller (ADF) and Philip and Perron (PP) Unit Root Tests.

	Variables	ADF				PP			
		At the Level		First Differentiation		At the Level		First Differentiation	
		T-Statistics	0.10	Test Statistics	0.10	T-Statistics	0.10	T-Statistics	0.10
Macroeconomic variables	lnNPLR	−0.7110	−2.6140	−2.977 **	−2.6160	−1.0060	−10.4800	−28.861 ***	−10.4600
	lnGDPGR	−3.4870 ***	−2.6140	−9.335 ***	−2.6160	−33.898 ***	−10.4800	−63.73 ***	−10.4600
	lnCPI	−0.1780	−2.6140	−3.232 **	−2.6160	−0.913 *	−10.4800	−11.298 ***	−10.4600
	lnDOCR	1.1930	−2.6140	−6.169 ***	−2.6160	0.3640	−10.4800	−34.838 ***	−10.4600
	lnUNEM	−1.7120	−2.6140	−5.145 ***	−2.6160	−2.3000	−10.4800	−45.254 ***	−10.4600
	lnEXR	−3.5180 ***	−2.6140	−4.798 ***	−2.6160	−2.269 **	−10.4800	−30.731 ***	−10.4600
Bank-specificvariables	lnBKLN	−0.3000	−2.6140	−5.661 ***	−2.6160	−0.2920	−10.4800	−32.355 ***	−10.4600
	lnLIQ	−2.4120	−2.6140	−3.213 **	−2.6160	−8.5110	−10.4800	−29.317 ***	−10.4600
	lnNOP	−2.763 *	−2.6140	−5.162 ***	−2.6160	−11.782*	−10.4800	−37.632 ***	−10.4600
	lnLDR	−1.951 ***	−2.6140	−3.76 ***	−2.6160	−4.6360	−10.4800	−24.115 ***	−10.4600
	lnDPR	−3.181 **	−2.6140	−4.51 ***	−2.6160	−8.2240	−10.4800	−20.525 ***	−10.4600

*, **, and *** stand for 10%, 5%, and 1% levels of significance, respectively.

4.2. ARDL Model

We constructed two different models to reduce the multi-collinearity problem among the variables. The co-integration relationship was examined among the determinants (i.e., analyzing the zero hypotheses (H_0: $\lambda = 1$, $\lambda = 2 \ldots \lambda_n = 0$). From the ARDL bounds test, it is apparent that (Table 4) the F statistics are 30.609 and 15.34 for the first and second models. The F values are significant, and in both models, the F statistics are greater than the upper limit. So, we reject the null hypothesis and agree that there are co-integrations among the determinants. Then, we used Akaike's information criterion (AIC) criterion to choose optimal lag lengths for each model (Table 5). For macroeconomic variables, the AIC selects the ARDL (4,3,4,3,2,1) specification and for industry-specific variables (3,3,4,1,4,2). The reason for using AIC is that AIC provides a smaller standard deviation than the Schwarz information criterion (SIC) when running in a model (Pesaran & Pesraran, 1997). We tested both long-run associations and short-run dynamics (error correction model) in the ARDL model (Tables 6 and 7). The coefficients were found to have multiple connotations between NPLs and macroeconomic and industry-specific variables.

Table 4. Pesaran/Shin/Smith (2001) ARDL (Autoregressive Distributed Lag) Bounds Test.

		At 10%		At 5%		At 2.5%		At 1%	
Category	F Statistics	Lower Limit	Upper Limit	Lower Limit	Upper Limit	Lower Limit	Upper Limit	Lower Limit	Upper Limit
Macro-economic	30.609	2.2600	3.3500	2.6200	3.7900	2.9600	4.1800	3.4100	4.6800
Industry-specific	15.337	2.2600	3.3500	2.6200	3.7900	2.9600	4.1800	3.4100	4.6800

Table 5. VAR (Vector Autoregression) Lag Order Selection Criteria.

Lag Rank		Akaike's Information Criterion (AIC)	Schwarz Information Criterion (SIC)
Macroeconomic Variables	0	−13.364	−13.1001
	1	−25.2891	−23.4417
	2	−27.2268	−23.7958 *
	3	−28.5331	−23.5186
	4	−29.3804 *	−22.7824
Industry-specific Variables	0	−2.9061	−2.64219
	1	−12.9529	−11.1055
	2	−13.3905	−9.95959
	3	−14.4065	−9.39201
	4	−18.4346 *	−11.8366 *

Note: * denotes the number lag(s).

Table 6. Long-Run coefficients of ARDL Model.

Macroeconomic			Industry-Specific		
Determinants	Coefficients	Standard Error	Determinants	Coefficients	Standard Error
lnGDPGR	−1.396011 **	0.5629	lnBKLN	−0.5203392 ***	0.0367
lnCPI	−0.9602321	0.7484	lnLIQ	2.669881 ***	0.5103
lnDOCR	1.066338 *	0.5631	lnNOP	−0.0192367 ***	0.0032
lnUNEM	−7.639355 ***	2.0093	lnLDR	3.790614 ***	0.3349
lnEXR	3.756394 ***	1.1450	lnDPR	−0.7667929 ***	0.1571
Cons	0.207973	0.2722	Cons	−3.784955 ***	0.6260
R-squared = 0.9618; Adj. R-squared = 0.8971			R-squared = 0.9338; Adj. R-squared = 0.8219		

*, **, and *** stand for 10%, 5%, and 1% levels of significance, respectively.

Table 7. Short-Run coefficients of ARDL Model.

Macroeconomic			Industry-Specific		
Determinants	**Coefficients**	**Standard Error**	**Determinants**	**Coefficients**	**Standard Error**
lnGDPGR	0.364553 ***	0.1142	lnBKLN	0.2050954	0.1857
lnCPI	−5.017027 ***	0.9689	lnLIQ	−2.247147 ***	0.4446
lnDOCR	−0.279248	0.1682	lnNOP	0.0092824 ***	0.0028
lnUNEM	2.445047 ***	0.2168	lnLDR	−1.591485 ***	0.3374
lnEXR	−0.8860041 **	0.3653	lnDPR	0.2151	0.2027
Cons	0.207973	0.2722	Cons	−3.784955 ***	0.6260
R-squared = 0.9618; Adj. R-squared = 0.8971			R-squared = 0.9338; Adj. R-squared = 0.8219		

*, **, and *** stand for 10%, 5%, and 1% levels of significance, respectively.

4.2.1. ARDL Long-Run Results

Among the macroeconomic variables, the results identified that lnGDPGR has a significant negative effect on the lnNPLR, meaning that as the economy becomes stronger, bad lending decreases. If there is an increase of 1% in economic growth, non-performing loans will decrease by 1.40% in the long run in Bangladesh.

lnCPI also has a negative relationship with lnNPLR, but in this case, the relationship is insignificant in the long run. Domestic credit growth (lnDOCR) and exchange rates (lnEXR) both have significant positive relationships with the bad loan ratio (lnNPLR) while unemployment (lnUNEM) in the country has a significant negative relation with increasing bad loans. With every 1% increase in both the domestic credit and exchange rates, there is a 1.07% and 3.76% increase in non-performing loans, respectively. Surprisingly, with the decrease of non-performing loans by 7.64%, there is a 1% increase in unemployment.

The long-run results of industry-specific variables show that bank loan growth (lnBKLN) has a negative association with the non-performing loan ratio (lnNPLR). Net operating profit (lnNOP) and deposit rates (lnDPR) also have the same impact over non-performing loans with significant p values, which means that with the growth of bank lending by 0.52%, there will be a decrease of 1% bad loan, which indicates healthy behavior by the banking sector. NPL reduces bank profitability by 0.02% when it increases by 1%, and also a 1% increase in lnNPLR reduces the capacity of the banks to provide depositors good returns, which is 0.76%. Finally, a 1% increase in lending rates (lnLDR) and liquidity (lnLIQ) increase non-performing loans by 3.79% and 2.67%, respectively.

In both models, the R^2, and the adjusted R^2 were remarkably good. The R^2 and the adjusted R^2 for macroeconomic variables are 0.9618 and 0.8971, respectively, while for industry-specific variables, it is 0.9338 and 0.8219, respectively, meaning the models fit quite well, which means that the models can explain 96.18% and 93.38% of the changes in non-performing loans.

4.2.2. ARDL Short-Run Results

The short-run outcomes suggest the growth of GDP has a significant positive influence on lnNPLR. Meaning that if there is a growth of 1% in GDP in Bangladesh, the non-performing loans of banks will rise by 0.36%. Then, only lnUNEM has a significant positive relation with NPLR. A 1% increase in unemployment will cause a 2.45% decrease in bad loans in the short run. The other three variables, lnCPI, lnDOCR, and lnEXR, affect lnNPLR negatively, with lnDOCR being the only insignificant variable. To be specific, a 1% increase in all these variables can cause a 5.01%, 0.27%, and 0.88% decrease consecutively in lnNPLR.

The short-run results of industry-specific variables show that bank loan growth (lnBKLN) has an insignificant positive relationship with non-performing loans (lnNPLR). Net operating profit (lnNOP) and deposit rates (lnDPR) also have the same impact over non-performing loans, which is statistically significant, while liquidity (lnLIQ) and lending rates (lnLDR) were found to have a statistically significant negative connection with non-performing loans.

4.3. Co-Integration Test

We found four co-integration relationships in the first model and for the second model, we found two co-integrating connections. We considered trace statistics to figure out the co-integrating equations at a the 5% level of significance. The existence of more than one co-integrating equation indicates a long-run convergence of the two models (Table 8).

Table 8. The Johansen Tests for Co-integration.

	Max. Rank	Parms	LL	Eigenvalue	T. Statistics	5% Critical Value
Macroeconomic Variables	0	42	485.4188		206.5194	94.1500
	1	53	527.6884	0.8919	121.9803	68.5200
	2	62	553.1712	0.7385	71.0147	47.2100
	3	69	570.5570	0.5995	36.2430	29.6800
	4	74	581.3974	0.4348	14.5622 *	15.4100
	5	77	588.6645	0.3178	0.0281	3.7600
	6	78	588.6785	0.0007		
Industry-specific Variables	0	42	273.84		112.7982	94.1500
	1	53	294.81	0.67	70.8531	68.5200
	2	62	308.84	0.52	42.7962 *	47.2100
	3	69	319.77	0.44	20.9224	29.6800
	4	74	325.67	0.27	9.1303	15.4100
	5	77	330.05	0.21	0.3664	
	6	78	330.24	0.01		

Note: * denotes the number of co-integrating equation(s) at 5% significance. At * we reject the null hypothesis with a 5% level of significance.

4.4. Vector Error Correction (Vec) Model Results

The VECM was applied to assess the long-run and short-run coefficients (Table 9). We found two lag periods for macroeconomic variables and four lag periods for industry-specific variables using the Schwarz information criterion. We selected the lag length of SIC criterions as it gives better results than AIC criterions. We then calculated the long and short-run coefficients, putting lag length outcomes in the VECM.

Table 9. Vector Error Correction Model (VECM) Results.

	Macroeconomic Variables				Industry-Specific Variables			
Description	Variables	Coefficient	Standard Error	T Statistics	Variable	Coefficient	Standard Error	T Statistics
Speed of Adjustment	ΔlnNPLR	−0.2557821 ***	0.0246683	−10.37	ΔlnNPLR	−0.1885038	0.1307467	−1.44
Short-run coefficients	ΔlnGDPGR	−0.6820223 ***	0.0918552	−7.42	ΔlnBKLN	−0.1901149	0.2513614	−0.76
	ΔlnCPI	0.6937023 ***	0.1355197	5.12	ΔlnLIQ	0.4885987 **	0.2136399	2.29
	ΔlnDOCR	−0.0501226	0.1408345	−0.36	ΔlnNOP	0.2759852	0.2599934	1.06
	ΔlnUNEM	−0.3287384	0.2686674	−1.22	ΔlnLDR	0.6160724 *	0.3157054	1.95
	ΔlnEXR	0.2371722	0.1514736	1.57	ΔlnDPR	0.7740481 ***	0.2054191	3.77
Long-run coefficients	lnGDPGR	0.4780902 **	0.2441085	1.96	lnBKLN	0.3681242 ***	0.0323276	11.39
	lnCPI	0.1832198	0.4663795	0.39	lnLIQ	−0.424397	0.3814911	−1.11
	lnDOCR	−0.5250594 **	0.2479925	−2.12	lnNOP	0.0602165 ***	0.0046823	12.86
	lnUNEM	6.997589 ***	0.6446684	10.85	lnLDR	−4.923853 ***	0.2398030	−20.53
	lnEXR	−3.293177 ***	0.5921451	−5.56	lnDPR	2.718319 ***	0.2358060	11.53

*, **, and *** stand for 10%, 5%, and 1% levels of significance, respectively.

The first model states that lnNPLR converges to long-run equilibrium with a 25.58% speed of adjustment every year by the influence of the variables, lnGDPGR, lnCPI, lnDOCR, lnUNEM, and lnEXR. The second model suggests an 18.85% speed of adjustment in lnNPLR by the influence of lnBKLN, lnLIQ, lnNOP, lnLDR, and lnDPR. The results from both the models recommend that long-run adjustment in the independent variables has substantial influence compared to short-run variables on NPLR. The long-run equations are explained in the following manner:

Model 1:

$$InNPLR_t = \beta_0 - \begin{array}{l} 0.4780902(InGDPGR)_t \\ -0.1832198(InCPI)_t + 0.5250594(InDOCR)_t \\ -6.997589(InUNEM)_t + 3.293177(InEXR)_t + \varepsilon_t \end{array} \tag{8}$$

Model 2:

$$InNPLR_t = \alpha_0 - \begin{array}{l} 0.3681242(InBKLN)_t \\ +0.424397(InLIQ)_t - 0.0602165(InNOP)_t + 4.923853(InLDR)_t \\ -2.718319(InDPR)_t + \varepsilon_t \end{array} \tag{9}$$

Model 1: In the case of macroeconomic variables, when lnGDPGR has a negative movement by 1%, non-performing loans lnNPLR will rise by 0.4780902%. lnCPI and lnUNEM have the same negative relationship as lnGDPGR, with 0.1832198% and 6.997589%, respectively. Meanwhile, domestic credit lnDOCR and exchange rates lnEXR, if appreciated by 1%, will cause an escalation in non-performing loans (lnNPLR) by 0.5250594% and 3.293177% respectively.

Model 2: Among industry-specific variables, when bank lending (lnBKLN) is decreased by 1%, non-performing loans (lnNPLR) will increase by 0.3681242%. Net operating profit (lnNOP) and deposit rates (lnDPR) also have an inverse relationship with lnNPLR. When lnNOP and lnDPR decrease by 1%, lnNPLR increases by 0.0602165%, and 2.718319% respectively. On the contrary, at a 1% increase in banks' liquidity (lnLIQ) and lending rates (lnLDR), bad loan (lnNPLR) is hyped by 0.424397% and 4.923853%, respectively.

To check if there is any autocorrelation, we performed the Lagrange-multiplier test (Table 10). Both models are free from the autocorrelation problem.

Table 10. VECM Diagnostic Tests (Lagrange-Multiplier Test).

Nature of Test	Industry-Specific Variables			Macroeconomic Variables		
	Lag Order	p Value	Interpretation	Lag Order	p Value	Interpretation
Auto-correlation test	Lag 1 Lag 2	0.7811 0.6193	No Autocorrelation	Lag 1 Lag 2	0.1264 0.8915	No Autocorrelation

4.5. Robustness of the Study

The overall stability of the models was examined through a few diagnostic tests of the ARDL model (Table 11). The Durbin–Watson tests (for autocorrelation) suggest that neither the macroeconomic nor the industry-specific variables have autocorrelations among them. Again, for the Jarque–Bera, Breusch–Godfrey (serial correlation test), and White's tests (homoscedasticity test), we cannot reject the zero hypothesis as all the coefficients are not significant, and hence, the models are normal; there is no serial correlation among the variables and the models are free from the heteroscedasticity problem. We checked autocorrelation for VECM and found no autocorrelation problem through the Lagrange-multiplier test. The CUSUM (cumulative sum) was tested to check the model stability (Figures 3 and 4). The model with macroeconomic variables seems okay, with a slight deviation in the middle. Again, the results of VECM are consistent with ARDL estimates as the signs of the coefficients are similar (Table 12).

Table 11. Diagnostic Tests for ARDL.

Tests Detail		Macroeconomic Variables		Industry-Specific Variables	
Tests Performed	**Nature of Tests**	**Score/p Value**	**Interpretation**	**Score/p Value**	**Interpretation**
Durbin-Watson d-statistic	Autocorrelation Test	2.2850	No Autocorrelation	2.4313	No Autocorrelation
Jarque-Bera test	Normality Test	0.2483	Normal	0.3731	Normal
Breusch-Godfrey LM test	Serial Correlation Test	0.2395	No Serial Correlation	0.0692	No Serial Correlation
White's test	Homoscedasticity Test	0.4215	Homoscedastic	0.4215	Homoscedastic

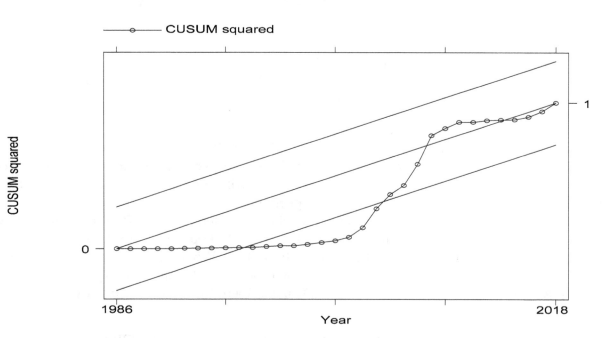

Figure 3. Cumulative Sum (CUSUM) Test for Macroeconomic Variables.

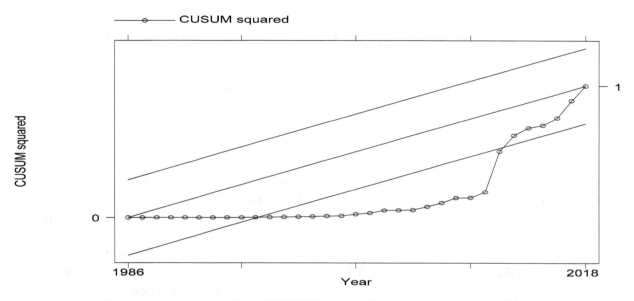

Figure 4. Cumulative Sum (CUSUM) Test for Industry-Specific Variables.

Table 12. Comparison of ARDL and VECM Coefficients.

	Macroeconomic Variables			Industry-Specific Variables	
Determinants	ARDL Coefficients	VECM Coefficients	Determinants	ARDL Coefficients	VECM Coefficients
lnGDPGR	−1.396011 **	−0.4780902 **	lnBKLN	−0.5203392 ***	−0.3681242 ***
lnCPI	−0.9602321	−0.1832198	lnLIQ	2.669881 ***	0.424397
lnDOCR	1.066338 *	0.5250594 **	lnNOP	−0.0192367 ***	−0.0602165 ***
lnUNEM	−7.639355 ***	−6.997589 ***	lnLDR	3.790614 ***	4.923853 ***
lnEXR	3.756394 ***	3.293177 ***	lnDPR	−0.7667929 ***	−2.718319 ***

*, **, and *** stand for 10%, 5%, and 1% levels of significance, respectively.

5. Conclusions

Throughout the study, we found significant shreds of evidence that our hypothesis of industry-specific and macroeconomic determinants influencing non-performing loans in Bangladesh is being established. To the best of our information, this research is the first to discover the impact of both industry-specific and macroeconomic determinants of NPLs in Bangladesh at a time horizon of 40 years. Also, very few studies, we found, had been conducted comparing the results in ARDL and VECM. Hence, it can be considered a robust study.

Long-run convergences of ARDL show that non-performing loans negatively impact economic growth. That means as the economy advances to good shape, entrepreneurs are more capable of repaying loans. The movement of exchange rates is another important factor, the consequence of which has a positive impact on NPLs. Results show as the exchange rate increases, entrepreneurs have to pay more on their imports causing a reduction in the capacity to repay. Again, with the increase in NPLs, unemployment rises in the short run, which can create instability in the economy as well.

Loan growth in the long run decreases non-performing loans. As the lending horizon has been increasing during the last decade in small and medium enterprises (SMEs) and micro-finances, non-performing loans have decreased proportionately. We may look into this fact in our future research as this is not the focal point of this study. In the short run, NPLs increase with loan growth. Banks' profitability decreases with higher NPLs as banks need to increase the base of loan loss provisions for future losses. This has a spillover effect on the lending interest rates and the deposit rates as well. Lending interest rates increase and deposit rates decrease with the growth of NPLs. Finally, the liquidity of banks needs to be handled carefully so that banks do not become too ambitious and make bad lending. There is a high chance of excess liquidity being wrongly managed by the bankers, as our research found a positive correlation between bad loans and liquidity. Central banks and policymakers can step into this to act as a guide in this regard. Banks may be controlled by implementing contractionary lending policies during an economic downturn and expansionary lending policies during economic growth to ensure their sustainability in the long run. Regulatory bodies may carefully monitor the growth of domestic credit and exchange rate fluctuation to scale down the impact of bad loans in the economy.

The results obtained piloting econometric examination can be used to project fundamental grounds of NPLs in the economy of Bangladesh. It will help policymakers of developing countries like Bangladesh to take enough measures to control NPLs or take precautions against it. The contribution of the current study puts light on future research. For example, future research can be conducted in the developing and emerging economies like Bangladesh.

Author Contributions: Conceptualization: P.K.B.; Methodology, P.K.B.; Formal analysis: P.K.B.; Investigation P.K.B.; Writing original draft preparation: P.K.B.; Writing review and editing: N.S.; Supervision: C.Z. All authors have read and agreed to the published version of the manuscript.

References

1. Norton, J.J.; Olive, C.D. Globalization of financial risks and international supervision of banks and securities firms: Lessons from the Barings debacle. *Int. Lawyer* **1996**, *30*, 301–344.
2. Klein, N. *Non-performing Loans in CESEE: Determinants and Impact on Macroeconomic Performance*; International Monetary Fund: Washington, DC, USA, 2013.
3. Louzis, D.P.; Vouldis, A.T.; Metaxas, V.L. Macroeconomic and bank-specific determinants of non-performing loans in Greece: A comparative study of mortgage, business and consumer loan portfolios. *J. Bank. Financ.* **2012**, *36*, 1012–1027. [CrossRef]
4. Podpiera, J.; Weill, L. Bad luck or bad management? Emerging banking market experience. *J. Financ. Stab.* **2008**, *4*, 135–148. [CrossRef]
5. Berger, A.N.; De-Young, R. Problem loans and cost efficiency in commercial banks. *J. Bank. Financ.* **1997**, *21*, 849–870. [CrossRef]
6. Demirgüç-Kunt, A.; Detragiache, E. The determinants of banking crises in developing and developed countries. *Staff. Pap.* **1998**, *45*, 81–109. [CrossRef]
7. González-Hermosillo, M.B. *Determinants of Ex-Ante Banking System Distress: A Macro-Micro Empirical Exploration of Some Recent Episodes*; International Monetary Fund: Washington, DC, USA, 1999.
8. Makri, V.; Tsagkanos, A.; Bellas, A. Determinants of non-performing loans: The case of Eurozone. *Panoeconomicus* **2014**, *61*, 193–206. [CrossRef]
9. Yang, C.-C. Reduction of non-performing loans in the banking industry: An application of data envelopment analysis. *J. Bus. Econ. Manag.* **2017**, *18*, 833–851. [CrossRef]
10. Barseghyan, L. Non-performing loans, prospective bailouts, and Japan's slowdown. *J. Monet. Econ.* **2010**, *57*, 873–890. [CrossRef]
11. Zeng, S. Bank non-performing loans (NPLS): A dynamic model and analysis in China. *Mod. Econ.* **2012**, *3*, 100. [CrossRef]
12. Fofack, H.L. *Nonperforming Loans in Sub-Saharan Africa: Causal Analysis and Macroeconomic Implications*; The World Bank: Washington, DC, USA, 2005.
13. Keeton, W.R.; Morris, C.S. Why do banks' loan losses differ. *Econ. Rev.* **1987**, *72*, 3–21.
14. Messai, A.S.; Jouini, F. Micro and macro determinants of non-performing loans. *Int. J. Econ. Financ. Issues* **2013**, *3*, 852–860.
15. Matthews, K. Risk management and managerial efficiency in Chinese banks: A network DEA framework. *Omega* **2013**, *41*, 207–215. [CrossRef]
16. Espinoza, R.A.; Prasad, A. *Nonperforming Loans in the GCC Banking System and Their Macroeconomic Effects*; International Monetary Fund: Washington, DC, USA, 2010; pp. 10–224.
17. Škarica, B. Determinants of non-performing loans in Central and Eastern European countries. *Financ. Theory Pract.* **2014**, *38*, 37–59. [CrossRef]
18. Chaibi, H.; Ftiti, Z. Credit risk determinants: Evidence from a cross-country study. *Res. Int. Bus. Financ.* **2015**, *33*, 1–16. [CrossRef]
19. Dimitrios, A.; Helen, L.; Mike, T. Determinants of non-performing loans: Evidence from Euro-area countries. *Financ. Res. Lett.* **2016**, *18*, 116–119. [CrossRef]
20. Partovi, E.; Matousek, R. Bank efficiency and non-performing loans: Evidence from Turkey. *Res. Int. Bus. Financ.* **2019**, *48*, 287–309. [CrossRef]
21. Ghosh, A. Banking-industry specific and regional economic determinants of non-performing loans: Evidence from US states. *J. Financ. Stab.* **2015**, *20*, 93–104. [CrossRef]
22. Godlewski, C.J. The determinants of multiple bank loan renegotiations in Europe. *Int. Rev. Financ. Anal.* **2014**, *34*, 275–286. [CrossRef]
23. Dey, B.K. Managing Nonperforming Loans in Bangladesh. 2019. Available online: https://www.adb.org/publications/managing-nonperforming-loans-bangladesh (accessed on 26 December 2019).
24. Vardar, G.; Özgüler, I.C. Short Term and Long Term Linkages among Nonperforming Loans, Macroeconomic and Bank-Specific Factors: An Empirical Analysis for Turkey. *Ege Akad. Bakış Derg.* **2015**, *15*, 313–326. [CrossRef]
25. Bardhan, S.; Mukherjee, V. Bank-specific determinants of nonperforming assets of Indian banks. *Int. Econ. Econ. Policy* **2016**, *13*, 483–498. [CrossRef]

26. Rajan, R.G. Why bank credit policies fluctuate: A theory and some evidence. *Q. J. Econ.* **1994**, *109*, 399–441. [CrossRef]

27. García-Marco, T.; Robles-Fernández, M.D. Risk-taking behaviour and ownership in the banking industry: The Spanish evidence. *J. Econ. Bus.* **2008**, *60*, 332–354. [CrossRef]

28. Boahene, S.H.; Dasah, J.; Agyei, S.K. Credit risk and profitability of selected banks in Ghana. *Res. J. Financ. Account.* **2012**, *3*, 6–14.

29. Sinkey, J.F.; Greenawalt, M.B. Loan-loss experience and risk-taking behavior at large commercial banks. *J. Financ. Serv. Res.* **1991**, *5*, 43–59. [CrossRef]

30. Liu, R. Comparison of Bank Efficiencies Between the US and Canada: Evidence Based on SFA and DEA. *J. Compet.* **2019**, *11*, 113–129. [CrossRef]

31. Kjosevski, J.; Petkovski, M.; Naumovska, E. Bank-specific and macroeconomic determinants of non-performing loans in the Republic of Macedonia: Comparative analysis of enterprise and household NPLs. *Econ. Res. Ekon. Istraživanja* **2019**, *32*, 1185–1203. [CrossRef]

32. Tanasković, S.; Jandrić, M. Macroeconomic and institutional determinants of non-performing loans. *J. Cent. Bank. Theory Pract.* **2015**, *4*, 47–62. [CrossRef]

33. Vogiazas, S.D.; Nikolaidou, E. Investigating the determinants of nonperforming loans in the Romanian banking system: An empirical study with reference to the Greek crisis. *Econ. Res. Int.* **2011**, *2011*. [CrossRef]

34. Rifat, A.M. An Analytical Study of Determinants of Non-Performing Loans: Evidence from Non-Bank Financial Institutions (NBFIs) of Bangladesh. *J. Bus. Technol. (Dhaka)* **2016**, *11*, 55–67. [CrossRef]

35. Shuman, M.A.R. Effect of Bank Specific Variables on the Non-Performing Loan Ratio: A case study on the Commercial Banks of Bangladesh. In Proceedings of the Annual Banking Conference, Dhaka, Bangladesh, 23–29 November 2015.

36. Parvin, A. Determinants of Problem Loan and Its Effect on the Financial Health: Evidence from Private Commercial Banks of Bangladesh. Proceedings of Welcome Message from Conference Chairs, Omaha, NE, USA, 28–31 September 2017.

37. Amir, M.K. Does excess bank liquidity impact non-performing loan? a study on Bangladeshi economy. *Int. J. Bus. Technopreneurship* **2019**, *9*, 287–298.

38. Islam, F.T. Evaluating Loan Loss Provisioning for Non-Performing Loans and Its Impact on the Profitability of Commercial Banks in Bangladesh. *Asian Financ. Bank. Rev.* **2018**, *2*, 33–41.

39. Rahman, M.; Hai, A. Factors Affecting Non-Performing Loan (NPL) of Private Commercial Banks in Bangladesh. *Amity Glob. Bus. Rev.* **2017**, *12*, 7–14.

40. Rahman, M.A.; Asaduzzaman, M.; Hossin, M.S. Impact of financial ratios on non-performing loans of publicly traded commercial banks in Bangladesh. *Int. J. Financ. Res.* **2016**, *8*, 181. [CrossRef]

41. Hasan, M.Z. Macroeconomic Determinants of Non-Performing Loans in Bangladesh: An ARDL Approach. *Sci. Res. J.* **2019**, *7*, 84–89.

42. Hasan, K.; Khan, R.S. Management of Non-Performing Loans (NPLs) of Banks in Bangladesh-An Evaluative study. *J. Econ. Financ.* **2013**, *1*, 1–15.

43. Rahman, B.; Jahan, N. Non-Performing Loans (NPLs) in Islamic Banks of Bangladesh: An Empirical Study. *world Rev. Bus. Res.* **2018**, *8*, 12–23.

44. Islam, M.Z.; Aktar, S.; Hossen, M.A.; Islam, M.S. Non-Performing Loan And Asset Utilization of Banks: Evidence From Bangladesh. *Rom. Econ. Bus. Rev.* **2018**, *13*, 31–39.

45. Islam, M.Z.; Islam, M.S. Non-Performing Loan As Eroding Factor of Capital Adequacy: Evidence From Banking Industry In Bangladesh. *Rom. Econ. Bus. Rev.* **2018**, *13*, 15–21.

46. Roy, S.; Dey, P.K.; Bhowmik, P. Non-performing loans in private commercial banks of Bangladesh: Macro-economic determinants and impacts. *Jahangirnagar J. Bus. Stud.* **2014**, *4*, 47–57.

47. Roy, J. Non-Performing Loan on Profitability: Evidence from Banking Sector of Dhaka Stock Exchange. *SSRN Electron. J.* **2015**, *1*, 13. [CrossRef]

48. Islam, M.S.; Nishiyama, S.-I. Non-Performing Loans of Commercial Banks in South Asian Countries: Adverse Selection and Moral Hazard Issues. *Asian Econ. Financ. Rev.* **2019**, *9*, 1091. [CrossRef]

49. Mondal, T. Sensitivity of non-performing loan to macroeconomic variables: Empirical evidence from banking industry of Bangladesh. *Glob. J. Manag. Bus. Res.* **2016**, *16*, 4-C.

50. Engle, R.F.; Granger, C.W. Co-integration and error correction: Representation, estimation, and testing. *Econom. J. Econom. Soc.* **1987**, *55*, 251–276. [CrossRef]

51. Hassler, U.; Wolters, J. Autoregressive distributed lag models and cointegration. In *Modern Econometric Analysis*; Springer: Berlin/Heidelberg, Germany, 2006; pp. 57–72.

52. Masih, M.; Hamdan, B. The impact of monetary policy on deposit and lending rates in industrial and developing countries: An application of ARDL approach. *J. Int. Financ. Econ.* **2008**, *8*, 114–122.

53. Mallick, H.; Agarwal, S. Impact of real interest rates on real output growth in India: A long-run analysis in a liberalized financial regime. *Singap. Econ. Rev.* **2007**, *52*, 215–231. [CrossRef]

54. Shrestha, M.B.; Chowdhury, K. *ARDL Modelling Approach to Testing the Financial Liberalisation Hypothesis*; Working Paper 05-15; Department of Economics, University of Wollongong: Wollongong, Australia, 2005. Available online: https://ro.uow.edu.au/commwkpapers/121 (accessed on 22 July 2019).

9

The Effect of Emotional Intelligence on Turnover Intention and the Moderating Role of Perceived Organizational Support: Evidence from the Banking Industry

Ha Nam Khanh Giao [1], Bui Nhat Vuong [1,*], Dao Duy Huan [2], Hasanuzzaman Tushar [3] and Tran Nhu Quan [4]

[1] Faculty of Air Transport, Vietnam Aviation Academy, Ho Chi Minh City 700000, Vietnam; khanhgiaohn@yahoo.com

[2] Vice Rector of Nam Can Tho University, Can Tho 94000, Vietnam; ddhuan51@yahoo.com.vn

[3] College of Business Administration, International University of Business Agriculture and Technology, Dhaka 1230, Bangladesh; tushar@iubat.edu

[4] Nida Business School-National Institute of Development Administration, Bangkok 10240, Thailand; quantrannhu@gmail.com

* Correspondence: nhatvuonga1@gmail.com

Abstract: The objective of this study is to investigate the impact of emotional intelligence on turnover intention, noting the mediating roles of work-family conflict and job burnout as well as the moderating effect of perceived organizational support. Survey data collected from 722 employees at banks in Vietnam was analyzed to provide evidence. Results from the partial least squares structural equation modeling (PLS-SEM) using the SmartPLS 3.0 program indicated that there was a negative effect of emotional intelligence on employees' turnover intention; this was mediated partially through work-family conflict and job burnout. Besides, this study indicated that perceived organizational support could decrease work-family conflict, job burnout and turnover intention of employees. It could also moderate the relationship between emotional intelligence and work-family conflict. This negative relationship was stronger for employees who work in a supportive environment. The main findings of this research provided some empirical implications for the Vietnamese banking industry. It implied that organizations in the service industry should try to improve their employees' work-family balance, reduce job burnout and take advantage of these emotional balances and supportive environments to create beneficial outcomes.

Keywords: emotional intelligence; work-family conflict; job burnout; employees' turnover intention; perceived organizational support; the Vietnamese banking industry

1. Introduction

In recent years, the notion of turnover intention has become a central attraction of research in various fields of managerial disciplines, therefore, prompting more and more executives/managers in different business sectors to take this concept into consideration to effectively manage their employees [1]. Employee turnover can have a variety of negative effects on organizations. For example, according to Allen et al. [2], replacing an employee can cost more than a year's salary for the position being filled. Hausknecht and Trevor [3] noted that turnover results in the loss of both social and human capital. In human services organizations, those negative effects can extend to the clients and the organization it serves. In the 21st century, the concept of job turnover intention is considered as a key concept in management for a successful career of an employee and business survival at all levels, predominantly in the service industry [4,5]. The particular characteristic of a service industry is "the contact and interaction between service providers (employees) and service acceptors (customers)" that infers that employees in the service industry have become a part of service products. Being a service ambassador, employees play an important role to satisfy customers with proper services. Therefore, understanding employees' emotions and feelings toward work is another recent concern that organizations are struggling to manage. The issue, then, is how individual employees manage their emotions effectively and lessen job turnover intention. Judeh [6] stated that emotional intelligence is a significant factor in interpreting and analyzing human behavior at work. Most successful service organizations understand their people's feelings and always have special concerns about any issues that may threaten the employees. However, it is broadly termed emotional intelligence (EQ) that enables an employee to work together with others toward achieving a common goal. In addition, emotional intelligence will enhance employees' suitable emotions in fulfilling customers' expectations that help to form a positive image of the organization [4,7].

Since joining the World Trade Organization (WTO) in 2007, Vietnam has taken part in significant economic growth in the last decade due to the improvement of the business environment and the high volume of foreign investments. Along with the achievement in the economy, the Vietnamese banking industry has also seen outstanding enlargement and development in terms of scale and service quality [8]. However, the increases in competition and financial innovation have led to extremely rapid expansion which has resulted in banking system problems in the past few years. Eventually, the government-initiated project 254 called "restructuring credit institutions system 2011–2015" was implemented by the Prime Minister in 2012. In response, the State Bank of Vietnam has pushed the commercial banks to merge with the project goal and reduce half of the number of banks. In such an unfavorable condition, employees in this sector have experienced a considerable fluctuation with the highest average voluntary turnover rate compared to other service sectors. As of 2019, the turnover rate was more than 25% each year [9] and 81% for turnover intention [10]. Restructuring the banking sector caused not only workforce transition among banks, but also between banking and non-banking sectors. High turnover can lead to compromised client care and increased organizational costs [11]. Service organizations, such as the banking industry, have an added burden with turnover given that they foster individual relationships between their counselors and their clients. When an employee leaves such an organization, a personal relationship with clients is broken. Moreover, the bank incurs the expense of finding and training new employees, and clients can suffer due to discontinuity of care [12]. Additionally, turnover results in decreased efficiency in carrying out job-related responsibilities [13]. Implementing new strategies and achieving organizational goals is hampered by high employee turnover [12]. Consequently, keeping intellectual capital for organizations is a crucial strategy for maintaining sustainable development.

With an increasing interest in employee turnover intention, numerous researches have been conducted to find out the predictors of employee turnover intention and discovered several factors including emotional intelligence (e.g., [14]), work-life conflict (e.g., [15]), job burnout (e.g., [16]), and a few others (e.g., [14,16]). Research has shown that emotional intelligence helps the employees to have control of their emotions and to understand the use of social skills that are helpful to the organization [17]. Emotional intelligence in individuals who lead can help organizations to reduce turnover intentions and retain valuable employees [18]. Avey et al. [19] asserted that emotional intelligence is one of the key factors that affect the turnover intention of an employee among other factors. Besides, prior studies have also confirmed that emotional intelligence strongly affects employees who intend to leave their jobs by causing work-family conflict [20] and job burnout [16]. In general, people's emotions change quickly based on the challenges in the workplace and also in family life. The work-family balance will enhance their suitable emotions in responding to customers' expectations that help to form a positive image of their organizations [7]. Hence, understanding an employee's emotions and feelings is a crucial issue for both employees and the organization in the service industry. Moreover, employees are among a company's most valuable assets. Therefore, employers need to understand burnout and its causes. Lu and Gursoy [16] pointed out that burnout is one of the best predictors of turnover intention because employees in customer service-based industries have to deal with customer demands, so they are at high risk for job burnout. They also noted that burnout is costly for organizations on two fronts, not only leading to higher turnover rates but also decreasing worker productivity.

Additionally, although there are tangible factors in work environments that have been described as antecedents to work-family conflict and job burnout, theory and empirical findings indicate that the nature of the work environment as sensed by the worker, that is, perceived organizational support, may be an important determinant of work-family conflict and job burnout in employees who work in the banking industry. Perceived organizational support refers to the general belief by an employee that support will be readily available from the organization when stressful situations arise and urgent needs are addressed [21]. Theorists posit that the availability of material aid and emotional support may reduce aversive psychological and psychosomatic reactions (e.g., emotional exhaustion) when stressful situations arise [22]. In supportive work environments, employees treat each other with fairness and respect and engage in effective open communication. These characteristics contribute to win-win solutions for the employee and the organization [21]. Thus, it is plausible that employees who perceive their work environments as supportive will experience work-family conflict and job burnout, and, conversely, bankers who perceive their work environments as unsupportive will experience more job burnout and work-family conflict.

In developed countries, much research has been conducted about the perceptions of subordinates in terms of emotional intelligence, perceived organizational support, work-family conflict, job burnout, and employee turnover intention and their significant mutual relationships [20,23], however, this topic has yet to receive considerable attention from scholars in developing or less developed countries, particularly in Vietnam. An extensive literature review informed that there has been no research conducted to examine the relationship between emotional intelligence and turnover intention of employees in Vietnamese organizations. Moreover, there is no empirical evidence that confirms the relationships of emotional intelligence, perceived organizational support, work-family conflict, job burnout, and turnover intention in one model. Specific to the financial sector, a banker with high emotional intelligence would perform effectively at enhancing customer enthusiasm and reducing customer frustration [24]. So, the need for understanding employee emotional intelligence is strongly considered in this research. Therefore, these twofold gaps have led the researchers to conduct this research to examine the mutual effects of emotional intelligence and perceived organizational support on work-family conflict and job burnout and subsequently explore its impact on the turnover intention of bankers in Vietnamese commercial banks. Besides, the moderating role of perceived organizational support on these relationships will be considered as well.

2. Literature Review

2.1. Emotional Intelligence

The Emotional Intelligence theory of Bar-On was first introduced in 1985 and was followed by a series of other subsequent developed versions (e.g., [25,26]). Emotional intelligence was found as having an important role in both building and maintaining successful social relationships, predicting specific aspects of situations involving social exchange, and it will either foster or hamper this exchange process [27]. Salovey and Mayer [28] stated that emotional intelligence is "the subset of social intelligence that involves the ability to monitor one's own and others' feelings and emotions, to discriminate among them and to use this information to one's thinking and actions". Besides, Ravichandran et al. [29] defined emotional intelligence as "the ability to recognize, understand, and assess one's own feelings as well as others and use this knowledge in thought and action". In line with this definition, Serrat [30] indicated that "emotional intelligence describes the ability, capacity, skill, or self-perceived ability to identify, assess, and manage the emotions of one's self, of others, and of groups". Possessing high emotional intelligence enables an individual employee to be more productive, optimistic, and resilient in both work and family life [31]. Mayer and Salovey [25] have established the scope of emotional intelligence into four dimensions including:

(1) *The self-emotions appraisal (SEA):* This dimension reflects the ability of a person to understand his/her own emotions and be able to express them properly, then apply the knowledge of those emotions to create beneficial outcomes.

(2) *The other emotions appraisal (OEA):* This component assesses the ability of an individual to observe and understand other's emotions. A person who has high capability in this dimension will be able to observe other people's emotions and predict other's emotional reactions;

(3) *The use of emotion (UOE):* This aspect evaluates the ability of an individual to access, generate and use his/her emotions to facilitate personal performance. People who rate highly in this ability will be able to return rapidly to normal psychological states after suffering depression or feeling upset;

(4) *The regulation of emotion (ROE):* This dimension mentions the ability of an individual to regulate his/her emotions to achieve an expected outcome and be able to remain balanced from psychological distress to solve problems.

2.2. Turnover Intention

Turnover intention is defined when an individual intends to leave their organization [32,33]. It is inevitable that turnover occurs in every organization in which some of the employees voluntarily leave the organization while others are discharged by the organization. Turnover is classified into two types, i.e., voluntary and involuntary turnover [34]. First, voluntary turnover happens when employees are not fulfilled with their current job and are ready to look for another job in another place. In other words, it is called turnover intention that refers to the desire to voluntarily leave an organization. Second, involuntary turnover happens when employees are fired by their organization. Either voluntary turnover or involuntary turnover creates serious consequences for the organization in today's business world including a number of difficulties in finding a replacement, recruitment, selection, training and development, socialization cost, and perception of service quality by customers [33,35,36]. Turnover intention involves a sequence of the process, thinking of leaving, intentions to search, and to leave [37]. Several researchers (e.g., [38,39]) also stated that turnover intention is one of the best predictors of employees' actual quitting.

2.3. Work-Family Conflict

The work-family conflict (WFC) refers to an incompatible demand that an individual employee faces difficulty in participating in both work and family roles [40]. Family and work are the inseparable two central areas of an adult's life [41,42]. Both sides assist to shape peoples' roles and define their identity. Greenhaus and Beutell [43] stated that work-family conflict arises from the "simultaneous pressures from both roles which indicate that the relationship between them is a reciprocal one". Disruptive events in either arena may have serious consequences for the individual and the conflict is bi-directional between work and family roles [44]. In other words, conflict on one side will have an impact on the other side, i.e., work stress causes family conflict (WFC) and family stress causes work conflict (FWC). In line with this notion, Boyar et al. [45] also conceptualized work-family conflict into two facets that include "work interfering with family (WIF) and family interfering with work (FIW)". Choi and Kim [46] posited that WIF appears when employees' experience at work interferes with their family lives. Conversely, FIW occurs when employees experience stress in family events that interfere with their work-life [47]. Bande, Fernández-Ferrín, Varela, and Jaramillo [23] argued that they are more common and closely associated with job satisfaction, exhaustion, and turnover intention. Moreover, Demerouti et al. [48] propositioned that work-family conflict is a crucial factor that causes job burnout. This can lead to absenteeism and increased turnover intention of an employee [49].

2.4. Job Burnout

While most people are aware of burnout, there is no specific, generally agreed definition of the term, leaving it to be defined differently in the literature over the years. Freudenberg [50], who is credited with coining the term job burnout, defined it as occurring when a person becomes psychologically worn out and exhausted due to excessive demand that could be internally or externally imposed. Pines et al. [51] viewed burnout as resulting from work tedium where the employee felt distressed and discontented with the job. In the end, the employee experienced a feeling of being emotionally and physically depleted from work. Kahn [52] viewed burnout as a syndrome of negative attitudes towards others and self, which then resulted in negative psychological and physical exhaustion for the person.

Maslach and Jackson [53] defined burnout as "a syndrome of emotional exhaustion and cynicism that occurs frequently among individuals who do people-work of some kind". Burnout is described as consisting of three aspects: emotional exhaustion, depersonalization, and reduced personal accomplishment. Firstly, emotional exhaustion is obtained when staff members feel severe emotional fatigue and feel diminished or have no ambition to work. Secondly, depersonalization is accomplished when employees get away from work and indicate an indifferent and callous attitude at firms. Lastly, reduced personal accomplishment is attained when people feel a lack of competence and successful work accomplishment. According to Maslach et al. [54], burnout has been known to lead to poor physical health. Psychological symptoms can occur, such as negative self-concept, perfectionism, irritability, feeling of being unappreciated, and depression [55].

3. Hypotheses

3.1. Emotional Intelligence and Turnover Intention

Raza et al. [56] stated that employees' emotional intelligence not only decreases frustration and stress in the workplace but also helps others to have less intention to quit. Optimistic emotions are influential from an individual perception and are indicative of cooperation and fairness within the organization [57]. Pessimistic emotions have negative effects on the organization as well as individuals. Those individuals who are upset have difficulty in assessing others' emotions accurately [58]. Emotional stress results in a lack of confidence, self-esteem, or motivation to reflect these limits. Employees tend to focus more on these negative emotions than they do their work and become disconnected physically and mentally, which results in underperformance and high turnover intention [59]. Emotional intelligence may be a key component to keep employees engaged and understand the emotional reasons for leaving decisions. Employees may use their emotional intelligence to better assess and understand the situation. Thus, emotional intelligence is considered a significant factor in predicting the turnover intention of employees which leads towards actual turnover [60]. There are several proposed theories that support a positive relationship between emotional intelligence and turnover intention: human capital theory, attraction-selection-attrition theory, and job embeddedness theory [61]. As employees continue to work for the same company, they become increasingly motivated to perform well; and, as their interests increasingly align with the company's values, their chances of leaving the company decrease [61]. Prior researches demonstrated a negative association between emotional intelligence and employees' turnover intention [60,62]. They stated that employees with higher emotional intelligence have very low intentions to quit. Based on the literature it is hypothesized that:

Hypothesis 1: *Emotional intelligence will reduce the turnover intention of bankers.*

3.2. Emotional Intelligence and Work-Family Conflict

Emotional intelligence and work-family conflict are two fundamental aspects of service organizations [63]. Both the organization and its employees are responsible for eliminating work-family conflict. Companies have their own policies and procedures to help their staff manage stress, but their employees still burn out. Certainly, individuals hold some responsibilities for regulating their own family balance, but they need organizational support. Organizations need to recognize and adapt employees' work and lives to win employee loyalty [64]. According to the content of resource theory, Hobfoll [65] has identified individual differences as resources causing the negative impacts of stressful events on individuals. Individuals who have more personal resources can deal with the loss of other kinds of resources, including resource loss caused by work-family conflict. "Emotional intelligence represents individual differences in the ability and capacity to monitor and recognize one's own and other's emotions and to use this information to regulate one's emotions and actions" [66]. Concerning the role of individuals, researchers have emphasized emotional intelligence is an essential factor in protecting employees from the beginning of the work-family conflict and stress to identify, acknowledge, and manage the emotions. Particularly, Suliman and Al-Shaikh [67] stated that in terms of conflict management, employees with an inflated level of emotional intelligence tended to have effective control with conflict. Indeed, people with high-ability of emotional intelligence tended to suffer less work-family conflict [63]. Accordingly, the following hypothesis is proposed:

Hypothesis 2. *Emotional intelligence will reduce the work-family conflict of bankers.*

3.3. Work-Family Conflict and Turnover Intention

Over the past several years, many researchers have believed that when experiencing work-family conflict, employees have a tendency to quit their job to eliminate the conflict. Employees may leave an organization because of the high stress of being overworked and limited personal time available to spend away from the office [68,69]. They do not want to choose between their personal lives and work, and, if they must, they will choose their personal lives. Employees leave when organizational rules are the cause of intolerable family stress and conflicts [68,69]. Greenhaus et al. [70] proved that being disappointed with family, work, and life leads to withdrawing from work. These studies demonstrated that when job-related retention grows too strong in the organization, one solution that employees can choose is to leave their firms. Allen and Armstrong [71] suggested that work-family conflict may cause employees to leave their jobs because the demands of work lead to frustration in the workplace and the strain from work makes it difficult to fulfill family duties. Employees took the emotions felt in the workplace home, as a result, they find it hard to concentrate on tasks. Similarly, some previous researchers examined and found that WFC has a significant effect on turnover intention [33,44,45]. Based on the foregoing review and previous research, it is hypothesized that:

Hypothesis 3: *Work-family conflict will increase the turnover intention of bankers.*

3.4. Emotional Intelligence and Job Burnout

It has been suggested that emotional intelligence enables individuals to control pressure and adapt easily with the challenge to avoid burnout [72]. In relation to job burnout, people who have elevated levels of emotional intelligence deal better with life's challenges and job stresses, which leads to good psychological and physical health [72] and makes them less likely to experience job burnout [73]. The fourth dimension of emotional intelligence enables a person to regulate their emotions quickly and work on emotive information effectively [74]. Regarding this matter, the emotionally intelligent individual helps employees choose appropriate approaches to cope with frustration and make a response more effectively relating to the emotional aspect. Employees with high levels of emotional intelligence can keep away from dysfunctional and angry emotions that would be a consequence of burnout [64]. Individuals with high-ability to manage their emotions would be less likely to experience burnout. Therefore, it could be hypothesized that:

Hypothesis 4: *Emotional intelligence will reduce job burnout.*

3.5. Work-Family Conflict and Job Burnout

The impact of the work-family conflict was investigated and the findings showed that work-family conflict was strongly influenced by lower job and family satisfaction, greater stress, and higher turnover intention [75]. Experiencing work-family conflict, individuals are subject to burnout that leads to the consequence of a conflict between work and family domains, which seems to result in draining their emotional and physical energy [23,76]. According to Hobfoll [65] in his conservation of resource theory, energy and time are resources that people attempt to maintain, protect, and create. In addition, "during recovery periods when not confronted with an immediate need for resources, individuals attempt to recover and stockpile resources to counter future losses" [76]. Hobfoll [65] perceived that work-family conflict expends an individual's energy and other sources and keeps them from "resource stockpiling" which is likely necessary to fend off other current and future resource demands. For this reason, individuals tend to suffer higher levels of burnout. People with a high level of work-family conflict are susceptible to burnout because conflicts inhibit individuals from accomplishing their work and family obligations. Consequently, work-family conflict could cause job burnout. Thus, the following hypothesis is presented:

Hypothesis 5: *Work-family conflict will increase job burnout.*

3.6. Job Burnout and Turnover Intention

Many researchers have found that job burnout is strongly associated with turnover intention [77,78]. Similarly, according to Layne et al. [79], the turnover intention corresponds with stress. Employees with a high level of stress are more likely to leave their organization and seek another opportunity. In addition, burnout will result in lower rates of organizational commitment and higher rates of turnover and turnover intention [80]. Hence, an employee experiencing a higher level of burnout results in a higher level of turnover intentions. Therefore, the following relationship is hypothesized:

Hypothesis 6: *Job burnout will increase turnover intention.*

3.7. The Mediating Role of Work-Family Conflict and Job Burnout

Basically, emotional intelligence is the ability to understand and to regulate one's own emotions effectively, as well as to apply these abilities to help achieve desired outcomes [81]. Normally, people who have high emotional intelligence tend to have good control over their emotions. They won't let negative emotions affect their life, work, and relationship with others. Rather, they know how to use their knowledge about emotions to enhance their interpersonal skills and to help them make good decisions without being affected by emotions. Employees with high emotional intelligence may properly balance the relationship between work and family and reduce job burnout thus resulting in less turnover intention. Previous research revealed the direct relationships between emotional intelligence and work-family conflict, job burnout [82,83], emotional intelligence and employees' turnover intention [60,62,84], work-family conflict, job burnout and employees' turnover intention [44,60]. Linking the associations outlined above, the authors argue that work-family conflicts and job burnout are likely to mediate the relationship between emotional intelligence and turnover intention. Based on the foregoing review and previous research, the hypotheses below are proposed:

Hypothesis 7: *Work-family conflict mediates the relationship between emotional intelligence and turnover intention of bankers.*

Hypothesis 8: *Job burnout mediates the relationship between emotional intelligence and turnover intention of bankers.*

3.8. Perceived Organizational Support

Perceived organizational support is theoretically defined as the employees' global beliefs about the extent to which the organization values their contributions and cares about their well-being [85]. The individual's perception about the degree to which their organization values their well-being is rooted in the nature of the give-and-take relationship between the workers and their organization [22]. Perceived organizational support theory suggests that when the emotional and social needs of the employee are fulfilled, there are positive outcomes for both the organization and the individual [21,85]. Perceived organizational support is expected to decrease negative psychological and psychosomatic reactions (e.g., burnout) to employees by providing supportive external resources.

According to the theory of perceived organizational support, the employee assigns the organization humanlike characteristics [85]. That is, employees view actions or behaviors by agents of the organizations as actions of the organization itself. Employees view favorable or unfavorable treatment directly by the organization representatives and indirectly through organizational policy as an indication of the extent to which the organization supports them. Employees who believe that their work environment is supportive are more likely to achieve personal and organizational goals, which leads to effectively balancing their work-family. Alternatively, unsupportive work environments foster a win-lose approach [21]. In unsupportive work environments, workers' individual goals are typically incompatible with other workers' goals or even organizational goals so that as one worker moves toward goal attainment, others are less likely to achieve their goals. It is plausible then that the extent to which an organization is perceived to be supportive or non-supportive can influence whether there is a positive outcome for both the employee and the organization and a reduction of work-family conflict as well as job burnout. Perceived organizational support is thought to reduce work-family conflict and job burnout by fostering the perception that material aid and emotional resources will be available when needed to deal with negative situations (e.g., work-family conflict, job burnout, and turnover intention). Besides, some scholars demonstrated that perceived organizational support could decrease work-family conflict (e.g., [86]), job burnout (e.g., [87]), and turnover intention (e.g., [88]). Therefore, the following hypotheses are suggested:

Hypothesis 9: *Perceived organizational support reduces the turnover intention of bankers.*

Hypothesis 10: *Perceived organizational support reduces the work-family conflict of bankers.*

Hypothesis 11: *Perceived organizational support reduces job burnout of bankers.*

3.9. Moderating Role of Perceived Organizational Support

Perceived organizational support theorists indicated that perceived organizational support reduces work-family conflict and job burnout because it provides external work environment physical and emotional resources to help employees deal with burnout as well as work-family conflict [86]. Individuals who have high emotional intelligence, work in environments where cooperative (i.e., supportive) values such as fair and respectful treatment of others are supported and are likely to diminish work-family conflict and job burnout [87]. Supportive work environments are characterized by effective open communication, helpfulness, fair and respectful treatment of others, and collaboration to achieve mutual goals leading to win-win solutions [89]. Moreover, the authors state that perceived organizational support could moderate the relationship between emotional intelligence and work-family conflict and job burnout because employees with high emotional intelligence have lower work-family conflict and job burnout levels. However, if the highly emotionally intelligent employees perceived low organizational support, their work-family conflict and job burnout levels could be increased, but if the highly emotionally intelligent employees perceived high organizational support, their work-family conflict and job burnout levels could be decreased as well. Thus, it is plausible that perceived organizational support may moderate or blunt the effects of emotional intelligence leading to a decrease in work-family conflict and job burnout. Based on the discussion above, the following hypotheses are proposed:

Hypothesis 12: *Perceived organizational support moderates the effect of emotional intelligence on work-family conflict. The negative relationship between EQ and WFC will be stronger for employees who work in a supportive environment.*

Hypothesis 13: *Perceived organizational support moderates the effect of emotional intelligence on job burnout. The negative relationship between EQ and JB will be stronger for employees who work in a supportive environment.*

3.10. Control Variables

Some researches (e.g., [90,91]) stated that employee demographic variables could be related to turnover intention. For example, Seyrek and Turan [91] argued that "both women and men are confronted with different demands from home, community and workplace in their life and these different groups compete for the person's time and energy. Especially for women, it can be difficult to cope with conflicts arising from playing different roles in workplace and family and this may lead to turnover intention". Although the impacts of individual characteristics of the employee on turnover intentions may differ in different environments, empirical studies in the banking industry context is scanty. Therefore, this study has been conducted exploring control variables (e.g., gender, marital status, age group, income, and educational level) in combination with turnover intention. The following hypotheses can be proposed (Figure 1):

Hypothesis 14: *There is a statistically significant relationship between control variables (e.g., gender, marital status, age group, income, and educational level) and turnover intention in the commercial banks of Vietnam.*

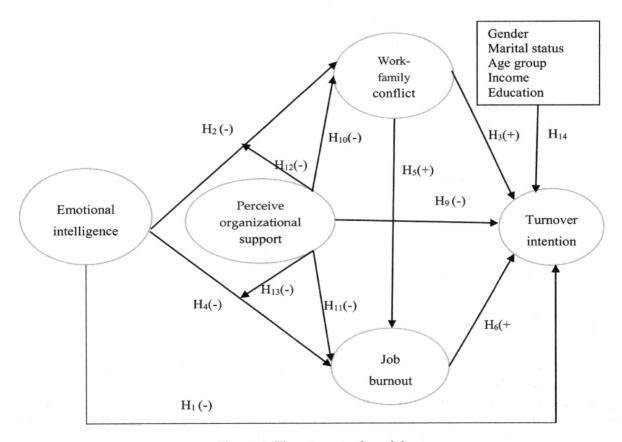

Figure 1. The conceptual model.

4. Research Methodology.

4.1. Procedure and Sampling Size

Respondents were the full-time employees of banks in Vietnam. The sample was selected using nonprobability technique-convenience sampling. First of all, the researchers collected a list of commercial banks in Vietnam. Thirty-five commercial banks were chosen to conduct the survey. The researchers contacted the concerned person in charge (i.e., human resource manager) over the phone prior to conducting the survey. The topic and purposes were explained clearly. Ten out of thirty-five banks allowed the researchers to collect data.

Based on the previous studies (e.g., [74,85,92–94]), a draft questionnaire was formed. The draft questionnaire was originally developed in the English language. Then the researchers translated the questions into the Vietnamese language and piloted the back-translation with the support of several English language experts. The current study consisted mainly of two stages including qualitative and quantitative research. For qualitative research, the Vietnamese version of the questionnaire was tested by an in-depth interview method in one week with ten employees from three banks to ensure if they understood the questions and revised Vietnamese terms which were unclear due to translation. Based on the comments of respondents, the survey questionnaire was modified properly.

The pilot study was sent to 50 employees working in the Vietnamese banking industry by a convenient method. The participants were asked to provide advice on elements of the survey that were confusing. They also provided recommendations on the wording and any questions they felt uncomfortable answering. Modifications were made to the instrumentation, specifically around grammatical errors and survey logic. The modified instrument was found to be reliable as the minimum Cronbach's Alpha of each factor equals to 0.743 (Table 1). The individual items were deemed to be valid for the research as for each dimension the Cronbach's alpha was above the acceptable threshold of 0.70 and the minimum value of corrected item-total correlation coefficients was higher than 0.3 [95]. Therefore, the reliability of the scales is sufficiently good to test the main survey.

Table 1. The quantitative pilot study analysis of 50 respondents.

Variables	Number of Items	Cronbach's Alpha	The Minimum Value of Corrected Item-Total Correlation
Self-emotion appraisal	4	0.851	0.481
Others' emotion appraisal	4	0.891	0.716
Use of emotion	4	0.865	0.608
Regulation of emotion	4	0.913	0.768
Perceived organizational support	7	0.897	0.513
Work interfere with family	5	0.928	0.724
Job burnout	4	0.906	0.714
Turnover intention	4	0.743	0.314

After finishing the main questionnaires, the authors distributed the questionnaires to 10 banks in the chosen sample. A total of 764 completed questionnaires were collected. Among these, 42 questionnaires were found invalid because the respondents answered one choice for all questions. Consequently, there were 722 valid questionnaires usable for further data analysis. Table 2 below shows the diverse information about the demographic profile of respondents.

Table 2. Statistics description.

N = 722		Frequency	Percent
Gender	Female	463	64.1
	Male	259	35.9
Marital status	Single	271	37.5
	Married	451	62.5
Age group	18–25	140	19.4
	26–35	349	48.3
	36–45	200	27.7
	>45	33	4.6
Income (1 million VND ≈ $ 43.25)	Under 10 million VND	220	30.5
	10–20 million VND	349	48.3
	20–30 million VND	117	16.2
	Above 30 million VND	36	5.0
Education	College/University	581	80.5
	Postgraduate	141	19.5

4.2. Measurement

All variables in the conceptual model were measured with multiple items, which were developed by prior scholars [74,85,92–94]. Particularly, an emotional intelligence scale was measured by 16 items of Wong and Law [74]. Sample items included (Self-emotion appraisal: e.g., *"Self-emotion appraisal I have a good sense of why I have certain feelings most of the time"*); (Others' emotion appraisal: e.g., *"I always know my friends' emotions from their behavior"*); (Use of emotion: e.g., *"I always set goals for myself and then try my best to achieve them"*); (Regulation of emotion: e.g., *"I am able to control my temper so that I can handle difficulties rationally"*). Perceived organizational support was measured by 7 items of Eisenberger, Huntington, Hutchinson, and Sowa [85]. Sample items for this construct were *"The organization really cares about my well-being"* and *"Help is available from the organization when I have a problem"*. The work-family conflict scale was measured by 5 items about work interference with family from Netemeyer, Boles, and McMurrian [92]. A sample item for this construct was *"The amount of time my job takes up makes it difficult to fulfill family responsibilities"*. The job burnout scale was measured by 4 items from Lee [93]. Sample items for this construct were *"I worry that this job is hardening me emotionally"* and *"I leave work feeling tired and rundown"*. Turnover intention scale was measured by 4 items of Vigoda [94]. A sample item for this construct was *"Next year I will probably look for a new job outside this organization"*. All items of these constructs were measured using a 5-point Likert scale ranging from 1 (strongly disagree) to 5 (strongly agree).

4.3. Partial Least Squares Regression

The statistical technique chosen to test the stated hypotheses was partial least squares (PLS) path analysis, otherwise known as partial least squares structural equation modeling (PLS-SEM). PLS-SEM is a statistical analysis technique for data exploration within the quantitative research discipline used to measure the observed variables collected from instruments to determine their influence on latent or unobserved variables [96]. Researchers have suggested the use of PLS-SEM due to its effective use as an analysis tool to support prediction models from empirical data [97,98]. Moreover, PLS-SEM is appropriate for analysis when different measurement scales are used in the research model because it allows optimal empirical assessment of a structural model. The use of PLS-SEM data analysis utilizes multi-item observations to measure the area under review as this has shown to be more reliable than using a single-item of observation, as this is shown to provide more accurate reflections on the latent variable. Moreover, PLS-SEM has the capability to calculate p-values through a bootstrapping technique if samples are independent and if the data is not required to be normally distributed [39,98]. Therefore, data analysis for this study was performed using PLS-SEM with the SmartPLS 3.0.

5. Research Results

Before performing PLS-SEM estimation for hypotheses testing, the validity and reliability of the multi-item measures should be assessed [99]. Convergent validity is the amount of variance between two or more items that agree when measuring similar constructs and is calculated using factor loadings. Hair, Hult, Ringle, and Sarstedt [98] stated that convergent validity will be suitable when the factor loadings are above 0.5. In Figure 2, the statistical results showed that all factor loadings were more than the threshold of 0.5. For example, the minimum factor loading for Use of emotion = 0.791, Regulation of emotion = 0.825, Self-emotion appraisal = 0.680, Others' emotion appraisal = 0.834, Emotional intelligence = 0.609, Perceived organizational support = 0.632, Work interference with family = 0.833, Job burnout = 0.818, and Turnover intention = 0.604. Besides, convergent validity will be confirmed when the average variance extracted (AVE) for each of the latent variables is greater than 0.5 [96]. As shown in Table 3 below, AVE values were reported for each of the variables ranging from 0.611 to 0.759 (perceived organizational support and emotional intelligence, respectively). Therefore, all constructs showed good convergent validity.

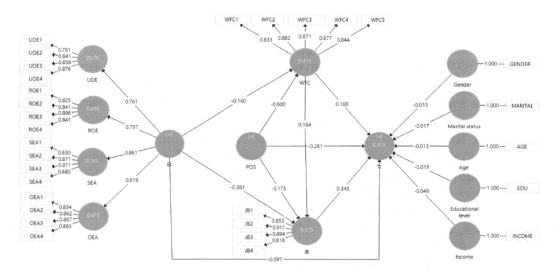

Figure 2. Measurement model.

Additionally, Hair, Hult, Ringle, and Sarstedt [98] recommended that discriminant validity can be shown through the correlation matrix. The square root of a construct's AVE value should be greater than the squared correlation with any other construct "since a construct shares more variance with its associated indicators than it does with any other construct" [96]. Table 2 indicated the correlation matrix of the constructs with the diagonal values. Square roots of AVE of latent constructs which were shown in the parentheses were higher than the correlation coefficient with any variable. For example, the AVE value of Others' emotion appraisal was 0.734 and the square root of its AVE was 0.857. This value was both higher than the correlation values in its column (0.069, 0.819, 0.050, −0.014, 0.055, −0.490, and 0.106) and its row (0.362, 0.481, 0.652, −0.383, 0.505, and −0.267). Therefore, discriminant validity for the constructs was established.

Next, the Cronbach's alpha and composite reliability values were used to assess construct reliability. According to Hair, Hult, Ringle, and Sarstedt [98], Cronbach's alpha and composite reliability values should be 0.7 or greater to be considered reliable in a model. As shown in Table 3 below, Cronbach's alpha and composite reliability values were more than 0.7. The minimum composite reliability and Cronbach's alpha values were 0.875 and 0.807, respectively. Furthermore, Hair, Hult, Ringle, and Sarstedt [98] also suggested the rho_A coefficient to measure the reliability for the partial least squares and this value should be greater than 0.7. According to Table 3, the rho_A values varied from 0.819 to 0.922. Consequently, the authors can verify that all constructs achieved good reliability.

Table 3. Construct reliability and validity.

	Cronbach's Alpha	rho_A	Composite Reliability	Average Variance Extracted (AVE)	Age	EI	Edu	Gen	Inc	JB	MS	OEA	POS	ROE	SEA	TI	UOE	WFC
Age	-	-	-	-	(1)													
EI	0.921	0.922	0.931	0.758	0.071	(0.871)												
Edu	-	-	-	-	0.108	-0.035	(1)											
Gen	-	-	-	-	0.149	0.028	-0.012	(1)										
Inc	-	-	-	-	0.083	0.078	0.077	-0.085	(1)									
JB	0.894	0.895	0.926	0.759	-0.028	-0.556	0.009	-0.063	0.058	(0.871)								
MS	-	-	-	-	0.124	0.016	0.050	-0.094	0.121	-0.076	(1)							
OEA	0.879	0.880	0.917	0.734	0.069	0.819	0.050	-0.014	0.055	-0.490	0.106	(0.857)						
POS	0.891	0.893	0.916	0.611	0.048	0.554	-0.061	0.030	0.018	-0.497	-0.020	0.362	(0.782)					
ROE	0.873	0.874	0.913	0.724	-0.016	0.797	-0.091	0.067	0.096	-0.525	-0.067	0.481	0.533	(0.851)				
SEA	0.810	0.819	0.877	0.642	0.091	0.861	-0.094	0.004	0.014	-0.407	-0.029	0.652	0.466	0.608	(0.801)			
TI	0.807	0.842	0.875	0.641	-0.058	-0.517	0.006	-0.055	-0.057	0.606	-0.047	-0.383	-0.601	-0.529	-0.418	(0.800)		
UOE	0.863	0.864	0.907	0.710	0.093	0.761	0.022	0.034	0.089	-0.360	0.042	0.507	0.424	0.460	0.534	-0.330	(0.842)	
WFC	0.913	0.915	0.935	0.742	-0.029	-0.472	0.051	-0.067	-0.072	0.462	0.000	-0.267	-0.677	-0.506	-0.395	0.555	-0.350	(0.862)

Notes: EI = Emotional intelligence; Edu = Educational level; Gen = Gender; Inc = Income; JB = Job burnout; MS = Marital status; OEA = Others' emotion appraisal; POS = Perceived organizational support; ROE = Regulation of emotion; SEA = Self-emotion appraisal; TI = Turnover intention; UOE = Use of emotion; WFC = Work interfere with family. Square roots of AVE of latent constructs were shown in the parentheses.

Finally, multicollinearity was assessed for all of the constructs. The variance inflation factor (VIF) indicator was suggested to measure multicollinearity issues. The VIF value should be less than a 5.00 tolerance level [95,98]. As shown in Table 4, the maximum inner VIF value of constructs was 2.190. Therefore, the collinearity of the latent variables was not a concern.

Table 4. Multicollinearitystatistic.

	JB	OEA	ROE	SEA	TI	UOE	WFC
Age					1.068		
EI	1.479	1.000	1.000	1.000	1.741	1.000	1.442
Edu					1.024		
Gen					1.054		
Inc					1.065		
JB					1.654		
MS					1.056		
POS	2.124				2.190		1.442
WFC	1.896				1.964		

Results from the PLS-SEM analysis are shown in Figure 3. Standardized path coefficients and p-values are reported. The findings are presented as follows:

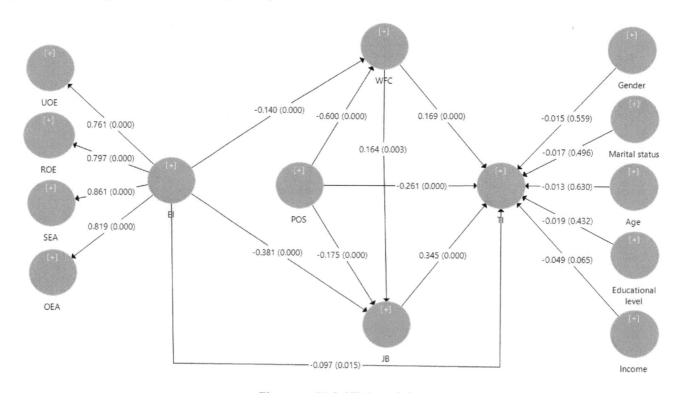

Figure 3. PLS-SEM model.

Hypothesis 1: the result showed that emotional intelligence had a negative and significant relationship with the turnover intention of bankers, (p-value = 0.015 and beta coefficient = −0.097) (Table 5). The results indicated that the more emotional intelligence, the greater the possibility that bankers will have low levels of turnover intention, which was consistent with the findings of the previous study of Akhtar, Shabir, Safdar and Akhtar [62] and Riaz, Naeem, Khanzada and Butt [60]. Emotional intelligence was related to bankers who had the propensity to leave his or her job based on a prolonged period of time being emotionally low regulated by employees' work. Thus, Hypothesis 1 was supported.

Table 5. Results of the relationship checking of the model's constructs.

Hypothesis	Relationship			PathCoefficient	Standard Deviation	T-Statistics	p-Values	Result
	EI	→	UOE	0.761	0.021	36.527	0.000	
	EI	→	ROE	0.797	0.016	50.307	0.000	
	EI	→	SEA	0.861	0.010	89.384	0.000	
	EI	→	OEA	0.819	0.013	64.661	0.000	
H_1	EI	→	TI	−0.097	0.040	2.435	0.015	Supported
H_2	EI	→	WFC	−0.140	0.032	4.392	0.000	Supported
H_3	WFC	→	TI	0.169	0.043	3.953	0.000	Supported
H_4	EI	→	JB	−0.381	0.030	12.527	0.000	Supported
H_5	WEC	→	JB	0.164	0.054	3.019	0.003	Supported
H_6	JB	→	TI	0.345	0.037	9.258	0.000	Supported
H_7	POS	→	TI	−0.261	0.050	5.164	0.000	Supported
H_{10}	POS	→	WFC	−0.600	0.033	18.423	0.000	Supported
H_{11}	POS	→	JB	−0.175	0.048	3.636	0.000	Supported
	Control variables							
	Gender	→	TI	−0.015	0.026	0.585	0.559	Not supported
	Age	→	TI	−0.013	0.028	0.483	0.630	Not supported
H_{14}	Edu	→	TI	−0.019	0.025	0.786	0.432	Not supported
	Income	→	TI	−0.049	0.026	1.846	0.065	Supported
	Marital status	→	TI	−0.017	0.025	0.681	0.496	Not supported

Hypothesis 2: the result found that emotional intelligence had a negative impact on work-family conflict with a standardized coefficient of −0.140 and p-value = 0.000, which corresponds with many studies (e.g., [63]) which suggested that emotional intelligence is one of the preliminary factors preventing employees from establishing work-family conflict. Subordinates with a good understanding of emotional intelligence would gain feelings of balancing her/his work and family. He or she not only senses that the work being performed is meaningful, but also exhibits the capability to take advantage of work-life balance to have mutual results: completing the job successfully and having a happy family life. Moreover, emotional intelligence helps employees figure out work-family conflicts and helps them to manage their emotions. In terms of conflict management, employees with better emotional intelligence tend to have better effective control with work-family conflict than others. Thus, emotional intelligence (self-emotion appraisal, others' emotions appraisal, use of emotion, regulation of emotion) are important for individual difference effects in regulating emotion in work-family life. Therefore, Hypothesis 2 was supported.

Hypothesis 3: This analysis found that work-family conflict had a positive and significant relationship with the turnover intention of bankers (p-value = 0.000 and beta coefficient = 0.169). It was connected to the studies of Khan, Nazir, Kazmi, Khalid, Kiyani, and Shahzad. [33] and Wang, Lee, and Wu [44]. Vietnamese bankers with higher work-family conflicts were found to have greater job turnover intentions. With a regression weight of 0.169, the results showed that bringing conflict from the workplace to employees' homes would likely force them to think of leaving their job. Moreover, in the banking sector, the majority of employees are women, and they may choose to leave an organization voluntarily because of family responsibilities, such as childbearing or child-rearing. Women are generally regarded as the caretakers for an elderly parent as well. As the secondary income earner in the household, a woman's income is characterized traditionally as non-crucial income, which is another common reason identified for turnover. Similarly, from a conventional perspective, women require the flexibility or support from an organization to fulfill family responsibilities. If these requirements cannot be fulfilled by a firm, the employee is more likely to leave voluntarily. Therefore, Hypothesis 3 3 was supported.

Hypothesis 4: The results showed that emotional intelligence had a negative impact on job burnout with the standardized coefficient of −0.381 and the p-value = 0.000 is consistent with research papers (e.g., [64]) which state that emotional intelligence strongly offers individuals control over the work pressures and the ability to adapt easily with challenges to avoid job burnout. In the relationship of emotional intelligence to job burnout, employees who have a moral or intellectual level of emotional intelligence deal better with life's challenges and job stresses, which leads to good psychological and physical health and seems to lessen employees' suffering from job burnout. Thus, Hypothesis 4 was supported.

Hypothesis 5: The results showed that work-family conflict had a positive impact on job burnout with the standardized coefficient of 0.164 and p-value =0.003, which is consistent with the findings of the previous studies of Bande, Fernández-Ferrín, Varela, and Jaramillo [23] and Golden [76]. Employees who experience stress from work-family conflict over a prolonged period of time get drained of energy, which eventually results in job burnout and vice versa. Indeed, the findings also showed that work-family conflict is associated with negative consequences (i.e., burnout) that affect both the work and family. Additionally, high values of work-family conflict may lead to contemporary feelings of emotional exhaustion, reduced personal accomplishment, and depersonalization. Therefore, Hypothesis 5 was supported.

Hypothesis 6: The results showed that job burnout had a positive impact on the turnover intention with the standardized coefficient of 0.345 and p-value = 0.000, which is consistent with the findings of the previous study of Gharakhani and Zaferanchi [78] and Scanlan and Still [77]. Job burnout is related to bankers in the commercial banks propensity to leave his or her job based on a prolonged period of time being emotionally overextended and exhausted by the employees' work. Thus, Hypothesis 6 was supported.

Hypothesis 7: According to Table 6, work-family conflict mediated the relationship between emotional intelligence and turnover intention due to the following reasons: first, the results in Table 5 revealed that the p-value for the direct path EI→TI was 0.015; EI→WFC was 0.000; WFC→TI was 0.000, which were statistically significant ($p < 0.05$). Second, the p-value of the indirect effect (EI→WFC→TI) was 0.000 (Table 6) which was statistically significant as well. Hence, the mediating role of work-family conflict exists [95]. Therefore, Hypothesis 7 was supported and this mediation was partial.

Table 6. The result of the mediating effect of work-family conflict and job burnout.

Hypothesis	Relationship	Direct Effect	Indirect Effect	Total Effect	Mediating Effect	Result
H$_7$	EI→WFC→ TI	−0.097 *	−0.024 ***	−0.252 ***	Partial Mediation	Supported
H$_8$	EI→JB→ TI		−0.131 ***			Supported

Note: *** =$p < 0.001$; * =$p < 0.05$.

Hypothesis 8: According to Table 6, job burnout mediated the relationship between emotional intelligence and turnover intention due to the following reasons: first, the results in Table 5 revealed that the p-value for the direct path EI→TI was 0.015; EI→WFC was 0.000; WFC→TI was 0.000, which were statistically significant ($p < 0.05$). Second, the p-value of the indirect effect (EI→JB→TI) was 0.000 (Table 6) which was statistically significant as well. Hence, the mediating role of job burnout exists [95]. Therefore, Hypothesis 8 was supported and this mediation was partial.

Hypothesis 9: The results showed that perceived organizational support had a negative and significant relationship with the turnover intention of bankers, (p-value = 0.000 and beta coefficient = −0.261) (Table 5). The result indicated that the more perceived organizational support, the greater the possibility that bankers will have low levels of turnover intention, which was consistent with the findings of Marchand and Vandenberghe [88]. Thus, Hypothesis 9 was supported.

Hypothesis 10: The results showed that perceived organizational support had a negative and significant relationship with work-family conflict, (p-value = 0.000 and beta coefficient = −0.600) (Table 5). The result indicated that the more perceived organizational support, the greater the possibility that bankers will have low levels of work-family conflict, which was consistent with the findings of Gurbuz, Turunc, and Celik [86]. Thus, Hypothesis 10 was supported.

Hypothesis 11: The results showed that perceived organizational support had a negative and significant relationship with the job burnout of bankers, (p-value = 0.000 and beta coefficient = −0.175) (Table 5). The results indicated that the more perceived organizational support, the greater the possibility that bankers will have low levels of job burnout, which was consistent with the findings of Caesens, Stinglhamber, Demoulin and De Wilde [87]. Thus, Hypothesis 11 was supported.

On the other hand, the findings showed that the component structure of emotional intelligence was a second-order structure. This result was consistent with emotional intelligence concepts [74], which stated that emotional intelligence was composed of four sub-components: self-emotion appraisal, others' emotions appraisal, use of emotion, and regulation of emotion. Regarding the dependency level of each variable to their subscales via arrows, the subscales of use of emotion had the smallest share and others' emotion appraisal had the largest share in stating emotional intelligence.

5.1. The Moderating Role of Perceived Organizational Support

Hypothesis 12 predicted that perceived organizational support would moderate the relationship between emotional intelligence and work-family conflict. The study showed that the moderating effect 1 of the interaction between emotional intelligence and perceived organizational support with work-family conflict was negative and statistically significant (p-value = −0.072 and beta coefficient = 0.006) (Figure 4). This finding proposed that perceived organizational support negatively moderated the relationship between emotional intelligence and work-family conflict. In other words, the negative relationship between EQ and WFC was stronger for employees who work in a supportive environment (Figure 5). Therefore, Hypothesis 12 is supported.

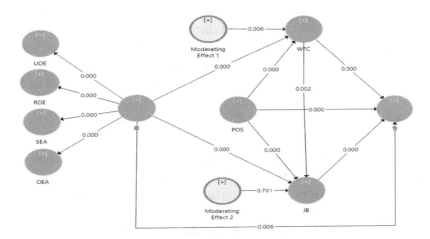

Figure 4. The moderating effect of perceived organizational support.

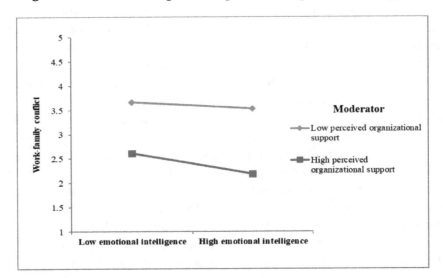

Figure 5. Perceived organizational support (POS) strengthens the negative relationship between emotional intelligence (EQ) and work stress causes family conflict (WFC).

Hypothesis 13 predicted that perceived organizational support would moderate the relationship between emotional intelligence and job burnout. The study showed that the moderating effect 1 of the interaction between emotional intelligence and perceived organizational support with job burnout was not statistically significant (p-value = 0.701) (Figure 4). Therefore, Hypothesis 13 was not supported.

Hypothesis 14: The results indicated income negatively related to turnover intention (p-value = 0.065) at the significance level of 10%, which means that bankers who had a high income tended to reduce turnover intention more than other bankers (beta coefficient = −0.019). This finding was different from some prior results of Seyrek and Turan [91] and Liu, Liu and Hu [90]. However, this study did not find the relationship between turnover intention and gender (p = 0.559; β = −0.015), age (p = 0.630; β = −0.013), educational level (p = 0.432; β = −0.049), and marital status (p = 0.496; β = −0.017), which was consistent with the findings of Seyrek and Turan [91] and Liu, Liu and Hu [90].

5.2. Model Fit

The coefficient of determination (R^2) is a measure of the model's predictive power. R^2 is the amount of variance in the endogenous (dependent) latent variables in the structural model explained by the exogenous (independent) constructs connected to it. R^2 values range from 0 to 1. The higher the R^2 coefficient, the better the construct is explained by the latent constructs in the structural model. The high R^2 coefficient also reveals that the values of the variables can be well predicted by the PLS path model [95,98,100]. The R^2 value for the turnover intention was 0.515 which indicated that 51.5% of the total variation of the endogenous construct turnover intention may be explained by the exogenous construct such as emotional intelligence, perceived organization support, work-family conflict, and job burnout (Figure 2). Moreover, R^2 values and the effect for endogenous latent variables in behavioral sciences can be assessed as 0.26 (large effect), 0.13 (moderate effect), and 0.02 (weak effect). Due to the fact that R^2 values for the turnover intention were greater than 0.26, the model of this study proved the model-data fit.

6. Discussion

Turnover is a costly consequence as recruiting, selecting, and training new members requires additional resources that might negatively affect the performance of a service organization. This study contributes to the existing body of literature supporting the role of emotional intelligence and perceived organizational support in turnover intention. It also focusses on the additional variables of work-family conflict and job burnout having a significant relationship in conjunction with emotional intelligence and perceived organizational support in influencing the turnover intention. Emotional intelligence and perceived organizational support are accounted for 47.2% and 37.5% of the variance in work-family conflict and job burnout, respectively. When work-family conflict and job burnout are added as the additional independent variables with emotional intelligence and perceived organizational support, the combination is accounted for 51.5% of the variance in turnover intention. These numbers may appear to be large; they are very important to banks looking to improve their retention. Being a banker can be an extremely stressful profession, emotionally intelligent bankers are better equipped to work in teams, deal with the job burnout, and interact with their customers. A better understanding of the relationship between emotional intelligence, perceived organizational support, work-family conflict, and turnover intention has the potential to help enhance the workplace as a whole.

An emotionally intelligent banker is more likely to be able to manage her/his tasks properly. Possessing the ability to communicate efficiently, appropriately, and quickly with customers, bankers will have more time for other tasks. It also can increase the accuracy of the banker's work if he or she is better able to understand the needs and wants of the customers in addition to a better understanding of the needs and wants of his/her family. A non-emotionally intelligent banker might struggle to communicate with the customer or misinterpret the customer's needs which can result in the delivery of inappropriate service. A less emotionally intelligent banker may also struggle to interact appropriately with the family members. This could leave the family with the impression that the banker is not caring for their loved one which could also leave the family dissatisfied with him/her, leading to an increase in work-family conflict.

Another way emotional intelligence can impact turnover intention is its effect on work-family conflict and job burnout. Employees with higher levels of emotional intelligence are more balanced in their job with family which in turn results in a lower level of job burnout. Emotionally intelligent bankers who can deal with the stressors of the workplace feel more confident and successful, so they have the potential to enjoy their jobs. This would decrease their likelihood of leaving the workplace. They would provide a greater contribution to the overall success of their unit and the bank. Bankers not possessing emotional intelligence would struggle to deal with the stress and demands of the workplace, which may make them more vulnerable to continue their jobs.

Additionally, the recent study of perceived organizational support included plentiful direct causal relations with turnover intention, and it illustrated that elevated employee perceptions of organizational support have been supportive of the reduced intention to quit. Besides, this research found that POS also reduced work-family conflict and job burnout. The negative relationship among POS, work-family conflict and turnover intention was consistent in relation to the previous researches of Marchand and Vandenberghe [88], Gurbuz, Turunc and Celik [86] and Caesens, Stinglhamber, Demoulin and De Wilde [87]. POS were key mechanisms in connecting voluntary turnover among employees. This research found that POS contributed to proactive employees' intent to retain their position in the organization. A positive perception of human resource management practices could lead employees to be less likely to quit as trust could form under a social exchange theory. Perceived organizational support is a belief emanating from the social exchange and the norm of reciprocity. According to organizational support theory, employees exchange valued organizational outcomes for the belief that the organization values their contribution and cares about their well-being as evidenced by tangible support as well as the fulfillment of intangible socio-emotional needs. In other words, employees who feel greater inducements might sense the obligation to repay the organization. Moroever, individuals who have stronger POS might be less likely to seek other jobs or consider turnover.

7. Conclusions

Keeping positive and motivated staff is a vital factor for commercial banks and has become a pressing matter for the board of directors. When a banker leaves his/her organization, the organization must absorb the cost of losing an employee such as the cost of recruiting a new employee, which consists of advertising, interviewing, choosing and hiring, and the cost of management activities, which consists of orientation and training. Thus, researchers have examined and proved the effect of emotional intelligence in jobs that required high interaction with others, such as bankers. Particularly, the study examined the effect of the emotional intelligence of commercial bank employees in Vietnam on the turnover intention of employees through the mediation of work-family conflict and job burnout. The findings strongly supported most of the proposed hypotheses. The results of testing have found correlations between a system of variables. The findings showed that emotional intelligence had a negative relationship with work-family conflict, job burnout, and turnover intention. The respondents in this study who had a high level of work-family conflict and job burnout will experience a high level of turnover intention. On the other hand, the high ability of emotional intelligence could lower the level of work-family conflict and job burnout which later could reduce employees' turnover intention.

In terms of emotional intelligence, this research reviewed the definition and dimensions of the emotional intelligence construct and argued its important role in reducing work-family conflict and job burnout issues which also decreased the turnover intention. Due to the importance of this issue, it is strongly recommended to promote the development of emotional intelligence and perceived organizational support to reduce work-family conflict, job burnout, and turnover intention.

Besides, the moderating role of perceived organizational support has not been found in any previous papers about emotional intelligence and turnover intention. Therefore, this study demonstrated the existence of the moderating role of perceived organizational support on these relationships. POS could decrease work-family conflict, job burnout, and turnover intention of employees. It could also moderate the relationship between emotional intelligence and work-family conflict. This negative relationship was stronger for employees who work in a supportive environment.

8. Managerial Implications

The results of this research study lead to many practical recommendations for both banking practitioners and managers of organizations desirous of improving work-related outcomes.

First of all, hiring employees with high levels of emotional intelligence could have a considerable impact on reducing organizational work-family conflict, job burnout, and turnover intention. Effective retention strategies often begin during the employee recruitment process. When choosing the right employee, the manager should strongly consider the personality, temperament, and capacity of candidates. People who are passionate and active will have strong emotion regulation ability. Thus, during the recruitment process, psychological tests and interviews are suggested methods to determine emotional intelligence. The psychological assessment usually includes a clinical interview, assessment of intellectual functioning (IQ), personality assessment, and behavioral assessment. A personality test is important because it allows the interviewer to thoroughly understand a person and their behavior which includes temperament, personality, interests, attitudes, values, motivation, and other non-cognitive factor characteristics. When interviewing candidates, the interviewer can be flexible and extend the interview to various aspects such as education, knowledge, experience, and achievement. By these approaches, the employer can properly judge the interviewee and select the qualified staff for the organization. In these ways, the organization can hire an employee with high levels of emotional intelligence which can help the organization keep its critical workforce.

Secondly, enhancing training for existing staff is considered. Since practical training can improve individual emotional intelligence levels, organizations may consider implementing Employee Assistance Programs (EAPs) to foster bankers' emotional competence. EAPs have been formed in American companies. EAPs are employee benefit programs that provide professional advice and guidance to help staff with personal problems or work-related conflicts that have a positive impact on reducing work-family conflict and turnover throughout the enterprise. Managers should develop and utilize EAPs in training employees.

Third, perceived organizational support could reduce work-family conflict, job burnout, and turnover intention. Thus, managers of organizations have fresh insight regarding how the delivery of supportive practices to their employees may result in an accretive improvement in organizational outcomes. Specifically, engaging in practices that instill within employees the belief that the organization values their contributions and cares about their well-being may achieve better, stronger outcomes when complemented by related but different organizational practices that increase job satisfaction and decrease work-family conflict, job burnout, and turnover intention to the organization. An employee's belief that the organization is supportive may better explain to management the variance in the levels of worker commitment, which in turn may add insight into how the effect of organizational support is transmitted to outcomes meaningful for organizational strategy execution.

Fourth, emotional intelligence interacts with perceived organizational support upon the intention to quit in a manner such that employees with higher levels of emotional intelligence will experience less work-family conflict and job burnout which will reduce their quitting intention. Management may, therefore, wish to screen potential hires for emotional intelligence, as well as implement training programs that will help employees perceive and better manage their emotions. Of equal importance is the finding that emotional intelligence appears to have an incremental effect upon outcomes as opposed to a basic foundational relation.

Finally, one of the positive ways to reduce the negative effects associated with work-family conflict, job burnout, and turnover intention is to provide a fair work environment. Fairness is a basic element that human beings need and is also a key factor in influencing people's emotions. This will create a pleasant atmosphere, and inspire all people in the organization to build up enthusiasm and be more positive. Besides, bankers must know clearly what to do for their customers and establish realistic expectations regarding performance. Managers should always be concerned about their employees and recognize and assist them to deal with problems effectively. A fair atmosphere is beneficial for the employee and the employer; if employees are treated well, then they are more likely to treat customers well. Furthermore, employees will retain positive emotions in the workplace, and the level of work-family conflict, job burnout, and turnover intention will reduce.

9. Limitations and Recommendations for Future Research

In this study, there were some limitations. First, this was a cross-sectional study. Future research should test the relations proposed with this study in longitudinal studies using a probability sampling technique, simple random sampling, to increase the generalization of the study. Secondly, multi-culture was another limitation of this project. Although emotional intelligence may be a universal construct, it is believed that the characteristics of the emotional intelligence of individuals may vary across cultures. However, emotional intelligence across cultural boundaries was not mentioned in the literature review. Finally, the survey method was the only method used in this study. Experimental study and field study should be considered in any future research.

Despite these limitations listed above, the present research has practical implications for managers in commercial banks. It is expected to expand the literature on turnover intention in Vietnamese commercial banks and will motivate further research from this scope. Obtaining actual turnover data is much better than turnover intention since there is still a gap between people who just have the intention to leave and those who ultimately leave their organization. This paper mainly studied the relationship between emotional intelligence, perceived organizational support, work-family conflict, and turnover intention. There are also other antecedents that predict turnover such as job satisfaction and employee engagement. These factors should also be involved in investigating the relationship between emotional intelligence and turnover intention.

Author Contributions: H.N.K.G. and B.N.V. proposed the research framework and, together with D.D.H. and T.N.Q. contributed to data collection; B.N.V. and H.T. analyzed the data and wrote the article; B.N.V. contributed to writing and revising article. All authors have read and agreed to the published version of the manuscript.

References

1. Li, N.; Zhang, L.; Xiao, G.; Chen, J.; Lu, Q. The relationship between workplace violence, job satisfaction and turnover intention in emergency nurses. *Int. Emerg. Nurs.* **2019**, *45*, 50–55. [CrossRef]
2. Allen, D.G.; Bryant, P.C.; Vardaman, J.M. Retaining talent: Replacing misconceptions with evidence-based strategies. *Acad. Manag. Perspect.* **2010**, *24*, 48–64.
3. Hausknecht, J.P.; Trevor, C.O. Collective Turnover at the Group, Unit, and Organizational Levels: Evidence, Issues, and Implications. *J. Manag.* **2011**, *37*, 352–388. [CrossRef]
4. Hassan, M.; Jagirani, T.S. Employee turnover in public sector banks of Pakistan. *Market Forces College of Management Sciences* **2019**, *14*, 119–137.
5. Lee, C.; Chon, K.S. An investigation of multicultural training practices in the restaurant industry: The training cycle approach. *Int. J. Contemp. Hosp. Manag.* **2000**, *12*, 126–134. [CrossRef]
6. Judeh, M. Emotional intelligence and retention: the moderating role of job involvement. *Int. J. Soc. Behav. Econ. Bus. Ind. Eng.* **2013**, *7*, 656–661.
7. Kusluvan, S. *Managing Employee Attitudes and Behaviors in The Tourism and Tourism Industry*; Nova Science Publishers: New York, NY, USA, 2003.
8. Leung, S. Banking and financial sector reforms in Vietnam. *ESEAN Econ. Bull.* **2009**, *26*, 44–57. [CrossRef]
9. NavigosGroup. Nhân viên ngân hàng thu nhập triệu đồng mỗi tháng vẫn nghỉ việc. Available online: https://news.zing.vn/nhan-vien-ngan-hang-thu-nhap-10-30-trieu-dong-moi-thang-van-nghi-viec-post82.html (accessed on 30 March 2019).

10. Cafef. Hàng nghìn nhân viên ngân hàng nghỉ việc từ đầu năm đến nay: Nhân sự ngành ngân hàng đang bước vào thời kỳ bị cắt giảm diện rộng? Available online: http://cafef.vn/hang-nghin-nhan-vien-ngan-hang-nghi-viec-tu-dau-nam-den-nay-nhan-su-nganh-ngan-hang-dang-buoc-vao-thoi-ky-bi-cat-giam-dien-rong-20191017104021499.chn (accessed on 12 December 2019).

11. Ducharme, L.J.; Knudsen, H.K.; Roman, P.M. Emotional exhaustion and turnover intention in human service occupations: The protective role of coworker support. *Sociol. Spectr.* **2007**, *28*, 81–104. [CrossRef]

12. Knight, D.K.; Becan, J.E.; Flynn, P.M. Organizational consequences of staff turnover in outpatient substance abuse treatment programs. *J. Subst. Abuse Treat.* **2012**, *42*, 143–150. [CrossRef]

13. McNulty, T.L.; Oser, C.B.; Aaron Johnson, J.; Knudsen, H.K.; Roman, P.M. Counselor turnover in substance abuse treatment centers: An organizational-level analysis. *Sociol. Inq.* **2007**, *77*, 166–193. [CrossRef]

14. Da Camara, N. Exploring the Relationship between Perceptions of Organizational Emotional Intelligence and Turnover Intentions amongst Employees: The Mediating Role of Organizational Commitment and Job Satisfaction. In *New Ways of Studying Emotions in Organizations*; Dulewicz, V., Ed.; Emerald Group Publishing Limited: Bentley, UK, 2015; Volume 11, pp. 295–339.

15. Chen, H.; Ayoun, B.; Eyoun, K. Work-Family conflict and turnover intentions: A study comparing China and U.S. hotel employees. *J. Hum. Resour. Hosp. Tour.* **2018**, *17*, 247–269. [CrossRef]

16. Lu, A.; Gursoy, D. Impact of job burnout on satisfaction and turnover intention: Do generational differences matter? *Journal of Hospitality & Tourism Research* **2013**, *40*, 210–235.

17. Alfonso, L.; Zenasni, F.; Hodzic, S.; Ripoll, P. Understanding The Mediating Role of Quality of Work Life on the Relationship between Emotional Intelligence and Organizational Citizenship Behaviors. *Psychol. Rep.* **2016**, *118*, 107–127. [CrossRef] [PubMed]

18. Mohammad, F.N.; Chai, L.T.; Aun, L.K.; Migin, M.W. Emotional intelligence and turnover intention. *Int. J. Acad. Res.* **2014**, *6*, 211–220.

19. Avey, J.M.; Luthans, F.; Jensen, S.M. Psychological capital: A positive resource for combating employee stress and turnover. *Hum. Resour. Manag.* **2009**, *48*, 677–693. [CrossRef]

20. O'Boyle, E.H.; Humphrey, R.H.; Pollack, J.M.; Hawver, T.H.; Story, P.A. The relation between emotional intelligence and job performance: A meta-analysis. *J. Organ. Behav.* **2011**, *32*, 788–818. [CrossRef]

21. Laschinger, H.K.; Purdy, N.; Cho, J.; Almost, J. Antecedents and consequences of nurse managers' perceptions of organizational support. *Nursing Economic* **2006**, *24*, 20–29.

22. Rhoades, L.; Eisenberger, R. Perceived organizational support: A review of the literature. *J. Appl. Psychol.* **2002**, *87*, 698–714. [CrossRef]

23. Bande, B.; Fernández-Ferrín, P.; Varela, J.A.; Jaramillo, F. Emotions and salesperson propensity to leave: The effects of emotional intelligence and resilience. *Ind. Mark. Manag.* **2015**, *44*, 142–153. [CrossRef]

24. Kidwell, B.; Hardesty, D.M.; Murtha, B.R.; Sheng, S. Emotional intelligence in marketing exchanges. *J. Mark.* **2011**, *75*, 78–95. [CrossRef]

25. Mayer, J.D.; Salovey, P. The intelligence of emotional intelligence. *Intelligence* **1993**, *17*, 433–442. [CrossRef]

26. Bar-On, R. The Bar-On model of emotional-social intelligence (ESI). *Psicothema* **2006**, *18*, 13–25. [PubMed]

27. Reis, D.L.; Brackett, M.A.; Shamosh, N.A.; Kiehl, K.A.; Salovey, P.; Gray, J.R. Emotional Intelligence predicts individual differences in social exchange reasoning. *NeuroImage* **2007**, *35*, 1385–1391. [CrossRef] [PubMed]

28. Salovey, P.; Mayer, J.D. Emotional intelligence. *Imagin. Cogn. Personal.* **1990**, *9*, 185–211. [CrossRef]

29. Ravichandran, K.; Arasu, R.; Kumar, S.A. The impact of emotional intelligence on employee work engagement behavior: An empirical study. *Int. J. Bus. Manag.* **2011**, *6*, 157–169. [CrossRef]

30. Serrat, O. Understanding and Developing Emotional Intelligence. In *Knowledge Solutions: Tools, Methods, and Approaches to Drive Organizational Performance*; Serrat, O., Ed.; Springer Singapore: Singapore, 2017; pp. 329–339.

31. Krishnaveni, R.; Deepa, R. Emotional intelligence–a soft tool for competitive advantage in the organizational context. *ICFAI J. Soft Ski.* **2011**, *5*, 51–62.

32. Tett, R.P.; Meyer, J.P. Job satisfaction, organizational commitment, turnover intention, and turnover: Path analyses based on meta-analytic findings. *Pers. Psychol.* **1993**, *46*, 259–293. [CrossRef]

33. Khan, M.R.U.; Nazir, N.; Kazmi, S.; Khalid, A.; Kiyani, T.M.; Shahzad, A. Work-life conflict and turnover intentions: Mediating effect of stress. *Int. J. Humanit. Soc. Sci.* **2014**, *4*, 92–100.

34. Dess, G.G.; Shaw, J.D. Voluntary turnover, social capital, and organizational performance. *Acad. Manag. Rev.* **2001**, *26*, 446–456. [CrossRef]

35. Saeed, I.; Waseem, M.; Sikander, S.; Rizwan, M. The relationship of turnover intention with job satisfaction, job performance, leader member exchange, emotional intelligence and organizational commitment. *Int. J. Learn. Dev.* **2014**, *4*, 242–256. [CrossRef]

36. Chan, S.H.J.; Ao, C.T.D. The mediating effects of job satisfaction and organizational commitment on turnover intention, in the relationships between pay satisfaction and work–family conflict of casino employees. *J. Qual. Assur. Hosp. Tour.* **2019**, *20*, 206–229. [CrossRef]

37. Mobley, W.H. *Employee Turnover: Causes, Consequences, and Control*; Addison-Wesley publishing: Philippines, PA, USA, 1982.

38. Griffeth, R.W.; Hom, P.W.; Gaertner, S. A meta-analysis of antecedents and correlates of employee turnover: Update, moderate tests, and research implications for the next millennium. *J. Manag.* **2000**, *26*, 463–488. [CrossRef]

39. Vuong, B.N.; Giao, H.N.K. The impact of perceived brand globalness on consumers' purchase intention and the moderating role of consumer ethnocentrism: An evidence from Vietnam. *J. Int. Consum. Mark.* **2020**, *32*, 47–68. [CrossRef]

40. Karatepe, O.M. The effects of work overload and work-family conflict on job embeddedness and job performance: The mediation of emotional exhaustion. *Int. J. Contemp. Hosp. Manag.* **2013**, *25*, 614–634. [CrossRef]

41. Durup, R.J.M. *An Integration Model of Work and Family Stress: Comparisons of Models*; Dahousie University: Halifax, NS, Canada, 1993.

42. Olorunfemi, D.Y. Family-work conflict, information use, and social competence: a case study of married postgraduate students in the faculty of education, University of Ibadan, Nigeria. *Libr. Philos. Pract.* **2009**, *235*, 1–7.

43. Greenhaus, J.H.; Beutell, N.J. Sources and conflict between work and family roles. *Acad. Manag. Rev.* **1985**, *10*, 76–88. [CrossRef]

44. Wang, I.A.; Lee, B.W.; Wu, S.T. The relationships among work-family conflict, turnover intention and organizational citizenship behavior in the hospitality industry of Taiwan. *Int. J. Manpow.* **2017**, *38*, 1120–1142. [CrossRef]

45. Boyar, S.; Maertz, C.; Person, A.; Keough, S. Work-family conflict: A model of linkages between work and family domain variables and turnover intentions. *J. Manag. Issues* **2003**, *15*, 175–190.

46. Choi, H.J.; Kim, Y.T. Work-family conflict, work-family facilitation, and job outcomes in the Korean hotel industry. *Int. J. Contemp. Hosp. Manag.* **2012**, *24*, 1011–1028. [CrossRef]

47. Mihelic, K.K.; Tekavcic, M. Work-family conflict: A review of antecedents and outcomes. *Int. J. Manag. Inf. Syst.* **2014**, *18*, 15–26. [CrossRef]

48. Demerouti, E.; Bakker, A.B.; Nachreiner, F.; Schaufeli, W.B. The job demands-resources model of burnout. *J. Appl. Psychol.* **2001**, *86*, 499–512. [CrossRef] [PubMed]

49. Davidson, M.J.; Cooper, C.L. *Shattering the Glass Ceiling, the Woman Manager*; Paul Chapman: London, UK, 1992.

50. Freudenberg, H.J. Staff burnout. *Journal of Soc. Issues* **1974**, *1*, 159–164. [CrossRef]

51. Pines, A.; Aronson, E.; Kafry, D. *Burnout: From Tedium to Personal Growth*; Free Press: New York, NY, USA, 1981.

52. Kahn, R.L. Job burnout: Prevention and remedies. *Public Welf.* **1978**, *36*, 61–63.

53. Maslach, C.; Jackson, S.E. The measurement of experienced burnout. *J. Occup. Behav.* **1981**, *2*, 99–113. [CrossRef]

54. Maslach, C.; Schaufeli, W.B.; Leiter, M.P. Job burnout. *Annu. Rev. Psychol.* **2001**, *52*, 397–422. [CrossRef] [PubMed]

55. Toker, S.; Biron, M. Job burnout and depression: unraveling their temporal relationship and considering the role of physical activity. *J. Appl. Psychol.* **2012**, *97*, 699–710. [CrossRef] [PubMed]

56. Raza, B.; Ali, M.; Naseem, K.; Moeed, A.; Ahmed, J.; Hamid, M. Impact of trait mindfulness on job satisfaction and turnover intentions: Mediating role of work–family balance and moderating role of work–family conflict. *Cogent Bus. Manag.* **2018**, *5*, 1–20. [CrossRef]

57. Webb, K.S. Why emotional intelligence should matter to management: A survey of the literature. *SAM Adv. Manag. J.* **2009**, *74*, 32.

58. Ramesar, S.; Koortzen, P.; Oosthuizen, R.M. The relationship between emotional intelligence and stress management. *SA J. Ind. Psychol.* **2009**, *35*, 1–10. [CrossRef]

59. Frost, P.J. *Toxic Emotions at Work*; Harvard Business School Press: Boston, MA, USA, 2003.

60. Riaz, F.; Naeem, S.; Khanzada, B.; Butt, K. Impact of emotional intelligence on turnover intention, job performance and organizational citizenship behavior with mediating role of political skill. *J. Health Educ. Res. Dev.* **2018**, *6*, 250. [CrossRef]

61. Ng, T.; Feldman, D. Organizational tenure and job performance. *J. Manag.* **2010**, *35*, 1220–1250. [CrossRef]

62. Akhtar, W.M.; Shabir, A.; Safdar, S.M.; Akhtar, S.M. Impact of emotional intelligence on turnover intentions: The role of organizational commitment and perceive organizational support. *J. Account. Mark.* **2017**, *6*, 1–7.

63. Lenaghan, J.A.; Buda, R.; Eisner, A.B. An examination of the role of emotional intelligence in work and family conflict. *J. Manag. Issues* **2007**, *19*, 76–94.

64. Carmeli, A. The relationship between emotional intelligence and work attitudes, behavior and outcomes: An examination among senior managers. *J. Manag. Psychol.* **2003**, *18*, 788–813. [CrossRef]

65. Hobfoll, S.E. Conservation of resources. A new attempt at conceptualizing stress. *Am. Psychol.* **1989**, *44*, 513–524. [CrossRef] [PubMed]

66. Gao, Y.; Shi, J.; Niu, Q.; Wang, L. Work–family conflict and job satisfaction: Emotional intelligence as a moderator. *Stress Health* **2013**, *29*, 222–228. [CrossRef]

67. Suliman, A.M.; Al-Shaikh, F.N. Emotional intelligence at work: links to conflict and innovation. *Employee Relations* **2007**, *29*, 208–220. [CrossRef]

68. Kaye, B.; Jordan-Evans, S. *Love 'Em or Lose 'Em: Getting Good People to Stay*; Berrett-Koehler Publishers, Inc: Williston, ND, USA, 2005.

69. Bilal, M.; Rehman, M.Z.; Raza, I. Impact of family friendly policies on employees' job satisfaction and turnover intention: A study on work-life balance at workplace. *Interdiscip. J. Contemp. Res. Bus.* **2010**, *2*, 379–395.

70. Greenhaus, J.H.; Parasuraman, S.; Collins, K.M. Career involvement and family involvement as moderators of relationships between work-family conflict and withdrawal from a profession. *J. Occup. Health Psychol.* **2001**, *6*, 91–100. [CrossRef]

71. Allen, T.D.; Armstrong, J. Further examination of the link between work–family conflict and physical health: The role of health-related behaviors. *Am. Behav. Sci.* **2006**, *49*, 1204–1221. [CrossRef]

72. Taylor, G.J. *Low Emotional Intelligence and Mental Illness*; Taylor & Francis: Philadelphia, PA, USA, 2001.

73. Moon, T.W.; Hur, W. Emotional intelligence, emotional exhaustion and job performance. *Soc. Behav. Personal.* **2011**, *39*, 1087–1096. [CrossRef]

74. Wong, C.-S.; Law, K. The effects of leader and follower emotional intel- ligence on performance and attitude: An exploratory study. *Leadersh. Q.* **2002**, *13*, 243–274. [CrossRef]

75. Aslam, R.; Shumaila, S.; Azhar, M.; Sadaqat, S. Work-family conflicts: Relationship between work-life conflict and employee retention-A comparative study of public and private sector employees. *Interdiscip. J. Res. Bus.* **2011**, *1*, 18–29.

76. Golden, T.D. Altering the effects of work and family conflict on exhaustion: Telework during traditional and nontraditional work hours. *J. Bus. Psychol.* **2012**, *27*, 255–269. [CrossRef]

77. Scanlan, J.N.; Still, M. Relationships between burnout, turnover intention, job satisfaction, job demands and job resources for mental health personnel in an Australian mental health service. *BMC Health Serv. Res.* **2019**, *19*, 62. [CrossRef]

78. Gharakhani, D.; Zaferanchi, A. The effect of job burnout on turnover intention with regard to the mediating role of job satisfaction. *Arumshealth* **2019**, *10*, 109–117. [CrossRef]

79. Layne, C.; Hohenshil, T.; Singh, K. The relationship of occupational stress, psychological strain, and coping resources to the turnover intensions of rehabilitation counselors. *Rehabil. Couns. Bull.* **2004**, *48*, 19–30. [CrossRef]

80. Khan, F.; Khan, Q.; Naz, A.; Khan, N. Job rotation on job burnout, organizational commitment: A quantitative study on medical staffs Khyber Pakhtunkhwa Pakistan. *J. Soc. Sci. Humanit. Stud.* **2017**, *3*, 11–18.

81. Mayer, J.D.; Salovey, P. What is Emotional Intelligence? In *Emotional Development and Emotional Intelligence: Educational Implications*; Salovey, P., Sluyter, D., Eds.; Basic Books: New York, NY, USA, 1997.

82. Sergio, R.P.; Dungca, A.L.; Gonzales, J.O. Emotional intelligence, work / family conflict, and work values among customer service representatives: Basis for organizational support. *J. East. Eur. Cent. Asian Res.* **2015**, *2*, 1–9. [CrossRef]

83. Weinzimmer, L.G.; Baumann, H.M.; Gullifor, D.P.; Koubova, V. Emotional intelligence and job performance: The mediating role of work-family balance. *J. Soc. Psychol.* **2017**, *157*, 322–337. [CrossRef]

84. Siddiqui, R.S.; Hasan, A. Relationship between emotional intelligence and employee turnover rate in FMCG organizations. *Pak. J. Commer. Social Sci.* **2013**, *7*, 198–208.

85. Eisenberger, R.; Huntington, R.; Hutchinson, S.; Sowa, D. Perceived organizational support. *J. Appl. Psychol.* **1986**, *71*, 500–507. [CrossRef]

86. Gurbuz, S.; Turunc, O.; Celik, M. The impact of perceived organizational support on work–family conflict: Does role overload have a mediating role? *Econ. Ind. Democr.* **2013**, *34*, 145–160. [CrossRef]

87. Caesens, G.; Stinglhamber, F.; Demoulin, S.; De Wilde, M. Perceived organizational support and employees' well-being: The mediating role of organizational dehumanization. *Eur. J. Work Organ. Psychol.* **2017**, *26*, 527–540. [CrossRef]

88. Marchand, C.; Vandenberghe, C. Perceived organizational support, emotional exhaustion, and turnover: The moderating role of negative affectivity. *Int. J. Stress Manag.* **2016**, *23*, 350–375. [CrossRef]

89. Kundu Subhash, C. Effects of supportive work environment on employee retention: Mediating role of organizational engagement. *Int. J. Organ. Anal.* **2017**, *25*, 703–722. [CrossRef]

90. Liu, B.; Liu, J.; Hu, J. Person-organization fit, job satisfaction, and turnover intention: An empirical study in the Chinese public sector. *Soc. Behav. Personal. Int. J.* **2010**, *38*, 615–626. [CrossRef]

91. Seyrek, İ.H.; Turan, A. Effects of individual characteristics and work related factors on the turnover intention of accounting professionals. *Int. J. Acad. Res. Account. Financ. Manag. Sci.* **2017**, *7*, 236–244. [CrossRef]

92. Netemeyer, R.G.; Boles, J.S.; McMurrian, R. Development and validation of work-family conflict and family-work conflict scales. *J. Appl. Psychol.* **1996**, *81*, 400–410. [CrossRef]

93. Lee, H.J. How emotional intelligence relates to job satisfaction and burnout in public service jobs. *Int. Rev. Adm. Sci.* **2017**, *84*, 729–745. [CrossRef]

94. Vigoda, E. Organizational politics, job attitudes, and work outcomes: Exploration and implications for the public sector. *J. Vocat. Behav.* **2000**, *57*, 326–347. [CrossRef]

95. Giao, H.N.K.; Vuong, B.N. *Giáo Trình Cao Học Phương Pháp Nghiên Cứu Khoa Học Trong Kinh Doanh Cập Nhật SmartPLS*; Nhà Xuất Bản Tài Chính: TP. Hồ Chí Minh, Việt Nam, 2019.

96. Fornell, C.; Larcker, D.F. Evaluating structural equation models with unobservable variables and measurement error. *J. Mark. Res.* **1981**, *18*, 39–50. [CrossRef]

97. Giao, H.N.K.; Vuong, B.N.; Quan, T.N. The influence of website quality on consumer's e-loyalty through the mediating role of e-trust and e-satisfaction: An evidence from online shopping in Vietnam. *Uncertain Supply Chain Manag.* **2020**, *8*. [CrossRef]

98. Hair, J.F.; Hult, G.T.M.; Ringle, C.M.; Sarstedt, M. *A Primer on Partial Least Squares Structural Equation Modeling (PLS-SEM)*; Sage Publication, Inc: Thousand Oaks, CA, USA, 2014.

99. Vuong, B.N.; Suntrayuth, S. The impact of human resource management practices on employee engagement and moderating role of gender and marital status: An evidence from the Vietnamese banking industry. *Manag. Sci. Lett.* **2020**, *10*, 1633–1648. [CrossRef]

100. Vuong, B.N.; Hieu, V.T.; Trang, N.T.T. An empirical analysis of mobile banking adoption in Vietnam. *Gestão e Soc.* **2020**, *14*, 3365–3393. [CrossRef]

10

Mobile Banking: An Innovative Solution for Increasing Financial Inclusion in Sub-Saharan African Countries

Alfonso Siano [1,*], **Lukman Raimi** [2], **Maria Palazzo** [1] and **Mirela Clementina Panait** [3]

[1] Department of Political and Communication Sciences, University of Salerno, 84084 Salerno, Italy; mpalazzo@unisa.it

[2] Department of Entrepreneurship and Management, American University of Nigeria, Lagos 23401, Nigeria; lukman.raimi@aun.edu.ng

[3] Department of Cybernetics, Economic Informatics, Finance and Accounting, Petroleum-Gas University of Ploiesti, 100680 Ploiesti, Romania; mirela.matei@upg-ploiesti.ro

[*] Correspondence: sianoalf@unisa.it

Abstract: Purpose—This research discusses emerging trends in financial inclusion, barriers and factors influencing mobile banking as an innovative solution for increasing financial inclusion in sub-Saharan Africa (SSA) with a specific focus on Nigeria. Design/methodology/approach—Using a qualitative meta-synthesis (QMS), an interpretivist research paradigm, authors provide an analytical tool for understanding the subject of inquiry by integrating findings from previous studies and relevant data from the reports of the Central Bank of Nigeria on emerging trends in financial inclusion. Findings—Three major factors emerged as drivers of mobile banking in Nigeria: (a) the ease of using mobile devices for personal banking transactions including prompt information about users' financial transactions (savings and withdrawals) immediately through SMS (short message service) alert (easy management of my account); (b) the security/safety concerns of theft and cyber fraud; (c) social influence of friends, relatives, policy makers and social trends. Implications—In contextualizing mobile banking in SSA and in Nigeria in particular, this paper contributes to exploring the growth in the use of mobile banking by linking it with the "value in use" (VIU) perspective. This approach of the service dominant logic involves three sub-constructs (experience, personalization, and relationship), which all validate and support the proposed assertion that mobile banking is adopted by users because of utility expectancy (perceived usefulness), effort expectancy (perceived ease of use), and social influence expectancy (opinions of friends/relatives). Originality/value—This research, although qualitative in nature, validates information technology (IT) adoption theories/perspectives and enriches the "value in use" approach.

Keywords: financial inclusion; innovative solution; mobile banking; Nigeria; sub-Saharan Africa (SSA); qualitative meta-synthesis (QMS); banking industry; digital transformation; value in use approach

1. Introduction

The global economy faces extreme poverty, slower growth, climate change, widening inequalities, unemployment, and growing inconstant working conditions, but the plight of sub-Saharan Africa (SSA) is worse because more than 204 million people are unemployed, and the worsening unemployment situation provides breeding grounds for forced labour, slavery and human trafficking [1]. Additionally, the report of the World Bank from 2019 [2] identified extreme poverty, growing public debt/debt risk, slow growth of the labour market, rising labour force, and gender disparities as the critical inhibiting factors holding back economic growth and sustainable development in SSA.

In the midst of the economic crisis explicated above, the people and businesses in the area, including Nigeria, suffer an extremely low level of financial inclusion [3,4]. Studies have explicated that the phenomenon of the lack of access (financial exclusion) to basic financial services is a global problem, but the problem is most pronounced in emerging economies including SSA [5,6].

At the global level, financial inclusion has occupied the attention of international organisations especially the agendas of the millennium development goals (MDGs) and sustainable development goals (SDGs). Some of the targets of the expired MDGs alert the United Nations member countries to the pressing issue of financial inclusion and its complexity. Specifically, the goals of fighting extreme poverty foundationally (MDG1); achieving gender equality to promote equal opportunities for women to access employment, social protection, and training (MDG3); and forging a global partnership for development (MDG 8) directly address financial inclusion challenges. Similarly, the targets of the ongoing SDGs that directly impact on financial inclusion include: no poverty (SDG1), zero hunger (SDG2), good health and wellbeing (SDG3), quality education (SDG4), decent work and economic growth (SDG8), industry, innovation, and infrastructure (SDG9), reduced inequality (SDG10), peace, justice and strong institutions (SDG16) and partnerships for the goals (SDG17).

In Nigeria, several attempts have been made by the government to improve financial inclusion through a number of public-sector led credit schemes and poverty alleviation programmes such as National Economy Reconstruction Fund (NERFUND); the People's Bank, Community Banking Models, the Bank of Industry (BOI), the Microfinance Institutions (MFIs) the Small and Medium Enterprises Equity Investment Scheme (SMEEIS), National Poverty Eradication Programme, Youth Enterprise with Innovation in Nigeria (You Win) Programme, Subsidy Reinvestment and Empowerment Programme or SURE-P, National Enterprise Development Programme or NEDEP and several others [7,8]. In spite of the financial inclusion intervention schemes, the National Financial Inclusion Strategy (drafted in 2012 and revised in 2018) and the "cash-less Nigeria policy", the efforts failed because of the government's inability to properly nurture its development programmes, weak reward system, dysfunctional structures and endemic poor programme implementation [8–11]. In the early 2000s, mobile banking emerged as an information technology (IT)-driven innovative technology, which greatly improved the degree of financial inclusion in the continent [5,12–15]. Mobile banking provides virtual access for individuals and businesses to procure financial transactions such as savings, funds' transfer, and stock market deals with banks at any convenient time and place [16]. The receptiveness to mobile banking is impressive, as the majority of the banks in Nigeria have adopted and introduced mobile banking applications. Additionally, mobile banking has thrived because Nigeria has the fastest growing telecommunication infrastructure in Africa and the third in the world [17]. The benefit of IT infrastructure is supported by the population of over 150 million people [18]. Providing an enabling environment for better and improved financial inclusion, Nigeria justifies the adoption and introduction of mobile banking to strengthen local and international efforts towards financial inclusion (the timely introduction of mobile phone technology in the continent within the last 10 years resulted in 82% mobile banking penetration in Nigeria, the highest penetration of mobile banking across developing markets [19].

It is possible to state that research on financial inclusion in SSA is just emerging [20–22]. To enrich the body of knowledge in this important field of financial inclusion, there is a need to explore empirical evidence. Financial inclusion, in fact, has been delayed in the continent prior to the liberalization of the financial sector in the 1980s, because many African banks were owned, controlled and heavily regulated by the governments as monopolies, a situation that restricted the adoption of innovative technologies in banking operations [3,6,23].

Thus, the purpose of this exploratory qualitative research is to critically discuss the emerging trends in financial inclusion, the barriers to financial inclusion and factors influencing mobile banking adoption as an innovative solution for increasing financial inclusion in SSA with a specific focus on Nigeria.

There are several parts to this paper. The first part presents the introduction of the thematic issue of mobile banking and financial inclusion. The second part focuses on the definition of financial inclusion and mobile banking from both managerial and academic perspectives, examining barriers to financial inclusion and factors influencing adoption of mobile banking in Nigeria. Then, this paper discusses methodology and proposes findings and discussions of thematic issues. The concluding part discusses the implications and recommendations on the mobile banking agenda and direction in sub-Saharan Africa.

2. Theoretical Background

2.1. Financial Inclusion: Definitions and Features

The need to achieve the sustainable development goals brings to the attention of the authorities a pressing issue, namely the complexity of the phenomenon, the multitude of tools that could be used to achieve the set targets, the large number of stakeholders involved or that may be involved and the lack of financial funds [24–27]. For these reasons, financial inclusion has become important, both at the microeconomic and macroeconomic levels, as it can be a tool for promoting the principles of sustainable development [28–36]. Financial inclusion is not only a concern of financial institutions that are trying to attract more and more categories of consumers and have a responsible attitude towards them but also of public authorities [33,37–42]. In fact, there are specialists who consider financial inclusion, for some countries, even a catalyst for sustainable development, a tool for poverty reduction and a facilitator of economic growth [27,43–45]. Financial inclusion is a complex concept in a continuous evolution taking into account the transformations that are taking place worldwide from an economic, social and political point of view. Financial inclusion refers to "access to and usage of appropriate, affordable, and accessible financial services" [46]. Given the complexity of the phenomenon and the importance of national and regional characteristics on it, financial inclusion presents multiple definitions in the literature, which emphasize certain aspects such as financial innovation, microfinance and the use of mobile phones [47]. According to the World Bank, which is a main international financial institution with preoccupations in this field, financial inclusion is defined as "access to useful and affordable financial products and services that meet their needs—transactions, payments, savings, credit and insurance—delivered in a responsible and sustainable way" [43].

Apiors and Suzuki (2018) consider that financial inclusion supposes "the full range of services (payments, savings, credit, and insurance), to specific quality features of delivery (for example, stability and affordability), inclusiveness (with special focus on the poor), and choice (offer of service by a range of institutions)" [48].

The concept of social inclusion emerged as a solution to the phenomenon of social exclusion that has been identified by geographers who have observed limited access of certain categories of citizens to basic financial services [49]. After the emergence of the concept of social exclusion, the 90s were characterized by intense scientific concerns regarding citizens' access to financial services for payment, savings, and credit, but also to insurance services. Subsequently, the European Commission focused on this issue, considering that financial exclusion is a component of the phenomenon of social exclusion that affects, in various forms, important categories of citizens of the European Union [45]. Financial exclusion targets people that "encounter difficulties accessing and/or using financial services and products in the mainstream market that are appropriate to their needs and enable them to lead a normal social life in the society in which they belong." It must be highlighted that the phenomenon of financial exclusion affects both developed and developing countries, but the share of the non-banked population is different across the world, depending on the level of development of that country [45].

Although the concept of financial exclusion has emerged in the UK [50], the phenomenon mainly affects developing countries characterized by a precarious financial infrastructure from an institutional, technical, legislative, or social point of view. Given the manifestation of the phenomenon of financial exclusion predominantly in developing countries, more and more definitions and approaches [51,52] focus on: (i) citizens' access to the formal or semi-formal financial sector composed of commercial banks, development finance institutions, post offices, microfinance banks, credit unions and cooperatives, (ii) improving the process of saving but also accessing loans, (iii) enhancing risk management, (iv) developing innovative financial solutions, (v) protection of consumer rights.

The concerns of international financial institutions such as the World Bank, development agencies, national market supervisors and regulators have intensified [53] in order to attract an increasing number of citizens to gain access to products and services. As the financial inclusion is a multidimensional concept [47], various categories of stakeholders from supply and demand sides must be involved. Public authorities and financial institutions must offer sustainable alternatives to consumers, and citizens must make efforts to increase the degree of financial education by participating in programs conducted in this regard by various entities [45,54–58]. Given the multiple crises and scandals that have particularly affected the banking market, financial institutions need to substantially improve their behaviour so as to inspire consumer confidence. Therefore, consumers are also required to use the proper financial services according to their ability to understand financial phenomena or income level [59,60]. In addition, in certain particular situations, such as immigrants, financial consumers have to overcome certain language, cultural, and religious barriers [45,48,61]. Consumers must not only show responsibility when making financial decisions but must also have the ability to learn and adapt to the new conditions of the financial market generated by the digitization of operations. Achieving the objectives set at national level, usually by launching financial inclusion strategies, therefore requires sustained efforts both by the population and by the financial authorities and institutions.

Given the large number of definitions [47], three dimensions of financial inclusion have been established, namely access (refers to physical proximity and affordability), usage (refers to regularity, frequency, duration of time used) and quality (refers to products well-tailored to clients' needs and to appropriate segmentation to develop products for all income levels). To the three dimensions, other specialists [44,62] added an additional dimension—choice (Figure 1).

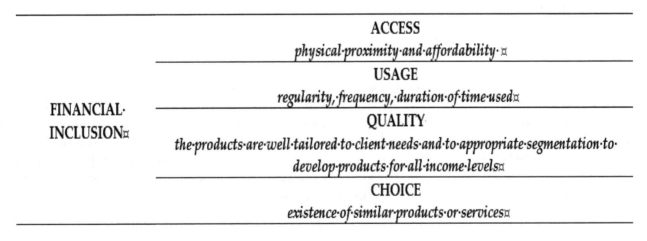

Figure 1. Dimensions of Financial Inclusion. Source [47].

Mobile banking largely stimulates and promotes financial inclusion in developing economies, especially in sub-Saharan Africa [13], mobile penetration promotes financial inclusion, and significantly reduces the probability of a household becoming poor [63–69]. Having briefly synthesized this complex topic, this paper will focus on the analysis of financial inclusion, taking into consideration Nigeria. Nigeria is one of the leaders on the African continent along with Kenya in the process of increasing the degree of financial inclusion through the use of mobile banking. In addition, the successful experiences registered in these countries have been models for other countries in the areas of implementation and development of mobile banking systems. Despite the similarities between the two countries in terms of the level of development, the degree of financial exclusion penetration rates in mobile phone usage, the structure of the banking system and the approach to the need to increase financial inclusion were undertaken with different instruments. The reluctance of the Central Bank of Nigeria to use this model based on a mobile phone company monopoly, the structure of the mobile phone market and the late launch of initiative that coincided with the onset of the 2008 international financial crisis made the results modest. Therefore, the model of "bank-led" (or a non-MNO-led-mobile network operators-led) ecosystem used in Nigeria generates different network externalities compared to mobile network operator systems used in Kenya [70–73].

2.2. Barriers to Financial Inclusion

In developing countries, financial exclusion is fuelled by the country's economic structure (mainly agriculture), the location of the majority of the population is in the rural areas with poor banking intermediation and low spread of money deposit bank branches across different parts of the country due to the policy of commercial financial institutions [27]. Other factors that limit the financial inclusion of the population are bureaucracy, high costs of banking products and services and distance [52,74,75].

Leveraging on past studies developed in Nigeria, Table 1 below clearly shows the degree of financial inclusion in the country measured in terms of five metrics, namely (a) % of adult using formal payment systems, (b) % of adult with savings accounts, (c) % of adult with credit from the bank, (d) % of adult with insurance policies, (e) % of adult with pension schemes and (f) % of adult financial exclusion.

Table 1. Access to financial services in Nigeria (2010–2018).

Focus Area	2010	2012	2014	2016	2018
% of Adult using Formal Payments System	22	20	24	38	40
% of Adult with Savings Accounts	24	25	32	36	24
% of Adult enjoying Credits	2	2	3	3	2
% of Adult with Insurance Policies	1	3	1	2	2
% of Adult with Pension Schemes	5	2	5	7	8
% of Adult Financial Exclusion	46.3	39.7	39.5	41.6	36.8

Source: [76].

The barrier of distance mentioned above is generated both by the weak representation in the territory of commercial banks, but also by the state of infrastructure that exacerbates the problem of moving citizens from rural areas to cities to make various financial operations [77]. Moreover, Table 2 below shows that weak representation of deposit money bank branches engenders the problem of financial inclusion in Nigeria. In fact, states in Northern Nigeria such as Adamawa, Jigawa, Bornu, Bauchi, and Kwara with a large population have very few bank branches, whereas smaller cosmopolitan states with a relatively low population have large bank branches.

Table 2. Number of deposit money bank branches in Nigeria by state 2010–2019.

	2010	2011	2012	2013	2014	2015	2016	2017	2018	2019
Number of Banks	24	24	21	24	24	25	25	26	27	29
Branches Abroad	2	2	2	1	1	2	2	2	2	2
Abia	146	125	138	147	144	135	142	137	135	135
Abuja (FCT)	398	359	379	397	380	369	421	437	382	390
Adamawa	67	79	63	61	47	47	57	64	66	60
Akwa-Ibom	99	92	100	94	92	103	106	114	88	102
Anambra	237	222	228	224	219	218	219	214	209	227
Bauchi	53	50	46	46	47	48	50	47	55	47
Bayelsa	37	37	37	38	38	38	38	39	35	35
Benue	75	57	73	76	67	63	69	71	78	65
Borno	79	68	71	69	83	72	60	61	58	56

Table 2. *Cont.*

	2010	2011	2012	2013	2014	2015	2016	2017	2018	2019
Cross-River	79	76	76	80	79	74	78	79	72	75
Delta	198	177	194	198	178	180	200	205	183	183
Ebonyi	35	45	33	33	59	61	37	36	59	42
Edo	183	162	188	192	144	165	178	188	159	177
Ekiti	80	60	64	76	91	87	86	92	76	77
Enugu	141	116	142	147	158	151	159	162	127	148
Gombe	40	36	36	37	43	41	36	37	65	34
Imo	104	97	100	102	110	105	98	100	99	94
Jigawa	39	37	36	38	63	66	38	36	43	34
Kaduna	183	170	169	171	154	164	168	173	169	157
Kano	193	186	183	183	174	170	178	179	195	161
Katsina	62	55	58	59	73	78	56	55	52	47
Kebbi	40	40	37	38	95	37	37	35	49	61
Kogi	80	77	82	84	88	80	79	82	70	71
Kwara	79	139	75	79	104	101	78	84	100	85
Lagos	1766	1453	1692	1678	1443	1486	1645	1686	1478	1624
Nasarawa	58	51	49	48	68	69	49	49	67	52
Niger	80	76	79	82	67	65	78	86	64	71
Ogun	175	402	161	154	137	142	154	172	153	169
Ondo	121	109	110	119	106	101	113	120	120	112
Osun	105	118	101	104	101	99	106	108	86	99
Oyo	236	203	223	237	347	343	222	237	195	223
Plateau	79	72	77	75	75	71	70	67	75	83
Rivers	302	246	310	311	292	275	312	319	275	301
Sokoto	53	53	52	52	43	45	53	52	60	47
Taraba	37	41	35	35	40	40	34	27	39	30
Yobe	35	35	33	35	38	41	34	31	27	29
Zamfara	35	33	34	40	39	38	30	31	38	34
TOTAL	5809	5454	5564	5639	5526	5470	5570	5714	5301	5437

Source: [78].

In addition, the rapid growth of the population in developing countries contributes to the deepening of the phenomenon of population impoverishment, and implicitly of social exclusion. Despite the efforts made by the public authorities in the banking sector and by the credit institutions, the population growth precedes the growth of the banked population, there are also multiple regional differences [45].

The ways of manifesting the phenomenon of financial inclusion and financial literacy differ depending on consumers' level of income and the development level of the countries [44,77,79]. In high-income countries, financial exclusion affects a small part of the population, and citizens have concerns about making sophisticated investments in the financial market and an investment plan for retirement [80]. In low-income countries, the concerns of financial authorities and institutions regarding financial inclusion are much more complex and lasting because they concern a considerable proportion of the population being attracted from the non-formal to the formal sector, and the causes of financial exclusion are generated by the economic situation, and not only the poor financial education of the population [80]. In these countries, citizens have problems when simply trying to open a bank account or purchase insurance.

In developing countries, the main cause of low financial inclusion is extreme poverty that affects a large part of the population. Citizens of these countries do not have bank accounts because they do not have enough money to save [47,52]. Studies conducted for African countries have revealed a positive link between per capita income and financial inclusion. Thus, the study conducted by Alenoghenain (2017) for 15 African countries for the period 2005–2014 showed that a high income per capita generates a higher financial inclusion [81].

Therefore, a phenomenon with multiple economic and social implications such as financial exclusion/inclusion has a complex of determining factors, and solving the problem requires a systemic approach and the involvement of several categories of stakeholders.

In addition, financial exclusion affects not only poor people and women but also migrants [44,82–84]. The trend of international migration has also generated financial problems, as migrants have to overcome certain psychological barriers generated by distrust in complex banking systems (compared to those in the country of origin), lack of financial education specific to developing countries or the time horizon (if the stay is prolonged, there is a change in attitude towards the banking system). The phenomenon of saving specific to migrants is followed by the periodic sending of large sums of money to the family in the country of origin, which is why having a bank account to make bank transfers is essential [85,86]. The frequency of remittances is different, being influenced by the needs of the family, the sex of the migrant, the prospects of opening a business in the country of origin or buying a home and by the intention to reunite the family in the destination country [61,87].

2.3. Drivers of Mobile Banking

The adoption of mobile banking has improved all aspects of financial transactions for both corporate and non-corporate customers of banks in Nigeria [21,88,89]. Conceptually, the term mobile banking is understood as the use of mobile devices for undertaking virtual financial transactions (especially savings, funds' transfer, and stock market transactions) with banks by customers at any convenient time and place [16]. Financial consumers are increasingly interested in achieving easy access to banking services and products, either to save money or to pay for goods or to send money to relatives or friends. In this sense, the statistical data provided by Global Findex [90] show the increase in the percentage of the population that makes domestic remittances. The intensification of the international migration process has also led to an increase in the frequency and value of the remittances sent by migrants to origin countries, mobile banking being a feasible solution that allows financial transfers but it also contributes to increasing the degree of financial education and financial inclusion in these countries. The feasibility of this method is also supported by the low costs generated by the intensification of competition between banks. From the consumers' perspective, the future of mobile banking depends on essentials such as ubiquity, instant connectivity, pro-active functionality, convenience, access to the service regardless of time and place, privacy, and savings in time and effort [91–93] (Singh 2012, Tiwari et al., 2016, Akturan and Tezcan, 2012). In addition, "The younger generations of the society seem to be fascinated by modern data and telecommunication services" [92]. The analysis of financial inclusion vis-à-vis mobile banking and information technology (IT) has to be embedded in IT adoption theories/perspectives. According to Bankole et al. (2011), the widely used theories in mobile banking [16] include the technology acceptance model (TAM), the extended technology acceptance model (TAM2), the theory of reasoned action (TRA), the theory of planned behavior (TPB) and the unified theory of use and acceptance of technology (UTAUT). Other specialists have focused on the task–technology fit (TTF) theory and the diffusion of innovation (DOI) in order to explain the determinants of the acceptance of mobile banking [94,95] (Munoz-Leiva et al. 2017, Sharma 2019). The technology acceptance model (TAM), the main influential model, focuses on two main issues—perceived usefulness and perceived ease of use—to explain the variance in users' intentions [96] (Luarn and Pin, 2005). According to Nasri and Charfeddine 2012, the "TPB suggests that in addition to attitudinal and normative influence, a third antecedent to the theory called perceived behavioral control, perceived behavioral (PBC), also influences behavioral intentions and actual behavior" [97]. Particularly, TAM and TPB were used by several researchers to investigate the factors influencing users' behavioural intentions towards mobile banking [16,98]. Summing up the insights from all the IT adoption theories, proponents argued that mobile banking is an off-shoot of IT that is adopted by users for financial transactions because of key factors, namely performance expectancy (perceived usefulness), effort expectancy (perceived ease of use), social influence (opinions of friends, relatives), facilitating conditions, trust and privacy, convenience and cost, user satisfaction and national culture [98–100].

Starting from these premises, the receptiveness of Nigerian customers towards mobile banking is impressive, as all banks have adopted and introduced mobile banking applications (the popular mobile banking apps in Nigeria include Diamond Mobile Banking, Stanbic IBTC Mobile Banking, First Bank Mobile Banking, Eco Bank Mobile Banking, Access Bank Mobile Banking, Fidelity Bank Mobile Banking and Sterling Bank Mobile Banking). Several factors have been identified by scholars as the determinants influencing mobile banking in the country. In a sequential order, the following are insights on factors influencing the adoption of mobile banking.

Anyasi and Otubu (2009) noted that mobile banking was adopted in Nigeria as a preferred means of accessing financial services with or without access to traditional banks, it also offers a way to lower the costs of transferring funds from place to place, while at the same time improving financial inclusion by bringing unbanked people into contact with the formal financial systems [101]. A decade ago, a result of the research of Oni et al. (2010) indicated that the e-banking system in Nigeria is widely adopted and preferred by customers because it is convenient, easy to use, time efficient, and appropriate for financial transactions. However, the users have concerns for the network security especially the privacy of transactions [102].

Moreover, Bankole et al. (2011) explained that utility expectancy and effort expectancy are major factors influencing behavioural intention to adopt mobile banking in Nigeria. Specifically, the ease of using a mobile device for personal banking transactions (easy management of accounts); the security and safety concerns of moving cash around regarding cyber fraud; and prompt information about users' financial transactions (savings and withdrawals) immediately through the SMS alert. However, the social influence of friends, relatives, colleagues at work and the service providers (banks) is not a major influence on mobile banking users in Nigeria [16].

Nevertheless, Aliyu et al. (2012) contended that the six critical success factors that influence the adoption of mobile banking in Nigeria include awareness, ease of use, security, cost, reduced reluctance to change and accessibility of mobile devices for undertaking financial transactions [103].

Furthermore, Balogun et al. (2013) affirmed that three factors largely influenced customers' satisfaction with different aspects of e-banking in Nigeria, such as telephone banking, mobile banking, point of sale terminals, smart cards, and television banking. These factors are the quality services provided by banks through SMS alerts and e-mail alerts; the second factor is access to the option of electronically opening a bank account, and the third factor is availability of automated teller machines in strategic locations for making withdrawals when needed without going into the banks [104].

However, Adewoyein (2013) reported that the adoption of mobile banking by customers is premised on a number of factors such as transactional convenience, better turn-around time (saving time), quick transaction alert, reduction in service cost and overall customer satisfaction [105]. Similarly, Njoku and Odumeru (2013) opined that seven factors positively influence the adoption of mobile banking in Nigeria, these include relative advantage that mobile banking gives to bank customers; less complexity of mobile technology; compatibility of mobile banking with customers' norms, belief, existing values, and past experience; perceived trialability/ease of mobile banking when experimented with by the customers; perceived observability/visibility of the outcomes of mobile banking to customers; age of customers using mobile banking; and educational qualification of customers using mobile banking [7].

Moreover, Agwu and Carter (2014) noted that the use of mobile phones for mobile banking has fundamentally changed the way Nigerians (as individuals and businesses) conduct financial transactions [106]. Particularly, mobile banking is more established than internet banking and ATM (automated teller machine) services because it has wider reach than both internet banking and mobile banking (effort expectancy).

Three factors identified by Tarhini et al. (2015) as key drivers of mobile banking adoption [107] in Nigeria include: (a) functionality factor that consists of awareness, ease of use and accessibility; (b) risks factors that comprise trust, security and privacy; and (c) context factor that includes convenience. From the viewpoints of Agu et al. (2016), mobile banking became a prominent feature in banking operations in the country because it is an effective technology for providing the growing population of customers with fast, accessible, reliable and quality services. Secondly, as an innovative option, mobile banking enables users carry out banking transactions anywhere and anytime and it provides an easy platform for paying for goods or services [108].

In the view of Khan and Ejike (2017), widespread adoption of mobile banking is influenced by access to technological domains, which enhance good knowledge regarding mobile devices, but the degree of convenience and satisfaction of usage are very low [109]. Additionally, Bagudu et al. (2017) explained that the singular and most important success factor for the widespread adoption of mobile banking in the country is access to functional mobile technology, which makes it easy for customers to carry out financial transactions on their mobile handsets with ease [110].

In SSA, there has been an increase in both registration and usage of financial inclusion tools such as mobile banking and related systems. This fact is corroborated by Bille et al., (2018) who reported that as of 2018 there has been an encouraging improvement in financial inclusion because unbanked people and the small and medium-sized enterprises (have been well integrated into the financial landscape in sub-Saharan Africa as a result of improved access to financial inclusion tools, which have been made accessible by the financial service providers, especially banks, microfinance institutions, different mobile network operators and licensed payment service providers [111]. Particularly, the World Bank report indicated that financial inclusion has reached over seven million new financial services users across SSA, from Senegal to Tanzania, from Nigeria to Zambia [111] (Bille et al., 2018).

3. Methodology

In view of the exploratory nature of this research, a qualitative meta-synthesis (QMS), an interpretivist research paradigm, provides a rich analytical tool for this study.

The qualitative meta-synthesis was applied as a suitable approach and essential stage towards enlarging the research and setting the basis for analysing the contributions of this paper [112]. This step makes it easy to identify boundaries of the conceptual content of the field and contribute to theory advances [113]. In line with the qualitative research tradition, a qualitative meta-synthesis is an analytical approach that is widely used in meta study to integrate different findings from diverse studies on the same subject of inquiry from different contexts [8,114].

The purpose of integrating findings and insights from groups of studies in a qualitative meta-synthesis is to develop an explanatory theory or model that explains the phenomenon being investigated better and richer [115]. With regard to steps involved in carrying out a sound QMS, Walsh and Downe (2005) proposed seven steps for using qualitative meta-synthesis in research [116].

(1) Framing a meta-synthesis exercise: our topic from the outset is framed for a qualitative meta-synthesis exercise.
(2) Locating relevant papers: we searched and located several papers on mobile banking within and outside SSA to gain richer insights on the subject of inquiry.
(3) Deciding what to include: after a literature audit of searched and located papers on mobile banking, we selected those related to mobile banking issues and financial inclusion in SSA in line with the qualitative meta-synthesis tradition.
(4) Appraising studies: the selected papers from SSA were then appraised to draw rich and meaningful information for making informed and evidence-based findings in line with the qualitative meta-synthesis tradition.
(5) Comparing and contrasting exercise: the findings in the selected papers from SSA were compared and contrasted.
(6) Reciprocating translation: we offered an explanation for the similar and opposing findings.

(7)   Synthesizing translation: the mixed findings extracted from different papers selected were then fused and synthesised to give a unique explanation for the trends and direction of mobile banking in relation to financial inclusion in SSA.

These steps were followed in the above study.

First of all, in order to manage the groundwork for the following QMS, and to identify emerging trends in financial inclusion, the key items were defined. In line with the mentioned definitions and features, but extending to related terms, "financial inclusion", "in-debtedness", "microfinance", "digital financial services", "mobile banking", and "Nigerian banks" were used for identifying related peer reviewed journal articles. The main reason for searching with these alternative items/terms was to ensure the comprehensive nature and content validity of our key terms.

The exploration for meaningful publications was conducted through databases such as Wiley, Elsevier, Scopus, Emerald, and Springer. The selection of these databases was based upon their use by academics in past systematic QMS in the fields of business, management, marketing, communication, and social sciences, along with the openness of the data for the analysis. In addition, the analysis was conducted by selecting only papers with a managerial/marketing perspective in peer-reviewed scientific journals published in the English language. Several papers in different languages or with a dissimilar focus were excluded. The list with articles used for this analysis is presented in Appendix A. The list of relevant papers was attained after removing duplicated articles and then exploring the filtered articles. Appendix A also refers to some relevant topics that are analysed in each paper, such as number of factors affecting mobile banking and type of specific factors affecting mobile banking.

Additionally, Appendices B and C show selected articles classified under several categories: number of research publications per year and classification based on number of determinants/factors able to influence mobile banking development. Moreover, for a meaningful selection of scholarly papers, a search for relevant articles on financial inclusion and mobile banking was carried out using a purposive sampling technique. Furthermore, 58 sampled articles that focused on Nigeria were systematically reviewed and synthesized with insights from the reports of the Central Bank of Nigeria to form integrated findings that explain the emerging trends in financial inclusion [117] and the barriers and factors influencing mobile banking in Nigeria.

The analysis and synthesis of papers aimed to reach two main objectives, first of all, briefly summarise existing research by identifying hot themes/matters; afterwards, contribute to shape the conceptual field of study. Obviously, the authors found it challenging to read everything about financial inclusion and mobile banking, especially if it is considered that the topic is not always called this label or the research is not always related to the selected country: Nigeria.

4. Findings and Discussions

Leveraging on the qualitative meta-synthesis, the findings that emerged could be classified into emerging trends on financial inclusion and the barriers and factors that influenced the adoption of mobile banking in Nigeria.

On the emerging trends of financial inclusion in connection with mobile banking, the research found that several attempts have been made by the government to improve financial inclusion in the country through a number of public-sector led credit schemes such National Economy Reconstruction Fund (NERFUND); the People's Bank, Community Banking Models, the Microfinance Institutions (MFIs), the Bank of Industry (BOI), the Small and Medium Enterprises Equity Investment Scheme (SMEEIS), National Poverty Eradication Programme, Youth Enterprise with Innovation in Nigeria (You Win) Programme, Subsidy Reinvestment and Empowerment Programme or SURE-P, National Enterprise Development Programme or NEDEP and several others (Table 3).

Table 3. Emerging trends in financial inclusion and mobile banking.

SN	Policies on Financial Inclusion	Governance Level	Target Audience
1	National Economy Reconstruction Fund (NERFUND)	National	Individuals and Businesses across Nigeria
2	People's Bank of Nigeria	National	Individuals, petty traders, artisans and small businesses across Nigeria
3	Community Banking Models	National	Individuals, petty traders, artisans and small businesses
4	Microfinance Institutions (MFIs)	National	Individuals, petty traders, artisans and small businesses
5	Bank of Industry (BOI)	National	Corporate entities—SMEs (small and medium-sized enterprises) across Nigeria
6	Small and Medium Enterprises Equity Investment Scheme (SMEEIS)	National	Corporate entities—SMEs across Nigeria
7	National Poverty Eradication Programme (NAPEP)	National	Individuals, petty traders, artisans and small businesses
8	Youth Enterprise with Innovation in Nigeria (You Win) Programme	National	Individuals, petty traders, artisans and small businesses
9	Subsidy Reinvestment & Empowerment Programme (SURE-P)	National	Individuals, petty traders, artisans and small businesses
10	Millennium Development Goals (MDGs)	International	National institutions, People and businesses
11	Sustainable Development Goals (SDGs)	International	National institutions, People and businesses

Source: authors, based on summary of reviewed literature on barriers to financial inclusion.

At the global level, financial inclusion has also occupied the attention of international organisations especially the agendas of the millennium development goals (MDGs) and sustainable development goals (SDGs). Some of the targets of the expired MDGs and SDGs alert the United Nations member countries to the pressing issue of financial inclusion and its complexity. Providing an enabling environment for better and improved financial inclusion in Nigeria justifies the introduction of mobile banking.

Considering the barriers to financial inclusion, this research identified a number of institutional and environmental barriers (Table 4). These barriers provided enabling grounds and springboards for the introduction of mobile banking in Nigeria. Financial inclusion intervention schemes failed because of the government's inability to properly nurture its development programmes, weak reward system, dysfunctional structures, and endemic poor programme implementation. Related to the barriers above are issues of bureaucracy of financial operations, high costs of banking products and services and distance of banks to the population.

With regard to drivers of mobile banking, this research identified three major factors as influencers of mobile banking in Nigeria; the ease of using a mobile device for personal banking transactions including prompt information about users' financial transactions (savings and withdrawals) immediately through the SMS alert (easy management of account); the security and safety concerns of moving cash around regarding cyber fraud; social influence of friends, relatives, policy makers and social trends. With regard to the contextualization of the findings, the three factors that emerged could be categorized as (a) utility expectancy (perceived usefulness), (b) effort expectancy (perceived ease of use), and (c) social influence expectancy (opinions of friends, relatives). Each of the three factors has specific elements assigned to them as shown in Table 5.

Table 4. Barriers to financial inclusion (summary of reviewed literature on barriers to financial inclusion).

SN	Nature of Barrier	Barrier Classification
1	Government's inability to properly nurture its financial inclusion interventions and programmes	Institutional factor
2	Dysfunctional structures and endemic poor programme implementation	Institutional factor
3	Structure of the economy (Agriculture-based economy)	Institutional factor
4	Location of the majority of the population	Environmental factor
5	Bureaucracy of financial operations	Environmental factor
6	High costs of banking products and services	Environmental factor
7	Distance of banks to the population.	Environmental factor
8	Number of money deposit bank branches	Environmental factor

Source: authors, based on summary of reviewed literature on barriers to financial inclusion.

Table 5. Contextualizing the factors influencing mobile banking (summary of reviewed literature on drivers of mobile banking).

SN	Value in Use (VIU)Sub-Constructs	Determinants/Drivers of Mobile Banking	Main Specific Factor Elements
1	Experience	Utility expectancy	Prompt, transaction notification, Trust and privacy, Satisfaction using mobile banking
2	Personalization	Effort expectancy	Convenience and cost, Ease of management, personal banking transactions
3	Relationship	Social influence expectancy	Influence of advert, opinions of friends and relatives, behavioural influence of people on mobile banking, institutional policy on cashless policy, other pressures

Source: authors, based on summary of reviewed literature on barriers to financial inclusion.

These three key factors seem to be in line with the complex perspective of the "value co-created in use", a very well-known facet of the service dominant logic (SDL) [118]. This approach considers value as co-created in use (VIU) because consumers assess and decide the value of a proposition based on their usage [119]. The VIU involves three sub-constructs: experience, personalization, and relationship.

Taking into consideration the first item, experience indicates an impressive, cognitive and/or emotional interface that creates essential value [118]. In our case, utility expectancy (perceived usefulness) can be perceived as a factor that is able to generate value for customers pushing them to use the banking sector's services as they are strongly based on setting a positive experience for these kind of potential clients through mobile banking.

On the other hand, personalization highlights the distinctiveness of the usage process, the value developed by individual needs [118]. In the current analysis, this is expressed by the effort expectancy (perceived ease of use). In fact, due to the fact that mobile banking is seen by customers as feasible and not too complicated, this also affects the perception that consumers have of banking services in general, before they were considered as misleading and problematic; nowadays, this trend is changing, setting the place for a new horizon in the sector.

Finally, relationship considers a mutual, continuing exchange and alliance not only among consumers, but also between the company and its clients, following an active communication setting [118]. The sub-construct of relationship, expressed in our study by the factor of social influence expectancy (opinions of friends, relatives), is able to empower current and potential consumers to resolve daily problems; thus, engendering mobile banking with a value that was not taken into account by people that until now decided to not use any kind of financial product [120].

5. Implications, Limitations and Future Research

This paper has the merit to deepen the understanding of current trends in financial inclusion. This topic can be considered nowadays as a catchphrase for banking specialists, researchers and other categories of stakeholders considering its implications on economic growth and achieving the SDGs [51,88,121]. Financial inclusion can be considered as an international challenge [122] but on the African continent, this issue is more stringent as there are high rates of financial exclusion and in addition, the heterogeneity generated by the specific economic situation, ethnic warfare, religious considerations and cultural perceptions is very high [123]. Little is known about emerging trends in financial inclusion and mobile banking, barriers to financial inclusion and factors influencing mobile banking especially in SSA and particularly in Nigeria. Exploring the trends, factors, barriers, and main items that impact on financial inclusion is essential, particularly in the African context where the level of financial inclusion is extremely low. Thus, this paper has contributed to the existing literature as it focuses on the importance of mobile banking as an innovative solution for increasing financial inclusion in a specific sub-Saharan African country: Nigeria.

Connecting back to previous conceptual research on VIU and SDL, a key theoretical contribution of this study lies in its extension of the boundary of this approach. Our study empirically illustrates the effects of VIU and of its variables in the field of mobile banking. In line with Ranjan and Read (2016) [118], our results empirically validate that consumers' VIU is due to personalized, memorable experiences and positive relationships with mobile banking features and applications. The three factors presented, in fact, not only increase consumers' propensity to continue to use mobile banking for the valuable services it provides to them but also nurtures a solid loyalty towards the banking sector that was never so developed before in the selected area.

From a managerial point of view, our findings regarding the applicability of SDL and the importance of VIU in mobile banking can be of special interest to managers and mobile app designers. Our results highlight that VIU is essential to boost financial inclusion towards banking services and financial products. From the VIU perspective, in fact, consumers are dynamically engaged in the value co-creation process, which relies on experience, personalization and relationship. This statement sets a challenge for managers and mobile app designers because for a client to play a role in the co-creation process, she/he have not only to download and utilize the app but log into the app for practitioners to attain her/his suggestions/comments/opinions. For instance, managers have to create more chances to co-create VIU with the client because the bank/financial institution needs to propose appropriate customized services and customer care that produce better experiences and set the basis for long term relationships with the customers. Additionally, leveraging on personalization is another key asset for managers, banks have to "push" clients to try new personalised financial services through mobile banking apps, offering to pioneer several incentives in order to reward their positive attitude towards the organisation and its services.

Moreover, this paper states that financial inclusion is a complex phenomenon and the solutions to reduce financial exclusion are economic, technical and social and have to be used in a mixed set up by public authorities and financial institutions.

For this reason, our work shows policy makers that the strategy of increasing financial inclusion must be based on the collaboration between different categories of stakeholders such as financial consumers, credit institutions, public authorities with supervisory and control attributions in financial markets, schools and universities.

From this perspective, this paper suggests that policy makers play an important role in creating online communities for consumers that use mobile banking. They could foster financial inclusion practices in virtual places, guiding users and acting as a reference point, or simply answer questions and solve doubts that consumers may have regarding using the financial products. In fact, policy makers should act as a "filter" between banks and users. This involves them being the first to catch customers' specific requests and needs and presenting them to banking managers.

Additionally, they can be useful in explaining how to use more complex software to banking clients who are now choosing to employ only services with a low level of complexity; in this case, policy makers can show to users that a major degree of personalization in services is not going to harm them, instead it should be preferred as it can give them more benefits. Actually, if they are involved in presenting these new personalised services, users could be more interested in approaching them as they trust these kind of players more than employees or spokespersons who are directly paid by banks and other financial institutions.

Having said that, these individuals should be rewarded for their important contribution inside the community with tax incentives, financial benefits, easy-terms loan, soft financing, etc. Actually, feedback posted in online communities can be also appreciated by managers, who can follow the users' point of view to find new ways to increase the level of personalization of services offered through mobile banking.

In addition, public service announcements and other kinds of social advertising should be created by policy makers to communicate to the public that financial inclusion (spread thanks to mobile banking) can highly benefit not only the economy of a country but also the whole society's lifestyle and level of education.

On the other hand, it must be highlighted that our analysis shows several limitations that provide some precious opportunities to future researchers in this underestimated area of research.

We acknowledge that the highlighted features of financial inclusion, explored in this paper, do not represent a comprehensive list of factors expressing all the potentialities hidden inside this concept as we took into consideration a specific country and its peculiarities. This proposes opportunities for further analyses in this vast area employing other specific methodologies and context-related factors.

Each of the labels chosen to conduct the qualitative meta-synthesis are strictly linked with the concept of financial inclusion but, of course, they are not part of an exhaustive list. Therefore, an increase in the labels used may help in the future to better understand how the concept has evolved through the years. Given the different approaches of central banks in Nigeria and Kenya to mobile money services, one of the areas that future studies should investigate is the adequacy of existing financial regulations and policies in SSA regarding mobile banking, particularly because mobile banking is an interface between financial services and telecoms. Another important raging issue that should be explored in the future is the moderating effect of culture on the relationship between mobile banking and financial inclusion in developing countries. Finally, as the financial inclusion represents a challenging area of research that is continuously evolving, we were unable to include all features of this topic in our analysis. In fact, what is clear now is that the main characteristics of financial inclusion may vary over time as they are highly affected by other factors and by technological developments. Therefore, we encourage future researchers to conduct a longitudinal analysis by including a wider range of factors, especially those related to the online world. Considering the intensification of the financial innovation process and the increase in the standard of living, consumers are oriented towards more and more complex products and services. For this reason, a future direction of research may be towards mobile financial services as a tool for financial inclusion. Such efforts will surely further contribute to the theoretical development of this research area.

6. Towards Conclusions

This study discusses the emerging trends in financial inclusion and the barriers and factors influencing mobile banking as an innovative solution for increasing financial inclusion in SSA with a specific focus on Nigeria. After a qualitative meta-synthesis of the literature and other secondary materials, it was found that mobile banking was introduced by the government and adopted by major banks in the country to strengthen national and international efforts towards financial inclusion in spite of institutional and environmental barriers engendering financial inclusion. Three major factors emerged from the qualitative meta-synthesis as drivers of mobile banking in Nigeria. Firstly, the ease of using a mobile device for personal banking transactions including prompt information about users' financial transactions (savings and withdrawals) immediately through the SMS alert (easy management of account). Secondly, the security and safety concerns of theft and of cyber fraud. Thirdly, social influence of friends, relatives, policy makers and social trends.

In contextualizing mobile banking in sub-Saharan Africa in general and Nigeria in particular, it could be stated that the growth of the use of mobile banking is largely supported by the IT adoption theories/perspectives, such as the technology acceptance model (TAM) and the extended technology acceptance model (TAM2), which all validate and support the assertion that technology is adopted by users because of (a) utility expectancy (perceived usefulness), (b) effort expectancy (perceived ease of use), and (c) social influence expectancy (opinions of friends, relatives).

Author Contributions: Conceptualization, A.S., L.R., M.P., M.C.P., methodology, L.R.; formal analysis, A.S., L.R., M.P., M.C.P., resources, A.S., L.R., M.P., M.C.P.; data curation, L.R.; writing—original draft preparation, A.S., L.R., M.P., M.C.P.; writing—review and editing, A.S., L.R., M.P., M.C.P.; visualization, A.S., L.R., M.P., M.C.P.; supervision, A.S., L.R., M.P., M.C.P.; project administration, A.S. All authors have read and agreed to the published version of the manuscript.

Acknowledgments: Although the views and ideas expressed in this article are those of Alfonso Siano, Lukman Raimi, Maria Palazzo and Mirela Clementina Panait; "Section 2.3" and "Section 3" are attributed to Lukman Raimi; "Section 2"; "Section 2.2" and "Section 4" are attributed to Mirela Clementina Panait; "Section 2.1" and "Section 5" are attributed to Maria Palazzo; while "Section 1" and "Section 6" is attributed to Alfonso Siano.

Appendix A

Table A1. Focus of Selected Paper.

Article	Title	Author	Year	Number of Factors Affecting Mobile Banking	Type of Specific Factors Affecting Mobile Banking
1	Toward an Understanding of Behavioural Intention to Use Mobile Banking	Luarn & Lin	2005	3	Perceived credibility, self-efficacy and financial cost
2	M-Commerce Implementation in Nigeria: Trends and Issues	Ayo, Ekong, Fatudimu & Adebiyi	2007	4	Patronage, quality of cell phones, lack of basic infrastructure and security issues
3	Internet Diffusion in Nigeria: is the 'Giant of Africa' waking up?	Muganda, Bankole & Brown	2008	1	Infrastructure
4	Mobile Commerce User Acceptance Study in China	Min & Qu	2008	7	Culture, user satisfaction, trust, privacy protection, quality, experience, and cost
5	Mobile phone technology in banking system: Its economic effect	Anyasi & Otubu	2009	3	Convenience, accessibility and affordability.
6	An Empirical Investigation of the Level of Users' Acceptance of E-Banking in Nigeria.	Oni, Aderonke & Ayo	2010	6	Convenience, ease of use, time saving, privacy, appropriateness for their transaction needs, and network security
7	Mobile phones and economic development in Africa	Aker & Mbiti	2010	3	Ease of use, fast services and reduced communication costs
8	Mobile banking adoption in Nigeria	Bankole, Bankole & Brown	2011	1	Cultural Values
9	An exploratory study on adoption of electronic banking: underlying consumer behaviour and critical success factors: case of Nigeria	Aliyu, Younus & Tasmin	2012	6	Accessibility, reluctance to change, cost/price, security concern, ease of use, and awareness

Table A1. *Cont.*

Article	Title	Author	Year	Number of Factors Affecting Mobile Banking	Type of Specific Factors Affecting Mobile Banking
10	Going cashless: Adoption of mobile banking in Nigeria	Njoku & Odumeru	2013	7	relative advantage, complexity, compatibility, observability, trialability, age and educational background
11	Global financial development report 2014: Financial inclusion	World Bank	2013	2	Economic growth and poverty alleviation
12	An investigative study on factors influencing the customer satisfaction with e-banking in Nigeria	Balogun, Ajiboye & Dunsin	2013	1	Quality of the service
13	Impact of mobile banking on service delivery in the Nigerian commercial banks.	Adewoye	2013	4	Transactional convenience, savings of time, quick transaction alert and save of service cost
14	Financial inclusion in Africa	Triki & Faye	2013		Broadening access, greater household savings, capital for investment, expansion of class of entrepreneurs, and human capital investment
15	The opportunities of digitizing payments	Klapper & Singer	2014	2	Access and Participation
16	International remittances and financial inclusion in Sub-Saharan Africa	Aga & Peria	2014	1	Increases the probability of households opening bank accounts
17	Mobile phone banking in Nigeria: benefits, problems and prospects	Agwu & Carter	2014	4	Cost of maintenance, Users' education, poverty and infrastructure availability.
18	Financial inclusion and innovation in Africa	Beck, Senbet & Simbanegavi	2015	3	Inclusive growth, financial deepening and access
19	Financial Inclusion: Can It Meet Multiple Macroeconomic Goals?	Sahay, Cihak, M & N'Diaye	2015	3	Access to credit, Savings and Economic growth
20	Can Islamic Banking Increase Financial Inclusion?	Ben Naceur, Barajas & Massara	2015	3	Access to Islamic banking products, improved savings, investment
21	User adoption of online banking in Nigeria: A qualitative study	Tarhini, Mgbemena, Trab & Masa' Deh	2015	3	Security, religion and culture
22	The determinants of financial inclusion in Africa	Zins & Weill	2016	4	Gender, economic status, education and age influence FI
23	Mobile banking–adoption and challenges in Nigeria	Agu, Simon & Onwuka	2016	5	Handset operability, Security, Scalability and reliability, Geographic distribution and Age
24	Financial inclusion in Africa: evidence using dynamic panel data analysis.	Gebrehiwot & Makina	2016	3	GDP per capita, mobile infrastructure and remoteness
25	Analysis of the determinants of financial inclusion in Central and West Africa	Soumaré, TchanaTchana & Kengne	2016	9	Gender, education, age, income, residence area, employment status, marital status, household size and degree of trust in financial institutions
26	Is the rise of Pan-African banking the next big thing in Sub-Saharan Africa	PWC	2017	2	Withdrawal of several Western banks and intra-regional trade linkages

Table A1. *Cont.*

Article	Title	Author	Year	Number of Factors Affecting Mobile Banking	Type of Specific Factors Affecting Mobile Banking
27	Mobile banking in Sub-Saharan Africa: setting the way towards financial development.	Rouse &Verhoef	2017	2	Extension of remote rural locations and introduction of innovative products
28	What determines financial inclusion in Sub-Saharan Africa?	Chikalipah	2017	1	Illiteracy is the major hindrance to FI
29	Financial inclusion, entry barriers, and entrepreneurship: evidence from China	Fan & Zhang	2017	3	Mitigation of credit constraints, boosting entrepreneurial activities and reducing information asymmetry in financial transactions
30	Determinants of financial inclusion in Sub-Sahara African countries	Oyelami, Saibu & Adekunle	2017	2	Demand side factors (level of income and literacy) and Supply side factors (Interest rate and bank innovation proxy by ATM usage).
31	An assessment of the impact of mobile banking on traditional banking in Nigeria	Khan & Ejike	2017	4	Good knowledge of mobile devices, access to mobile banking, convenience and satisfaction of usage
32	The effect of mobile banking on the performance of commercial banks in Nigeria	Bagudu, Mohd Khan & Roslan	2017	1	More access to mobile handsets
33	Financial inclusion as a tool for sustainable development	Voica	2017	3	Sustainable development, Consumer protection and economic literacy
34	The effect of financial inclusion on welfare in sub-Saharan Africa: Evidence from disaggregated data	Tita & Aziakpono	2017	3	Increase in formal opening of bank accounts, financial infrastructure and economic activities
35	Infrastructure deficiencies and adoption of mobile money in Sub-Saharan Africa	Mothobi & Grzybowski	2017	2	physical infrastructure and level of income
36	Mobile Money and Financial Inclusion in Sub-Saharan Africa: the Moderating Role of Social Networks	Bongomin, Ntayi, Munene & Malinga	2018	1	Existence of social networks of strong and weak ties among mobile money users
37	Can mobile money help firms mitigate the problem of access to finance in Eastern sub-Saharan Africa?	Gosavi	2018	2	Access to finance, or lines of credit
38	EFInA Access to Financial Services in Nigeria 2010–2018 survey	EFInA	2018	4	Number of banked population, awareness & knowledge, institutional exclusion and affordability
39	The Global Findex Database 2017: Measuring financial inclusion and the FinTech revolution	Demirguc-Kunt, Klapper, Singer, Ansar & Hess	2018	0	
40	Financial Inclusion and Per Capita Income In Africa: Bayesian VAR Estimates.	Alenoghena	2019	3	Per capital incomes, deposit interest rate and the internet
41	M-PESA and Financial Inclusion in Kenya: Of Paying Comes Saving?	Van Hove & Dubus	2019	2	Phone owners, Better educated
42	Migrant remittances and financial inclusion among households in Nigeria.	Ajefu & Ogebe	2019	2	Receipt of remittances increases the use of formal financial services and migrant networks
43	The Impact of Mobile Money on the Financial Performance of the SMEs in Douala, Cameroon	Talom & Tengeh	2019	3	Access to the internet, cost and efficiency

Table A1. *Cont.*

Article	Title	Author	Year	Number of Factors Affecting Mobile Banking	Type of Specific Factors Affecting Mobile Banking
44	Digitising Financial Services: A Tool for Financial Inclusion in South Africa?	Shipalana	2019	3	Tackle poverty, promote inclusive development and address the SDGs
45	See the best Nigerian mobile banking apps in H1 2019	Benson	2019	2	Access to mobile device, network connection
46	Financial Inclusion and Achievements of Sustainable Development Goals (SDGs)	Ma'ruf &Aryani	2019	2	Achievement of SGDs and poverty alleviation
47	Financial inclusion and sustainable development in Nigeria.	Soyemi, Olowofela & Yunusa	2019	6	Accessibility, reluctance to change, cost/price, security concern, ease of use, and awareness
48	Financial inclusion in sub-Saharan Africa: Recent trends and determinants	Asuming, Osei-Agyei, L.G. & Mohammed	2019	6	Age, education, gender, wealth, growth rate of GDP and access to financial institutions
49	Enhancing Financial Inclusion in ASEAN: Identifying the Best Growth Markets for Fintech	Loo	2019	4	Commercial bank branches, Demand deposit from the rural areas, loan to rural areas and human capital development
50	Social and Financial Inclusion through Nonbanking Institutions: A Model for Rural Romania.	Yue, Cao, Duarte, Shao & Manta	2019	3	Access to financial services, communication technologies, digital mobile platforms
51	Do mobile phones, economic growth, bank competition and stability matter for financial inclusion in Africa?	Chinoda & Kwenda	2019	4	Mobile phones, economic growth, bank competition and stability impact financial inclusion
52	Financial Inclusion Condition of African Countries	Chinoda & Kwenda	2019	2	Access and usage factors affect financial inclusion
53	Mobile telephony, financial inclusion and inclusive growth	Abor, Amidu & Issahaku	2019	3	Mobile penetration, pro-poor development and improved livelihoods
54	Financial Inclusion in Ethiopia: Is It on the Right Track?	Berhanu Lakew & Azadi	2020	3	Barriers are preference for informal saving club, unemployment and low income
55	Readiness for banking technologies in developing countries	Berndt, Saunders & Petzer	2020	2	Access to innovative banking technologies and technology readiness of the people
56	Financial Inclusion	World Bank	2020	3	Quality of life, poverty reduction, facilitating investments in health, education, and businesses
57	Financial exclusion in OECD countries: A scoping review	Caplan, Birkenmaier & Bae	2020	6	Dominant issues covered in FI are conceptualization, contributors, and impacts of FI. Less covered are measurement, prevention, and contemporary practice trends in financial exclusion.
58	Financial inclusion-and the SDGs	UN Capital Development Fund	2020	3	Promotes investment, consumption and resource mobilization

Source: authors, based on the summary of the reviewed literature.

Appendix B. Year-Wise Distribution of Research Publications

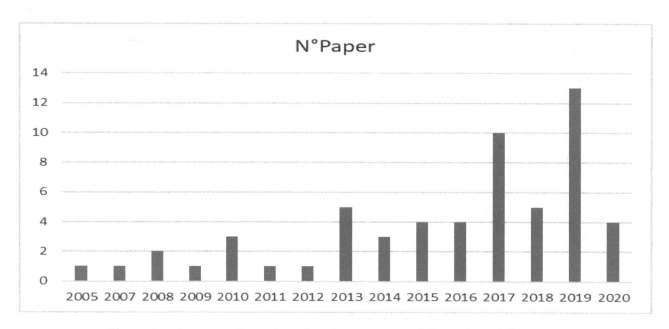

Figure A1. Source: authors, based on the summary of the reviewed literature.

Appendix C. Year-Wise Distribution of Specific Factors Affecting Mobile Banking Explored by Former Publications

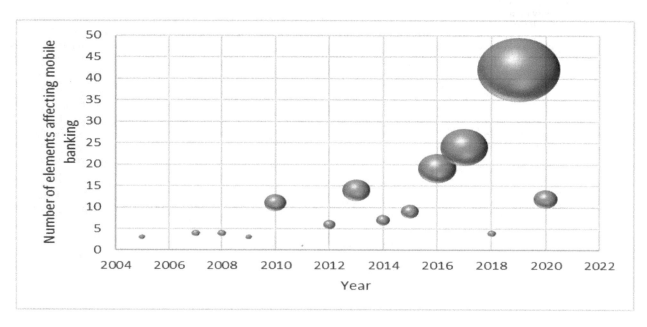

Figure A2. Source: authors, based on the summary of the reviewed literature.

References

1. United Nations Development Programme Goal 8: Decent Work and Economic Growth. 2020. Available online: https://www.undp.org/content/undp/en/home/sustainable-development-goals/goal-8-decent-work-and-economic-growth.html (accessed on 24 February 2020).
2. World Bank The World Bank in Africa. 2019. Available online: https://www.worldbank.org/en/region/afr/overview (accessed on 18 March 2020).
3. Amankwah-Amoah, J.; Boso, N.; Debrah, Y.A. Africa rising in an emerging world: An international marketing perspective. *Int. Mark. Rev.* **2018**, *35*, 550–559. [CrossRef]

4. Amankwah-Amoah, J.; Egbetokun, A.; Osabutey, E.L. Meeting the 21st century challenges of doing business in Africa. *Technol. Forecast. Soc. Chang.* **2018**, *131*, 336–338. [CrossRef]

5. Aker, J.C.; Mbiti, I.M. Mobile phones and economic development in Africa. *J. Econ. Perspect.* **2010**, *24*, 207–232. [CrossRef]

6. Rouse, M.; Verhoef, G. Mobile Banking in Sub-Saharan Africa: Setting the Way Towards Financial Development. *MPRA Paper No. 78006.* 2017, pp. 1–21. Available online: https://mpra.ub.uni-muenchen.de/78006/1/MPRA_paper_78006.pdf (accessed on 15 April 2020).

7. Njoku, A.C.; Odumeru, J.A. Going cashless: Adoption of mobile banking in Nigeria. *Niger. Chapter Arab. J. Bus. Manag. Rev.* **2013**, *62*, 1–9.

8. Raimi, L. Imperative of meta-study for research in the field of corporate social responsibility and emerging issues in corporate governance. In *The Handbook of Research Methods on Corporate Social Responsibility*; Crowther, D., Lauesen, L.M., Eds.; Handbook Series: Edgar Elgar, UK, 2017.

9. Amuda, Y.J.; Embi, N.A.C. Alleviation of Poverty among OIC Countries through Sadaqat, Cash Waqf and Public Funding. *Int. J. Trade Econ. Finance* **2013**, *4*, 405–407. [CrossRef]

10. Ihugba, O.A.; Odii, A.; Njoku, A. Theoretical Analysis of Entrepreneurship Challenges and Prospects in Nigeria. *Int. Lett. Soc. Humanist. Sci.* **2014**, *5*, 21–34. [CrossRef]

11. Rjoub, H.; Aga, M.; AbuAlRub, A.; Bein, M.A. Financial Reforms and Determinants of FDI: Evidence from Landlocked Countries in Sub-Saharan Africa. *Economics* **2017**, *5*, 1. [CrossRef]

12. Asuming, P.O.; Osei-Agyei, L.G.; Mohammed, J.I. Financial Inclusion in Sub-Saharan Africa: Recent Trends and Determinants. *J. Afr. Bus.* **2019**, *20*, 112–134. [CrossRef]

13. Bongomin, G.O.C.; Ntayi, J.M.; Munene, J.C.; Malinga, C.A. Mobile Money and Financial Inclusion in Sub-Saharan Africa: The Moderating Role of Social Networks. *J. Afr. Bus.* **2018**, *19*, 361–384. [CrossRef]

14. Talom, F.S.G.; Tengeh, R.K. The Impact of Mobile Money on the Financial Performance of the SMEs in Douala, Cameroon. *Sustainability* **2019**, *12*, 183. [CrossRef]

15. Coffie, C.P.K.; Zhao, H.; Mensah, I.A. Panel Econometric Analysis on Mobile Payment Transactions and Traditional Banks Effort toward Financial Accessibility in Sub-Sahara Africa. *Sustainability* **2020**, *12*, 895. [CrossRef]

16. Bankole, F.O.; Bankole, O.O.; Brown, I. Mobile Banking Adoption in Nigeria. *Electron. J. Inf. Syst. Dev. Ctries.* **2011**, *47*, 1–23. [CrossRef]

17. Ayo, C.K.; Ekong, U.O.; Fatudimu, I.T.; Adebiyi, A.A. M-Commerce Implementation in Nigeria: Trends and Issues. *J. Internet Bank. Commer.* **2007**, *12*, 1–15.

18. Muganda, N.O.; Bankole, F.O.; Brown, I. Internet Diffusion in Nigeria: Is the 'Giant of Africa' waking up? In Proceedings of the 10th Annual Conference on World Wide Web Applications, Cape Town, South Africa, 3–5 September 2008.

19. Benson, E.A. *See the Best Nigerian Mobile Banking Apps in H1 2019*; Nairametrics Publication: Lagos, Nigeria, 2019; Available online: https://nairametrics.com/2019/07/17/the-best-mobile-banking-apps-in-nigeria/ (accessed on 20 April 2020).

20. Chikalipah, S. What determines financial inclusion in Sub-Saharan Africa? *Afr. J. Econ. Manag. Stud.* **2017**, *8*, 8–18. [CrossRef]

21. Mothobi, O.; Grzybowski, L. Infrastructure deficiencies and adoption of mobile money in Sub-Saharan Africa. *Inf. Econ. Policy* **2017**, *40*, 71–79. [CrossRef]

22. Gosavi, A. Can Mobile Money Help Firms Mitigate the Problem of Access to Finance in Eastern sub-Saharan Africa? *J. Afr. Bus.* **2018**, *19*, 343–360. [CrossRef]

23. Beck, T.; Senbet, L.; Simbanegavi, W. Financial Inclusion and Innovation in Africa: An Overview. *J. Afr. Econ.* **2015**, *24*, i3–i11. [CrossRef]

24. Gebrehiwot, K.G.; Makina, D. Financial inclusion in Africa: Evidence using dynamic panel data analysis. In Proceedings of the Conference on Inclusive Growth and Poverty Reduction in the IGAD Region, Addis Abeba, Ethiopia, 24–25 October 2016; p. 49.

25. Sahay, R.; Cihak, M.; N'Diaye, P.; Barajas, A.; Mitra, S.; Kyobe, A.; Mooi, Y.; Yousefi, R. Financial Inclusion: Can it Meet Multiple Macroeconomic Goals? *Staff. Discuss. Notes* **2015**, 1–33. [CrossRef]

26. Ma'Ruf, A.; Aryani, F. Financial Inclusion and Achievements of Sustainable Development Goals (SDGs) in ASEAN. *GATR J. Bus. Econ. Rev.* **2019**, *4*, 147–155. [CrossRef]

27. Soyemi, K.A.; Olowofela, O.E.; Yunusa, L.A. Financial inclusion and sustainable development in Nigeria. *J. Econ. Manag.* **2020**, *39*, 105–131. [CrossRef]

28. Ene, C. Current Issues Regarding the Protection of Retail Investors on the Capital Market within the European Union. *USV Ann. Econ. Public Adm.* **2017**, *17*, 35–44.

29. Fan, Z.; Zhang, R. Financial Inclusion, Entry Barriers, and Entrepreneurship: Evidence from China. *Sustainability* **2017**, *9*, 203. [CrossRef]

30. Grigorescu, A.; Cerchia, A.E.; Oachesu, M.M.; Udroiu, F. Enhancing Internet Banking-Solutions for Customer Relationship Management. *Saudi J. Bus. Manag. Stud.* **2017**, *2*, 38–43.

31. Voica, M.C. Financial inclusion as a tool for sustainable development. *Rom. Econ. Rev.* **2017**, *44*, 121–129.

32. Abor, J.Y.; Amidu, M.; Issahaku, H. Mobile Telephony, Financial Inclusion and Inclusive Growth. *J. Afr. Bus.* **2018**, *19*, 430–453. [CrossRef]

33. Iacovoiu, V.B. An Empirical Analysis of Some Factors Influencing Financial Literacy. *Econ. Insights Trends Chall.* **2018**, *VII*, 23–31.

34. Loo, M.K.L. Enhancing Financial Inclusion in ASEAN: Identifying the Best Growth Markets for Fintech. *J. Risk Financ. Manag.* **2019**, *12*, 181. [CrossRef]

35. Yue, X.-G.; Cao, Y.; Duarte, N.; Shao, X.-F.; Manta, O.P. Social and Financial Inclusion through Nonbanking Institutions: A Model for Rural Romania. *J. Risk Financ. Manag.* **2019**, *12*, 166. [CrossRef]

36. Lakew, T.B.; Azadi, H. Financial Inclusion in Ethiopia: Is It on the Right Track? *Int. J. Financ. Stud.* **2020**, *8*, 28. [CrossRef]

37. Berndt, A.D.; Saunders, S.G.; Petzer, D.J. Readiness for banking technologies in developing countries. *S. Afr. Bus. Rev.* **2010**, *14*, 47–76.

38. Sapepa, K.; Roberts-Lombard, M.; Van Tonder, E. The Relationship between Selected Variables and Customer Loyalty within the Banking Environment of an Emerging Economy. *J. Soc. Sci.* **2015**, *43*, 115–123. [CrossRef]

39. Deigh, L.; Farquhar, J.; Palazzo, M.; Siano, A. Corporate social responsibility: Engaging the community. *Qual. Mark. Res. Int. J.* **2016**, *19*, 225–240. [CrossRef]

40. Deigh, G.L.A. Corporate Social Responsibility in the Banking Sector of a Developing Country: A Ghanaian Perspective. Ph.D. Thesis, University of Bedfordshire, Luton, UK, 2016.

41. Deigh, L.; Palazzo, M.; Farquhar, J.; Siano, A. Creating a national identity through community relations: The context of a developing country. In Proceedings of the 22nd International Conference on Corporate and Marketing Communications. CMC2017—Challenges of Marketing Communications in a Globalized World, Zaragoza, Spain, 4–5 May 2017.

42. Grigorescu, A.; Oprisan, O.; Condrea, E. Other economico-social factors of the saving process. *HOLISTICA-J. Bus. Public Adm.* **2017**, *8*, 41–48. [CrossRef]

43. World Bank. 2020. Available online: https://www.worldbank.org/en/topic/financialinclusion/overview (accessed on 20 March 2020).

44. Shipalana, P. Digitising Financial Services: A Tool for Financial Inclusion in South Africa? *SAIIA. Occas. Pap.* **2019**, *31*, 1–38.

45. Caplan, M.A.; Birkenmaier, J.; Bae, J. Financial exclusion in OECD countries: A scoping review*. *Int. J. Soc. Welf.* **2020**, 1–14. [CrossRef]

46. Klapper, L.; Singer, D. *The Opportunities of Digitizing Payments*; The World Bank: Washington, DC, USA, 2014; pp. 1–33.

47. Triki, T.; Faye, I. *Financial Inclusion in Africa*; African Development Bank: Tunis, Tunisia, 2013; pp. 1–74.

48. Apiors, E.K.; Suzuki, A. Mobile money, individuals' payments, remittances, and investments: Evidence from the Ashanti Region, Ghana. *Sustainability* **2018**, *10*, 1409. [CrossRef]

49. Leyshon, A.; Thrift, N. The restructuring of the U.K. financial services industry in the 1990s: A reversal of fortune? *J. Rural. Stud.* **1993**, *9*, 223–241. [CrossRef]

50. Wilson, T.A. Supporting social enterprises to support vulnerable consumers: The example of community development finance institutions and financial exclusion. *J. Consum. Policy* **2012**, *35*, 197–213. [CrossRef]

51. Tita, A.F.; Aziakpono, M.J. The effect of financial inclusion on welfare in sub-Saharan Africa: Evidence from disaggregated data. *Econ. Res. S. Afr. Work. Pap.* **2017**, *679*, 1–29.

52. Soumaré, I.; Tchana, F.T.; Kengne, T.M. Analysis of the determinants of financial inclusion in Central and West Africa. *Transnatl. Corp. Rev.* **2016**, *8*, 231–249. [CrossRef]

53. Anghelache, C.; Niță, D.O.G. Analiza statistică aincluziunii financiare. *Rom. Stat. Rev. Suppl.* **2019**, *9*, 3.

54. Lorena, I.P.; Florin, R.; Iuliana, T.A. Needs of local sustainable development. *Ann. Fac. Econ.* **2011**, *1*, 91–97.

55. Matei, M.; Voica, M.C. Social Responsibility in the Financial and Banking Sector. *Econ. Insights-Trends Chall.* **2013**, *2*, 115–123.

56. Ene, C.; Panait, M. The financial education-Part of corporate social responsibility for employees and customers. *Rev. Romana Econ.* **2017**, *44*, 145–154.

57. Brezoi, A.G. Ethics and Corporate Social Responsibility in the Current Geopolitical Context. *Econ. Insights-Trends Chall.* **2018**, *7*, 45–52.

58. Tăbîrcă, A.I.; Ivan, O.R.; Radu, F.; Djaouahdou, R. Qualitative Research in WoS of the Link between Corporate Social Responsibility and Corporate Financial Performance. *Valahian J. Econ. Stud.* **2019**, *10*, 107–118. [CrossRef]

59. Matei, M. Responsabilitatea socială a corporaţiilor şi instituţiilor şi dezvoltarea durabilă a României. *Bucharest. Expert Publ. House* **2013**. Available online: https://www.amfiteatrueconomic.ro/temp/Articol_1014.pdf (accessed on 2 December 2020).

60. Iacovoiu, V.; Stancu, A. Competition and Consumer Protection in the Romanian Banking Sector. *Amfiteatru Econ.* **2017**, *19*, 381.

61. Kapur, D. Remittances: The new development mantra? *Remit. Dev. Impact Future Prospect.* **2005**, *2*, 331–360.

62. FinScope, 2015, FinScope South Africa 2015. Available online: http://www.finmark.org.za/wp-content/uploads/2016/03/Broch_FinScopeSA2015_Consumersurvey_FNL.pdf (accessed on 17 April 2020).

63. Okello Candiya Bongomin, G.; Ntayi, J.M.; Munene, J.C.; Nabeta, I.N. Financial inclusion in rural Uganda: Testing interaction effect of financial literacy and networks. *J. Afr. Bus.* **2016**, *17*, 106–128. [CrossRef]

64. Klein, M.; Mayer, C. *Mobile Banking and Financial Inclusion: The Regulatory Lessons*; Frankfurt School of Finance and Management: Frankfurt, Germany, 2011; pp. 1–31.

65. Donovan, K. Mobile Money for Financial Inclusion. *Inf. Commun. Dev.* **2012**, *61*, 61–73.

66. Mago, S.; Chitokwindo, S. The Impact of Mobile Banking on Financial Inclusion in Zimbabwe: A Case for Masvingo Province. *Mediterr. J. Soc. Sci.* **2014**, *5*, 221.

67. Mutsune, T. No Kenyan left behind: The model of Financial Inclusion through Mobile banking. *Rev. Bus. Financ. Stud.* **2015**, *6*, 35–42.

68. Okello Candiya Bongomin, G.; Munene, J.C. Analyzing the Relationship between Mobile Money Adoption and Usage and Financial Inclusion of MSMEs in Developing Countries: Mediating Role of Cultural Norms in Uganda. *J. Afr. Bus.* **2019**, 1–20. [CrossRef]

69. Ouma, S.A.; Odongo, T.M.; Were, M. Mobile financial services and financial inclusion: Is it a boon for savings mobilization? *Rev. Dev. Financ.* **2017**, *7*, 29–35. [CrossRef]

70. Bakari, I.H.; Idi, A.; Ibrahim, Y. Innovation determinants of financial inclusion in top ten African countries: A system GMM approach. *Mark. Manag. Innov.* **2018**, *4*, 99. [CrossRef]

71. Dafe, F. Ambiguity in international finance and the spread of financial norms: The localization of financial inclusion in Kenya and Nigeria. *Rev. Int. Politi-Econ.* **2020**, *27*, 500–524. [CrossRef]

72. Lepoutre, J.; Oguntoye, A. The (non-)emergence of mobile money systems in Sub-Saharan Africa: A comparative multilevel perspective of Kenya and Nigeria. *Technol. Forecast. Soc. Chang.* **2018**, *131*, 262–275. [CrossRef]

73. Williams, I. Regulatory frameworks and Implementation patterns for Mobile Money in Africa: The case of Kenya, Ghana and Nigeria. In *Aalborg University Conference Paper*; National Information Technology Agency: Accra, Ghana, 2013.

74. World Bank Group. *Global Financial Development Report 2014: Financial Inclusion*; World Bank Publications: Washington, DC, USA, 2013; Volume 2.

75. Prince, W.; Fantom, N. *World Development Indicators 2014*; The World Bank: Washington, DC, USA, 2014; pp. 1–137.

76. EFInA Access to Financial Services in Nigeria 2010–2018 Survey. Available online: https://www.efina.org.ng/wp-content/uploads/2019/01/A2F-2018-Key-Findings-11_01_19.pdf (accessed on 24 February 2020).

77. Oyelami, L.O.; Saibu, O.M.; Adekunle, B.S. Determinants of financial inclusion in Sub-Sahara African countries. *Covenant J. Bus. Soc. Sci.* **2017**, *8*, 104–116.

78. Central Bank of Nigeria/Nigerian Deposit Insurance Corporation (2020). Available online: https://ndic.gov.ng/ (accessed on 24 February 2020).

79.   UN Capital Development Fund (UNCDF). Available online: https://www.uncdf.org/financial-inclusion-and-the-sdgs (accessed on 24 February 2020).

80.   Demirguc-Kunt, A.; Klapper, L.; Singer, D.; Ansar, S.; Hess, J. *The Global Findex Database 2017: Measuring Financial Inclusion and the Fintech Revolution*; The World Bank: Washington, DC, USA, 2018.

81.   Alenoghena, R.O. Financial Inclusion and Per Capita Income in Africa: Bayesian VAR Estimates. *Acta Univ. Danub. Acon.* **2017**, *13*, 201–221.

82.   Conroy, K.; Goodman, A.R.; Kenward, S. Lessons from the Chars Livelihoods Programme, Bangladesh (2004–2010). In Proceedings of the CPRC International Conference, Manchester, UK, 8–10 September 2010.

83.   Anghelache, C.; Partachi, I.; Anghel, M.G. Remittances, a factor for poverty reduction. *Rom. Stat. Rev. Suppl.* **2017**, *65*, 59–66.

84.   Van Hove, L.; Dubus, A. M-PESA and Financial Inclusion in Kenya: Of Paying Comes Saving? *Sustainability* **2019**, *11*, 568. [CrossRef]

85.   Aga, G.A.; Peria, M.S.M. *International Remittances and Financial Inclusion in Sub-Saharan Africa*; The World Bank: Washington, DC, USA, 2014.

86.   Ajefu, J.B.; Ogebe, J.O. Migrant remittances and financial inclusion among households in Nigeria. *Oxf. Dev. Stud.* **2019**, *47*, 319–335. [CrossRef]

87.   Giuliano, P.; Ruiz-Arranz, M. Remittances, financial development, and growth. *J. Dev. Econ.* **2009**, *90*, 144–152. [CrossRef]

88.   Zins, A.; Weill, L. The determinants of financial inclusion in Africa. *Rev. Dev. Financ.* **2016**, *6*, 46–57. [CrossRef]

89.   PWC. Is the rise of Pan-African Banking the Next Big Thing in Sub-Saharan Africa? 2017. Available online: https://www.pwc.com/gx/en/issues/economy/global-economy-watch/rise-of-pan-african-banking.html (accessed on 1 September 2019).

90.   World Bank, Global Findex Data. Available online: https://globalfindex.worldbank.org/ (accessed on 10 November 2020).

91.   Singh, A.B. Mobile Banking Based Money Order for India Post: Feasible Model and Assessing Demand Potential. *Procedia Soc. Behav. Sci.* **2012**, *37*, 466–481. [CrossRef]

92.   Tiwari, R.; Buse, S.; Herstatt, C. Customer on the move: Strategic implications of mobile banking for banks and financial enterprises. In Proceedings of the 8th IEEE International Conference on E-Commerce Technology, San Francisco, CA, USA, 26–29 June 2006; p. 81.

93.   Akturan, U.; Tezcan, N. Mobile banking adoption of the youth market. *Mark. Intell. Plan.* **2012**, *30*, 444–459. [CrossRef]

94.   Munoz-Leiva, F.; Climent-Climent, S.; Liébana-Cabanillas, F. Determinants of intention to use the mobile banking apps: An extension of the classic TAM model. *Span. J. Mark. ESIC* **2017**, *21*, 25–38. [CrossRef]

95.   Sharma, S.K. Integrating cognitive antecedents into TAM to explain mobile banking behavioral intention: A SEM-neural network modeling. *Inf. Syst. Front.* **2017**, *21*, 815–827. [CrossRef]

96.   Luarn, P.; Lin, H.-H. Toward an understanding of the behavioral intention to use mobile banking. *Comput. Hum. Behav.* **2005**, *21*, 873–891. [CrossRef]

97.   Nasri, W.; Charfeddine, L. Factors affecting the adoption of Internet banking in Tunisia: An integration theory of acceptance model and theory of planned behavior. *J. High Technol. Manag. Res.* **2012**, *23*, 1–14. [CrossRef]

98.   Zhou, T.; Lu, Y.; Wang, B. Integrating TTF and UTAUT to explain mobile banking user adoption. *Comput. Hum. Behav.* **2010**, *26*, 760–767. [CrossRef]

99.   Wang, Y.S.; Lin, H.H.; Luarn, P. Predicting consumer intention to use mobile service. *Inf. Syst. J.* **2006**, *16*, 157–179. [CrossRef]

100. Min, Q.; Ji, S.; Qu, G. Mobile commerce user acceptance study in China: A revised UTAUT model. *Tsinghua Sci. Technol.* **2008**, *13*, 257–264. [CrossRef]

101. Anyasi, F.I.; Otubu, P.A. Mobile phone technology in banking system: Its economic effect. *Res. J. Inf. Technol.* **2009**, *1*, 1–5.

102. Oni, A.A.; Ayo, C.K. An Empirical Investigation of the Level of Users' Acceptance of E-Banking in Nigeria. *J. Internet Bank. Commer.* **2010**, *15*, 1–13.

103. Aliyu, A.A.; Younus, S.; Tasmin, R.B.H.J. An exploratory study on adoption of electronic banking: Underlying consumer behaviour and critical success factors: Case of Nigeria. *Bus. Manag. Rev.* **2012**, *2*, 1–6.

104. Balogun, O.J.; Ajiboye, F.; Dunsin, A.T. An Investigative Study on Factors Influencing the Customer Satisfaction with E-Banking in Nigeria. *Int. J. Acad. Res. Econ. Manag. Sci.* **2013**, *2*, 64–73.

105. Adewoye, J.O. Impact of mobile banking on service delivery in the Nigerian commercial banks. *Int. Rev. Manag. Bus. Res.* **2013**, *2*, 333–344.

106. Agwu, P.E.; Carter, A.L. Mobile phone banking in Nigeria: Benefits, problems and prospects. *J. Internet Bank. Commer.* **2014**, *3*, 50–70.

107. Tarhini, A.; Mgbemena, C.; Trab, M.S.A.; Masa'Deh, R. User adoption of online banking in Nigeria: A qualitative study. *J. Internet Bank. Commer.* **2015**, *20*, 132.

108. Agu, B.O.; Simon, N.P.N.; Onwuka, I.O. Mobile banking–adoption and challenges in Nigeria. *Int. J. Innov. Soc. Sci. Humanit. Res.* **2016**, *4*, 17–27.

109. Khan, H.U.; Ejike, A.C. An assessment of the impact of mobile banking on traditional banking in Nigeria. *Int. J. Bus. Excell.* **2017**, *11*, 446–463. [CrossRef]

110. Bagudu, H.D.; Khan, S.J.M.; Roslan, A.H. The Effect of Mobile Banking on the Performance of Commercial Banks in Nigeria. *Int. Res. J. Manag. IT Soc. Sci.* **2017**, *4*, 71–76.

111. Bille, F.S.; Buri, S.; Crenn, T.A.; Denyes, L.S.; Hassam, C.V.T.; Heitmann, S.; Martinez, M. *Digital Access: The Future of Financial Inclusion in Africa*; The World Bank: Washington, DC, USA, 2018; pp. 1–97.

112. Denyer, D.; Tranfield, D. Using qualitative research synthesis to build an actionable knowledge base. *Manag. Decis.* **2006**, *44*, 213–227. [CrossRef]

113. Lee, J. 10 year retrospect on stage models of e-Government: A qualitative meta-synthesis. *Gov. Inf. Q.* **2010**, *27*, 220–230. [CrossRef]

114. Raimi, L.; Uzodinma, I. Trends in Financing Programmes for the Development of Micro, Small and Medium Enterprises (MSMEs) in Nigeria: A Qualitative Meta-synthesis. In *Contemporary Developments in Entrepreneurial Finance. FGF Studies in Small Business and Entrepreneurship*; Moritz, A., Block, J., Golla, S., Werner, A., Eds.; Springer: Cham, Switzerland, 2020.

115. Finlayson, K.W.; Dixon, A. Qualitative meta-synthesis: A guide for the novice. *Nurse Res.* **2008**, *15*, 59–71. [CrossRef]

116. Walsh, D.; Downe, S. Meta-synthesis method for qualitative research: A literature review. *Methodol. Issues Nurs. Res.* **2005**, *50*, 204–211. [CrossRef]

117. Central Bank of Nigeria. Annual Statistical Bulletin. 2020. Available online: https://www.cbn.gov.ng/documents/Statbulletin.asp (accessed on 24 February 2020).

118. Ranjan, K.R.; Read, S. Value co-creation: Concept and measurement. *J. Acad. Mark. Sci.* **2016**, *44*, 290–315. [CrossRef]

119. Vargo, S.L.; Lusch, R.F. Evolving to a new dominant logic for marketing. *J. Mark.* **2004**, *68*, 1–17. [CrossRef]

120. Bonsu, S.K.; Darmody, A. Co-creating second life: Market—Consumer cooperation in contemporary economy. *J. Macromarket.* **2008**, *28*, 355–368. [CrossRef]

121. Chinoda, T.; Kwenda, F.; McMillan, D. Do mobile phones, economic growth, bank competition and stability matter for financial inclusion in Africa? *Cogent Econ. Financ.* **2019**, *7*, 1622180. [CrossRef]

122. Chinoda, T.; Kwenda, F. Financial Inclusion Condition of African Countries. *Acta Univ. Danub. Acon.* **2019**, *15*, 242–266.

123. Ben Naceur, S.; Barajas, A.; Massara, A. Can Islamic Banking Increase Financial Inclusion? *Int. Monet. Fund.* **2015**, 213–252. [CrossRef]

11

Peer-to-Peer Lending and Bank Risks: A Closer Look

Eunjung Yeo [1] and Jooyong Jun [2],*

[1] School of Business Administration, Chung-Ang University, Seoul 06974, Korea; ejyeo@cau.ac.kr
[2] Department of Economics, Dongguk University, Seoul 04620, Korea
* Correspondence: jooyong@dongguk.edu

Abstract: This study examined how the expansion of peer-to-peer (P2P) lending affects bank risks, particularly insolvency and illiquidity risks. We compared a benchmark case wherein banks are the only players in the loan market with a segmented market case wherein the loan market is segmented by borrowers' creditworthiness, P2P lending platforms operate only in the low-credit market segment, and banks operate in both low- and high-credit segments. For the segmented market case compared with the benchmark one, we find that, while banks' insolvency risk increases, their illiquidity risk decreases such that their overall risk also decreases. Our results imply that sustainable P2P lending requires an appropriate differentiation of roles between banks and P2P lending platforms—P2P lending platforms operate in the low-credit segment and banks' involvement in P2P lending is restricted—so that the growth of P2P lending is not adverse for bank stability.

Keywords: peer-to-peer lending; bank risk; insolvency risk; illiquidity risk

JEL Classification: G21, G23

1. Introduction

Peer-to-peer (P2P) lending—also known as FinTech credit, crowd-finance, or marketplace lending—refers to credit activities through online P2P lending platforms that provide direct matching between investors and borrowers and split loans into payment-dependent notes. (Committee on the Global Financial System (CGFS) of Bank for International Settlements (BIS) provided the differences among P2P lending business models: some simply match lenders and borrowers, while others reflect the loans on their balance sheets [1].) P2P lending often targets borrowers with low- and mid-level credit ratings, a group facing a reduced supply of bank loans since the collapse of the subprime loan markets and the global financial crisis of 2008. P2P lending has also demonstrated its usefulness in financial inclusiveness and as a substitute for bank loans by expanding its range of credit offers to borrowers with low-credit ratings [2] as well as by providing more investment opportunities for small institutions and retail investors [3].

P2P lending has grown dramatically in size and scale over the past decade, drawing attention from both investors and regulatory agencies [1,3]. On the one hand, unclear regulations and policy guidelines have sometimes plagued these platforms, hindering the application of new and innovative information technologies that could reduce intermediation costs and improve user experiences. (For example, in 2015, the Financial Supervisory Service of Korea suspended operations of the P2P lending platform "8 Percent" after concluding that the matching platform should be required to have the same certification as other financial institutions providing credit.) On the other hand, in terms of banking and financial stability, these regulations are reasonable. The lingering effects of the global financial crisis have become the "new normal," and, in reality, P2P lending platforms have at times failed to properly allocate credit. (In May 2016, the LendingClub, one of the best-known P2P lending platforms, was accused of providing USD 22 million in loans to underqualified borrowers. Afterwards then-CEO Renaud Laplache and three other directors resigned or were dismissed.)

Direct investments through P2P lending platforms have the following characteristics. First, the notes traded via FinTech platforms are often unsecured [4,5]. Second, P2P lending platforms often subdivide loans into a number of mini-bonds (or notes) and provide aftermarket trading functionality, both of which enhance liquidity. (In some credit markets, wherein raising funds through banks may be difficult, other funding methods are gaining in popularity, such as small-scale divisions of bonds or direct investments. In the UK, for example, small- and medium-sized enterprises use so-called mini-bonds as a means of marketing and financing. These enterprises issue bonds to their customers, who can choose discounted products rather than receiving interest payments [4].) For example, by paying a fee equal to 1% of the sales price, LendingClub investors can trade their dividend notes in the associated aftermarket (the Note Trading Platform) before they expire. Third, P2P lending platforms typically provide loans for borrowers with low- and mid-level credit ratings. This group has faced a credit gap, or a reduced supply of loans from banks, since the global financial crisis.

Despite its growing popularity, the effects of P2P lending on major bank risks have not been investigated thoroughly. (CGFS [1] provide an expository note about this issue.) Direct investments via P2P lending platforms are supposed to be duration-matched, and they cannot be liquidated until the maturity date. This means that P2P lending is designed not to create a short-term liquidity problem. (In practice, however, some P2P lending platforms adopt more complicated originate-to-distribute approaches. LendingClub is an example: After investors and borrowers are matched, the investment funds raised by LendingClub are transferred to the WebBank (located in Utah, US), which originates from the loan and returns it to LendingClub. LendingClub then divides the loan into "payment-dependent notes" by units of USD 25, and distributes them to investors, the proceeds of which fund specific loans to borrowers. The principal and interest are paid to the loan note holders. Note that, if LendingClub initiated the loan directly, without going through a bank or depository agency, the activity would be considered as an unauthorized shadow banking activity.) Further, notes (of split loans) invested and traded through P2P lending platforms are mainly unsecured bonds (i.e., with no collateral). This implies that the contagious effects of loan defaults would be limited. Still, P2P lending platforms make commissions on initial loan brokerages and exchanges of notes in the associated aftermarkets, while investors mostly bear the risks of borrowers' defaults. (In this sense, P2P lending has some features of an originate-to-distribute model [6]. Phillips [7] uses the features as a basis for criticism of P2P lending.) Thus, P2P lending platforms would be more focused on increasing fee revenues than on proper evaluations of creditworthiness, leading to an increase in the proportion of non-performing loans. To the extent that P2P lending and bank loans act more as substitutes than as complements, competition between banks and P2P lending platforms may hamper banking prudence, given the aforementioned incentives.

Considering these characteristics and the aforementioned gap in the literature, we theoretically analyzed the effects of P2P lending on two major bank risks: (in)solvency risk and (il)liquidity risk. The idea of separating banks' illiquidity and insolvency risks was first introduced by Bagehot [8], who argued that the market itself cannot fully address the problems of an interim liquidity shock. Some researchers have criticized this view e.g., [9], but recent studies such as by Rochet and Vives [10] and Freixas and Ma [11] have supported it. The Bank for International Settlements also supports this view, having introduced the liquidity coverage ratio (LCR) and the net stable funding ratio (NSFR) requirements in Basel III. (LCR requires that a bank should hold adequate stock of unencumbered high-quality liquid assets to meet its liquidity needs for a 30 calendar day liquidity stress scenario [12]. NSFR is defined as the amount of available stable funding relative to the amount of required stable funding. This ratio should be at least 100% on an ongoing basis [13].)

Finally, while we let P2P lending refer to general lending activities rather than financing with a specific purpose, we want to note the study by Petruzzelli et al. [14], who focus on the role of crowdfunding in supporting sustainability-oriented initiatives. They find that in terms of economic importance, P2P lending becomes the most relevant crowd-finance form, (Lending-based crowdfunding collected a global volume of funds about $25 billion in 2015 [14].) implying that P2P lending should be an important issue in sustainable finance. The rest of the paper proceeds as follows. Section 2 presents the theoretical background and Section 3 describes the model. Section 4 analyzes the major bank risks—insolvency and liquidity risks—by comparing two cases: in the benchmark case, only banks exist, and in the other case, both banks and P2P platforms exist. Section 5 discusses the effects of competition on bank risks, and the importance of the isolation of P2P lending from the banking sector. Section 6 concludes the paper.

2. Theoretical Background

In this study, we compared two cases: (i) the benchmark, in which only banks exist in a single loan market, and (ii) the case wherein the loan market is segmented by borrowers' creditworthiness and P2P lending platforms operate only in the low-credit segment. Our results show that compared with the benchmark case, when P2P lending platforms and banks operate in the low-credit market the (i) insolvency risk of individual banks increases; (ii) illiquidity risk of individual banks decreases; (iii) banks' total credit risk—the sum of both risks—also decreases.

First, regarding insolvency risk, borrowers in the low-credit segment would choose higher-risk, higher-return projects because the interest rate applied to the low-credit market segment would be higher than that applied to the benchmark case, as in Boyd and De Nicolo [15]. As a result, the likelihood of borrowers' defaults on individual bank loans increases in the low-credit segment, leading to higher insolvency risk. Second, regarding illiquidity risk, the proportion of protected deposits in a bank's deposit portfolio would increase with loan market segmentation, as a result of banks substituting for P2P lending platforms. This would lower the level of critical cash flow that would prevent a bank run, resulting in a lower illiquidity risk. Third, in the segmented market case, a bank's combined credit risk is smaller than that in the benchmark case, implying that the decreased illiquidity risk would be great enough to cancel out the increased insolvency risk.

We further investigated the effect of competition and the implication of the separation of P2P lending and banking and find that competition is more likely to reduce the combined credit risk in the segmented market case than in the benchmark case. This result also implies that once banks begin to participate in P2P lending, either directly or indirectly, it would adversely affect the combined risk because it would lessen the competition in the segmented market case. Our results imply that sustainable P2P lending requires an appropriate separation of roles between banks and P2P lending platforms. If P2P lending platforms and banks are differentiated in their roles for separate market segments, the spread of the former may not pose a significant problem in terms of bank risks. Regulatory agencies, however, would have to limit P2P lending platforms' brokerage of mini-bonds or notes outside their associated aftermarkets. At the same time, they may have to prevent banks or their subsidiaries from joining the trades of split notes in the aftermarkets of P2P lending platforms and let the banks focus on the high-credit market segments and protected deposits business.

Before the mid-2000s, studies on inter-bank competition focused on analyzing the impact of competition on financial stability [16–18]. Often, as competition increases, banks become more risk-seeking (See Carletti [19] for more details on previous studies on bank competition and financial stability). However, recent studies have suggested that this is not necessarily the case [15,20,21]. The U-shaped relationship between bank competition and bank failure has been confirmed by both theoretical [15] and empirical analyses [21]. These studies are traditional, homogeneous inter-bank competition analyses, and they do not involve financial institutions that do not follow the deposit-loan model.

More recent studies have investigated the coexistence of P2P lending platforms and banks. Thakor and Merton [22] suggested that banks have a stronger incentive to manage a trust, but P2P lending platforms tend to experience more adverse effects from a loss of trust. De Roure et al. [23]

found that P2P lenders tend to be bottom fishers, P2P loans are riskier, and the risk-adjusted interest rates for P2P loans are lower than those for bank loans. Tang [24] found that P2P platforms are essentially substitutes for banks and mostly serve the same borrower population, despite their unique potential. Finally, Vallee and Zeng [25] and Balyuk [26] studied the informational role of P2P lending and its relationship with investors and banks, respectively.

A strand of the recent banking literature has adopted global games, which are games of incomplete information wherein each player obtains a private signal about the true state with a small amount of noise, and his/her higher-order beliefs also affect the outcome [27,28]. Goldstein and Pauzner [29] and Rochet and Vives [10] are two well-known global game-based bank run models. Goldstein and Pauzner [29] directly extend the Bryant–Diamond–Dybvig (BDD) model [30,31] by incorporating the actual interim liquidity needs of consumer-depositors. Our study is close to Rochet and Vives [10] and Freixas and Ma [11], who focus on depositors' speculative runs on unprotected bank deposits. Nevertheless, it is distinct because we extend the model to incorporate the situation wherein heterogeneous types of financial institutions co-exist in the market.

In addition to the finance literature, studies such as Cusumano [32], Einav et al. [33], and Sundararajan [34] emphasize the positive aspects of competition in platform economies, which open the chance of entry for small players and enhance efficiency. However, their focus is often the sharing of horizontally diversified, and sometimes idle, "physical" facilities. Due to this difference, there are limitations to applying the implications to the case of P2P lending in the current paper.

To the best of our knowledge, this study is one of the first works, if not the first, to implement a full theoretical analysis of the effects of the competition between P2P lending platform and banks on bank failure risks, specifically in the strand of microeconomic banking literature such as Rochet and Vives [10], Goldstein and Pauzner [29] and Freixas and Ma [11], which consider only homogeneous banks. This study also provides related policy implications that it is necessary for a regulatory authority to supervise the P2P lending platforms separately from the existing banking sector to promote the sustainable development of alternative lending.

3. Model

We follow the basic settings and notations of Freixas and Ma [11], (Freixas and Ma [11] can also be regarded as an extension of the BDD model, which is the de facto standard model and the starting point in the microeconomics of banking.) with modifications, extensions, and clarifications where necessary.

3.1. Players and Settings

As per the standard Bryant–Diamond–Dybvig (BDD) model, we consider a one-good, three-period ($t = 0, 1, 2$) economy wherein all agents are assumed to be risk-neutral. There are two types of investors: *depositors* who deposit their liquidity in banks, and *P2P lenders* who lend directly to entrepreneurs (borrowers) via P2P lending platforms and hold these entrepreneurs' loan notes. Similar to the BDD model, depositors are assumed to be homogeneous. At $t = 1$, the depositors decide whether to withdraw their deposits early, and the lenders trade notes amongst themselves in the accompanying aftermarket. When depositors withdraw their deposits early at $t = 1$, they incur a penalty. (In Rochet and Vives [10], unprotected deposits are mostly wholesale deposits such as certificates of deposit, and early withdrawals stop the rolling over of these deposits.) However, unlike the BDD model, we do not consider any unanticipated consumption needs at $t = 1$, which are likely to be covered by protected demand deposits such as checking accounts. We assume that depositors are interested only in the rates of return from their investments, as modeled in Rochet and Vives [10] for example, and that their decisions on the early withdrawal of their deposits solely depend on their speculation on the likelihood of realization of the promised return at $t = 2$.

P2P lending platforms do not take deposits; they only match lenders and borrowers and earn fee revenue per match. Loans via P2P lending platforms are split into payment-dependent *notes* and can be traded in the accompanying aftermarkets at $t = 1$, similar to that in the (incomplete) market example of Diamond and Dybvig [31]. We assume that trades of notes occur only between P2P lenders, limiting the effects of trades within P2P lending platforms and preventing the "hacking" of the market e.g., [35]. Moreover, we assume that banks cannot identify a borrower's type, default risk, or creditworthiness. However, we assume that P2P platforms, with their new technology, can correctly identify whether a borrower's type is higher or lower than a threshold.

Borrowers are entrepreneurs who are cashless but have long-term and productive, yet potentially risky, projects classified by their type $b \in (0, B]$, with a higher b indicating the safer entrepreneur. Each entrepreneur's project requires a unit of the loan at $t = 0$ which is to be paid back with the gross rate of return from the loan $r(> 1)$, when the project is completed at $t = 2$. There is a threshold type $\hat{B}$ such that $\hat{B} > 1/(x - r)$. Here, x denotes the gross rate of return from an entrepreneur's successful project. Borrowers of $b < \hat{B}$ and $b \geq \hat{B}$ are classified as Group 1 and Group 2, respectively. We assume that there exists a difference in the maximum value of r for Group 1 and for Group 2, respectively, which the borrowers in each group are willing to accept. Banks are supposed to be unable to identify which group a potential borrower belongs to. In contrast, P2P lending platforms, often considered to have more advanced technology, are supposed to correctly identify whether a borrower is in Group 1 or Group 2, although not the exact value of b, which creates the possibility of market segmentation.

A bank's portfolio of deposits at $t = 0, 1 + F$, consists of the following: F is the portion of demand deposit, given the amount of loan is normalized as one, in the benchmark case with banks only, and F' in the case of P2P lending platforms also operate. (For the remainder of the paper, we use the same approach using the apostrophe.) At $t = 2$, the sum of the liquidity reserve and recouped loan with return D (and D'), $F + D$ (and $F' + D'$), must be delivered to depositors if the bank is solvent where $D > 1$ (and $D' > 1$). $F + D$ is the promised, but not all of it is necessarily protected. Note that, although not exactly the same, F is related to the liquidity reserve; a higher value of F implies that the proportion of savings deposits is lower. We assume that there is no equity in the bank's portfolio. For simplicity, we assume that if a bank fails at $t = 2$, it returns nothing but F (and F') to the depositors. As Diamond [36] noted, increased participation in direct financing causes the banking sector to shrink, primarily through the reduced holdings of long-term assets, implying the possibility of $F' > F$. Finally, we assume that the size of deposits is less than the demand for loans, causing excess demand for loans.

A P2P lending platform does not have a depository function (i.e., $F = 0$) and it only matches P2P lenders and borrowers. We assume that all P2P lenders are homogeneous: every P2P lender has an equal share of the loans given to all borrowers such that each P2P lender has the same homogeneous loan portfolio. We also assume that the (average) investment at $t = 0$ is normalized as 1. Thus, a P2P lender's ex-post gross rate of return at $t = 2$ is the cash flow generated from successful loans. When banks and credit markets co-exist, we assume that no cross-participation—depositors' purchase of notes or lenders' purchase of loan claims—is allowed at $t = 1$. Thus, any transaction that occurs in the secondary markets attached to P2P platforms does not affect the money market. Finally, we assume that all rates are exogenous unless specified.

3.2. Timing of Game

At $t = 0$, loans are jointly financed by a continuum of investors. For simplicity, a P2P lender is homogeneous and assumed to hold split notes of all types of borrowers' loans, in the same way as (unprotected) deposits are diversified via bank.

At $t = 1$, an investor, indexed by i, receives a private noisy signal $s_i = \theta + \epsilon_i$ about a random cashflow generated from the (unit) loan portfolio, denoted by θ. Here, ϵ_i is i.i.d. and follows a probability distribution with zero mean and a small but non-zero standard deviation of σ. Each depositor who chooses to withdraw his/her deposit early will recover $qD(< D/R$ or $q < 1/R)$ by paying an early withdrawal penalty of $(1 - q)D$ where $q \in (0, 1)$ is the proportion of a deposit that one can recover from early withdrawal, given that the bank has not failed at $t = 1$. Similarly, at $t = 1$, lenders decide whether to sell or buy the diversified notes in the aftermarket. Both depositors' and P2P lenders' decisions at $t = 1$ depend on their observations of private signals.

Provided an early withdrawal of savings deposit (or loan) is requested, the bank should liquidate its long-term financial claims with discount, which generates an expected cash flow of θ multiplied by the discount factor $\frac{1}{1+\lambda}$ where λ is the discount rate. (This can be regarded as the haircut rate of the financial products in the money market. During the repo run in the last global financial crisis of 2007–2008, the average haircut on bilateral repo transactions, except for U.S. Treasuries, rose from zero in early 2007 to almost 50% at the peak of the crisis in late 2008 [37].) We assume $\frac{1}{1+\lambda} \leq q$, which means that a bank's early liquidation of long-term assets is costlier than a depositor's early liquidation of short-term assets or deposits. If the bank's ex-post cash flow at $t = 2$ (i.e., which is the sum of the recovered loan and the value of its remaining assets) is less than the amount to be redeemed, bank failure occurs.

In case of lending via P2P lending platforms, the notes are assumed to be traded within the associated aftermarkets where lenders are randomly matched and trade their notes; if lender i and j, whose signals satisfy $s_i > s_j$ without loss of generality, are matched, then j sells her/his (portfolio of) notes to i at s_j. (In fact, only a fraction of the notes and not the whole portfolio would be traded in the aftermarkets. This assumption helps to avoid theoretical problems with the measurement from abusing the law of large numbers. This setting also implies that no speculative trade in the sense of Harrison and Kreps [38] would occur.) Thus, the traded notes would be "discounted" proportional to the risk or standard deviation. (For example, if we assume that noise ϵ_j follows $N(0, \sigma^2)$, the amount of the discount can be approximated as $\sigma/\sqrt{3}$.) Note that based on our assumptions, which limit the effects of trades within associated P2P lending platforms, transactions in aftermarkets do not have any spillover effect in the banking sector.

At $t = 2$, if the bank is solvent, it delivers the promised amount $F + D$ (and $F' + D'$), and F (and F') otherwise. For investments via P2P lending platforms, the cash flow generated from loans (excluding non-performing loans) is recovered for an individual lender i.

3.3. Borrowers' Type and Market Segmentation

Although P2P lending platforms seek to maximize the number of matches between lenders and borrowers, we argue that P2P lending platform eventually match loans only for borrowers in Group 1, and segment the loan market, based on the empirical findings by De Roure et al. [23], Tang [24]. (In this study, we combined the finding from De Roure et al. [23]—P2P lenders tend to be bottom fishers and P2P loans are riskier, with that from Tang [24]—P2P lending platforms are essential substitutes for banks, as a stylized fact for our setting. We also want to note that [39] observe a similar kind of vertical separation of the hospitality market after the entry of Airbnb. In a separate study, we investigated a condition for this type of endogenous market segmentation to occur. The key idea is that when the loan supply from banks fails to clear the loan demand due to external conditions (e.g., prudence regulation and credit rationing), the P2P lending platform can choose to either (i) compete in both market segments with a single rate, or (ii) let banks cover *everyone* in the high-credit market and capture the bigger excess loan demand as well as compete only in the low-credit market. In some cases, choosing the latter is better for P2P lending platforms.) Henceforth, we use Market 1 to denote the market segment for low-credit borrowers (Group 1) and Market 2 to denote high-credit borrowers (Group 2). When the loan market is segmented, the gross rate of return from a loan in Market 2, denoted by r_2, is supposed to be lower than that in Market 1, denoted by r_1, namely $r_1 > r_2$.

Similar to the early withdrawal of unprotected deposits, the P2P lending notes can be traded at $t = 1$ with a discount proportional to the standard deviation of private signal σ. Because we assume that investors would not switch between banks and P2P platforms at $t = 1$, (For example, without this assumption, depositors of unprotected bank deposits could withdraw early and purchase the notes at $t = 1$.) trades in the aftermarkets do not have any influence on the banking sector. Table 1 summarizes the investment characteristics classified by institutional settings, timing, decision, and cash flows.

Table 1. Timing, decision, and cash flows for different institutional settings.

Investment (and Decision)	Banks Only (Single Market)	Banks (Segmented Market)	P2P Platforms (Low-Credit Segment)
Demand deposit (protected, at t = 0)	F	F'	0
Loan (unprotected, at t = 0)	1	1	1
Investor's choice at t = 1	Withdrawal(of qD) or waiting	Withdrawal(of qD') or waiting	Trades (with discount) between lenders
Investor's return at t = 2 (bank failure)	F	F'	Cash flow from performing loans
Investor's return at t = 2 (bank solvency)	$D + F$	$D' + F'$	

3.4. Cash Flow from Loans

We adopt the result of the cash flow model by Freixas and Ma [11] which derives the probability of success according to the type of borrower b as follows

$$\Pr(b) = \begin{cases} 1 & \text{if } b \in [1/(x-r), B] \\ b(x-r) & \text{if } b \in (0, 1/(x-r)). \end{cases}$$

Note that there exists a unique threshold type of entrepreneur that determines whether a loan is risk-free or risky. Assume that b follows a uniform distribution $U(0, B]$ and that B is sufficiently high so that loans would be riskless for a large proportion of borrowers. In the same loan market, (or market segment), banks and P2P lending platforms are assumed to treat borrowers equally. That is, differentiating the rate on loans for each type of borrowers is impossible. The ratio of risk-free to total loans is derived as

$$\alpha \equiv (B - 1/(x-r))/B = 1 - 1/(B(x-r)). \tag{1}$$

The greater the value of α, the more secure is the loan portfolio.

Equation (2) is the first derivative of α with respect to r, represented as

$$\partial\alpha/\partial r = -1/(B(x-r)^2) < 0, \tag{2}$$

implying that as the exogenous gross rate of return on loan r increases, the proportion of risk-free loans α decreases.

Let γ be the ratio of *non-performing* loans to risky loans. From a unit loan provided to borrowers, the total cash flow generated referred to as θ, can be expressed as

$$\theta \equiv \alpha r + (1-r)[0 \cdot \gamma + r \cdot (1-\gamma)] = r - (1-\alpha)r\gamma. \tag{3}$$

We assume that γ follows a uniform distribution $U[0,1]$. (Freixas and Ma [11] show that γ follows a uniform distribution between 0 and 1 if entrepreneurs know the exact value of b; moreover, b follows a uniform distribution $(0, B]$; and their utility functions are a specific form of the quadratic function. However, we use the result as an exogenous condition due to the symmetric uninformedness of entrepreneur types in our model, and the negative, deterministic correlation between entrepreneur type and the gross rate of return from a project.) Then, the expected value of the ratio of the non-performing loan to the risky loan, $E(\gamma)$, is $1/2$. (Consequently, the volatility of the cash flow is determined only by the ratio of risk-free loans, α.) and the expected gross rate of return from loans, which is also the expected gross rate of return from investment via P2P lending platforms, is $(1+\alpha)r/2$.

Finally, it should be noted that not all of the entrepreneurs would be able to get a loan from banks regardless of their types without P2P lending for the following reasons. First, the canonical credit rationing problem e.g., ref. [40] can occur: all type of borrowers want to get a loan with a given gross rate of return less than r_L, and some of them are even willing to pay higher rates, but the loan supply is less than the demand. Second, we have assumed that the amount of deposits is not sufficient to cover the entire demand for loans. Note that only one of these two constraints is binding.

4. Comparison of Risks

Following Rochet and Vives [10] and Freixas and Ma [11], we consider only speculative runs by depositors and treat (in)solvency risk and (il)liquidity risk separately. We first use the case wherein only banks exist as a benchmark and compare the result with that of the segmented market case with both banks and P2P lending platforms; furthermore, we investigate how individual risks and total credit risk change under different circumstances.

4.1. Insolvency Risk

4.1.1. Benchmark: Only Banks Exist

Insolvency occurs if the ex-post cash flow θ from the unit loan is smaller than the total amount of bank deposits $F + D$ that must be paid back at $t = 2$. That is if inequality condition,

$$\theta = r - (1 - \alpha)r\gamma \geq F + D, \tag{4}$$

is *not* satisfied, the bank can be considered as insolvent. From Equation (4), the critical level of the loan loss for determining solvency, γ_{SR}, is derived as

$$\gamma_{SR} = (r - (F + D))/((1 - \alpha)r). \tag{5}$$

Note that γ follows a uniform distribution in $[0, 1]$. The (in)solvency risk, or the probability that a bank faces the solvency problem, is denoted by ρ_{SR} and derived as $\rho_{SR} \equiv 1 - \gamma_{SR}$. By simple rearrangement in terms of the market gross rate of return from the loan, this is expressed as

$$\rho_{SR} \equiv 1 - \gamma_{SR} = (F + D - \alpha r)/(1 - \alpha)r \tag{6}$$

4.1.2. Co-Existence of Banks and P2P Lending Platforms

Now, we investigate the segmented market case of banks and P2P lending platforms co-existing in the low-credit market segment (Market 1) while only banks exist in the high-credit one (Market 2). Unlike a bank, a P2P lending platform itself does not face the problem of insolvency, as the lenders directly take on the default risk of their loans. The cash flow condition for the bank's soundness is now represented as

$$\hat{\theta} = \frac{\beta\hat{B}}{B}[r_1 - (1 - \alpha_1)r_1\gamma] + \frac{B - \hat{B}}{B}r_2 \geq F' + D' \tag{7}$$

where β is the share of applicants for whom banks provide a loan in Market 1, which satisfies

$$\frac{r_2}{r_1} = \frac{B - \beta\hat{B}}{B - \hat{B}}\frac{1 + \alpha_1}{2}$$

such that the expected cash flows from both a unit loan via banks and via P2P lending are the same. Note that $\alpha_1 = (\hat{B} - 1/(x - r_1))/\hat{B} < \alpha$, and $\alpha_2 = 1$.

From Equation (7), in the segmented market case, the critical level of loan loss, denoted by $\hat{\gamma}_{SR}$, is derived as

$$\hat{\gamma}_{SR} = \frac{\beta r_1 + (B - \hat{B})r_2/\hat{B} - B(F' + D')/\hat{B}}{\beta(1 - \alpha_1)r_1}. \tag{8}$$

The change in the bank's profit from the benchmark is represented by

$$\delta(r - (F + D)) = \hat{r} - (F' + D') \qquad (9)$$

where $\hat{r} = \frac{\hat{B}}{B}\beta r_1 + \frac{(B - \hat{B})}{B}r_2$, which is supposed to be less than r due to competition, represents the bank's gross rate of return, or revenue, on unit loan from both market segments, and $\delta(< 1)$ reflects the decrease in the bank's loan–deposit margin compared with the benchmark case. Given the assumptions and Equation (8), the following inequality

$$\hat{\gamma}_{SR} = \frac{\delta(r - (F + D))}{\hat{B}/B(1 - \alpha_1)\beta r_1} = \frac{B\delta r(1 - \alpha)}{\hat{B}\beta r_1(1 - \alpha_1)}\gamma_{SR} = \frac{\delta r(x - r_1)}{\beta r_1(x - r)}\gamma_{SR} < \gamma_{SR}$$

is sufficiently satisfied if β is not sufficiently smaller than δ, implying that the impact of P2P lending on banks' profit reduction is greater than that on their market share in the low-credit segment.

To facilitate comparison with the benchmark results, suppose that $F + D = F' + D' = R$, which means that the future value of the normalized deposit portfolio in the benchmark case and that in the segmented market case are the same. Note that, in this case, the amount of the protected bank deposit, denoted by F', is greater than that in the benchmark case (i.e., $F' > F$) due to the lower rate of return on loan and, consequently, savings deposits. Then, from $\hat{r} - (F' + D') < r - (F + D) + \hat{B}(\beta - 1)r_1/B$, Equation (9) leads to the following inequality

$$(1 - \delta)(r - (F + D)) > (1 - \beta)r_1\hat{B}/B.$$

Given that $\hat{B}r_1/B > 1/2$, and $r - (F + D)$, which is the loan–deposit spread, would not be greater than $1/2$ in any reasonable case, $1 - \delta$ must be greater than $1 - \beta$, or $\beta > \delta$. Thus, given that $F + D = F' + D' = R$, the insolvency risk of a bank, $\hat{\rho}_{SR} = 1 - \hat{\gamma}_{SR}$, is greater than that in the benchmark, ρ_{SR}, which leads to the following proposition.

Proposition 1. *When a loan market is segmented by borrowers' capability and when P2P lending platforms and banks operate simultaneously in the low-credit segment, an individual bank's insolvency risk is greater than that in the benchmark case.*

4.2. Liquidity Risk

4.2.1. Benchmark: Only Banks Exist

We now examine the case of bank failure due to insufficient liquidity caused by depositors' early withdrawal. This situation can occur when a bank is forced to liquidate its long-term assets due to the early withdrawal of many depositors at $t = 1$, even though in the absence of early withdrawals, the bank would not face a soundness problem and it could repay the debt sufficiently at $t = 2$.

Let q be the proportion of a deposit that one can recover from early withdrawal at $t = 1$, and let λ, satisfying $1/(1 + \lambda) < q$ as assumed above, be the discount rate applied to a bank's (long-term) loan sold at $t = 1$, which would generate cash flow θ without the early withdrawal request. The condition that the liquidity problem never occurs at $t = 1$ is expressed as

$$\theta/(1 + \lambda) > qD,$$

implying that the present value of cash flow θ discounted by $1 + \lambda$ is greater than the highest possible recovered amount in early withdrawal.

Let L be the ratio of depositors who take early withdrawals, or run, at $t = 1$. In this case, the level of L at which the bank can survive at $t = 1$ but experiences failure at $t = 2$ is determined by the following inequality

$$(1 - L)D > \theta - F - L(1 + \lambda)qD. \tag{10}$$

The liquidity risk arises when the deposit to be returned at $t = 2$ is greater than the remaining liquidity from the cash flow θ, deducted by the protected deposit F, and by the liquidity that has flowed out due to early withdrawal at $t = 1$, $L(1 + \lambda)qD$. The probability of each depositor's belief that a bank will *not* fail at $t = 2$ due to illiquidity is the probability that L *does not satisfy* Equation (10), which is

$$\Pr\left(L \leq \frac{\theta - F - D}{[(1 + \lambda)q - 1]D} = L^*\right). \tag{11}$$

Whether a depositor i chooses to withdraw early at $t = 1$ or not is influenced by his/her private signal, $s_i = \theta + \epsilon_i$, and his/her forecasts about other depositors' behavior, which are reflected by L. Note that depositor i's strategy is influenced by other depositors' *belief* on L upon observing his/her private signal s_i. Then, ultimately, this depositor must consider the *belief on other depositors' beliefs*, which violates the common knowledge assumption and corresponds with the setting of a global game [28].

Following convention, we first apply the *Laplacian property* [28] to our setting: any investor i's *belief* about the ratio of early withdrawal L follows $U[0, 1]$. Depositors are supposed to use the switching strategy, which is proven to be optimal if the Laplacian Property is satisfied [28]. If depositor i chooses a switching strategy, he/she chooses either to run if the signal is below a certain threshold level or to wait until maturity.

The threshold level of the cash flow for an early withdrawal decision, referred to as s^*, is determined when the expected value of the early withdrawal at $t = 1$ equals that of the maturity withdrawal at $t = 2$, or

$$qD = \Pr(\text{survive at } t = 2|s = s^*) \cdot D,$$

given that $\Pr(\text{survive at } t = 1|s = s^*) = 1$, or $\alpha r > (1 + \lambda)qD$. Given that the Laplacian Property is satisfied, in a Perfect Bayesian Equilibrium, the likelihood of other investors' decision to run would behave like a random variable drawn from the uniform distribution of $U[0, 1]$. (Moving away from the switching point, this belief may not actually be uniform. However, according to Morris and Shin [28], as long as the payoff advantage of running on the bank is decreasing in θ, the Laplacian action coincides with the equilibrium action.) From the Equation (11), we can infer that

$$\Pr(\text{survive at } t = 2|s = s^*) = \Pr(L \leq L^*) = (\theta - F - D)/([(1 + \lambda)q - 1]D)$$

as L follows $U[0, 1]$. Note that the probability of solvency at $t = 2$ is continuous. Thus, the expected payoff from waiting is also continuous and monotone decreasing in L, and thus, monotone increasing in θ. The threshold cash flow level θ^*, under which a bank run may occur, is derived as

$$\theta^* = F + D + q[(1 + \lambda)q - 1]D. \tag{12}$$

Note that s^* is *uniquely* determined, $s^* = \theta^*$. Let $\underline{\theta} = F + D$, and $\bar{\theta} = F + (1 + \lambda)qD$, which satisfy $\underline{\theta} < \theta^* < \bar{\theta}$. Then, a depositor has to run for any $L \in [0, 1]$ if $\theta < \underline{\theta}$ and wait if $\theta > \bar{\theta}$, which means that the *limit dominance property* [28] is satisfied. Thus, we can conclude that our setting of the global game satisfies all the required properties in Proposition 2.1 of Morris and Shin [28] for the existence of a unique switching strategy $s^* = \theta^*$. (While not incorrect, the explanation of the global game model in Freixas and Ma [11] uses the setting of Carlsson and Van Damme [27], where the state variable is an unbounded real number (i.e., $\theta \in \mathbf{R}$) and neither upper nor lower dominance exists.)

Let $\mu = 1 + q[(1 + \lambda)q - 1] > 1$ for simplicity of notation. If the bank becomes illiquid, despite it being solvent at $t = 2$, and a run on the bank would occur, the range of cash flow would be

$$F + D < \theta \leq F + \mu D.$$

Similar to ρ_{SR}, we can define the probability of (il)liquidity risk, ρ_{LR}, as

$$\rho_{LR} = \frac{(\mu - 1)D}{(1 - \alpha)r}. \tag{13}$$

The total credit risk of a bank, $\rho_{TR} = Pr(\theta < \theta^*)$, is the sum of the insolvency risk ρ_{SR} and the illiquidity risk ρ_{LR}, which is derived as

$$\rho_{TR} = \frac{(F + \mu D) - \alpha r}{(1 - \alpha)r}. \tag{14}$$

4.2.2. Co-Existence of Banks and P2P Lending Platforms

Again, we investigate the segmented market case, in which P2P lending platforms enter and operate in the low-credit market segment (Market 1). Considering that loans in the high-credit segment (Market 2) are supposed to be riskless and early withdrawal is not likely to occur, we focus only on Market 1.

Note that the trades of notes in the associated aftermarket at $t = 1$ do not influence depositors outside P2P lending platforms. Then, we can adapt Equation (10), which describes the condition for the illiquidity problem for an otherwise solvent bank, for the segmented market case as

$$(\hat{B}/B)(1 - L)D' \geq \hat{\theta} - F' - L(\hat{B}/B)(1 + \lambda)qD'.$$

The threshold cash flow that makes early withdrawal and waiting indifferent without actual insolvency, $\hat{\theta}^*$, is then derived as

$$\hat{\theta}^* = F' + (\hat{B}/B)(1 + q[(1 + \lambda)q - 1])D' = F' + \mu(\hat{B}/B)D'. \tag{15}$$

Given the assumptions, we find that the cash flow threshold level $\hat{\theta}^*$ is lower than θ^*, derived from the benchmark case. The liquidity risk in the segmented market case is derived as

$$\hat{\rho}_{LR} = \frac{F' + \mu(\hat{B}/B)D' - (F' + D')}{(\hat{B}/B)(1 - \alpha_1)r_1} = \frac{(\mu - (B/\hat{B}))D'}{(1 - \alpha_1)r_1} \tag{16}$$

In the worst case, the cash flow would be generated only from risk-free loans. Given that $B > \hat{B}$, $D' < D$, $\alpha_1 < \alpha$, and $r < r_1$, we derive the following proposition.

Proposition 2. *The probability of a bank's (il)liquidity risk is lower when the market is segmented by borrower types and banks compete with P2P platforms than that in the benchmark case, or when $\hat{\rho}_{LR} < \rho_{LR}$.*

As in the benchmark case, the total credit risk of a bank in the segmented market case, $\hat{\rho}_{TR} = Pr(\hat{\theta} < \hat{\theta}^*)$, the sum of the insolvency risk, $\hat{\rho}_{SR}$, and the illiquidity risk, $\hat{\rho}_{LR}$, is derived as

$$\hat{\rho}_{TR} = \hat{\rho}_{SR} + \hat{\rho}_{LR} = 1 - \frac{\delta B(r - (F + D))}{\beta \hat{B}(1 - \alpha_1)r_1} + \frac{(\mu - (B/\hat{B}))D'}{(1 - \alpha_1)r_1}$$

$$< 1 - \frac{B(r - (F' + D'))}{\hat{B}(1 - \alpha_1)r_1} + \frac{(\mu - 1)D'}{(1 - \alpha_1)r_1} = \frac{(1 - \alpha_1)r_1}{(1 - \alpha_1)r_1} - \frac{B(r - (F' + D'))}{\hat{B}(1 - \alpha_1)r_1} + \frac{(\mu - 1)D'}{(1 - \alpha_1)r_1}, \tag{17}$$

by assuming $\beta > \delta$. The right-hand side of Equation (17) is less than $\rho_{TR} = (F + \mu D - \alpha r)/((1 - \alpha)r)$ if the inequality

$$\frac{\hat{B}}{B}(1 - \alpha_1)r_1 + F' + D' - r + \frac{\hat{B}}{B}(\mu - 1)D' < \frac{r_1(x - r)}{r(x - r_1)}(F + \mu D - \alpha r)$$

is satisfied, which can be rewritten as

$$\frac{r_1}{B(x - r_1)} + F' + D' - r + \frac{\hat{B}}{B}(\mu - 1)D' < \frac{r_1(x - r)}{r(x - r_1)}(F + D - r + (\mu - 1)D) + \frac{r_1}{\hat{B}(x - r_1)} \qquad (18)$$

Given A3, $D' < D$ and $\hat{B} < B$, we can conclude that the inequality condition of Equation (18) is always satisfied, which leads to Proposition 3

Proposition 3. *Given the assumptions, the total credit risk of a bank is lower when the loan market is segmented by borrower types and P2P lending platforms operate in the low-credit market segment than that in the benchmark case.*

The insolvency risk rises when the loan market is segmented by credit ratings because banks as well as P2P lending platforms charge higher interest rates in the low-credit segment than they would in the benchmark case, which leads borrowers to choose high-risk, high-return projects, as in Boyd and De Nicolo [15]. In contrast, the decrease in illiquidity risk occurs because the ratio of protected deposits in a bank's portfolio would be higher in the segmented market case. Then, the effect of lowering the cash flow threshold that would trigger a bank run would dominate the effect from the increase in the ratio of risky loans in the low-credit market segment. Note that our model is mainly designed for analyzing the risks of individual institutions; it is not suitable for contagion or systemic risk. Still, our result implies that expecting a minimal impact from P2P lending on contagion and systemic risk in the banking sector is not overstretching. (Freixas and Ma [11] used the same global game approach for the analysis of system risk with strong assumptions about the contagion; it is a simultaneous, non-sequential event that affects only the discount rate.)

Note that our results are mainly derived from the assumptions that (i) P2P lending platforms operate only in the segmented market for borrowers with low-credit ratings while banks operate in both the low- and high-credit market segments; (ii) lending is direct and loans are treated as split notes (non-secured mini-bonds); (iii) only lenders can trade split notes in the associated aftermarket.

5. Extension

5.1. Competition Effects

Two common effects of competition on the soundness of banks are (i) the risk-shifting effect, which is the result of lower risk-seeking tendencies among borrowers as loan rates decline with intensified competition, and (ii) the buffer-reduction effect, which is the lowered capacity of banks to absorb loan loss as loan–deposit margins decline with intensified competition and deteriorating profitability. The effect of competition on the soundness of banks mainly depends on which effect dominates. As the benchmark for this discussion, we again adopt the results of Freixas and Ma [11], which we summarize as follows.

Considering that the risk-free loan ratio α is also a function of the gross rate of return from a loan r, the first derivative of the benchmark insolvency risk ρ_{SR} is as follows:

$$\frac{\partial \rho_{SR}}{\partial r} = \frac{-1}{(1 - \alpha)^2 r^2} \frac{\partial \alpha}{\partial r}(r^2 - x(F + D)). \qquad (19)$$

Equation (2) shows that α is monotonically decreasing in r. Thus, the insolvency risk ρ_{SR} increase in r, or declines as the competition intensifies, only when $r^2 - x(F + D) > 0$, which is a necessary and sufficient condition. In other words, given that all other conditions remain the same, competition in the loan market initially reduces banks' rates of return on loans and contributes to the reduction of insolvency risk. However, once the rate falls below a threshold (or $r^2 - x(F + D) < 0$), it leads to decreased buffering capital and increased insolvency risk. The first derivative of the illiquidity risk ρ_{LR} with respect to r in the benchmark case is as follows:

$$\frac{\partial \rho_{LR}}{\partial r} = (\mu - 1)\frac{-D}{(1-\alpha)^2 r^2}\left(\frac{\partial(1-\alpha)}{\partial r}r + (1-\alpha)\right) < 0. \tag{20}$$

As competition intensifies, the rate of return on loan r decreases and, consequently, the illiquidity risk increases.

Finally, from Equation (14), we conclude that the total credit risk ρ_{TR} increases with respect to r if and only if $r^2 - x(F + \mu D) > 0$. In other words, under the threshold level, $\tilde{r} = \sqrt{x(F + \mu D)}$, the risk-shifting effect no longer dominates the buffer reduction effect, or competition causes the total credit risk to be higher.

Now, we examine the segmented market case. Suppose the rate of return on a loan in Market 2, r_2, is fixed, and we focus on the rate of return on a loan in Market 1, r_1, and the competition effects in the low-credit market segment between banks and P2P lending platforms. Equation (8) implies that $\hat{\gamma}_{SR}$ monotone decreases in r_1 in a way that is similar to the benchmark case. That is, the insolvency risk of a bank, $\hat{\rho}_{SR} = 1 - \hat{\gamma}_{SR}$, decreases, and competition reduces the insolvency risk until r_1 reaches the threshold level. However, the risk then increases if the interest rate further decreases below the threshold level. From Equation (16), we conclude that competition in Market 1 reduces the illiquidity risk of a bank.

The effect on a bank's total credit risk is similar to that observed in the benchmark case. Instead of the exact threshold rate of return from a loan, we use the approximation derived from Equation (18) to determine the threshold level as

$$r_1^2 > x_1(F' + (1 + \hat{B}/B(\mu - 1))D').$$

Given that $x_1 > x$, and $F' + (1 + \hat{B}/B(\mu - 1))D' < F + \mu D$, whether the threshold value of r_1, $\tilde{r}_1 = \sqrt{x_1(F' + (1 + \hat{B}/B(\mu - 1))D')}$, is greater or not than that of the benchmark case $\tilde{r}$ depends on the values of these variables.

Proposition 4 shows that the threshold rate of return on a loan in Market 1 is likely to be lower than that in the benchmark case. That is, the risk-shifting effect—the upside—is likely to dominate the buffer-reduction effect—the downside—for a lower level of threshold rate in the segmented market case than in the benchmark case.

Proposition 4. *Given $F + D = F' + D'$, the threshold rate of Market 1 in the segmented market case, $\tilde{r}_1$, is lower than $\tilde{r}$, the threshold rate in the benchmark case (i.e., $\tilde{r}_1 < \tilde{r}$).*

Proof. We want to show that $x_1(F' + (1 + \hat{B}/B(\mu - 1))D') < x(F + \mu D)$. Given that $x_1 \approx x$, we can rewrite the inequality as

$$F' - F' = D - D' < \mu D - D' - \hat{B}(\mu - 1)D'/B,$$

which leads to

$$\hat{B}(\mu - 1)D'/B < (\mu - 1)D.$$

As $\hat{B}/B \leq 1$ and $D' < D$, we conclude that the inequality holds true. □

Proposition 4 also implies that competition is more likely to reduce the combined credit risk in the segmented market case than in the benchmark case.

5.2. Implication for the Separation of P2P Lending and Banking

So far in our analysis, we have strictly limited bank participation in P2P lending and assumed that only individual lenders can buy split notes and trade them in an associated aftermarket. Given the stringent regulations that prohibit shadow banking that includes P2P lending, it is doubtful that P2P lending platforms would be allowed to take deposits or mediate loans for borrowers with high credit ratings. In contrast, banks could use their subsidiaries and invest in and/or trade payment-dependent notes via P2P lending platforms, (For example, as stated in Vallee and Zeng [25], financial institutions like banks could combine their information with that of P2P lending platforms and use this higher-quality information to purchase split notes) or they could even operate their own P2P lending platforms.

Once banks begin purchasing split notes via P2P lending platforms, they would replace the "loans" that the banks would otherwise provide. These could also be used as another source of interim liquidity in the aftermarket, which would be less conspicuous to monitoring authorities than the money market. From the analysis of competition effects in the previous subsection, however, we expect that reduced competition in the low-credit market segment, along with the lax separation of P2P lending and banking, would lead to a higher rate of return on loan r_1. It would also increase an individual bank's liquidity and total credit risk.

Another possibility is the banks' direct participation in P2P lending. From the perspective (and within the limitations) of our model, unlike banks purchasing split notes via P2P lending platforms, competition in the low-credit market segment (Market 1) would not decrease, although banks would now hold more payment-dependent split notes. If banks choose to buy more notes in the aftermarket after observing their private signals, their liquidity reserves would decrease, which would lead to a higher rate of the haircut in the money market, as suggested by the higher discount rate λ. If a bank chooses to sell more notes in the aftermarket, the sales themselves would decrease the expected value of the split notes. This would be bad news for the bank, which could, in turn, lead to an increase in the probability of a run on an otherwise solvent bank. In all, allowing banks to participate in P2P lending would counter the purpose of Basel III, which requires stronger prudential regulation of bank liquidity.

6. Concluding Remarks

Since the global financial crisis of 2007–2008, direct finance via P2P lending has emerged and rapidly grown as a new vehicle for borrowers without high credit ratings, especially among households and small- and mid-sized enterprises. The growth of P2P lending may have two countervailing effects on banking. One is that banks are less exposed to risky loans and interim liquidity needs, which tend to be better served by P2P lending platforms and their associated aftermarkets. The other is that banks must compete against P2P lending platforms, reducing the liquidity buffers that they need to maintain solvency.

In this study, we investigated the effects of P2P lending on major bank risks: (in)solvency risk and (il)liquidity risk. Specifically, considering the characteristics of direct investments through P2P lending platforms, we compared two cases: (i) the benchmark case, in which only banks exist in a single loan market, and (ii) a segmented market case in which the loan market is segmented by borrowers' creditworthiness, P2P lending platforms operate only in the low-credit segment, and banks operate in both low-and high-credit segments. For the segmented market case, as compared with the benchmark one, we find that while banks' insolvency risk increases, their illiquidity risk decreases such that their overall risk also decreases.

We also find that competition between banks and P2P lending platforms is more likely to reduce the combined credit risk, the sum of (in)solvency, and (il)liquidity risks, in the segmented market case than in the benchmark one. This result implies that once banks begin to participate in P2P lending either directly or indirectly, it would create an adverse effect on the combined risk because it would lessen the competition in the segmented market case. In all, sustainable P2P lending requires an appropriate differentiation of roles between the banking sector and P2P lending so that P2P lending platforms focus more on borrowers with low-credit ratings, while banks focus more on the high-credit market segment and protected deposits.

To the best of our knowledge, this study is one of the first works, if not the first, to implement a full theoretical analysis of the effects of the competition between P2P lending platform and banks on bank failure risks, specifically in the strand of microeconomic banking literature such as Rochet and Vives [10], Freixas and Ma [11], Goldstein and Pauzner [29].

Note that our results are valid only if P2P lending platforms adhere to more primitive, direct forms of financing (e.g., issuing and circulating payment-dependent notes), without handling shadow deposits, derivatives or secured loans. If these platforms expand their business scope and develop more highly leveraged or complex products strongly linked to and affected by other markets and tradings, the implications of the results would be investigated. This is because our assumption that the effects of aftermarket trades of notes stay within the scope of P2P lending platforms would be no longer valid. Finally, we do not fully examine the strategic behaviors of P2P lending platforms in this study. Apart from filling this gap, future studies can (i) empirically investigate how P2P lending platforms affect bank risks under different regulatory frameworks in different economies, and (ii) explore how the role of P2P lending platforms differs from that of banks in advanced economies.

Author Contributions: For this research article, contributing roles are as follows: Conceptualization, E.Y. and J.J.; formal analysis, E.Y. and J.J.; funding acquisition, E.Y.; investigation, J.J.; methodology, J.J.; project administration, E.Y.; writing—original draft, J.J.; writing—review and editing, E.Y. All authors have read and agreed to the published version of the manuscript.

Acknowledgments: We thank Inho Lee, Takeshi Nakata and, specifically, Yun Woo Park for helpful comments and suggestions.

Abbreviations

The following abbreviations are used in this manuscript:

P2P   Peer-to-Peer
BDD   Bryant–Diamond–Dybvig

References

1.   CGFS. FinTech credit: Market structure, business models and financial stability implications. In *Committee on the Global Financial System Report*; Bank for International Settlements and Financial Stability Board. 2017. Available online: https://www.bis.org/publ/cgfs_fsb1.htm (accessed on 29 July 2017)

2.   Bord, V. M.; Santos, J. A. The Rise of the Originate-to-Distribute Model and the Role of Banks in Financial Intermediation. In *Federal Reserve Bank of New York Economic Policy Review*; Federal Reserve Bank of New York: New York, NY, USA, 2012; pp. 21–34.

3.   Buchak, G.; Matvos, G.; Piskorski, T.; Seru, A. Fintech, regulatory arbitrage, and the rise of shadow banks. *Natl. Bureau Econ. Res.* **2017**, *130*, 453–483.

4.   Menon, N. Mini-Bonds—So Good Things Come in Small Packates? ReedSmith LLP. 2015. Available online: http://www.structuredfinanceinbrief.com/2015/05/mini-bonds-so-good-things-come-in-small-packages/ (accessed on 29 July 2017).

5. Musatov, A.; Perez, M. Shadow banking reemerges, posing challenges to banks and regulators. *Econ. Lett.* **2016**, *11*, 1–4.

6. Purnanandam, A. Originate-to-distribute model and the subprime mortgage crisis. *Rev. Financ. Stud.* **2010**, *24*, 1881–1915. [CrossRef]

7. Phillips, M. The Incentive Problem at the Heart of Peer-to-Peer Lending. Quartz. 2014. Available online: https://qz.com/310682/the-incentive-problem-at-the-heart-of-peer-to-peer-lending/ (accessed on 29 July 2017).

8. Bagehot, W. *Lombard Street: A Description of the Money Market*; Scribner, Armstrong & Company: New York, NY, USA, 1873.

9. Goodfriend, M.; King, R.G. *Financial Deregulation, Monetary Policy, and Central Banking*; Working paper 88-1; Federal Reserve Bank of Richmond: Richmond, VA, USA, 1988.

10. Rochet, J.C.; Vives, X. Coordination failures and the lender of last resort: Was Bagehot right after all? *J. Eur. Econ. Assoc.* **2004**, *2*, 1116–1147. [CrossRef]

11. Freixas, X.; Ma, K. Banking Competition and Stability: The Role of Leverage. Discussion Paper Series no. 2014-048, CentER. 2014. Available online: https://papers.ssrn.com/sol3/papers.cfm?abstract_id=2488426 (accessed on 29 July 2017).

12. BCBS. Basel III: The Liquidity Coverage Ratio and liquidity risk monitoring tools. Basel Committee on Banking Supervision, Bank for International Settlements. 2013. Available online: https://www.bis.org/publ/bcbs238.pdf (accessed on 29 July 2017).

13. BCBS. Basel III: The Net Stable Funding Ratio. Basel Committee on Banking Supervision, Bank for International Settlements. 2014. Available online: https://www.bis.org/bcbs/publ/d295.pdf (accessed on 29 July 2017).

14. Petruzzelli, A.M.; Natalicchio, A.; Panniello, U.; Roma, P. Understanding the crowdfunding phenomenon and its implications for sustainability. *Technol. Forecast. Soc. Chang.* **2019**, *141*, 138–148. [CrossRef]

15. Boyd, J.H.; De Nicolo, G. The theory of bank risk taking and competition revisited. *J. Financ.* **2005**, *60*, 1329–1343. [CrossRef]

16. Besanko, D.; Thakor, A.V. Collateral and Rationing: Sorting Equilibria in Monopolistic and Competitive Credit Markets. *Int. Econ. Rev.* **1987**, *28*, 671–689. [CrossRef]

17. Keeley, M.C. Deposit insurance, risk, and market power in banking. *Am. Econ. Rev.* **1990**, *80*, 1183–1200.

18. Edwards, F.R.; Mishkin, F.S. The Decline of Traditional Banking: Implications for Financial Stability and Regulatory Policy. NBER Working Paper no. 4993, National Bureau of Economic Research. 1995. Available online: http://www.nber.org/papers/w4993 (accessed on 29 July 2017).

19. Carletti, E. Competition and regulation in banking. *Handb. Financ. Intermediation Bank.* **2008**, *126*, 449–482.

20. Allen, F.; Gale, D. Competition and Financial Stability. *J. Money Credit Bank.* **2004**, *36*, 453–480. [CrossRef]

21. Martinez-Miera, D.; Repullo, R. Does competition reduce the risk of bank failure? *Rev. Financ. Stud.* **2010**, *23*, 3638–3664. [CrossRef]

22. Thakor, R.T.; Merton, R.C. *Trust in Lending*; NBER Working Paper no.24778; National Bureau of Economic Research: Cambridge, MA, USA, 2018. Available online: http://www.nber.org/papers/w24778 (accessed on 29 July 2020).

23. De Roure, C.; Pelizzon, L.; Thakor, A.V. *P2P Lenders Versus Banks: Cream Skimming or Bottom Fishing?* SAFE Working Paper No. 206; Goethe University Frankfurt, SAFE-Sustainable Architecture for Finance in Europe: Frankfurt, Germany, 2019.

24. Tang, H. Peer-to-peer lenders versus banks: Substitutes or complements? *Rev. Financ. Stud.* **2019**, *32*, 1900–1938. [CrossRef]

25. Vallee, B.; Zeng, Y. Marketplace lending: A new banking paradigm? *Rev. Financ. Stud.* **2019**, *32*, 1939–1982. [CrossRef]

26. Balyuk, T. *Financial Innovation and Borrowers: Evidence from Peer-to-Peer Lending*; Working Paper 2802220; Rotman School of Management: Toronto, ON, Canada, 2018.

27. Carlsson, H.; Van Damme, E. Global games and equilibrium selection. *Econometrica* **1993**, *61*, 989–1018. [CrossRef]

28. Morris, S.; Shin, H.S. Global Games: Theory and Applications. Discussion Paper, no.1275r, Cowles Foundation. 2001. Available online: https://papers.ssrn.com/sol3/papers.cfm?abstract_id=284813 (accessed on 29 July 2017).

29. Goldstein, I.; Pauzner, A. Demand–deposit contracts and the probability of bank runs. *J. Financ.* **2005**, *60*, 1293–1327. [CrossRef]

30. Bryant, J. A model of reserves, bank runs, and deposit insurance. *J. Bank. Financ.* **1980**, *4*, 335–344. [CrossRef]

31. Diamond, D.W.; Dybvig, P.H. Bank runs, deposit insurance, and liquidity. *J. Political Econ.* **1983**, *91*, 401–419. [CrossRef]

32. Cusumano, M.A. How traditional firms must compete in the sharing economy. *Commun. ACM* **2014**, *58*, 32–34. [CrossRef]

33. Einav, L.; Farronato, C.; Levin, J. Peer-to-peer markets. *Annu. Rev. Econ.* **2016**, *8*, 615–635. [CrossRef]

34. Sundararajan, A. *The Sharing Economy: The End of Employment and the Rise of Crowd-Based Capitalism*; MIT Press: Cambridge, MA, USA, 2016.

35. Jacklin, C.J. Demand deposits, trading restrictions, and risk sharing. *Contract. Arrange. Intertemporal Trade* **1987**, *1*, 26–47.

36. Diamond, D.W. Liquidity, banks, and markets. *J. Political Econ.* **1997**, *105*, 928–956. [CrossRef]

37. Gorton, G.; Metrick, A. Securitized Banking and the Run on Repo. *J. Financ. Econ.* **2012**, *104*, 425–451. [CrossRef]

38. Harrison, J.M.; Kreps, D.M. Speculative investor behavior in a stock market with heterogeneous expectations. *Q. J. Econ.* **1978**, *92*, 323–336. [CrossRef]

39. Roma, P.; Panniello, U.; Nigro, G.L. Sharing economy and incumbents' pricing strategy: The impact of Airbnb on the hospitality industry. *Int. J. Prod. Econ.* **2019**, *214*, 17–29. [CrossRef]

40. Stiglitz, J.E.; Weiss, A. Credit rationing in markets with imperfect information. *Am. Econ. Rev.* **1981**, *71*, 393–410.

12

How to Achieve Sustainable Development of Mobile Payment through Customer Satisfaction—The SOR Model

Su-Chang Chen [1], Kuo Cheng Chung [1,*] and Ming Yueh Tsai [2]

[1] Department of Marketing and Logistics Management, National Penghu University of Science and Technology, Magong City, Penghu County 88046, Taiwan; csc@npu.edu.tw

[2] Land Bank of Taiwan, Taipei City 10047, Taiwan; a0989411830@gmail.com

* Correspondence: d9732004@gmail.com

Abstract: In recent years, due to smartphones being more popular and the wireless network infrastructure improving, individuals are no longer constrained by the workflow on personal computers. Therefore, business operators are constantly launching new mobile application services for everyday life. This study mainly explores how mobile payment adopts the determinants, and adds utilitarian value, hedonic value and salesperson performance as antecedences to understand whether utilitarian value, hedonic value and salesperson behavior can affect satisfaction through determinants, as well as to understand consumers' mobile payment usage intention through the stimulus-response model. The research objectives of this study are mainly mobile payment users in Taiwan. 425 valid questionnaires were received. This study uses a structural equation model to analyze the data. This study's results indicate that utilitarian value, hedonic value and salesperson selling behaviors positively affects customers' satisfaction, which customers' satisfaction positively affects mobile payment usage intention. The research results could provide mobile payment operators with references in the design and implementation of the mobile payment and application process, thereby accelerating the popularization of mobile payment.

Keywords: stimulus-response model; utilitarian value; Hedonic value; salesperson selling behaviors; customer satisfaction

1. Introduction

Research Background and Motives

With the popularization of the 4G mobile network and the diversified development of smart phone applications, the time spent by Taiwanese on mobile phones is increasing year by year. According to the report of the Institute for Information Industry, 51.5% of the people belong to moderate users of mobile phones, while 28.1% spend more than 5 h on mobile phones every day, making them heavy users [1]. It is worth noting that entertainment content has become the focus of the use of these mobile phones.

Consumers can pay for things in stores by scanning the bar codes, or sensing through their mobile phones, as long as their mobile phones are bound to their credit cards, bank accounts or electronic wallets, sparing them the trouble of carrying credit cards and cash.

According to the estimation of Statista, an international research institute, global mobile payment transactions will grow from 391.4 billion USD in 2018 to 1 trillion USD in 2021 and 1.3 trillion USD in 2022, with an annual composite growth rate (CAGR) of 35.7%, while the number of global mobile payment users is looking forward to growing up to 970,000,000 by 2022, which number was 530,000,000 in 2018, and its annual composite growth rate is 16.2% [2]. Pursuant to the statistical data of the Institute for Information Industry, the penetration rate of mobile payment in 2017 is 39.7%, which is a growth in multiple compared with 19% in 2015.

In response to consumers' willingness to use mobile payments, many studies suggest that strategies which improve the usability and ease of use of mobile payments enhance customer value, and the reduced perceived risks will increase the customers' willingness to use mobile payments. The survey of the Institute for Information Industry [3] finds that about 39.7% of Taiwanese smart phone users used mobile payment in 2017, and consumers' perception of mobile payment increased from 84% in 2016 to 91% in 2017. The above data show that consumers' experience and perception of mobile payment is significantly improved. However, the proportion of mobile payment is still low compared with other payment markets. Although the acceptance of mobile payment among the public is gradually increasing, mobile payment has not reached the expected popularity. With the advent of the Banking 4.0 era, the behavioral patterns of financial consumers changes dramatically. Key factors for progress include consumers' perceived value, as it can attract new consumers and retain the original consumers [4]. Cognition and emotion would affect consumers' willingness to use technology services [5]. From the perspective of system design, consumers' use of mobile payment seems to bring more convenience to their life and it deserves to be their preference. Lee et al. (2004) points out that personal anxiety about technology will affect users' willingness to use mobile payment [6]. So as to achieve the popularization of mobile payment, we should not only strengthen the demand side (the perceived value of consumers), but also consider the supply side (the willingness of stores to provide good mobile payment services, including the salesperson's behaviors). The main purpose of many companies launching mobile pay is to utilize the convenient consumption model to assist the integration of online and offline virtual channels, cultivating loyal member customers and also grasping the contours of consumers' behavior based on consumers' big data. Then they shall launch products that are closest to customers' needs and propose the marketing strategy, so that the company can grasp the customers' consumption trends and respond to the market environment.

In review of literatures on the research of mobile payment use intentions in recent years, Lee et al. (2009) studies the interaction between the mobile payment platform and customers, pointing out that consumers will have an impact on network externality [7]. Consumers tend to use mobile payment under peer influence, while their purchase decisions are not easily subject to the influences of web advertising and promotion. Through the analysis based on innovation diffusion theories, Sharma (1999) brings up that trust is the most significant factor in mobile payment [8]. Customers make decisions on the use of mobile payment mainly according to the reputation, convenience and specifications of the payment platform. In the past studies, there is rare research on the intention to use mobile payment from the point of view of customer demand, except for Wang (2008) from interviews with mobile payment users' switching behavior, based on the Push-Pull-Mooring Theory, which came to the finding that privacy concerns are the determinant on consumers' decisions about whether to use the mobile payment [9]. Our study aims to understand the impacts of environmental stimulus and internal psychological state on consumers' intentions to use mobile payment from the view of points of customer demand, in order to compensate for the lack of previous literature on mobile payment, and to achieve the goal of sustainable operation. This study uses a stimulus-response model to analyze customers' consumption psychology.

2. Literature Review

2.1. Mobile Payment

As of late, with the consistent innovation and developing of Internet technology and e-commerce, mobile devices have become an inseparable companion of people in their daily life. They can use smart devices in their hands for socializing, playing games, sending and receiving e-mails, browsing messages, taking photos, or even shopping. Among them, the payment method has changed from simple cash or credit to mobile payment. Therefore, more and more people worldwide are using mobile payment. According to EMarketer (2018) research, 34.9% of smart phone users will pay through mobile phones in retail channels at least every six months [10]. Advances in mobile payment technology have reduced technology barriers to mobile payment, and coupled with the rise of financial service Apps and the expanding accessibility of mobile devices, we believe that mobile payment will become more common and simple in the future [11]. Consumers can apply to the credit card issuing bank for this e-wallet. The e-wallet stores users' profiles, facilitating consumers to use it online. The operating mechanism is that the buyer's credit information will be encrypted before transmitting it to the seller's server. After the bank receives the encrypted data, the confirmation message is also encrypted into the credit card data, and this then transmits to the relevant bank network. Mobile payment is to use a Smartphone as an electronic wallet, so that consumers can use several services and pay for physical goods without using coins or credit cards. There are five types of mobile payment methods: SMS-based transfer payments, mobile bill payments, wireless application protocol payments (WAP), application payments (APP) and Near-field communication payments (NFC).

Mobile payment can be divided into two different types: Remote payment and short-range payment. Remote payment allows consumers to access financial accounts remotely, and can remit money or get other online services by using mobile devices and mobile websites, including mobile banking, mobile network payment, and so on [12]; short-range payment is also known as mPOS payment, which refers to payments that occur when customers and merchants are very close. In this type of payment, the vouchers of transactions displayed on cell phones and traded over short distances uses barcode scanning or radio frequency identification (RFID) technology [13]. In other words, consumers and physical store owners must make transactions face to face. Commodity trade and services occur in adjacent fields, for example, paying for transport tolls, dinner or shopping payment services in physical stores. Offline physical transactions use mobile tools and the merchants' equipment to transmit data to complete the cash flow. At present, there are two common ways of information communication, namely NFC sensing and bar code scanning. Mobile payment with NFC sensing technology requires consumers to install the mobile payment App on their mobile devices and store a variety of payment tools. Businessmen must build POS terminals for NFC payment [14]. This study considers mobile payment as a kind of payment, with smart phones as the tools to complete the transaction for purchases in physical stores, by using non-cash financial instruments with certification steps through specific transmission technologies or devices.

2.2. SOR (Stimulus-Organism-Response) Framework (Stimulas-Response Model)

Mehrabian and Russell (1974) originally proposed Stimulus-Organism-Response (S-O-R) from environmental psychology [15]. In the S-O-R framework, it is assumed that stimulus has an impact on the emotional state of an individual. This internal processing involves the individual's cognitive and emotional responses, such as the perception of stimuli; response represents the individual's behavioral outcomes, which can show that SOR is a physical and intangible form [16]. SOR stimulates individual's emotional and cognitive state through environmental cues, leading to certain behavioral outcomes [17]. Using the SOR model in the study of consumer behavior is helpful to distinguish environmental stimuli from consumers' internal and external behavior. Therefore, this S-O-R framework is considered to be a popular psychological theory in consumer behavior research [18].

The target of this study is to scrutinize consumers' consumption behavior of mobile payment from their cognitive and emotional responses through the S-O-R framework, the Stimulus factors consumer's hedonic value and utilitarian value and salesperson selling behaviors during this study. The reason is that consumers are exposed to the situational stimulus in the use of mobile payment in physical stores. Organism refers to the users' emotional and cognitive state, including their views, experiences and evaluations, and its factor selected in this study is satisfaction. Finally, Response is the intention of use. The study of Hossain et al. (2018) using SOR for mobile payment is the only one that uses stimulus-organism-response (SOR) as the study framework to understand the customer's purchase intentions and satisfaction of using mobile payments [19].

On the whole, when consumers are using mobile payment, the stimulation of perceived value which comprises hedonic value and utilitarian value and salesperson selling behaviors will affect their inner cognitive state (satisfaction) and their behavioral response (intention to use mobile payment).

2.3. Utilitarian Value

Value can influence consumers' views and considerations in purchasing products. In the same shopping situation, consumers with different shopping values will show different consumption behaviors [20]. Perceived value has two consumption values: Hedonic value and utilitarian value [21]. These two levels of value gave a complete picture of consumers' values [22]. Babin et al. (1994) points out that the utilitarian value represents that the usefulness, functionality and cognition of the tools and tasks related to consumption are essentially means to achieve goals [21]. Overby and Lee (2006) argue that the utilitarian value is the consumer's assessment of the cost and substantial advantages of products, services and prices after considering their characteristics [23]. Lowe and Alpert (2015) point out that the consumers' product perceptions, such as concepts, technological novelty and comparative advantages, all affect their hedonic and utilitarian values [24]. Overby and Lee (2006) point out that consumers mostly consider rational factors, i.e., judgment of economic benefits in terms of money, convenience and time cost [23].

2.4. Hedonic Value (HV)

Jong et al. (2010) believe that consumers with hedonic motivation would give themselves reasons to indulge themselves in shopping, with reasons including the elements of fun, happiness, joy and excitement [25]. Hedonism is related to the desire to pursue happiness and self-realization. Babin et al. (1994) regards shopping as enjoyment, which can relax the mood, relieve the pressure in the real life, and arouse a happy response naturally in the inner heart [21].

Roy and Ng (2012) argue that hedonic value is the comparatively strong emotion that consumers usually have toward a product [26]. They would consider all kinds of feelings that a product can bring, and evaluate the costs they would pay and the experienced benefits they would get, such as the feelings of pleasure, enjoyment and escaping from reality [23]. Soman (2003) puts forward the concept of payment transparency and regards mobile payment as an intangible way of payment which indirectly reduces customers' pain in payment, and thus reduces their negative emotions, so that consumers may pay more attention to the benefits of purchasing products than to the costs of using mobile devices to pay for them [27–29]. In terms of the development of hedonic value, Chitturi et al. (2007) put forward the principle of "hedonic advantage", that is, when all products to be purchased meet or exceed the standard value of utility and hedonism, consumers will pay more attention to hedonic benefits when choosing products [30]. Chitturi et al. (2008) indicate that consumers' pleasure could be generated through the promotion activities of stores, or when the products themselves could satisfy consumers' hedonic demands [31].

2.5. Salesperson Selling Behaviors

In the retail environment, the interaction between salesperson and customers is an important behavioral relationship. Jones et al. (2005) point out that because of the rapid changes in information technology and customer preferences, consumers' requirements for products and services and their expectations for salespersons are getting higher and higher [32]. Some consumers like to interact with salespersons when shopping, thereby establishing business friendship between salesmen and consumers, which often involves emotional elements [33]. Many enterprises begin to emphasize the customer-oriented marketing concept. How to improve customer value, customer satisfaction, service quality and retain customers has become the direction that enterprises must think about [34].

Service behavior is defined as the behavior of a salesperson after the initial point of sale by Ahearne et al. (2007) [35]. This ongoing behavior aims at cultivating and developing exchange relationships, and identifies five aspects of the salesperson's service behavior: Diligence, information communication, induction, sportsmanship and empathy. Darian et al. (2005) defines salesperson selling behavior as the consumers' feelings brought by the interaction between the salesperson and consumers in the shopping procedure [36]. Salespersons assume a significant job in sales, as they contact and interact with customers on behalf of the manufacturers. The success of marketing strategy mainly depends on the salesperson [37]. For consumers, the friendliness of salespersons has an important impact on whether they could feel comfortable or stress-free during the shopping process. Rapp et al. (2014) interpret that a salesperson is like a knowledge broker, whose important job is to obtain information about their merchandise and industries, in order to explain and resolve customers' matters [38]. Therefore, salespeople should constantly enrich their knowledge about new products, so as to make an adequate product introduction to customers. Meanwhile, if the salesperson responds to the information needed by the customer in time, it will help the customer save time cost, and avoid negative emotions. Sharma (1999) points out that if retailers want to improve customer service, they should pay attention to the salesperson's selling behaviors, as when consumers feel the positive emotions conveyed by the salesperson, the message transmission and persuasion will be improved [8]. Lee and Dubinsky (2003) believe that not only the store environment will affect customers' purchasing mood, but the interaction between salespersons and customers will also promote the customers' purchasing mood [39]. With technological advances and rapid changes, consumers' unfamiliarity with the use of equipment may inhibit their adoption of the equipment. Friendly salespeople should use sales service technology to help inexperienced consumers to extend their consumer experience rather than to act as barriers.

2.6. Mobile Payment Usage Intention

The Rational Behavior Theory (TRA) proposed by Fishbein and Ajzen (1975) holds that we can predict individual behavior, and behavioral intention can also influence individual behavior, that is too say, the actual behaviors can be predicted through behavioral intention, which is a method of people's intention to engage in a particular behavior [40]. The key indicator in measuring the use of information technology is Behavioral intention, and it is the basis for developing information technology as well.

Behavioral intention is an individual's belief in what he wants to do in certain situations [41]. Zeithaml et al. (1996) divide behavioral intention into positive intention and negative intention. When consumers have positive intention, they will generate positive word-of-mouth, and then recommend products or services to their friends and relatives; if they have negative intention, they may choose to change products or reduce the number of purchases [42]. When behavioral intention is applied to the degree of an individual's willingness to use the technology information system in the future, that is, when an individual intends to use the system subjectively, he has generated the usage intention [43]. Consumers' usage intention is related to their experience of trying the products or services, as well as the continuous of consumers to use the products or services if they have positive usage experience [44].

A research on the usage intention of interactive information is proposed by Lin et al. (2008), and it states a model which shows that the usage intention is positively affected by satisfaction. Usage intention is usually considered to be as a prior variable for consumers' actual use of a mobile service [45,46].

3. Research Design

3.1. Research Structure

This research is based on the S-O-R framework, supplemented by the two consumption values (hedonic value and utilitarian value) proposed by Babin et al. (1994), and combined with the external factor of salesperson selling behavior, which are integrated into the three main constructs of "utilitarian value", "hedonic value" and " salesperson selling behavior" as the external stimulus influencing individuals (stimulus), which further influences the consumers' mobile payment usage intention (response) by influencing customer satisfaction (organism) [21].

3.2. Hypothesis Deduction

Customers' perceived value originates from their personal experience and interaction with the products or services [47]. Understanding the value of products or services from a user's perspective is long considered a successful customer strategy, and is usually related to the overall business performance [48]. Terpstra and Verbeeten (2014) find that many studies show that the relevance between perceived value and customer satisfaction, along with customers' perceived service value, positively affects customer satisfaction [49]. According to the past literature, empirical studies of traditional retailers have confirmed that perceived value positively affects the customers' satisfaction in most cases, and similar conclusions have been drawn from researches on online shopping websites and e-commerce [50,51]. In light of the above literature, we deduce some hypotheses listed in the following on the mobile payment context in this study:

H1. *Utilitarian value has a positive impact on customer satisfaction.*

Although the relative importance of hedonic value and utilitarian value is different, hedonic value may be regarded as the user's psychological needs compared with the basic functional needs of utilitarian value [52]. Past literatures show that hedonic value is an important factor affecting satisfaction [12]. Yoo et al. (2010) also propose that in the interactive relationship between suppliers and purchasers, customers experience intimate relationships, making e-commerce users happier [53]. According to the above literature, our study deduces the following hypothesis in mobile payment context:

H2. *Hedonic value has a positive impact on customer satisfaction.*

Mobile payment is a new technology for Taiwanese consumers. Every new technology must be considered from a consumer perspective before its launch. Therefore, the salesperson assumes a significant job in the promotion. When the consumer uses the electronic wallet, all the personal data can be integrated on one mobile phone. However, there are many banks and telecommunications companies that are actively investing in how to make the most adhesive with consumers through the relationship between salespeople and customers. The salesperson's behavior and attitudes directly affect consumers' satisfaction [19]. The interaction between salespersons and consumers is very important. Compared with competitors, assuming that the salespersons can offer consumers with more merchandises' knowledge, they will create higher added value for customers, which will affect the performance of their retail stores [36].

Lee and Dubinsky (2003) hold that the reliability, professionalism, empathy, friendliness, enthusiasm, similarity and professionalism of salespersons all affect customers' mood and satisfaction in their consumption, and then affect their purchase intention [39]. Amyx and Bhuian (2009) find that the customer evaluation of salesperson selling behavior reflects customers' satisfaction of the service and brand loyalty [54]. In addition, scholars support the concept that adaptive sales could have distinctive customer satisfaction, for example, supplier satisfaction, and satisfaction with services/products [55,56]. In light of the above literature, this study deduces the following hypothesis in the mobile payment context:

H3. *Salesperson selling behaviors have a positive impact on customer satisfaction.*

Practical value and hedonic motivation are important factors affecting consumers' online shopping, and are also important for repeat purchasing intention [22,57]. In the past literature, some scholars propose that cognition and emotion would influence consumers' willingness to use technology services [5]. In terms of mobile services, Pihlstrom and Brush (2008) propose that money, convenience and emotional value would influence repurchase intention [58]. In light of the above literature, this study deduces the following hypotheses in the mobile payment context:

H4. *Utilitarian value has a positive impact on mobile payment usage intention.*

H5. *Hedonic value has a positive impact on mobile payment usage intention.*

The salespeople of electronic payment are very important to the consumer because they have usefulness, emotion and security [19]. In addition, they can also understand consumers' needs and deliver the opinions of consumers to the company. The salesperson's empathy (cognition and emotion) and professionalism (sales wisdom and communication ability) have an impact on product sales. Salesperson's characteristics will affect consumers' repurchase intention [59]. Kennedy et al. (2001) also believes that salesperson's professional ability and sales skills will affect customers' satisfaction with salesperson and repurchase [60]. Haas and Kenning (2014) hold that salespersons have influences in determining customers by providing information [61]. The salesperson is also an important factor influencing purchase intention [62]. In light of the above literature, this study deduces the following hypothesis in the mobile payment context:

H6. *Salesperson behaviors have a positive impact on mobile payment usage intention.*

Satisfaction means the comprehensive evaluation of a service or a product after consumption, which includes the satisfaction degree at the cognitive and emotional levels. The satisfaction degree serves as a basis for the judgment of the successive consumers' behavioral intentions [63]. Customer satisfaction can lead to subsequent behavioral intention, like repurchase intention and behavioral intention [64,65]. Expectation uncertainty theory is universally used to disclose customer satisfaction [66]. Satisfaction comes from the comparison between the performance and expectation perception. On the assumption that the performance meets customer expectations, it is satisfactory; otherwise, when performance is lower than customer expectations, it is unsatisfactory. In addition, Chen et al. (2012) mentions that the subject of expectation uncertainty theory is that repurchase behavior depends on satisfaction [67]. Satisfied customers often tend to make positive word-of-mouth, and have a strong intention to keep using the service [68]. The research structure is shown in Figure 1. This study deduces the following hypothesis, in light of the above literature:

H7. *Customer satisfaction has a positive impact on mobile payment usage intention.*

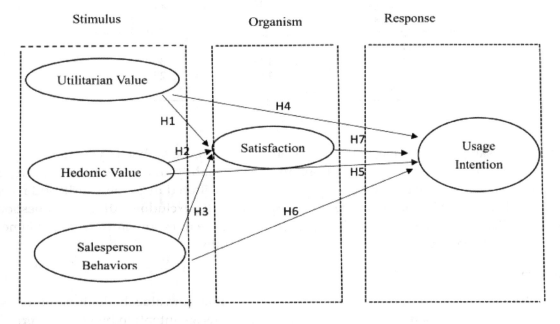

Figure 1. Research model.

3.3. Definition of Variables and Questionnaire Design

The reason why we do this study is to scrutinize the relationship between the mobile payment users' satisfaction formed by their perceived utilitarian value, hedonic value and salesperson selling behaviors and their usage intention. This study adopts a method of investigation and research, and a structured questionnaire as the research tool. The subjects of this study are those who have experiences of using mobile payment in consumption in physical stores in Taiwan. Questionnaire data is received online. The content of the questionnaire was developed by collating the items of the scales already developed by experts and scholars that incorporate three segments: The initial segment is the experience of using mobile payment, the second segment consists of the questionnaire items, in order of utilitarian value, hedonic value and salesperson selling behaviors, customer satisfaction and mobile payment usage intention. Likert's 7-point scale was used as the measurement scale to quantify the data filled in by the respondents, ranging from 1 to 7 points, with 1 point representing "Strongly Disagree" and 7 points representing "Strongly agree", and finally, the third part is the basic data. Based on the research purpose and the need of research hypothesis, this study makes use of the operational characteristics of the structural equation model to measure the causal relationship between the measurement dimensions. The statistical software IBM SPSS AMOS 22 was used to make the model analysis and statistical software IBM SPSS Statistics 22 was used for statistical analysis of data (see Table 1).

Table 1. The demographic characteristics of the sample.

	Frequency	Percentage
Gender		
Female	201	47.3
Male	224	52.7
Age		
20–	5	1.2
21–30	47	11.1
31–40	181	42.5
41–50	124	29.2
51+	68	16.0
Education		
Diploma	35	8.2
Bachelor	286	67.3
Masters and Ph.D.	104	24.5
Income		
20,000–	13	3.0
20,001–35,000	47	11.1
35,001–50,000	128	30.1
50,001–65,000	110	25.9
65,001+	127	29.9

3.4. Sample Data

In this study, samples were selected mainly from users who use mobile payment, mainly through an online questionnaire. The online questionnaires were mainly distributed through My Survey network platform. The questionnaires of this study were distributed in October 2018 and received in February 2019. The entire 526 questionnaires were received. After excluding 101 invalid questionnaires, there remained 425 valid questionnaires. The respondents of the questionnaires were consumers with experience in mobile payment in Taiwan in the past six months.

3.5. Measurement

In this study, analysis was made on five dimensions: Utilitarian value, hedonic value, salesperson selling behaviors, customer satisfaction and mobile payment usage intention by using Likert's 7-point Scale from 1 ("strong disagree") to 7 ("strong agreement"). The definition of utilitarian value is the consumers' assessment of the actual advantages and costs of using mobile payment services, with reference to [23]. The definition of Hedonic value is the degree to which consumers acquire emotional and sensory experience in using mobile payment services, with references to [68]. The salesperson selling behaviors are defined as the feelings brought to consumers by interaction between salesperson and consumer in the sales process, with reference to 36]. Customer satisfaction is the consumers' overall evaluation of use of the mobile payment service, with reference to [64]. Mobile payment usage intention is considered to be the willingness of people to pay through the mobile vehicle, with reference to [69,70].

4. Data Analysis

4.1. Reliability and Validity Analysis

We use Harman's factor test method to conduct exploratory factor analysis (EFA) on all items in this study. Table 2 shows that five factors are extracted, and the explanatory power of the first factor is 34.265%, which was less than 50%. We can infer that there was no serious deviation in common method in the sample data of this study. In addition, we use single factor confirmatory factor analysis (CFA) for the test, which included all of the 25 items in the single-factor test. The results of the test indicate that the factor load level of 12 items exceeds 0.5, and none of the items is significantly higher than the load level of 0.5. The model values of this single factor validation analysis show that not all the constructional correlations in this study are derived from common method variations.

Table 2. Initial eigenvalues.

Component	Eigenvalues	Variance (%)	Cumulative Variance (%)
1	8.566	34.265	34.265
2	3.646	14.584	48.848
3	3.003	12.012	60.860
4	1.640	6.560	67.421
5	1.408	5.630	73.051

In terms of reliability, the combination reliability can be used as a test of internal consistency. It could be found through Table 3 that the values of combination reliability (CR) are from 0.846 to 0.9421, and all of them are larger than 0.6, indicating that each dimension of the measurement model has a certain degree of reliability. Table 3 shows the measurement model. Among them, the values of average variance extracted (AVE) were between 0.599 and 0.699, all larger than 0.5. In addition, the values of AVE open root sign are also larger than the correlation coefficient of each construct, which means that each construct has discriminant validity. This study conducts verification of discriminant validity according to the two criteria put forward by Gaski and Nevin (1985): If (1) the correlation coefficient between two constructs is less than 1; (2) the correlation coefficient between two constructs is less than the individual reliability coefficients Cronbach's α, and thus it indicates that the two constructs have discriminant validity. In addition, using Fornell and Larcker's (1981) method, we got the third criterion for verification of the discriminant validity: (3) If the correlation coefficient of the two constructs is less than the square root of AVE, it indicates that the two constructs have discriminant validity [71,72]. In addition, we use SPSS 22.0 and AMOS 22.0 to analyze the correlation coefficient matrix of measurement variables in this study, with the analysis data received in the table, all of which conform to the above three criteria for verification of the discriminant validity, showing a good validity of each dimension. In Table 4, all CR values of the structural model are greater than 0.7, which verifies that the measurement items of each dimension have internal consistency, and all AVE values are larger than 0.5. Therefore, the proposed framework has convergent validity and the measurement model of this study has good convergent validity, discriminant validity and reliability.

Table 3. Main statistics.

Constructs	MLE Estimates		Composite Reliability (CR)	Average of Variance Extracted (AVE)
	Factor Loading (λ_x/λ_y)	Measurement (δ/ε)		
Utilitarian Value			0.889	0.068
UV1	0.824 ***	0.321		
UV2	0.846 ***	0.284		
UV3	0.816 ***	0.334		
UV4	0.781 ***	0.390		
Hedonic Value			0.936	0.678
HV1	0.849 ***	0.279		
HV2	0.793 ***	0.371		
HV3	0.822 ***	0.324		
HV4	0.827 ***	0.316		
HV5	0.821 ***	0.326		
HV6	0.813 ***	0.339		
HV7	0.839 ***	0.296		
Salesperson Behaviors			0.882	0.599
SB1	0.721 ***	0.480		
SB2	0.800 ***	0.360		
SB3	0.815 ***	0.336		
SB4	0.753 ***	0.433		
SB5	0.765 ***	0.415		
Satisfaction			0.874	0.636
Sat1	0.849 ***	0.279		
Sat2	0.839 ***	0.296		
Sat3	0.792 ***	0.373		
Sat4	0.699 ***	0.511		
Usage Intention			0.920	0.699
UI1	0.856 ***	0.267		
UI2	0.775 ***	0.399		
UI3	0.797 ***	0.365		
UI4	0.856 ***	0.267		
UI5	0.892 ***	0.204		

Note: UV: Utilitarian HV: Hedonic SB: Salesperson Behaviors US: Usage ***; $p < 0.001$.

Table 4. Correlation matrix for measurement scales.

Constructs	Utilitarian Value	Hedonic Value	Salesperson Behaviors	Satisfaction	Usage Intention
Utilitarian Value	0.817				
Hedonic Value	0.214	0.823			
Salesperson Behaviors	0.132	0.166	0.773		
Satisfaction	0.520	0.231	0.227	0.797	
Usage Intention	0.356	0.572	0.284	0.376	0.836

4.2. Model Fitness Analysis and Results

The results of the basic fit criteria are that the error variance of the theoretical model is not negative, the load of standardization factors is not less than 0.50 or more than 0.95, and all of them reach a significant level, and no higher standard errors are found (see Table 5). Therefore, the basic fitness of the research model should reach an acceptable level. The absolute fit measure index of the overall fitness of the model is as follows: $\chi^2 = 556.336$, d.f. = 265, GFI = 0.908, AGFI = 0.887. Except that AGFI is slightly lower than the standard, various indices are in the criteria, and the index of incremental fit: NFI = 0.926, CFI = 0.908, both within the acceptable range; the brief fit measurement index is: PNFI = 0.818, PGFI = 0.740, both within the acceptable range (>0.500). On the whole, judging from all indices, in this study, the overall fitness of the theoretical model is good.

The significance of the internal structural fitness of the model in evaluating this model's parameters, and the reliability of the indices and potential variables, can evaluated from whether the CR of the potential variables is above 0.70, whether the AVE of the potential variables is above 0.5, or whether the Individual Item Reliability is above the acceptable level of 0.5. Both the CR and AVE reach the standard value. On the whole, the evaluation results of the CR and AVE of potential variables show that this study's theoretical model has great fitness of internal structure.

Table 5. Standard coefficients and significance values.

Paths			Path Coefficients	Hypotheses	Test Results
Utilitarian Value	→	Satisfaction	0.624 ***	H1	Supported
Hedonic Value	→	Satisfaction	0.136 **	H2	Supported
Salesperson Behaviors	→	Satisfaction	0.320 ***	H3	Supported
Utilitarian Value	→	Usage Intention	0.173 **	H4	Supported
Hedonic Value	→	Usage Intention	0.528 **	H5	Supported
Salesperson Behaviors	→	Usage Intention	0.245 ***	H6	Supported
Satisfaction	→	Usage Intention	0.130 **	H7	Supported

Note: ***; $p < 0.001$; **; $p < 0.005$.

4.3. Mediation Effect Analysis

There are three mediating effects in this study. Customers' satisfaction has a mediating effect on the mobile payment usage intention and the utilitarian value. Customers' satisfaction has a mediating effect on hedonic value and mobile payment usage intention. Customers' satisfaction has a mediating effect on salesperson selling behaviors and mobile payment usage intention.

In this study, the results of the Sobel test show that the result of values of this Sobel test are all greater than 1.96 (Sobel, 1982), and that all 95% confidence intervals for 5000 simulation analyses through Bootstrapping analysis did not include 0 (Efron and Tibshirani, 1993) [73,74]. The study indicates that customer satisfaction has significant impacts on utilitarian value, hedonic value, salesperson selling behaviors and mobile payment usage intention (see Table 6).

Table 6. Sobel test and bootstrapping confidence interval of mediator effects.

IV	M	DV	Sobel Test	Bootstrapping 95%Confidence I			
				Percentile CI		Biased Method CI	
				Lower	Upper	Lower	Upper
UV	PS	UI	4.683	0.077	0.189	0.075	0.201
HV	PS	UI	3.898	0.032	0.0954	0.0351	0.117
SSB	PS	UI	3.9787	0.0516	0.1515	0.0548	0.513

5. Conclusions and Suggestions

5.1. Conclusions

Empirical research shows that consumers' utilitarian value, hedonic value and salesperson selling behaviors positively affect customers' satisfaction, and Utilitarian value is considered to be an assessment of all the utilitarian costs and benefits. Hedonic value refers to the emotions about products, services and activities generated on the basis of hedonic activities, focusing on the experiences of the product purchasing process. For the first purpose, we can find that customer perceived value which comprises hedonic value and utilitarian value, also salesperson selling behaviors, all have positive impacts on customer satisfaction.

When people use mobile payment, they also enjoy the pleasure of consumption. The salesperson will explain the usage of mobile payment according to consumers' perception and will operate it to show to consumers. When consumers feel the behavior of the salesperson, their satisfaction will be relatively improved. Therefore, the perceived value which comprises hedonic value and utilitarian value and salesperson selling behavior has positively affected customers' satisfaction. In the part of customer satisfaction, this study finds that consumers' utilitarian value, hedonic value and salesperson selling behavior have positive impacts on customer satisfaction. This shows that customers tend to attach more importance to the acquisition of immediate benefits.

Many customers think that they will feel the existence of individual uniqueness at the moment of mobile payment, making them feel different from others, which will lead to the improvement of customer satisfaction. In terms of salesperson selling behavior, it can be clearly found that when consumption is made through mobile payment, the salesperson's introduction and assistance in actual operation will greatly improve customer satisfaction and will make the customers more likely to use mobile payment and consider mobile payment as one of the most critical options for payment. In short, when customers use the mobile payment function and consume through mobile payment, they will understand the satisfaction brought by mobile payment, and have relatively greater intention to use mobile payment. Consumer's perceived value, which comprises hedonic value and utilitarian value, comes from their perception. When consumers feel the convenience and happiness brought on by mobile payment, or feel the good performance of salesmen in the operation process, they will have greater intention to use mobile payment during consumption.

Therefore, operators can make use of the utilitarian value or hedonic value of mobile payment to create topics, encourage consumers to use mobile payment in consumption, and make use of the explanations of salesmen to make consumers more willing to use mobile payment. The mediating mechanism of customer satisfaction can assist the consumers' hedonic value and utilitarian value, the salesperson selling behaviors and the mobile payment usage intention.

The study finds that customer perceived value (utilitarian and hedonic) and salesperson selling behaviors can improve customer usage intention through customer satisfaction. It means that when promoting mobile payment products, the sellers shall first make customers free from vigilance towards the usage of mobile payment, so that customers can slowly tend towards mobile payment. In addition, they shall explain the mobile payment functions to customers. After trying the usage of mobile payment, customers can understand the convenience of mobile payment and experience the pleasant atmosphere brought by new payment means. In addition, if there is a salesperson to guide them, it can reduce customers' doubts about mobile payment and increase their mobile payment usage intention. Therefore, customer perceived value and salesperson selling behaviors can increase mobile payment usage intention through customer satisfaction.

5.2. Suggestions

1. Stores can share free Internet or WIFI and improve the security of mobile network transmission. Many consumers are less willing to use mobile payment because they do not have access to the Internet, or the signal is very weak during their consumption.

2. Business operators can adopt cross-industry alliances to provide more diversified and preferential promotion programs or lottery activities. Consumers will be more willing to use mobile payment if they can enjoy promotion programs together with lottery activities in consumption.

3. Business operators can strengthen the promotion and marketing of mobile payment through online social media. To popularize mobile payment, in addition to the cooperation and promotion of government policies, businesses operators can strengthen the promotion and marketing of mobile payment through online social media. The study finds that salesperson performance is significantly correlated with satisfaction. Because the mobile payment function is more reliable and faster, it is recommended that the company can regularly hold employee on-the-job training, so that employees can immediately operate it to reduce customers' waiting time. This study adopts the cross-section method, and that may be this study's main limitation, so it is only based on observing the data at a certain point in time as the basis for inference and verification. Therefore, it is impossible to understand

the relationship between variables in the longitudinal section, and the inference and development of causality have limitations.

Author Contributions: Conceptualization and data curation: S.-C.C., formal analysis and methodology: K.C.C., writing-review and editing: M.Y.T.

References

1. Institute for Information Industry. Taiwanese People Are More Sticky Phones! Nearly 80% of the People Use Mobile Phones Every Day for More Than 2 Hours. 2018. Available online: https://www.iii.org.tw/Press/NewsDtl.aspx?nsp_sqno=2081&fm_sqno=14 (accessed on 1 December 2018).
2. Statista. The Key to Mobile Payment and Electronic Payment. 2018. Available online: https://www.statista.com/study/39303mobile-payment-usage-worldwide/ (accessed on 2 December 2018).
3. Institute for Information Industry. Nearly 40% of Mobile Phone Users Have Used Mobile Payment Line Pay, Apple Pay Has the Highest Awareness. 2018. Available online: https://mic.iii.org.tw/news.aspx?id=486 (accessed on 1 December 2018).
4. Al-Sabbahy, H.Z.; Ekinci, Y.; Riley, M. An investigation of perceived value dimensions: Implications for hospitality research. *J. Travel Res.* **2004**, *42*, 226–234. [CrossRef]
5. Kulviwat, S.; Bruner, G.C.; Kumar, A.; Nasco, S.A.; Clark, T. Toward a unified theory of consumer acceptance technology. *Psychol. Mark.* **2007**, *24*, 1059–1084. [CrossRef]
6. Lee, C.P.; Warkentin, M.; Choi, H. The role of technological and social factors on the adoption of mobile payment technologies. In Proceedings of the 10th Americas Conference on Information Systems (AMCIS 2004), New York, NY, USA, 6–8 August 2004; pp. 2781–2786.
7. Lee, M.; Kim, Y.; Fairhurst, A. Shopping value in online auctions: Their antecedents and outcomes. *J. Retail. Consum. Serv.* **2009**, *16*, 75–82. [CrossRef]
8. Sharma, A. Does the salesperson like customers? A conceptual and empirical examination of the persuasive effect of perceptions of the salesperson's affect toward customers. *Psychol. Mark.* **1999**, *16*, 141–162. [CrossRef]
9. Wang, Y.S. Assessing e-commerce systems success: A respecification and validation of the DeLone and McLean model of IS success. *Inf. Syst. J.* **2008**, *18*, 529–557. [CrossRef]
10. Emarketer. 2018. Available online: https://www.emarketer.com/content/emarketer-releases-new-global-proximity-mobile-payment-figures (accessed on 1 December 2018).
11. Qin, Z.; Sun, J.; Wahaballa, A.; Zheng, W.; Xiong, H. A secure and privacy preserving mobile wallet with outsourced verification in cloud computing. *Comput. Stand. Interfaces* **2017**, *54*, 55–60. [CrossRef]
12. Kim, C.; Mirusmonov, M.; Lee, I. An empirical examination of factors influencing the intention to use mobile payment. *Comput. Hum. Behav.* **2010**, *26*, 310–322. [CrossRef]
13. Qasim, H.; Abu-Shanab, E. Drivers of mobile payment acceptance: The impact of network externalities. *Inf. Syst. Front.* **2015**, *8*, 1–14. [CrossRef]
14. Morosan, C.; DeFranco, A. It's about time: Revisiting UTAUT2 to examine consumers' intentions to use NFC mobile payments in hotels. *Int. J. Hosp. Manag.* **2016**, *53*, 17–29. [CrossRef]
15. Mehrabian, A.; Russell, J.A. *An Approach to Environmental Psychology*; MIT Press: Cambridge, MA, USA, 1974.
16. Jacoby, J. Stimulus-organism-response reconsidered: An evolutionary step in modeling (consumer) behavior. *J. Consum. Psychol.* **2002**, *12*, 51–57. [CrossRef]
17. Chan, T.K.; Cheung, C.M.; Lee, Z.W. The state of online impulse-buying research: A literature analysis. *Inf. Manag.* **2017**, *54*, 204–217. [CrossRef]
18. Chang, H.J.; Eckman, M.; Yan, R.N. Application of the stimulus-organism-response model to the retail environment: The role of hedonic motivation in impulse buying behavior. *Int. Rev. Retail* **2011**, *21*, 233–249. [CrossRef]
19. Hossain, M.S.; Zhou, X. Impact of m-payments on purchase intention and customer satisfaction: Perceived flow as mediator. *Int. J. Sci. Bus.* **2018**, *2*, 503–517.
20. Scarpi, D. Hedonic and utilitarian behaviour in specialty shops. *Mark. Rev.* **2005**, *5*, 31–44. [CrossRef]
21. Babin, B.J.; Darden, W.R.; Griffin, M. Work and/or Fun: Measuring hedonic and utilitarian shopping value. *J. Consum. Res.* **1994**, *20*, 644–656. [CrossRef]

22. Ryu, K.; Han, H.; Jang, S. Relationships among hedonic and utilitarian values, satisfaction and behavioral intentions in the fast-casual restaurant industry. *Int. J. Contemp. Hosp. Manag.* **2010**, *22*, 416–432. [CrossRef]

23. Overby, J.W.; Lee, E.J. The effects of utilitarian and hedonic online shopping value on consumer preference and intentions. *J. Bus. Res.* **2006**, *59*, 1160–1166. [CrossRef]

24. Lowe, B.; Alpert, F. Forecasting consumer perception of innovativeness. *Technovation* **2015**, *45–46*, 1–14. [CrossRef]

25. Jong, U.K.; Woong, J.K.; Sang, C.P. Consumer perceptions on Web advertisements and motivation factors to purchase in the online shopping. *Comput. Hum. Behav.* **2010**, *26*, 1208–1222.

26. Roy, R.; Ng, S. Regulatory focus and preference reversal between hedonic and utilitarian consumption. *J. Consum. Behav.* **2012**, *11*, 81–88. [CrossRef]

27. Soman, D.T. The effect of payment transparency on consumption: Quasi-experiments from the field. *Mark. Lett.* **2003**, *14*, 173–183. [CrossRef]

28. Raghubir, P.; Srivastava, J. Monopoly money: The effect of payment coupling and form on spending behavior. *J. Exp. Psychol. Appl.* **2008**, *14*, 213–225. [CrossRef] [PubMed]

29. Chatterjee, P.; Rose, R.L. Do payment mechanisms change the way consumers perceive products? *J. Consum. Res.* **2012**, *38*, 1129–1139. [CrossRef]

30. Chitturi, R.; Raghunathan, R.; Mahajan, V. Form versus function: How the intensities of specific emotions evoked in functional versus hedonic trade-offs mediate product preferences. *J. Mark. Res.* **2007**, *44*, 702–714. [CrossRef]

31. Chitturi, R.; Raghunathan, R.; Mahajan, V. Delight by design: The role of hedonic versus utilitarian benefits. *J. Mark.* **2008**, *72*, 48–63. [CrossRef]

32. Jones, E.; Brown, S.P.; Zoltners, A.A.; Weitz, B.A. The changing environment of selling and sales management. *J. Pers. Sell. Sales Manag.* **2005**, *25*, 105–110.

33. Price, L.L.; Arnould, E.J.; Deibler, S.L. Consumers' emotional responses to service encounters: The influence of the service provider. *Int. J. Serv. Ind. Manag.* **1995**, *6*, 34–63. [CrossRef]

34. Siu, N.Y.M.; Cheung, J.T. A measure of retail service quality. *Mark. Intell. Plan.* **2001**, *19*, 88–97. [CrossRef]

35. Ahearne, M.; Jelinek, R.; Jones, E. Examining the effect of salesperson service behavior in a competitive context. *J. Acad. Mark. Sci.* **2007**, *35*, 603–616. [CrossRef]

36. Darian, J.C.; Wiman, A.R.; Tucci, L.A. Retail patronage intentions: The relative importance of perceived prices and salesperson service attributes. *J. Retail. Consum. Serv.* **2005**, *12*, 15–23. [CrossRef]

37. Johnson, M.S.; Sivadas, E.; Kashyap, V. Response bias in the measurement of salesperson orientations: The role of impression management. *Ind. Mark. Manag.* **2009**, *38*, 1014–1024. [CrossRef]

38. Rapp, A.; Bachrach, D.G.; Panagopoulos, N.; Ogilvie, J. Salespeople as knowledge brokers: A review and critique of the challenger sales model. *J. Pers. Sell. Sales Manag.* **2014**, *34*, 245–259. [CrossRef]

39. Lee, S.; Dubinsky, A. Influence of salesperson characteristics and customer emotion on retail dyadic relationships. *Int. Rev. Retail Distrib. Consum. Res.* **2003**, *13*, 23–36. [CrossRef]

40. Fishbein, M.; Ajzen, I. *Belief, Attitude, Intention, and Behavior: An Introduction to Theory and Research*; Addison-Wesley: Boston, MA, USA, 1975.

41. Fishbein, M.; Ajzen, I. *Understanding Attitudes and Predicting Social Behavior*; Prentice-Hall: Englewood Cliffs, NJ, USA, 1980.

42. Zeithaml, V.A.; Berry, L.L.; Parasuraman, A. The behavioral consequences of service quality. *J. Mark.* **1996**, *60*, 31–46. [CrossRef]

43. Taylor, S.; Todd, P.A. Understanding information technology usage: A test of competing models. *Inf. Syst. Res.* **1995**, *6*, 144–176. [CrossRef]

44. Zhang, X.; Prybutok, V.R. A consumer perspective of e-service quality. *IEEE Trans. Eng. Manag.* **2005**, *52*, 461–477. [CrossRef]

45. Lin, C.P.; Huang, H.N.; Joe, S.W.; Ma, H.C. Learning the determinants of satisfaction and usage intention of instant messaging. *Cyber Psychol. Behav.* **2008**, *11*, 262–267. [CrossRef] [PubMed]

46. Shin, D.H. Towards an understanding of the consumer acceptance of mobile wallet. *Comput. Hum. Behav.* **2009**, *25*, 1343–1354. [CrossRef]

47. Turel, O.; Serenko, A.; Bontis, N. User acceptance of wireless short messaging services: Deconstructing perceived value. *Inf. Manag.* **2007**, *44*, 63–73. [CrossRef]

48. DeSarbo, W.S.; Jedidi, K.; Sinha, I. Customer value analysis in a heterogeneous market. *Strateg. Manag. J.* **2001**, *22*, 845–857. [CrossRef]

49.   Terpstra, M.; Verbeeten, F.H.M. Customer satisfaction: Cost driver or value driver? Empirical evidence from the financial services industry. *Eur. Manag. J.* **2014**, *32*, 499–508. [CrossRef]

50.   Eggert, A.; Ulaga, W. Customer perceived value: A substitute for satisfaction in business markets. *J. Bus. Ind. Mark.* **2002**, *17*, 107–118. [CrossRef]

51.   Hsu, H. An empirical study of web site quality, customer value, and customer satisfaction based on e-shop. *Bus. Rev.* **2006**, *5*, 190–193.

52.   Oliver, R.L. *Satisfaction: A Behavioral Perspective on the Consumer*; Routledge: New York, NY, USA, 2014.

53.   Yoo, W.S.; Lee, Y.; Park, J. The role of interactivity in e-tailing: Creating value and increasing satisfaction. *J. Retail. Consum. Serv.* **2010**, *17*, 89–96. [CrossRef]

54.   Amyx, D.; Bhuian, S. Salesperf: The salesperson service performance scale. *J. Pers. Sell. Scdes Manag.* **2009**, *29*, 367–376. [CrossRef]

55.   Román, S.; Juan Martín, P. Does the hierarchical position of the buyer make a difference? The influence of perceived adaptive selling on customer satisfaction and loyalty in a business-to-business context. *J. Bus. Ind. Mark.* **2014**, *29*, 364–373. [CrossRef]

56.   Román, S.; Iacobucci, D. Antecedents and consequences of adaptive selling confidence and behavior: A dyadic analysis of salespeople and their customers. *J. Acad. Mark. Sci.* **2009**, *38*, 363–382. [CrossRef]

57.   Bridges, E.; Florsheim, R. Hedonic and utilitarian shopping goals: The online experience. *J. Bus. Res.* **2008**, *61*, 309–314. [CrossRef]

58.   Pihlstrom, M.; Brush, G.J. Comparing the perceived value of information and entertainment moible services. *Psychol. Mark.* **2008**, *25*, 732–755. [CrossRef]

59.   Pilling, B.K.; Eroglu, S. An empirical examination of the impact of salesperson empathy and professionalism and merchandise slability on retail buyers evaluations. *J. Pers. Sell. Sales Manag.* **1994**, *14*, 45–58.

60.   Kennedy, M.S.; Ferrell, L.K.; LeClair, D.T. Consumers' trust of salesperson and manufacturer: An empirical study. *J. Bus. Res.* **2001**, *51*, 73–86. [CrossRef]

61.   Haas, A.; Kenning, P. Utilitaria and hedonic motivators of shoppers' decision to consult with salespeople. *J. Retail.* **2014**, *90*, 428–441. [CrossRef]

62.   Sun, T.R.; Yazdanifard, R. Review of physical store factors that influence impulsive buying behavior. *Int. J. Manag. Account. Econ.* **2015**, *2*, 1048–1054.

63.   Chea, S.; Luo, M.M. Post-adoption behaviors of e-service customers: The interplay of cognition and emotion. *Int. J. Electron. Commer.* **2008**, *12*, 29–56. [CrossRef]

64.   Anderson, E.W.; Sullivan, M.W. The antecedents and consequences of customer satisfaction for firms. *Mark. Sci.* **1993**, *12*, 125–143. [CrossRef]

65.   Gotlieb, J.B.; Grewal, D.; Brown, S.W. Consume. satisfaction and perceived quality: Complementary or divergent constructs? *J. Appl. Psychol.* **1994**, *79*, 875–885. [CrossRef]

66.   Chou, S.W.; Min, H.T.; Chang, Y.C.; Lin, C.T. Understanding continuance intention of knowledge creation using extended expectation-confirmation theory: An empirical study of Taiwan and China online communities. *Behav. Inf. Technol.* **2010**, *29*, 557–570. [CrossRef]

67.   Chen, S.C.; Yen, D.C.; Hwang, M.I. Factors influencing the continuance intention to the usage of Web 2.0. *Comput. Hum. Behav.* **2012**, *28*, 933–941. [CrossRef]

68.   Chen, J.H.; Fu, J.R. On the effects of perceived value in the mobile moment. *Electron. Commer. Res. Appl.* **2018**, *27*, 118–128. [CrossRef]

69.   Escobar-Rodríguez, T.; Carvajal-Trujillo, E. Online purchasing tickets for low cost carriers: An application of the unified theory of acceptance and use of technology (UTAUT) model. *Tour. Manag.* **2014**, *43*, 70–88. [CrossRef]

70.   Schierz, P.G.; Schilke, O.; Wirtz, B.W. Understanding consumer acceptance of mobile payment services: An empirical analysis. *Electron. Commer. Res. Appl.* **2010**, *9*, 209–216. [CrossRef]

71.   Gaski, J.F.; Nevin, J.R. The differential effects of exercised and unexercised power sources in a marketing channel. *J. Mark. Res.* **1985**, *22*, 130–142. [CrossRef]

72.   Fornell, C.R.; Larcker, F.F. Structural equation models with unobservable variables and measurement error. *J. Mark. Res.* **1981**, *18*, 39–51. [CrossRef]

13

Digital Financial Inclusion and Farmers' Vulnerability to Poverty

Xue Wang * and Guangwen He

College of Economics and Management, China Agricultural University, Beijing 100083, China;
hegwen@cau.edu.cn
* Correspondence: wangxue078@126.com.

Abstract: Access to finance is often cited as a key factor for sustainable poverty alleviation, but expanding access to the poor remains an important challenge for financial institutions. Much hope has, therefore, been placed in the transformative power of digital financial inclusion. However, evidence on the relationship between digital financial inclusion and poverty is limited. This paper is one of the first attempts to study the effects of digital financial inclusion on farmers' vulnerability to poverty in China, using survey data on 1900 rural households. Vulnerability to poverty, here defined as the likelihood of poverty in the future, is measured by the Asset-Based Vulnerability model. In our survey, the proportion of farmers using digital financial services is 35.63%. Our estimations show that farmers' use of digital financial services have positive effects on reduction in their vulnerability. We also find that such effects rely mainly on improvement in farmers' ability to cope with risk, that is, alleviating their vulnerability induced by risk. Further investigation reveals that digital financial services provided by ICT companies have a larger impact on farmers' vulnerability than that provided by traditional banks. The lessons learned from China's digital financial inclusion is valuable for other developing countries where financial exclusion looms large.

Keywords: digital financial inclusion; risk-coping ability; vulnerability to poverty; instrumental variable estimation

1. Introduction

Expanding access to finance is often cited as one of the most important poverty alleviation policies [1]. However, it is well recognized that financial institutions face challenges in expanding access to the poor [2]. The government in China, as in many other developing counties, has actively employed numerous policies to improve financial services in rural areas [3], often with disappointing results [4]. Despite the variety of financial institutions—such as Rural Commercial Banks, Agricultural Banks, Postal Savings Banks, Village and Township Banks, and Credit-Only Companies—in Chinese rural areas [5], as pointed out by He et al. [6], farmers remain underserved or excluded by the traditional banking sector because of the fundamental questions of high transaction cost, information asymmetry, and the shortage of collateral.

Much hope has, therefore, been placed in the growth of financial digital innovations. The term "digital financial inclusion", defined as digital access to and use of formal financial services by underserved and excluded populations [7], has attracted attention from many researchers and policy makers. In particular, in 2016, when China was the leader of the G20, the G20 Global Partnership for Financial Inclusion (GPFI) developed a set of High-Level Principles (HLPs) for digital financial inclusion that encourage governments to use digital technologies to foster inclusive finance. In this decade, successful business models for digital financial inclusion have emerged worldwide, following the introduction in Kenya in 2007 of M-Pesa, a key innovation initially developed for peer-to-peer (P2P) payment—mobile money. Using SMS, it is used mainly for money transfer and cash storage, primarily through mobile network operators [8]. The service was first expanded to Tanzania, and then to Afghanistan, South Africa, India, Romania, and most recently to Albania.

In China, digital financial inclusion differs in important ways, using a completely different model [9]. Unlike M-Pesa, mobile financial services in China are offered mainly by third-party payment platforms based on smartphone apps, such as those offered by Alipay or WeChat. In addition, digital financial inclusion is more than a payment innovation in China, which has a broad range of digital financial products and services, such as online banks, peer-to-peer (P2P) online lending, online fund sales, online crowdfunding, and online insurance [10].

Digital finance, also known as internet finance or FinTech, has experienced explosive development in China since 2013, when Yu'ebao (Yu'ebao is an online sales platform for money market funds, which was launched by Alibaba's Ant Financial Services in June 2013), an online fund sales platform was launched, and in 2016 the term "digital financial inclusion" began to draw attention when it was formally proposed in G20 HLPs. The providers of digital financial services in China can be divided into two groups—information and communication technologies (ICT) companies providing financial services, such as Alibaba or JD.com, and financial institutions applying ICT to their traditional services, such as the E-Housekeeper services of the Agricultural Bank [11], which are both crucial to financial inclusion goals [12]. In fact, providers of such financial services have actively expanded their business in rural China, including e-commerce platforms, P2P lending platforms and traditional financial institutions (see Appendix A Table A1). The Peking University Digital Finance Development Index (IFDI) shows the rapid development of digital finance at the county level across 30 provinces of China (see Appendix A Figure A1). The IFDI measures the growth in China's digital finance with rich data from Ant Financial Services. Several recent papers find a positive correlation between digital financial inclusion and rural economic activities, such as self-employment, income growth, and improvement in income distribution [13,14].

However, evidence on the relationship between digital financial inclusion and poverty reduction remains limited, especially at the micro level. This paper is one of the first attempts to provide evidence from rural China regarding the impact of digital financial inclusion on farmers' vulnerability to poverty. Vulnerability to poverty, defined here as the possibility that a household will fall below the poverty line in the future, is an ex-ante poverty indicator, while poverty represents an ex-post welfare outcome. Vulnerability to poverty is a better indicator in China, given that its government has pledged to lift all people out of poverty by 2020, when what really matters is vulnerability of a household, that is, poverty prevention is more important than alleviation. Using survey data on 1900 rural households, this paper first applies the Asset-Based Vulnerability model to measure farmers' vulnerability to poverty, then rely on an instrumental variable (IV) and two-stage least squares (2SLS) regression to study the effects of farmers' use of digital financial services on their vulnerability to poverty. We also examine the potential channels through which digital financial services may affect farmers' vulnerability to poverty.

The remainder of the paper is organized as follows. Section 2 first reviews the existing literature and then develops our hypothesis. Section 3 presents the research design. Section 4 reports the estimate results including the endogeneity tests. Section 5 presents additional robustness checks, and Section 6 concludes with a brief discussion of policy implications.

2. Literature Review and Hypothesis Development

2.1. Literature Review for Vulnerability to Poverty

The concept "vulnerability to poverty" was initially coined by the World Bank [15], which defined it as the possibility that a household will fall below the poverty line in the future. Poverty is an ex-post welfare condition, whereas vulnerability is an ex-ante poverty indicator of a household's ability to cope with risks [16,17]. In fact, the expanding literature on vulnerability has produced a multitude of definitions and corresponding approaches [18], including vulnerability as expected poverty (VEP), vulnerability as low expected utility (VEU), and vulnerability as uninsured exposure to risk (VER), among which the VEP approach is dominant [17–19]. However, as noted by Carter and Barrett [20], the VEP approach, as well as many other approaches, fails to unpack the nature and sources of vulnerability.

This paper thus adopts the Asset-Based Vulnerability approach developed by Chiwaula et al. [18], who combined the VEP approach and measured farmers' vulnerability based on their asset endowments. This approach allows us to decompose vulnerability into structural vulnerability and risk-induced vulnerability and thereby identify the sources of vulnerability. Structural vulnerability refers to a situation in which a household moves in and out of poverty in the future mainly because of changes in the level of assets (e.g., land endowment), while risk-induced vulnerability is when a household moves in and out of poverty because of positive or negative risk events [19], such as excessive rainfall or drought. It is important to distinguish structural from risk-induced vulnerability, which allows us to establish whether the farmers' vulnerability is driven by structural factors or risk events.

2.2. Literature Review on Digital Financial Inclusion

After the important stages of microcredit, microfinance and financial inclusion, the development of financial inclusion has arrived at a fourth stage: digital financial inclusion, which stresses the importance of ICT in expanding the scale and deepening the reach of financial services [7]. As the first stage, microcredit was coined initially to refer to institutions, such as the Grameen Bank of Bangladesh, that were founded to provide small loans to the poor [4]. By the early 1990s, the term "microcredit" was pushed to a much broader concept "microfinance," meaning the supply of a range of financial services, such as savings, mutual funds, insurance, loans, and so on [21]. Another important departure has involved the shift from "microfinance" to "financial inclusion," which was put forward by United Nations and CGAP in 2006. Historically, traditional financial institutions like Grameen Bank developed microcredit, microfinance and financial inclusion based on manual and field-based operation, a structure that weakened their efficiency in serving the poor [22]. Relying on ICT, the development of financial inclusion comes to a fourth stage: digital financial inclusion, a radical innovation that can be a changer for the population at the bottom of the pyramid [7,11]. As noted by Hart and Prahalad [22], doing business with population at the bottom of the pyramid requires radical innovations in technology and business models.

Digital financial inclusion refers broadly as digital access to and use of formal financial services by underserved and excluded populations [7]. This term began to attract attention mainly due to the success of M-PESA, a payment technology innovation introduced in Kenya in 2007 [8]. In Kenya, mobile money is used mainly for digital payments [23]. Several recent papers also provide some evidence on positive [8,24] or negative [23] correlations between this payment tool and economic activity. Digital financial inclusion in China, however, represents more than a payment instrument. It has been recognized as a new financial format, which includes three basic business: digital payments, digital investments, and digital financing.

The existing literature pointes out several important differences between traditional and digital financial inclusion. First, digital financial services greatly reduce transaction costs in rural areas because of their lower marginal cost [10,12,25]. Relying on ICT, such financial services need not establish physical outlets. Although new digital technologies often face higher initial costs to establish digital system, their marginal cost then tends toward zero with the increase of business volume [25,26]. Second, digital finance may overcome information asymmetry by developing ICT [27,28]. Online products and services, such as online shopping platforms and online social networks, produce a large amount of information on individuals [27], which will alleviate information asymmetry between individuals and financial institutions [13]. Finally, digital technology may improve access to credit for farmers who lack collateral [29]. Based on big data analysis, cloud computing, and other technologies, digital finance, such as P2P lending, uses new credit score mechanisms to create collateral-free loan products [25]. In summary, digital financial inclusion is considered a great method for alleviating financial constraints faced by farmers, especially those who are vulnerable [26]. In fact, the digital financial inclusion movement has made inroads around the world in the past decade. For instance, Grameen Bank, as the best-known microfinance institution, has broadly developed online business model to automate its operation [22].

2.3. Hypotheses Development

Based on the nature and sources of vulnerability to poverty, as mentioned above, the literature notes that farmers' vulnerability can be directly decomposed into two parts: structural vulnerability, in which households remain at a low level of consumption in the future because they have low asset endowments, and risk-induced vulnerability, in which households face consumption fluctuations in the future because of stochastic events. Figure 1 motivates our research by revealing these two channels through which digital financial inclusion affects farmers' vulnerability.

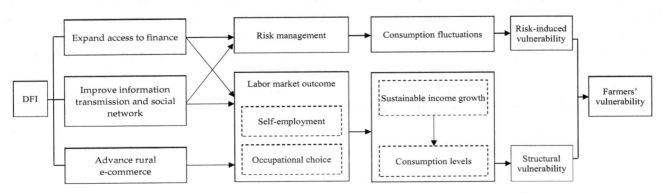

Figure 1. Logit Relationship between Digital Financial Inclusion (DFI) and Farmers' Vulnerability.

Access to digital financial services provides farmers with a more proactive way to cope with risks and thereby reduces fluctuations in their consumption and vulnerability. The intuition for this "primary impact channel" is first related to digital financing, through which farmers who lack collateral can expand access to formal loans based on big data analysis. Internet technology enables a rich information database to be established rapidly. The database in rural China includes three categories: direct credit data collected by traditional banks, information on individuals collected from online platforms, such as e-commerce platform and online social networks, and public information collected by governments, such as tax and social security records. Second, digital technology, as a way of lowering participation costs, makes it easier for farmers to manage their cash flows and savings and thereby improve their ability to cope with risk [30]. In addition, through associated internet-based financial services, farmers can draw on a wider network of social support in response to negative shocks, because they can receive more remittances more quickly from more people [31].

Farmers with higher use of digital finance are more likely to achieve sustainable income growth and consumption improvement through labor market outcomes, a "secondary impact channel". First, having a smaller asset endowment is often cited as the key reason the poor remain poor, especially small farmers. Thus, access to finance plays a fairly important role in both initial investment in production activities and their subsequent expansion [32]. Digital financing, as He and Li [14] noted, enables Chinese farmers to transform and expand their production activities. In addition, the use of digital financial services may improve information transmission and expand social networks, both of which are key factors for small farmers. Second, as the Klapper and Singer [31] reported, digital finance is a critical factor in advancing the expansion of e-commerce, which creates more opportunities and changes occupational choices. It allows farmers to move out of agriculture and into business and thereby obtain sustainable income growth [33].

Based on the theoretical analysis, our hypotheses can therefore be stated as follows:

H1: *Farmers' use of digital financial services has positive effects on alleviating their vulnerability to poverty.*

H2a: *Risk management is a potential channel through which digital financial services affect fluctuations in consumption and thereby alleviate farmers' vulnerability induced by risk events, that is, risk-induced vulnerability.*

H2b: *The labor market outcome is a potential channel through which digital financial services affect consumption levels and thereby alleviate farmers' vulnerability induced by structural factors, that is, structural vulnerability.*

3. Research Design

3.1. Sample and Data

In this paper, we rely on the China Rural Financial Inclusion Survey Data 2018, conducted by the China Agricultural University, which includes a set of questions on the use of digital financial services. The data were collected through a stratified random sample survey of 1979 rural households through face-to-face interviews in July 2018. The survey was designed and conducted as follows: first, we selected Shandong, Henan and Guizhou provinces in the eastern, central, and western regions of China, respectively; second, in each province, we chose three counties based on their level of gross domestic product per capita; third, in each county, we chose three townships based on their level of economic development; and, fourth, in every township, we randomly chose two villages, in which the number of farm households is between 30 and 50. After deleting questionnaires with missing data, we ended up with 1900 valid samples for analysis (see Table 1).

Table 1. Districts studied and sample size.

Province	Shandong	Henan	Guizhou	Total
Counties	3	3	3	9
Townships (three per county)	9	9	9	27
Villages (two per township)	18	18	18	54
Farmers in all villages	666	691	543	1900

3.2. Variable Definition and Measurement

3.2.1. Measuring Farmers' Use of Digital Financial Services

Payment, investment, and financing are key aspects of digital financial inclusion. Therefore, following Guo et al. [10] and He and Li [14], we measure farmers' use of digital financial services in terms of digital payments, digital investments, and digital financing. The corresponding survey questions are shown in Table 2.

Table 2. Questions and possible responses about the use of digital financial services.

Type	Questions and Possible Responses
Payment	Question 1: Which digital payment methods have you used? a. online banking transfer; b. mobile banking transfer; c. Alipay; d. Wechat pay; e. other digital payment methods; f. none
Investment	Question 2: Have you invested in the following financial products? a. bonds; b. funds; c. bank wealth management products; d. foreign assets; e. gold; f. derivatives; g. stocks; h. online investment; i. online crowdfunding; j. none
financing	Question 3: Have you ever used the internet to borrow money or to raise money? a. yes; b. no

In Question 1, digital payment takes a value of 1 for any response other than f, and 0, otherwise. In Question 2, digital investment takes a value of 1 for any response other than i or j, and 0, otherwise. In Question 3, digital financing takes a value of 1 if the response is a, and 0, otherwise. Digital financial services use here is a dummy variable that equals 1 if the value of digital payment, digital investment, or digital financing is 1, which means that the respondent has used digital financial services, and 0, otherwise.

In our sample, the proportion of farmers using digital financial services is 35.63%. The proportion of farmers using digital payment instruments is 35.58%. The proportion of farmers using digital investment and digital financing is 0.3% and 0.6%, respectively, both of which are relatively low compared with digital payment. These results are similarly to those of a study on the Global Findex Database 2017 [9], which shows that in China 40% of adults in rural and urban areas use digital payment.

3.2.2. Measuring Farmers' Vulnerability to Poverty

This paper applies the Asset-Based Vulnerability Approach, proposed by Chiwaula et al. [18], to measure farmers' vulnerability to poverty. Carter and Barrett [20] developed an Asset-Based Poverty Approach that established a functional relationship between assets and welfare indicators, such as consumption. The Asset-Based Vulnerability Approach introduces risk to the Asset-Based Poverty Approach by incorporating the variance of income or consumption [18]. Defined as the likelihood that a household will move into or out of poverty in the future, farmers' vulnerability can be calculated as

$$
V_h = \Pr(V_h \le Z) = \begin{cases} 0 & if \left[\hat{E}(C_h) - \sqrt{\hat{V}(C_h)}\right] \ge Z \\ \frac{Z - \left[\hat{E}(C_h) - \sqrt{\hat{V}(C_h)}\right]}{2\sqrt{\hat{V}(C_h)}} & if \left[\hat{E}(C_h) - \sqrt{\hat{V}(C_h)}\right] < Z \le \left[\hat{E}(C_h) + \sqrt{\hat{V}(C_h)}\right] \\ 1 & if \left[\hat{E}(C_h) + \sqrt{\hat{V}(C_h)}\right] \le Z \end{cases} \tag{1}
$$

where V_h is a household's vulnerability to poverty. $\Pr(\cdot)$ is the likelihood that household consumption will fall below the poverty line in the future. Z is the poverty line, and C_h is per capita consumption expenditure. $\hat{E}(C_h)$ of a given household is structural (or expected) consumption, and the approach assumes that this structural consumption is defined by the household stock of assets. $\sqrt{\hat{V}(C_h)}$ is the standard deviation of structural consumption. $\hat{E}(C_h) - \sqrt{\hat{V}(C_h)}$ is the lower consumption bound, and $\hat{E}(C_h) + \sqrt{\hat{V}(C_h)}$ is the upper consumption bound. In the presence of risk, household consumption has stochastic variations between the upper and lower bounds.

The approach applies model (1) to measure a specific household's vulnerability and uses a 50% cut-off to identify the structural and risk-induced vulnerability to poverty. The different categories are defined as:

a. Structural vulnerability ($StruV_h$), if $V_h \ge 0.5$

b. Risk-induced vulnerability ($RiskV_h$), if $0 < V_h \le 0.5$

c. Never poor, if $V_h = 0$

Furthermore, the approach specifies an asset-based consumption Equation (2), which allows us to estimate expected consumption $\hat{E}(C_h)$ and variance in consumption $\hat{V}(C_h)$ using a three-step feasible generalized least squares (FGLS) procedure. (Following Chiwaula et al. [18], the first step of FGLS applies ordinary least squares (OLS) to estimate Equation (2). In the second step, the log of the squared residuals is regressed on the same variables as in the first step. The last step corrects for inefficiency of the OLS model by weighting it with the square root of the predicted values of the second step.) The equation is specified as follows:

$$
\ln(C_h) = \beta_0 + \beta_1 Asset_h + \beta_2 X_h + e_h \tag{2}
$$

where C_h is per capita consumption expenditure. Here, $Asset_h$ is understood to broadly include productive capital, human capital, financial capital, and social capital. X_h represents a number of control variables.

Using the FGLS estimation, this approach predicts $\hat{E}(C_h)$ and $\hat{V}(C_h)$, which we apply to estimate a household's vulnerability level.

We then calculate V_h, a household's vulnerability, using the Chinese poverty line of RMB 2300 and the international poverty line of \$1.90 USD, respectively. In our sample, based on the international poverty line, the average vulnerability is 0.03, which is lower than 0.08, the result derived by Wan et al. [33], who used the same approach to calculate Chinese farmers' vulnerability in 2004. The decomposition of the vulnerability in our study, as in theirs, shows that the proportion of farmers with structural vulnerability and risk-induced vulnerability is 0.79% and 12.37%, respectively. The results-based poverty line of RMB 2300 remain unchanged.

3.2.3. Control Variables

This study includes three categories of control variables: household characteristics, household-head characteristics, and the ability to manage risk. Household characteristics include household size, labors, and land area. Household-head characteristics include age, education level, and financial literacy. The ability to manage risk includes job security, access to formal bank loans, and informal insurance networks. The definitions of these variables and descriptive statistics are in Table 3. To reduce noise in the data, we drop the top and bottom 0.05% outliers on the continuous variables.

Table 3. Definition and description of variables.

Variable Labels	Definition of Variables	Mean	S.D.	Min	Max
size	Household size	4.319	1.767	1	10
labor	Proportion of labor in a household	0.416	0.293	0	1
land	Land area (measured in mu [a])	5.436	4.496	0	24.25
h_age	Age of household head	51.330	12.360	21	77
h_age²	Age of household head, squared	2787	1240	441	5929
h_edu	Education of household head (1 = 0–8 years of education; 2 = 9–15 years of education; 3 = >15 years of education)	1.614	0.535	1	3
h_finknow	Level of financial knowledge by household head (1 = lowest; 2 = low; 3 = high; 4 = highest)	0.550	0870	0	4
worksecur	Number of migrant workers	0.941	1.014	0	4
fincap	Having access to bank loans or not (1 = yes; 0 = no)	0.800	0.400	0	1
socialcap	Number of relatives proving assistance	7.771	8.118	0	40

[a.] One mu equals to 666.666 m².

3.3. Econometric Model

To test H1, we construct the following Ordinary Least Squares (OLS) regression model:

$$V_h = \alpha_0 + \alpha_1 DFI_h + \alpha_2 X_h + \varepsilon_h \tag{3}$$

where h is a household. V_h is farmers' vulnerability calculated on basis of the Chinese poverty line of RMB 2300 and the international poverty line of \$1.90, respectively; the range is [0, 1]. DFI_h equals 1 if a household uses digital financial services, and 0, otherwise. X_h represents additional control variables, and ε_h is the error term.

The OLS estimate may be biased for various reasons, such as omitted-variable bias or reverse causality. In order to address these potential problems, we instrument the digital financial services use index with the average value of the digital financial services use index of the same age group in the same county. Following Bucher and Lusardi [34] and He and Li [14], we assume that famers are more likely to use digital financial services when they are exposed to an environment in which many other people use them (this is beyond the control of the respondent). The age groups are divided as follows: 18–30, 40–50, 50–60, and over 60.

To test H2, we construct the following Logit regression model:

$$Prob(Vtype_h = k|DFI_h, X_h) = \frac{exp(\alpha_0 + \alpha_1 DFI_h + \alpha_2 X_h + \varepsilon_h)}{1 + \sum_{k=1}^{K} exp(\alpha_0 + \alpha_1 DFI_h + \alpha_2 X_h + \varepsilon_h)} \tag{4}$$

where k takes a value of 0 if a household will never be poor, a value of 1 if a household has risk-induced vulnerability, and a value of 2 if a household has structural vulnerability. Other variables are the same as in model (3).

4. Empirical Results

4.1. Does Digital Financial Inclusion Have an Effect on Farmers' Vulnerability?

We first investigate the impact of farmers' use of digital financial services on their vulnerability to poverty. Table 4 presents the regression results of OLS. Columns (1) to (3) in Table 4 use farmers' vulnerability calculated on basis of the Chinese poverty line of RMB 2300 as dependent variables. All estimations control for county dummy variables. Column (1) shows the relationship without other control variables. In column (2), we gradually add the relatively exogenous control variables, such as household size, dependency ratio, land area, and age of household head. In column (3), we control for all variables. Similarly, columns (4) to (6) in Table 4 use vulnerability calculated according to the international poverty line of $1.90 as dependent variables, which are also results of OLS regressions.

Table 4. Impacts of farmers' use of digital financial services on their vulnerability to poverty: OLS results.

Poverty line	RMB 2300 a Year Per Capita			$1.90 a Day Per Capita		
	(1)	(2)	(3)	(4)	(5)	(6)
DFI	−0.032 ***	−0.009 ***	−0.006 **	−0.032 ***	−0.009 ***	−0.006 *
	(0.003)	(0.003)	(0.003)	(0.003)	(0.003)	(0.003)
size		0.018 ***	0.019 ***		0.017 ***	0.019 ***
		(0.002)	(0.002)		(0.002)	(0.002)
labor		0.028 ***	0.018 ***		0.027 ***	0.018 ***
		(0.006)	(0.006)		(0.006)	(0.005)
land		−0.001 ***	−0.001 ***		−0.001 ***	−0.001 ***
		(0.000)	(0.000)		(0.000)	(0.000)
h_age		−0.006 ***	−0.006 ***		−0.006 ***	−0.006 ***
		(0.001)	(0.001)		(0.001)	(0.001)
h_age²		0.000 ***	0.000 ***		0.000 ***	0.000 ***
		(0.000)	(0.000)		(0.000)	(0.000)
h_edu			−0.015 ***			−0.015 ***
			(0.003)			(0.003)
h_finknow			0.002			0.002
			(0.001)			(0.001)
worksecur			−0.006 ***			−0.006 ***
			(0.002)			(0.002)
fincap			−0.014 ***			−0.014 ***
			(0.005)			(0.005)
socialcap			−0.000			−0.000
			(0.000)			(0.000)
County	Yes	Yes	Yes	Yes	Yes	Yes
Observations	1900	1900	1900	1900	1900	1900
R-squared	0.084	0.304	0.320	0.084	0.303	0.319

Note: The poverty lines are adjusted according to purchasing power parity (PPP) according to the World Bank in 2015 and the Chinese consumer price index (CPI) of rural residents in 2017. Robust standard errors are in parentheses. ***, **, * denote the significance at 1%, 5% and 10% level, respectively.

The results in Table 4 indicate that the use of digital financial services is likely to reduce farmers' vulnerability to poverty regardless of which poverty line is considered. In columns (1) to (3) in Table 4, the coefficients of *DFI* are significantly negative whether with or without control variables, suggesting that farmers' use of digital financial services have positive effects on reducing their vulnerability to poverty. Results in columns (4) to (6) in Table 4 show that the relationship between digital financial services use and farmers' vulnerability remains negative and statistically significant. Suri and Jack [24] obtain similar results, finding that using mobile money in Kenya has a significant impact on poverty reduction. Their analysis focuses mainly on digital payments, whereas ours considers digital payment as well as digital investment and digital financing.

Considering that the OLS regression may be biased, we further rely on an instrumental variable (IV) mentioned in Section 3 and two-stage least squares (2SLS) regression to deal with potential endogeneity. Table 5 presents both first- and second-stage 2SLS regression results. The 2SLS models here use vulnerability based on the poverty lines of RMB 2300 and $1.90 USD, as in the OLS models in Table 4. At the same time, we also gradually added the controls variables in the 2SLS models. The first-stage regressions in columns (1) to (6) in Table 5 show that the Cragg–Donald F-statistics and Hansen J-statistics are significant, suggesting that our IV is valid. The second-stage regressions in columns (1) to (6) show that the coefficients of *DFI* are significantly negative, which confirms the relationship between digital finance and vulnerability while mitigating endogeneity concerns.

Table 5. Impacts of farmers' use of digital financial services on their vulnerability to poverty: 2SLS results.

Poverty Line	RMB 2300 a Year Per Capita			$1.90 a Day Per Capita		
	(1)	(2)	(3)	(4)	(5)	(6)
	2SLS_Second Stage					
DFI	−0.075 ***	−0.035 **	−0.032 *	−0.074 ***	−0.035 **	−0.032 *
	(0.007)	(0.015)	(0.018)	(0.007)	(0.015)	(0.018)
Exogenous control variables		Yes	Yes		Yes	Yes
Potential endogenous control variables			Yes			Yes
County	Yes	Yes	Yes	Yes	Yes	Yes
Observations	1900	1900	1900	1900	1900	1900
R-squared	0.031	0.291	0.308	0.031	0.290	0.307
	2SLS_First Stage					
Average *DFI* of same age group in the same township	1.000 ***	0.694 ***	0.543 ***	1.000 ***	0.694 ***	0.543 ***
	(0.025)	(0.068)	(0.067)	(0.025)	(0.068)	(0.067)
Cragg–Donald F-statistic	929.735	115.223	73.174	929.735	115.223	73.174
Hansen J-statistic	0.000	0.000	0.000	0.000	0.000	0.000

Note: The poverty lines are adjusted according to purchasing power parity (PPP) according to the World Bank in 2015 and the Chinese consumer price index (CPI) of rural residents in 2017. Exogenous control variables and Potential endogenous control variables are the same as in Table 4. For more details on the impact of control variables on vulnerability, see Appendix A Table A2. Robust standard errors are in parentheses. ***, **, * denote the significance at 1%, 5% and 10% level, respectively.

4.2. How Does Digital Financial Inclusion Affect Vulnerability: Structural or Risk-Induced?

The regression results above show the positive impact of farmers' use of digital financial services on reduction in their vulnerability. In this section, we go one step further by investigating the channels through which digital financial services play a role in reducing farmers' vulnerability. We decompose vulnerability into structural vulnerability induced by the low asset endowments and risk-induced vulnerability due to stochastic events. Table 6 presents the Logit regression results for vulnerability with the poverty line of RMB 2300 in Panel A and $1.90 USD in Panel B, respectively.

Table 6. Impact Channels of Digital Financial Services on Farmers' Vulnerability.

Panel A	RMB 2300 a Year Per Capita					
	(1)	(2)	(3)	(4)	(5)	(6)
	$RiskV_h$	$StruV_h$	$RiskV_h$	$StruV_h$	$RiskV_h$	$StruV_h$
DFI	−2.314 ***	−15.447	−1.586 ***	−14.916	−1.329 ***	−15.038
	(−8.150)	(−0.020)	(−3.960)	(−0.030)	(−3.110)	(−0.020)
Exogenous controls			Yes	Yes	Yes	Yes
Possible endogenous controls					Yes	Yes
County	Yes	Yes	Yes	Yes	Yes	Yes
Observations	1900		1900		1900	1900

Panel B	$1.90 USD a Day Per Capita					
	(1)	(2)	(3)	(4)	(5)	(6)
	$RiskV_h$	$StruV_h$	$RiskV_h$	$StruV_h$	$RiskV_h$	$StruV_h$
DFI	−2.297 ***	−15.682	−1.564 ***	−16.509	−1.299 ***	−14.998
	(−8.100)	(−0.020)	(−3.910)	(−0.020)	(−3.050)	(−0.020)
Exogenous controls			Yes	Yes	Yes	Yes
Possible endogenous controls					Yes	Yes
County	Yes	Yes	Yes	Yes	Yes	Yes
Observations	1900	1900	1900	1900	1900	1900

Note: For more details on the impact of control variables on vulnerability, see Appendix A Table A3. Robust standard errors are in parentheses. *** denotes the significance at 1% level.

The results in Table 6 indicate a significant and positive impact of digital financial services use on reducing risk-induced vulnerability, suggesting that digital financial inclusion may alleviate poverty vulnerability primarily through the channel of coping with risk. Panel A in Table 6 shows that the coefficients of DFI are negative and significant at the 1% level in columns (1), (3), and (5), while the coefficients of DFI are not significant in columns (2), (4), and (6). These results indicate that the use of digital financial services has a significant impact only on risk-induced vulnerability. The results in Panel B in Table 6 show that the coefficients of DFI are negative and significant at the 1% level only in columns (1), (3), and (5), which is consistent with the results in Panel A. Zhang and Yin [35] obtain similar results, finding that financially inclusive services provided by commercial banks have a greater impact on farmers' risk-induced vulnerability than on structural vulnerability.

4.3. Further Analysis: Different Providers of Digital Financial Services

The providers of digital financial services in China can be divided into two groups—ICT companies providing financial services, and financial institutions applying ICT to their traditional services [11,36]. Compared with traditional banks, the ICT companies have a comparative advantage in information technology and collection mechanisms. Having established that farmers' use of digital financial services has a positive effect on reducing their vulnerability to poverty, we further investigate whether digital financial services provided by ICT (DFI_ICT) have a larger impact than that provided by traditional banks (DFI_Bank). We measure DFI_ICT and DFI_Bank based on Question 1 in Table 3. In Question 1, DFI_ICT takes a value of 1 if the response is c or d, and 0, otherwise; DFI_Bank takes a value of 1 if the response is a or d, and 0, otherwise. At the same time, we also separately instrument the DFI_ICT and DFI_Bank index with the average value of the DFI_ICT and DFI_Bank index of the same age group in the same township.

We separately investigate the impact of DFI_ICT and DFI_Bank on farmers' vulnerability to poverty. Table 7 presents both OLS and second-stage 2SLS regression results. The Cragg–Donald F-statistics and Hansen J-statistics are significant, suggesting that our IV is valid. The results in Table 7 shows that the coefficients of DFI_ICT are significantly negative in Columns (2), (4), (6), and (8), while the coefficients of DFI_Bank are not significant in Columns (1), (3), (5), and (7). These results indicate that different providers of digital financial services result in a heterogeneous effect, and only *DFI_ICT* has a positive effect on reducing farmers' vulnerability to poverty.

Table 7. Impacts of different providers of digital financial services on farmers' vulnerability.

Poverty Line	RMB 2300 a Year Per Capita				$1.90 a Day Per Capita			
	OLS		2SLS_Second Stage		OLS		2SLS_Second Stage	
	(1)	(2)	(3)	(4)	(5)	(6)	(7)	(8)
DFI_Bank	0.003		0.014		0.003		0.014	
	(0.003)		(0.014)		(0.003)		(0.014)	
DFI_ICT		−0.005 *		−0.037 *		−0.005 *		−0.037 *
		(0.003)		(0.019)		(0.003)		(0.019)
Controls	Yes	Yes	Yes	Yes	Yes	Yes	Yes	Yes
County	Yes	Yes	Yes	Yes	Yes	Yes	Yes	Yes
Observations	1900	1900	1900	1900	1900	1900	1900	1900
R-squared	0.320	0.320	0.318	0.301	0.318	0.319	0.317	0.300
Cragg–Donald F-statistic			132.328	70.253			132.328	70.253
Hansen J-statistic			0.000	0.000			0.000	0.000

Note: Robust standard errors are in parentheses. * denotes the significance at 10% level.

5. Additional Robustness Checks

Our main results above show that farmers with higher use of digital finance are associated with lower vulnerability, a finding that is robust to the different choices of poverty line and to instrumental variable estimation. In this section, we present further robustness checks and these results further confirm the positive effect of digital financial inclusion on reduction in farmers' vulnerability to poverty.

First, we use an alternative variable to measure farmers' use of digital financial services in order to reduce the possibility of measurement error. Specially, we construct the frequency of farmers' use of digital payments (*DP_Num*) based on the following survey question.

Question 4: How often do you use the digital payment?
a. Never; b. Only once or twice; c. Sometimes; d. Often

In Question 4, *DP_Num* takes a value of 0 if the response is a, 1 if the response is b, 2 if the response is c, and 3 if the response is d. We instrument the *DP_Num* index with the average value of the *DP_Num* index of the same age group in the same township. Results of OLS and 2SLS regressions in Table 8 show that *DP_Num* has a significant impact on farmers' vulnerability regardless of which poverty line is considered.

Table 8. Impacts of frequency of farmers' use of digital payments on their vulnerability.

Poverty Line	RMB 2300 a Year Per Capita			$1.90 USD a Day Per Capita		
	OLS	2SLS_First	2SLS_Second	OLS	2SLS_First	2SLS_Second
	(1)	(2)	(3)	(4)	(5)	(6)
DP_Num	−0.004 ***		−0.036 ***	−0.004 ***		−0.035 ***
	(0.001)		(0.012)	(0.001)		(0.012)
Average *DP_Num* in same age group in the same township		0.647 ***			0.647 ***	
		(0.084)			(0.084)	
Controls	Yes	Yes	Yes	Yes	Yes	Yes
County	Yes	Yes	Yes	Yes	Yes	Yes
Observations	1900	1900	1900	1900	1900	1900
R-squared	0.321	0.269	0.261	0.319	0.269	0.260
Cragg–Donald F-statistic		67.401			67.401	
Hansen J-statistic		0.000			0.000	

Note: Robust standard errors are in parentheses. *** denotes the significance at 1% level.

Second, we further calculate farmers' vulnerability according to a higher international poverty lines of \$3.20 USD, which is more typical of national poverty lines found in lower income economies. Results of OLS and 2SLS regressions in Table 9 show that the coefficients of *DFI* remain significantly negative while using the higher international poverty lines.

Table 9. Impacts of farmers' use of digital financial services on their vulnerability to poverty (poverty line: \$3.20 USD a day per capita).

	OLS	2SLS_First	2SLS_Second
	(1)	(2)	(3)
DFI	−0.033 ***		−0.107 **
	(0.008)		(0.045)
Average *DFI* of same age group		0.543 ***	
in the same township		(0.067)	
Controls	Yes	Yes	Yes
Counties	Yes	Yes	Yes
Observations	1900	1900	1900
R-squared	0.575	0.417	0.561
Cragg–Donald *F*-statistic		73.174	
Hansen *J*-statistic		0.000	

Note: Robust standard errors are in parentheses. ***, ** denote the significance at 1% and 5% level, respectively.

6. Conclusions and Policy Implication

After the important stages of microcredit, microfinance, and financial inclusion, the development of financial inclusion has arrived at a fourth stage: digital financial inclusion, which has experienced explosive growth in China. However, evidence on the relationship between digital financial inclusion and poverty reduction remains limited, especially at the micro level. Using survey data on 1900 farmers in rural China, this paper sheds light on this relationship and its potential impact channels. The main conclusions are as follows.

First, farmers' broader participation in digital financial inclusion has a sizable positive effect on reduction in their vulnerability. Our empirical results show that farmers' vulnerability tends to be alleviated as a result of the use of digital financial services. Digital financial services are different from traditional financial services and have a great potential to expand farmers' access to finance. It also has a potential impact on information transmission, social networks and e-commerce.

Furthermore, the effect of digital financial services provided by ICT companies is more pronounced than that provided by traditional banks. We split the sample based on the provider types and the results show that digital financial services provided only by ICT companies have a statistically significant effect. Compared with traditional banks, the ICT companies have a comparative advantage in information technology and collection mechanisms, which further strengthens the potential impact of digital financial services on information transmission, social networks and e-commerce.

Second, our results shed a light on a channel through which digital financial inclusion reduces farmers' vulnerability. To investigate the potential impact channels, we decompose farmers' vulnerability into structural vulnerability induced by asset endowments and risk-induced vulnerability due to risk events. Our empirical results show that the use of digital financial services has a significant impact on risk-induced vulnerability but not on structural vulnerability. These results, as a theoretical prediction, highlight the channel of ability to cope with risk through which digital financial inclusion can reduce fluctuations in consumption and thereby alleviate farmers' vulnerability.

Our results have important policy implications. One direct policy implication is that farmers' access to and use of digital financial services, especially digital financing, should be expanded. First, more targeted efforts and programs may be needed to improve farmers' understanding of digital financing. According to our survey data, 80.76% of the respondents seemed unwilling to borrow money through the P2P platforms or online banks because they were unfamiliar with the tools or worried about security. Therefore, financial knowledge is as important as infrastructure, such as the internet penetration rate or smartphone, for expanding farmers' participation in digital financial inclusion. Second, a rich information database is one of the most important parts of the development of digital financial models. To improve information transmission and collection, policy makers should stimulate the development of rural e-commerce, which provides invaluable data about farmers' buying habits, as well as selling conditions.

For instance, based on the rich data on buyers and sellers collected from the e-commerce platform, Ant Financial of the Alibaba Group established three digital financial products targeting farmers in rural areas. At the same time, local governments can support the availability of information by establishing a public information sharing system, including direct credit information, such as credit default records, and indirect information, such as tax and social security records.

In addition, paying attention to the effect of digital financial services on sustainable income growth is crucial if policy makers wish to reduce farmers' vulnerability through digital financial inclusion. Our results show that digital financial services have little impact on labor market outcomes which has a direct effect on structural vulnerability induced by lower asset endowments. This is consistent with the evidence showing that digital finance reduces the level of farmers' demand for credit for production but that increases their demand for credit for consumption [37]. Therefore, more targeted products and services for credit for production should be encouraged to expand in China's rural areas.

Author Contributions: Conceptualization, X.W. and G.H.; Formal analysis, X.W.; Investigation, X.W. and G.H.; Methodology, X.W.; Writing—original draft, X.W. and G.H.; Writing—review and editing, X.W. All authors have read and agreed to the published version of the manuscript.

Appendix A

Table A1. Key providers of digital financial services in rural areas in China.

Types of Providers	Examples of Providers	Main Online Services
e-commerce platforms	Ant Financial Services [a] JD.com [b]	Payment, Insurance, Lending Investment, Crowdfunding, Lending
P2P lending platforms	CreditEase [c] Yi Longdai [d]	Lending Lending
Financial institutions	Agricultural Bank of China [e]	E-Housekeeper app including payment, investment, lending, and other services

[a] Ant Financial Services of Alibaba group has produced three products for rural areas: Wangnong payment, Wangnong insurance, and Wangnong Lending, which have reached RMB 180 million, RMB 1.5 billion, and RMB 213 billion, respectively, at the end of June 2017. [b] JD.com proposed "Finance to Country" strategy in 2015, since which its digital financial services have involved 1700 counties and 300,000 villages. [c] CreditEase, as the largest P2P firm in the world, has a lending product targeting at farmers' financial demand for their production and entrepreneurship. [d] Yi Longdai is a P2P platform proving online lending primarily for rural areas. [e] To develop digital finance in rural areas, this bank designed a smartphone app—E-Housekeeper—through which farmers can expand access to payment, investment, lending and other services without physical outlets.

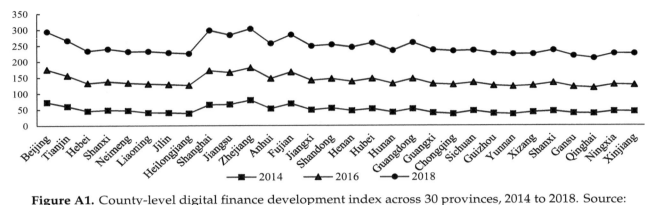

Figure A1. County-level digital finance development index across 30 provinces, 2014 to 2018. Source: authors' calculations based on the Peking University IFDI.

Table A2. Impacts of digital inclusive finance on vulnerability to poverty: 2SLS results.

Poverty Line	RMB 2300 a Year Per Capita			$1.90 USD a Day Per Capita		
	(1)	**(2)**	**(3)**	**(4)**	**(5)**	**(6)**
			2SLS_second stage			
DFI	−0.075 ***	−0.035 **	−0.032 *	−0.074 ***	−0.035 **	−0.032 *
	(0.007)	(0.015)	(0.018)	(0.007)	(0.015)	(0.018)
size		0.018 ***	0.020 ***		0.018 ***	0.019 ***
		(0.002)	(0.002)		(0.002)	(0.002)
labor		0.027 ***	0.018 ***		0.027 ***	0.018 ***
		(0.006)	(0.005)		(0.006)	(0.005)
land		−0.001 ***	−0.001 ***		−0.001 ***	−0.001 ***
		(0.000)	(0.000)		(0.000)	(0.000)
h_age		−0.007 ***	−0.007 ***		−0.007 ***	−0.007 ***
		(0.001)	(0.001)		(0.001)	(0.001)
h_age^2		0.000 ***	0.000 ***		0.000 ***	0.000 ***
		(0.000)	(0.000)		(0.000)	(0.000)
h_edu			−0.012 ***			−0.012 ***
			(0.004)			(0.004)
h_finknow			0.005 *			0.005 *
			(0.002)			(0.002)
worksecur			−0.007 ***			−0.007 ***
			(0.002)			(0.002)
fincap			−0.013 ***			−0.013 ***
			(0.005)			(0.005)
socialcap			−0.000			−0.000
			(0.000)			(0.000)
County	Yes	Yes	Yes	Yes	Yes	Yes
Observations	1900	1900	1900	1900	1900	1900
R-squared	0.031	0.291	0.308	0.031	0.291	0.307
			2SLS_first stage			
instrument	1.000 ***	0.694 ***	0.543 ***	1.000 ***	0.694 ***	0.543 ***
	(0.025)	(0.068)	(0.067)	(0.025)	(0.068)	(0.067)
size		0.004	0.008		0.004	0.008
		(0.005)	(0.005)		(0.005)	(0.005)
labor		−0.048	−0.026		−0.048	−0.026
		(0.030)	(0.030)		(0.030)	(0.030)
land		0.001	−0.001		0.001	−0.001
		(0.002)	(0.002)		(0.002)	(0.002)
h_age		−0.016 ***	−0.015 ***		−0.016 ***	−0.015 ***
		(0.005)	(0.005)		(0.005)	(0.005)
h_age^2		0.000 *	0.000 *		0.000 *	0.000 *
		(0.000)	(0.000)		(0.000)	(0.000)

Table A2. *Cont.*

Poverty Line	RMB 2300 a Year Per Capita			$1.90 USD a Day Per Capita		
	(1)	(2)	(3)	(4)	(5)	(6)
h_edu			0.079 ***			0.079 ***
			(0.018)			(0.018)
h_finknow			0.097 ***			0.097 ***
			(0.011)			(0.011)
worksecur			−0.014			−0.014
			(0.010)			(0.010)
fincap			0.040 *			0.040 *
			(0.021)			(0.021)
socialcap			0.003 ***			0.003 ***
			(0.001)			(0.001)
County	Yes	Yes	Yes	Yes	Yes	Yes
Cragg–Donald F-statistic	929.735	115.223	73.174	929.735	115.223	73.174
Hansen J-statistic	0.000	0.000	0.000	0.000	0.000	0.000

Note: Robust standard errors in parentheses: ***, **, * denote the significance at 1%, 5% and 10% level, respectively.

Table A3. Impact mechanism of digital finance on vulnerability to poverty.

Panel A	RMB 2300 a Year Per Capita					
	(1)	(2)	(3)	(4)	(5)	(6)
	$RiskV_h$	$StruV_h$	$RiskV_h$	$StruV_h$	$RiskV_h$	$StruV_h$
DFI	−2.314 ***	−15.447	−1.586 ***	−14.916	−1.329 ***	−15.038
	(−8.150)	(−0.020)	(−3.960)	(−0.030)	(−3.110)	(−0.020)
size			1.083 ***	2.276 ***	1.272 ***	2.516 ***
			(0.080)	(0.286)	(0.096)	(0.342)
labor			4.084 ***	17.734 ***	3.874 ***	16.557 ***
			(0.521)	(3.633)	(0.567)	(3.950)
land			−0.123 ***	−0.289 **	−0.136 ***	−0.313 **
			(0.029)	(0.135)	(0.031)	(0.146)
h_age			0.202 *	0.371	0.220 *	0.173
			(0.114)	(0.761)	(0.122)	(0.825)
h_age^2			−0.000	−0.000	−0.001	0.001
			(0.001)	(0.006)	(0.001)	(0.006)
h_edu					−1.162 ***	−1.851 *
					(0.240)	(1.026)
h_finknow					−0.331 *	−1.141
					(0.196)	(1.263)
worksecur					−0.316 **	−0.338
					(0.127)	(0.468)
finca					−0.351	−2.429 **
					(0.258)	(1.057)
socialcap					−0.037 **	0.089
					(0.018)	(0.102)
County	Yes	Yes	Yes	Yes	Yes	Yes
Observations	1900	1900	1900	1900	1900	1900

Table A3. *Cont.*

Panel B	$1.90 USD a Day Per Capita					
	(1)	(2)	(3)	(4)	(5)	(6)
	$RiskV_h$	$StruV_h$	$RiskV_h$	$StruV_h$	$RiskV_h$	$StruV_h$
DFI	−2.297 ***	−15.682	−1.564 ***	−16.509	−1.299 ***	−14.998
	(−8.100)	(−0.020)	(−3.910)	(−0.020)	(−3.050)	(−0.020)
size			1.083 ***	2.273 ***	1.264 ***	2.504 ***
			(0.080)	(0.286)	(0.095)	(0.342)
labor			4.125 ***	17.775 ***	3.917 ***	16.596 ***
			(0.523)	(3.636)	(0.568)	(3.954)
land			−0.120 ***	−0.286 **	−0.132 ***	−0.309 **
			(0.029)	(0.134)	(0.031)	(0.146)
h_age			0.193 *	0.362	0.211 *	0.161
			(0.113)	(0.760)	(0.121)	(0.825)
h_age^2			−0.000	−0.000	−0.000	0.002
			(0.001)	(0.006)	(0.001)	(0.006)
h_edu					−1.108 ***	−1.794 *
					(0.238)	(1.024)
h_finknow					−0.355 *	−1.160
					(0.196)	(1.262)
worksecur					−0.311 **	−0.332
					(0.127)	(0.469)
fincap					−0.320	−2.398 **
					(0.258)	(1.056)
socialcap					−0.035 *	0.091
					(0.018)	(0.102)
County	Yes	Yes	Yes	Yes	Yes	Yes
Observations	1900	1900	1900	1900	1900	1900

Note: Robust standard errors in parentheses: ***, **, * denote the significance at 1%, 5% and 10% level, respectively.

References

1. Bruhn, M.; Love, I. The Real Impact of Improved Access to Finance: Evidence from Mexico. *J. Financ.* **2014**, *69*, 1347–1376. [CrossRef]
2. Braverman, A.; Guasch, J.L. Rural Credit Markets and Institutions in Developing Countries: Lessons for Policy Analysis from Practice and Modern Theory. *World Dev.* **1986**, *14*, 1253–1267. [CrossRef]
3. Kochar, A. Branchless Banking: Evaluating the Doorstep Delivery of Financial Services in Rural India. *J. Dev. Econ.* **2018**, *135*, 160–175. [CrossRef]
4. Armendáriz, B.; Morduch, J. *The Economics of Microfinance*; MIT Press: Cambridge, MA, USA, 2010.
5. Wang, X.; He, G.W. The Banking Competition and Deepening of Financial Inclusion in Rural China: A Stratified Analysis between Poor and Non-poor Counties. *Chin. Rural Econ.* **2019**, *4*, 55–72. (In Chinese)
6. He, G.W.; He, J.; Guo, P. Rethinking the Credit Demand and Availability of Farm Household. *Issues Agric. Econ.* **2018**, *2*, 38–49. (In Chinese)
7. Lauer, K.; Lyman, T. Digital Financial Inclusion: Implications for Customers, Regulators, Supervisors, and Standard-Setting Bodies. In *Consultative Group to Assist the Poor (CGAP) Brief*; Consultative Group to Assist the Poor (CGAP): Washington, DC, USA, 2015.
8. Beck, T.; Pamuk, H.; Ramrattan, R.; Uras, B.R. Payment Instruments, Finance and Development. *J. Dev. Econ.* **2018**, *133*, 162–186. [CrossRef]
9. Demirguc-Kunt, A.; Klapper, L.; Singer, D.; Ansar, S.; Hess, J. *The Global Findex Database 2017: Measuring Financial Inclusion and the Fintech Revolution*; The World Bank: Washington, DC, USA, 2018.
10. Guo, F.; Kong, S.T.; Wang, J. General Patterns and Regional Disparity of Internet Finance Development in China: Evidence from the Peking University Internet Finance Development Index. *China Econ. J.* **2016**, *9*, 253–271. [CrossRef]
11. Huang, Y.P.; Shen, Y.; Wang, J.Y.; Guo, F. Can the Internet Revolutionise finance in China? *China's New Sources Econ. Growth* **2016**, *115*. [CrossRef]

12. Huang, Y.P.; Wang, X. Building an Efficient Financial System in China: A need for stronger market discipline. *Asian Econ. Policy Rev.* **2017**, *12*, 188–205. [CrossRef]

13. Guo, F.; Wang, J.Y.; Wang, F.; Kong, T.; Zhang, X.; Cheng, Z.Y. *Measuring China's Digital Financial Inclusion: Index Compilation and Spatial Characteristics*; Working Paper; Institute of Digital Finance, Peking University: Beijing, China, 2019.

14. He, J.; Li, Q.H. Digital Finance and Farmers' Entrepreneurship. *Chin. Rural Econ.* **2019**, *1*, 112–126.

15. World Bank. *World Development Report 2000/2001, Attacking Poverty*; Oxford University Press: New York, NY, USA, 2001. (In Chinese)

16. Azeem, M.M.; Mugera, A.W.; Schilizzi, S.; Siddique, K.H. An Assessment of Vulnerability to Poverty in Punjab, Pakistan: Subjective Choices of Poverty Indicators. *Soc. Indic. Res.* **2017**, *134*, 117–152. [CrossRef]

17. Chaudhuri, S.; Jalan, J.; Suryahadi, A. *Assessing Household Vulnerability to Poverty from Cross-Sectional Data: A Methodology and Estimates from Indonesia*; Columbia University Discussion Paper No.0102-52; Columbia University: New York, NY, USA, 2002.

18. Chiwaula, L.S.; Witt, R.; Waibel, H. An Asset-Based Approach to Vulnerability: The Case of Small-Scale Fishing Areas in Cameroon and Nigeria. *J. Dev. Stud.* **2011**, *47*, 338–353. [CrossRef] [PubMed]

19. Günther, I.; Harttgen, K. Estimating Household's Vulnerability to Idiosyncratic and Covariate Shocks: A Novel Method Applied in Madagascar. *World Dev.* **2009**, *37*, 1222–1234. [CrossRef]

20. Carter, M.R.; Barrett, C.B. The Economics of Poverty Rraps and Persistent Poverty: An Asset-Based Approach. *J. Dev. Stud.* **2006**, *42*, 178–199. [CrossRef]

21. Karlan, D.; Morduch, J. Access to finance in Handbook of development economics. *Elsevier* **2010**, *5*, 4703–4784.

22. Hart, S.; Prahalad, C.K. The fortune at the bottom of the pyramid. *Strategy Bus.* **2002**, *26*, 54–67.

23. Hove, L.V.; Dubus, A. M-PESA and Financial Inclusion in Kenya: Of Paying Comes Saving? *Sustainability* **2019**, *11*, 568. [CrossRef]

24. Suri, T.; Jack, W. The Long-Run Poverty and Gender Impacts of Mobile Money. *Science* **2016**, *354*, 1288–1292. [CrossRef]

25. Liao, G.; Yao, D.; Hu, Z. The Spatial Effect of the Efficiency of Regional Financial Resource Allocation from the Perspective of Internet Finance: Evidence from Chinese Provinces. *Emerg. Mark. Financ. Trade* **2019**, 1–13. [CrossRef]

26. Xie, P.; Zhou, C. Research on Internet-Based Finance Mode. *J. Financ. Res.* **2012**, *12*, 1211–1222. (In Chinese)

27. Mishkin, F.S.; Strahan, P.E. What will Technology Do to Financial Structure? *Natl. Bur. Econ. Res.* **1999**. [CrossRef]

28. Gomber, P.; Koch, J.A.; Siering, M. Digital Finance and FinTech: Current Research and Future Research Directions. *J. Bus. Econ.* **2017**, *87*, 537–580. [CrossRef]

29. Bruett, T. How Disintermediation and the Internet are Changing Microfinance. *Community Dev. Invest. Rev.* **2007**, *3*, 44–50.

30. Apiors, E.; Suzuki, A. Mobile Money, Individuals' Payments, Remittances, and Investments: Evidence from the Ashanti Region, Ghana. *Sustainability* **2018**, *10*, 1409. [CrossRef]

31. Klapper, L.; Singer, D. The Opportunities of Digitizing Payments. Available online: https://www.openknowledge.worldbank.com/handle/10986/19917 (accessed on 11 October 2019).

32. Beck, T.; Lu, L.; Yang, R. Finance and Growth for Microenterprises: Evidence from Rural China. *World Dev.* **2015**, *67*, 38–56. [CrossRef]

33. Wan, G.H.; Liu, F.; Zhang, Y. Decomposition of Poverty Vulnerability from the Perspective of Assets: Based on China Empirical Analysis of Farmers' Panel Data. *Chin. Rural Econ.* **2014**, *4*, 4–19. (In Chinese)

34. Bucher-Koenen, T.; Lusardi, A. Financial Literacy and Retirement Planning in Germany. *J. Pension Econ. Financ.* **2011**, *10*, 565–584. [CrossRef]

35. Zhang, D.H.; Yin, Z.C. Financial Inclusion, Risk Coping and Rural Household Poverty. *Chin. Rural Econ.* **2018**, *4*, 54–73. (In Chinese)

36. Xu, J. China's internet finance: A critical review. *China World Econ.* **2017**, *4*, 78–92. [CrossRef]

37. Fu, Q.Z.; Huang, Y.P. Digital Finance's Heterogeneous Effects on Rural Financial Demand: Evidence from China Household Finance Survey and Inclusive Digital Finance Index. *J. Financ. Res.* **2018**, *11*, 68–84. (In Chinese)

Permissions

The contributors of this book come from diverse backgrounds, making this book a truly international effort. This book will bring forth new frontiers with its revolutionizing research information and detailed analysis of the nascent developments around the world.

We would like to thank all the contributing authors for lending their expertise to make the book truly unique. They have played a crucial role in the development of this book. Without their invaluable contributions this book wouldn't have been possible. They have made vital efforts to compile up to date information on the varied aspects of this subject to make this book a valuable addition to the collection of many professionals and students.

This book was conceptualized with the vision of imparting up-to-date information and advanced data in this field. To ensure the same, a matchless editorial board was set up. Every individual on the board went through rigorous rounds of assessment to prove their worth. After which they invested a large part of their time researching and compiling the most relevant data for our readers.

The editorial board has been involved in producing this book since its inception. They have spent rigorous hours researching and exploring the diverse topics which have resulted in the successful publishing of this book. They have passed on their knowledge of decades through this book. To expedite this challenging task, the publisher supported the team at every step. A small team of assistant editors was also appointed to further simplify the editing procedure and attain best results for the readers.

Apart from the editorial board, the designing team has also invested a significant amount of their time in understanding the subject and creating the most relevant covers. They scrutinized every image to scout for the most suitable representation of the subject and create an appropriate cover for the book.

The publishing team has been an ardent support to the editorial, designing and production team. Their endless efforts to recruit the best for this project, has resulted in the accomplishment of this book. They are a veteran in the field of academics and their pool of knowledge is as vast as their experience in printing. Their expertise and guidance has proved useful at every step. Their uncompromising quality standards have made this book an exceptional effort. Their encouragement from time to time has been an inspiration for everyone.

The publisher and the editorial board hope that this book will prove to be a valuable piece of knowledge for researchers, students, practitioners and scholars across the globe.

List of Contributors

Huidong Sun, Guping Cheng and Qinghua Fu
Economics and Management School, Wuhan University, Wuhan 430072, China

Mustafa Raza Rabbani
Department of Finance and Accounting, College of Business Administration, Kingdom University, Riffa 40434, Bahrain

Naveed Ahmad
UCP Business School, University of Central Punjab, Lahore 54000, Pakistan

Muhammad Safdar Sial
Department of Management Sciences, COMSATS University Islamabad (CUI), Islamabad 44000, Pakistan

Malik Zia-Ud-Din
Faculty of Law, Islamia University, Bahawalpur 63100, Pakistan

Angelos Dassios and Junyi Zhang
Department of Statistics, London School of Economics, Houghton Street, London WC2A 2AE, UK

Jelena Kabulova and Jelena Stankevičienė
Faculty of Business Management, Vilnius Gediminas Technical University, Saul᾽ etekio al. 11, LT-10223 Vilnius, Lithuania

Andrea Pérez, María del Mar García de los Salmones and Elisa Baraibar-Diezt
Business Administration Department, University of Cantabria, 39005 Santander, Spain

Luning Shao, Jianxin You, Tao Xu and Yilei Shao
School of Economics and Management, Tongji University, Shanghai 200092, China

Mengdi Fang, Feifei Jin and Chengsong Wu
School of Business, Anhui University, Hefei 230601, China

Jinpei Liu
Department of Industrial and Systems Engineering, North Carolina State University, Raleigh, NC 27695, USA

Huayou Chen
School of Mathematical Sciences, Anhui University, Hefei 230601, China

Francesco Manta, Annunziata Tarulli and Domenico Morrone
Faculty of Economics and Management, LUM Jean Monnet University, 70010 Casamassima (Ba), Italy

Pierluigi Toma
Department of Economics and Management, University of Salento, 73100 Lecce, Italy

Changjun Zheng and Probir Kumar Bhowmik
School of Management, Huazhong University of Science and Technology, Wuhan 430074, China

Niluthpaul Sarker
Department of Accounting and Information Systems, Jagannath University, Dhaka 1100, Bangladesh

Ha Nam Khanh Giao and Bui Nhat Vuong
Faculty of Air Transport, Vietnam Aviation Academy, Ho Chi Minh City 700000, Vietnam

Dao Duy Huan
Vice Rector of Nam Can Tho University, Can Tho 94000, Vietnam

Hasanuzzaman Tushar
College of Business Administration, International University of Business Agriculture and Technology, Dhaka 1230, Bangladesh

Tran Nhu Quan
Nida Business School-National Institute of Development Administration, Bangkok 10240, Thailand

Alfonso Siano and Maria Palazzo
Department of Political and Communication Sciences, University of Salerno, 84084 Salerno, Italy

Lukman Raimi
Department of Entrepreneurship and Management, American University of Nigeria, Lagos 23401, Nigeria

Mirela Clementina Panait
Department of Cybernetics, Economic Informatics, Finance and Accounting, Petroleum-Gas University of Ploiesti, 100680 Ploiesti, Romania

Eunjung Yeo
School of Business Administration, Chung-Ang University, Seoul 06974, Korea

Jooyong Jun
Department of Economics, Dongguk University, Seoul 04620, Korea

Su-Chang Chen and Kuo Cheng Chung
Department of Marketing and Logistics Management, National Penghu University of Science and Technology, Magong City, Penghu County 88046, Taiwan

Ming Yueh Tsai
Land Bank of Taiwan, Taipei City 10047, Taiwan

Xue Wang and Guangwen He
College of Economics and Management, China Agricultural University, Beijing 100083, China

Index

Printed in the USA
CPSIA information can be obtained
at www.ICGtesting.com
JSHW051405091023
49903JS00006B/287